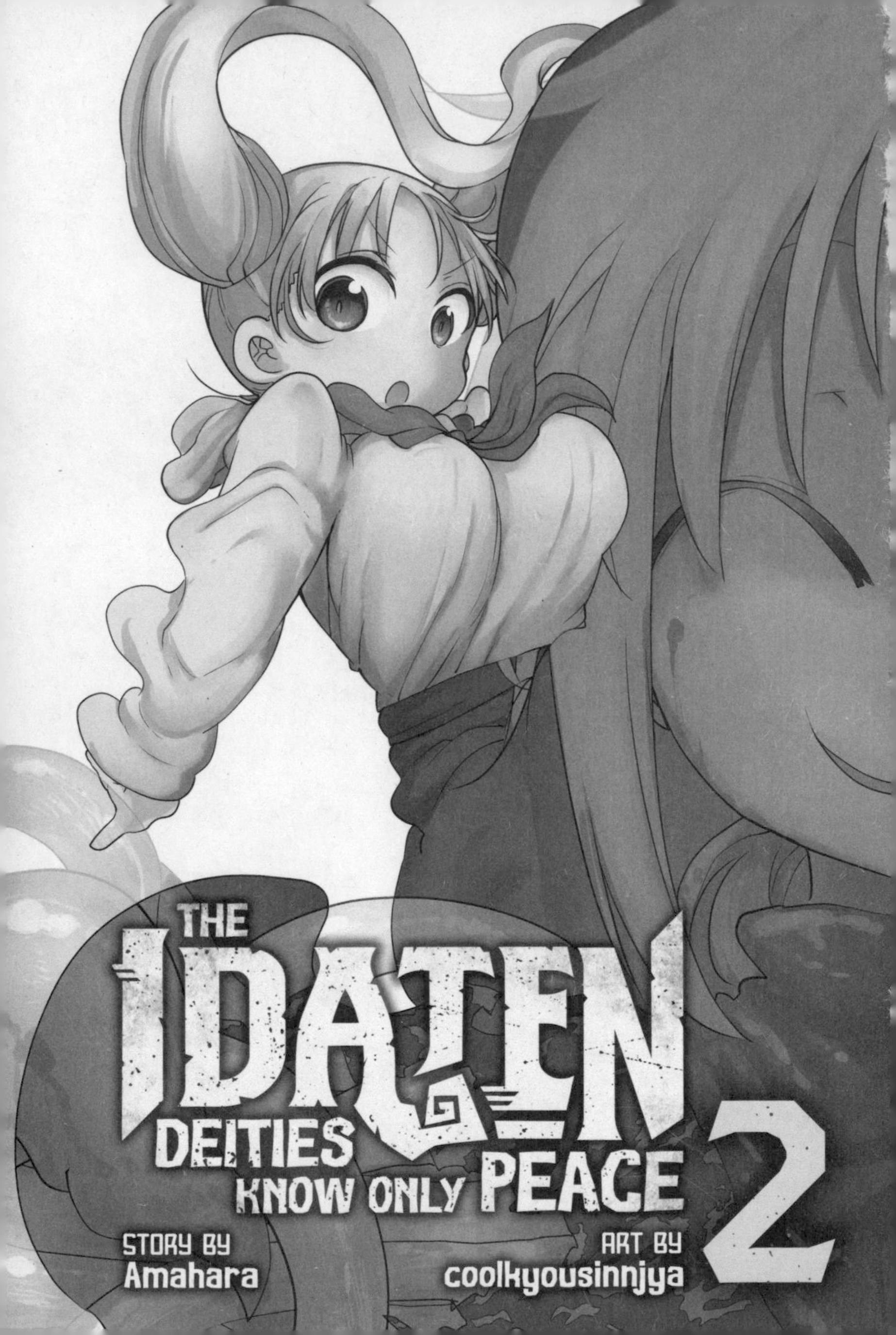
THE IDATEN DEITIES KNOW ONLY PEACE
2
STORY BY
Amahara
ART BY
coolkyousinnjya

THE IDATEN 2 DEITIES KNOW ONLY PEACE

CONTENTS

Cover Design: Natsuki Kubo (nartis)

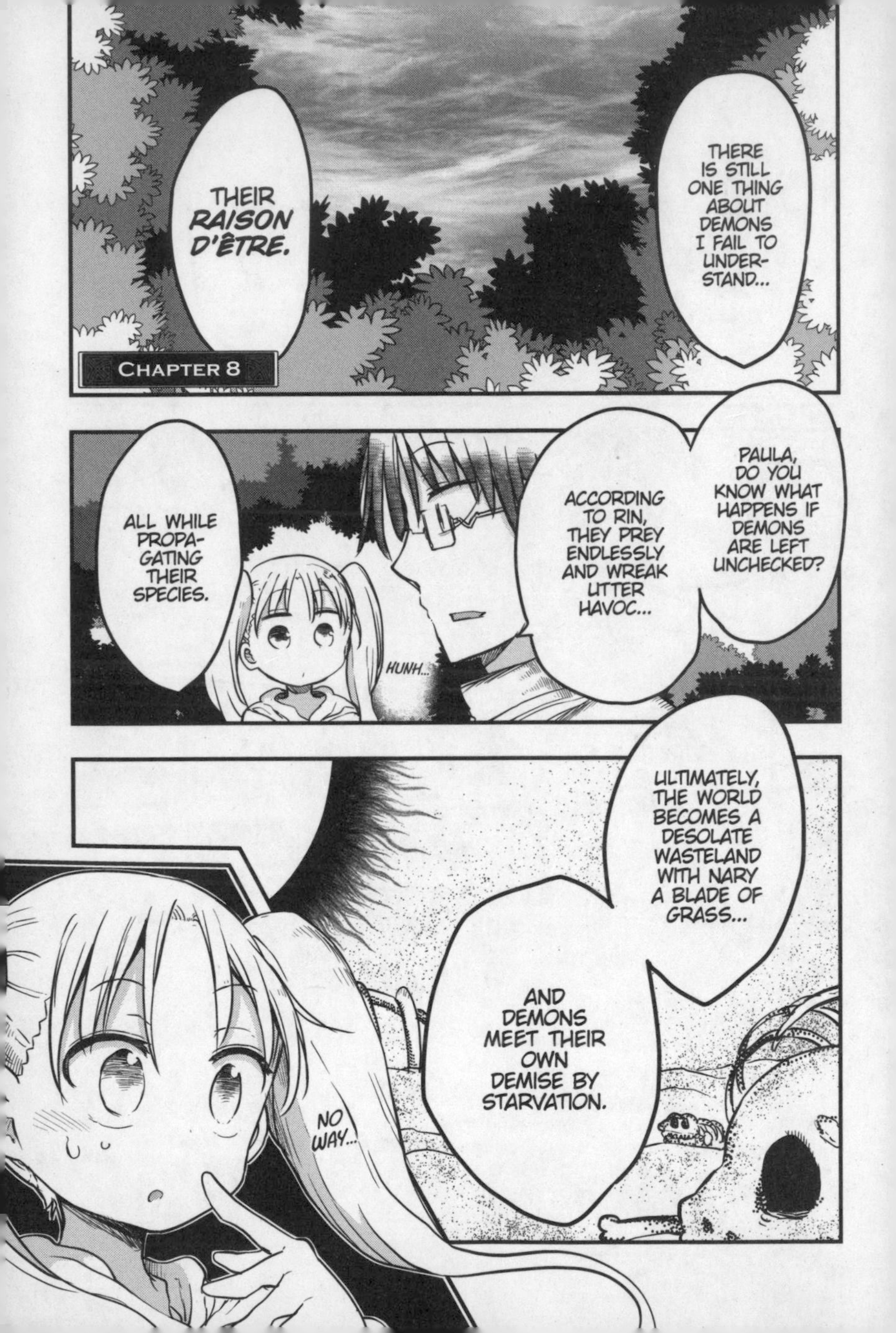
THERE IS STILL ONE THING ABOUT DEMONS I FAIL TO UNDERSTAND...
THEIR RAISON D'ÊTRE.
CHAPTER 8
PAULA, DO YOU KNOW WHAT HAPPENS IF DEMONS ARE LEFT UNCHECKED?
ACCORDING TO RIN, THEY PREY ENDLESSLY AND WREAK UTTER HAVOC...
HUNH...
ALL WHILE PROPAGATING THEIR SPECIES.
ULTIMATELY, THE WORLD BECOMES A DESOLATE WASTELAND WITH NARY A BLADE OF GRASS...
AND DEMONS MEET THEIR OWN DEMISE BY STARVATION.
NO WAY...

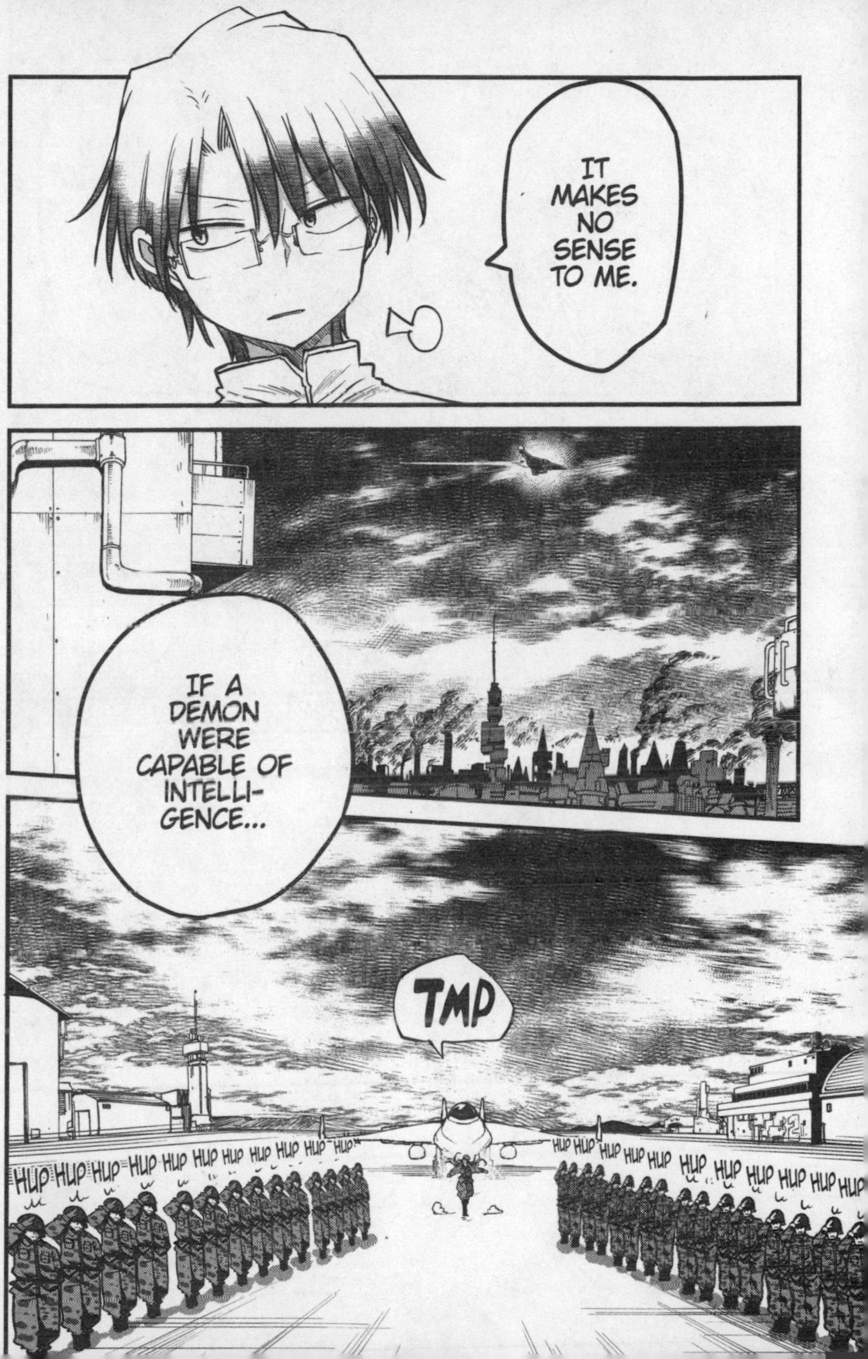
IT MAKES NO SENSE TO ME.
IF A DEMON WERE CAPABLE OF INTELLI-GENCE...
TMP
HUP HUP HUP HUP HUP HUP HUP HUP HUP
HUP HUP HUP HUP HUP HUP HUP HUP HUP HUP HUP HUP HUP HUP HUP

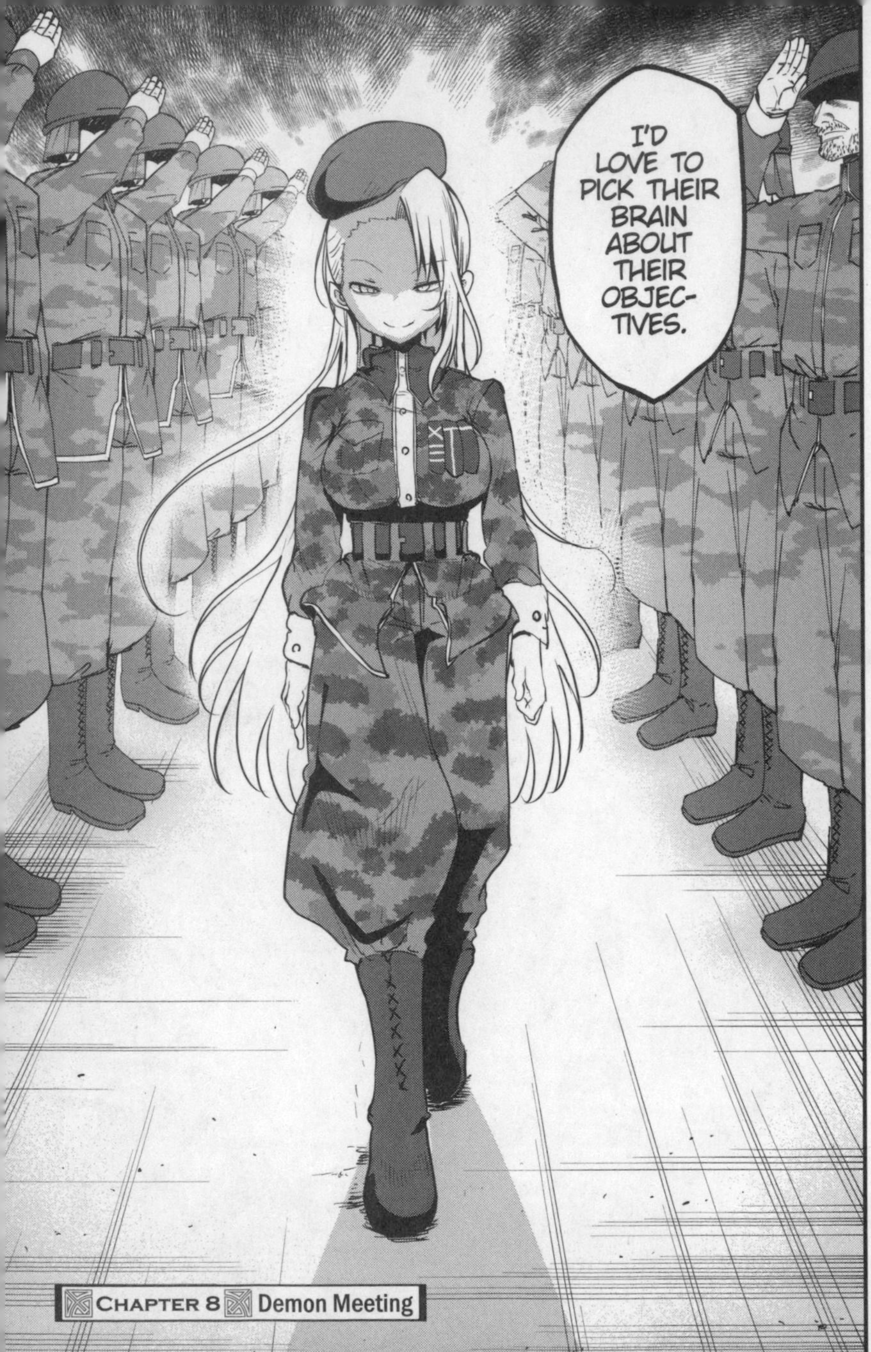
I'D LOVE TO PICK THEIR BRAIN ABOUT THEIR OBJECTIVES.
CHAPTER 8 Demon Meeting

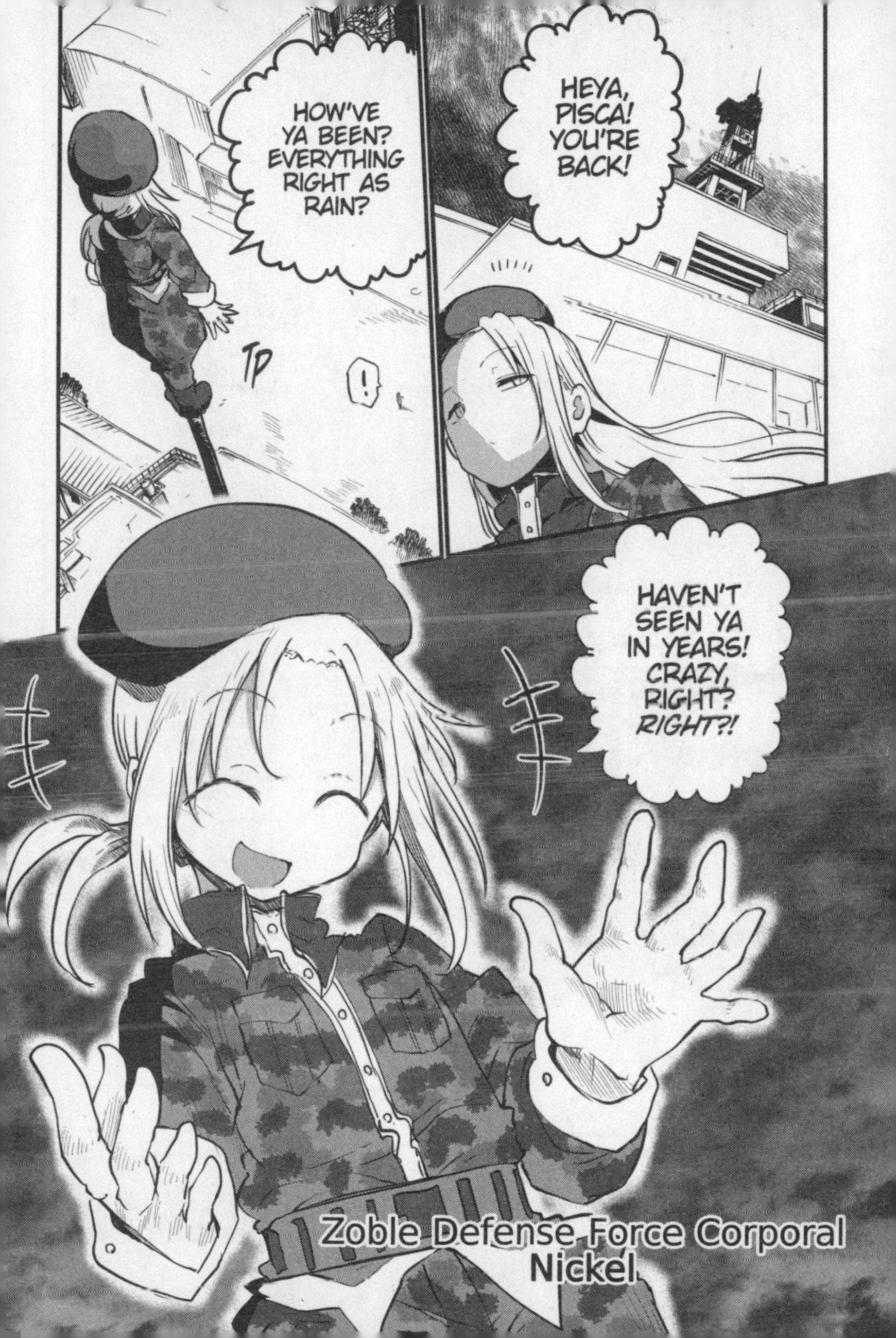
HEYA, PISCA! YOU'RE BACK!
HOW'VE YA BEEN? EVERYTHING RIGHT AS RAIN?
!
TP
HAVEN'T SEEN YA IN YEARS! CRAZY, RIGHT? *RIGHT?!*
Zoble Defense Force Corporal
Nickel

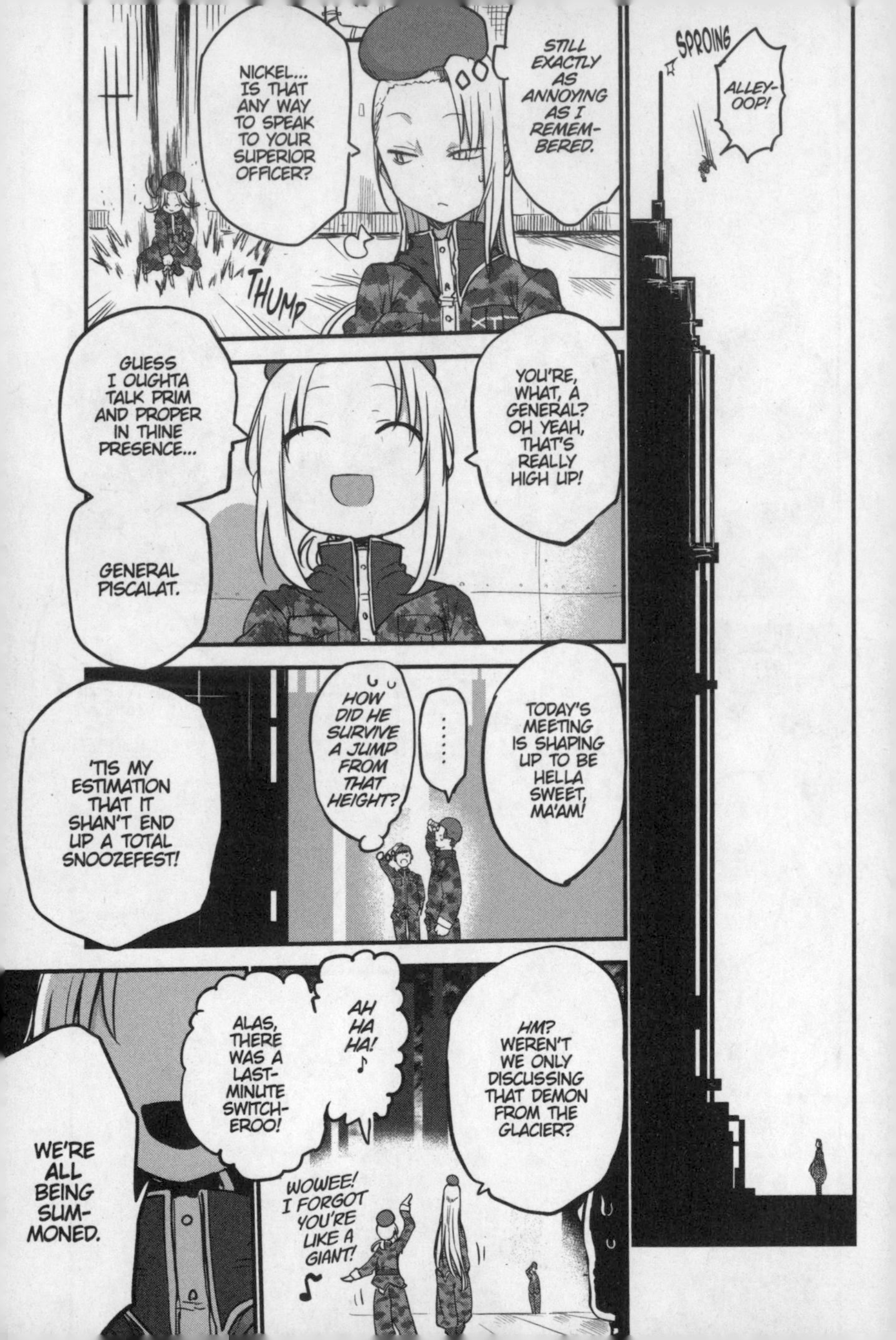
SPROING
ALLEY-OOP!
STILL EXACTLY AS ANNOYING AS I REMEMBERED.
NICKEL... IS THAT ANY WAY TO SPEAK TO YOUR SUPERIOR OFFICER?
THUMP
YOU'RE, WHAT, A GENERAL? OH YEAH, THAT'S REALLY HIGH UP!
GUESS I OUGHTA TALK PRIM AND PROPER IN THINE PRESENCE...
GENERAL PISCALAT.
TODAY'S MEETING IS SHAPING UP TO BE HELLA SWEET, MA'AM!
......
HOW DID HE SURVIVE A JUMP FROM THAT HEIGHT?
'TIS MY ESTIMATION THAT IT SHAN'T END UP A TOTAL SNOOZEFEST!
HM? WEREN'T WE ONLY DISCUSSING THAT DEMON FROM THE GLACIER?
AH HA HA! ♪
ALAS, THERE WAS A LAST-MINUTE SWITCHEROO!
WOWEE! I FORGOT YOU'RE LIKE A GIANT!
WE'RE ALL BEING SUMMONED.

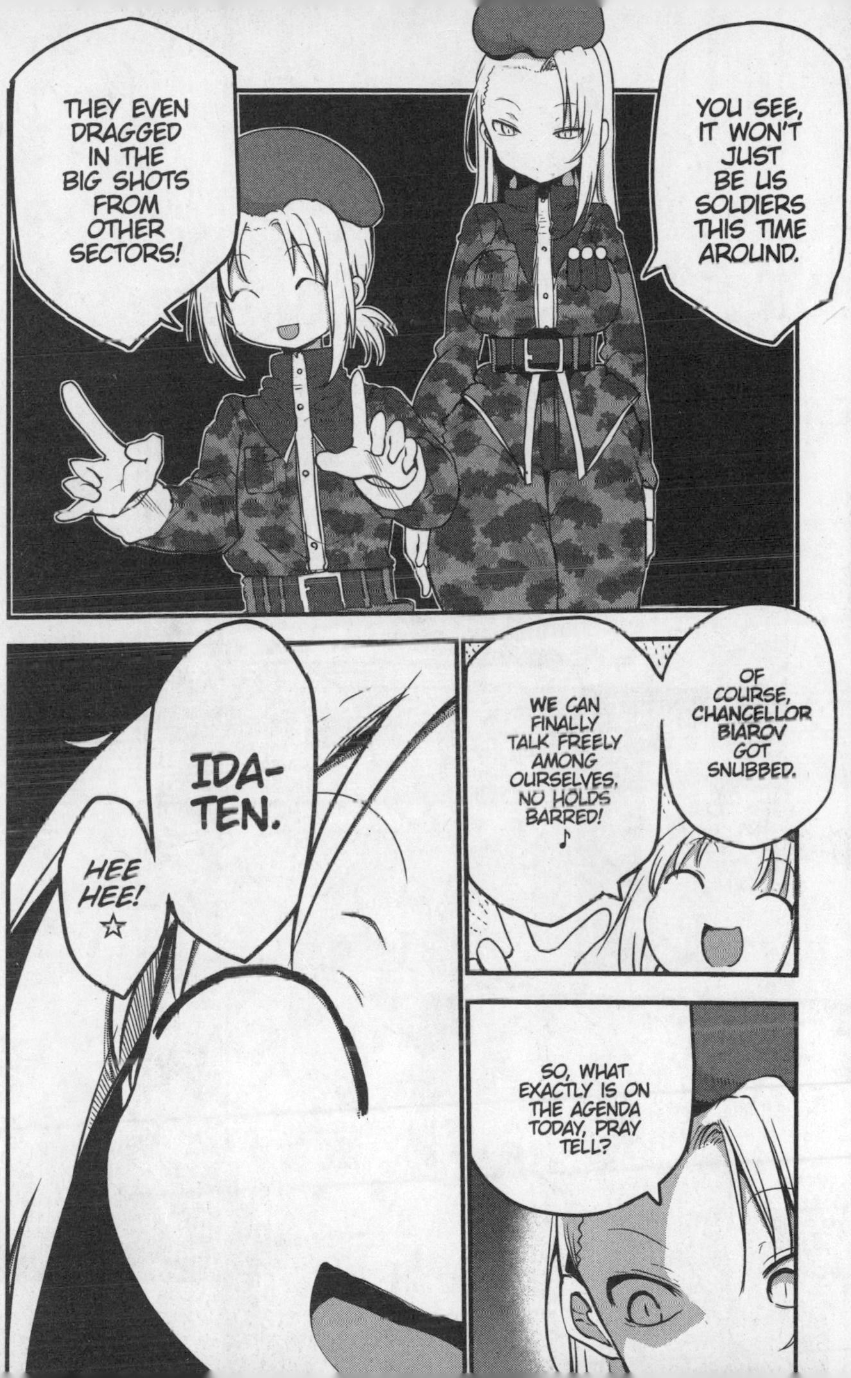
YOU SEE, IT WON'T JUST BE US SOLDIERS THIS TIME AROUND.
THEY EVEN DRAGGED IN THE BIG SHOTS FROM OTHER SECTORS!
OF COURSE, CHANCELLOR BIAROV GOT SNUBBED.
WE CAN FINALLY TALK FREELY AMONG OURSELVES, NO HOLDS BARRED! ♪
SO, WHAT EXACTLY IS ON THE AGENDA TODAY, PRAY TELL?
IDA-TEN.
HEE HEE! ☆

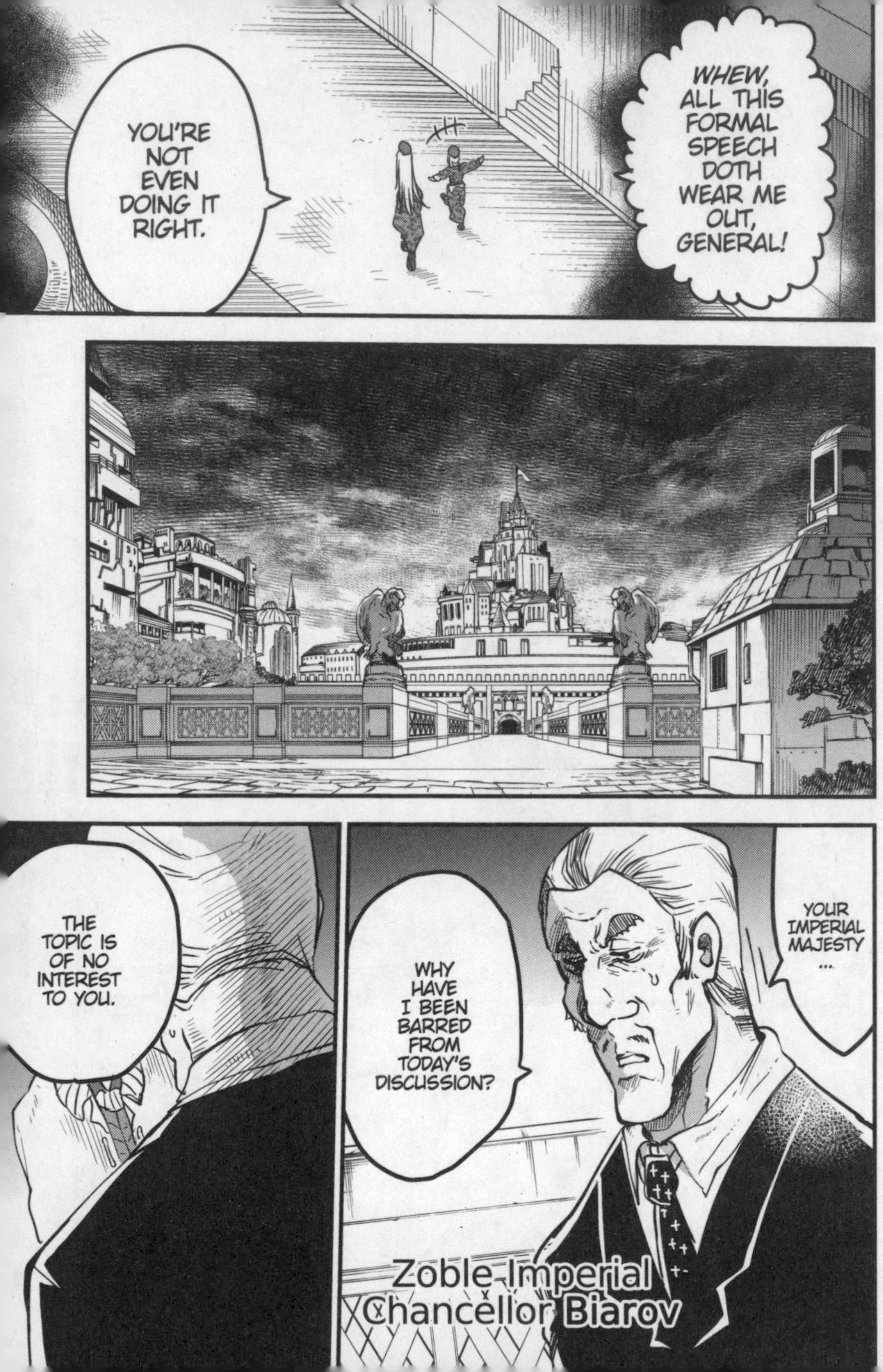
WHEW, ALL THIS FORMAL SPEECH DOTH WEAR ME OUT, GENERAL!
YOU'RE NOT EVEN DOING IT RIGHT.
YOUR IMPERIAL MAJESTY...
WHY HAVE I BEEN BARRED FROM TODAY'S DISCUSSION?
Zoble Imperial Chancellor Biarov
THE TOPIC IS OF NO INTEREST TO YOU.

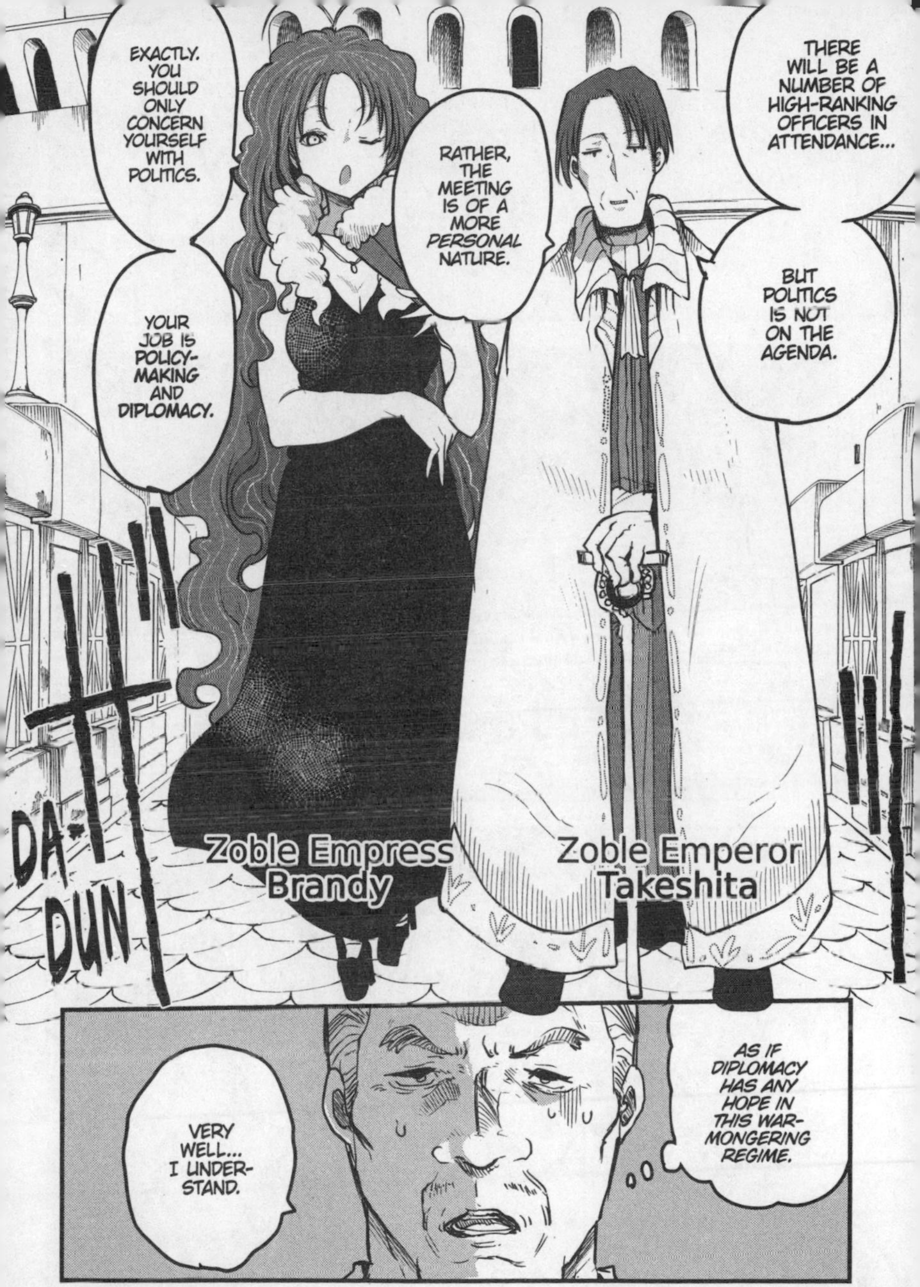
THERE WILL BE A NUMBER OF HIGH-RANKING OFFICERS IN ATTENDANCE...
BUT POLITICS IS NOT ON THE AGENDA.
RATHER, THE MEETING IS OF A MORE PERSONAL NATURE.
EXACTLY. YOU SHOULD ONLY CONCERN YOURSELF WITH POLITICS.
YOUR JOB IS POLICY-MAKING AND DIPLOMACY.
Zoble Emperor Takeshita
Zoble Empress Brandy
DA-DUN
AS IF DIPLOMACY HAS ANY HOPE IN THIS WAR-MONGERING REGIME.
VERY WELL... I UNDER-STAND.

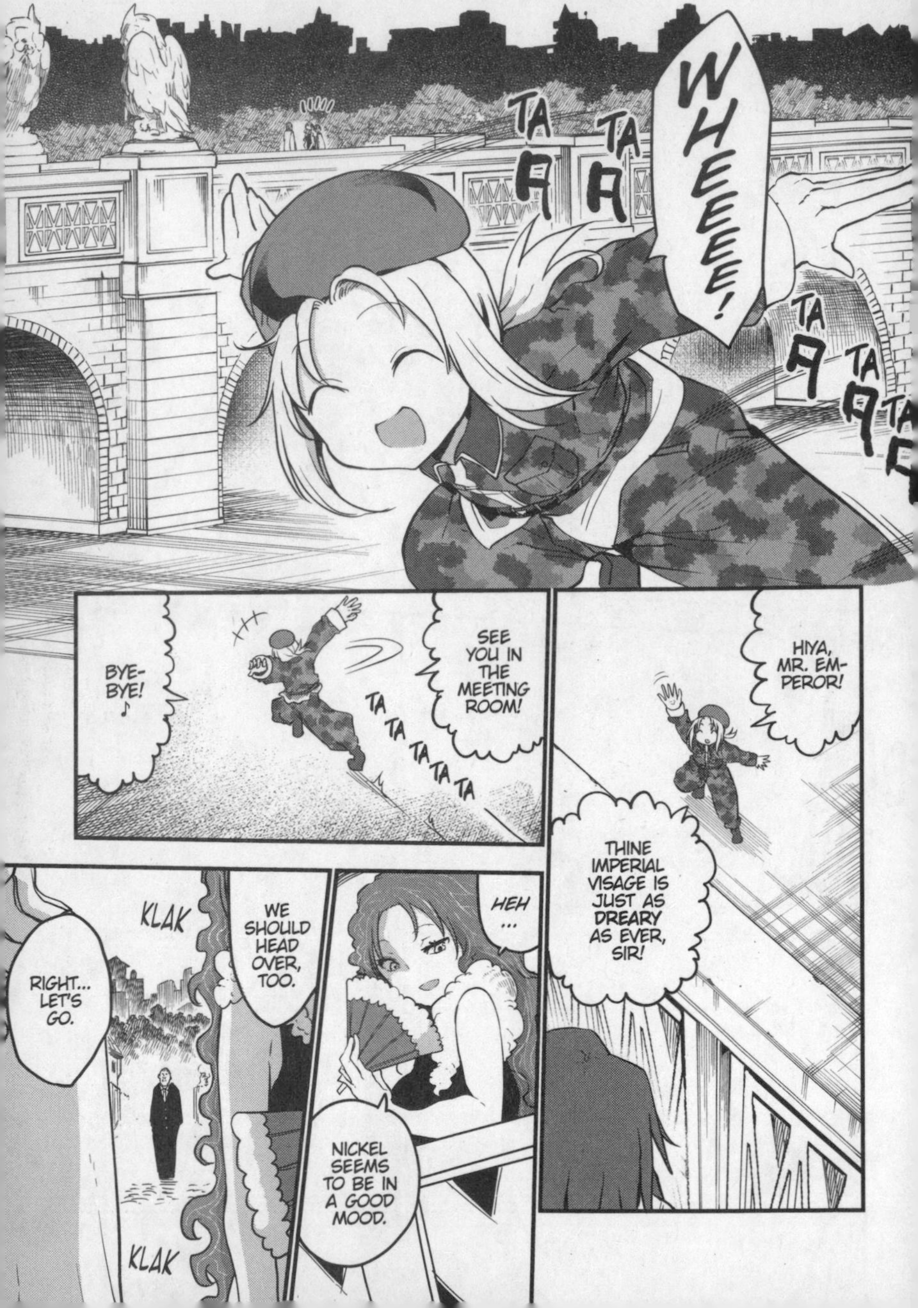
WHEEEEE!
TA TA TA TA
TA TA
HIYA, MR. EMPEROR!
THINE IMPERIAL VISAGE IS JUST AS DREARY AS EVER, SIR!
SEE YOU IN THE MEETING ROOM!
BYE-BYE! ♪
TA TA TA TA TA
HEH...
NICKEL SEEMS TO BE IN A GOOD MOOD.
KLAK
WE SHOULD HEAD OVER, TOO.
RIGHT... LET'S GO.
KLAK

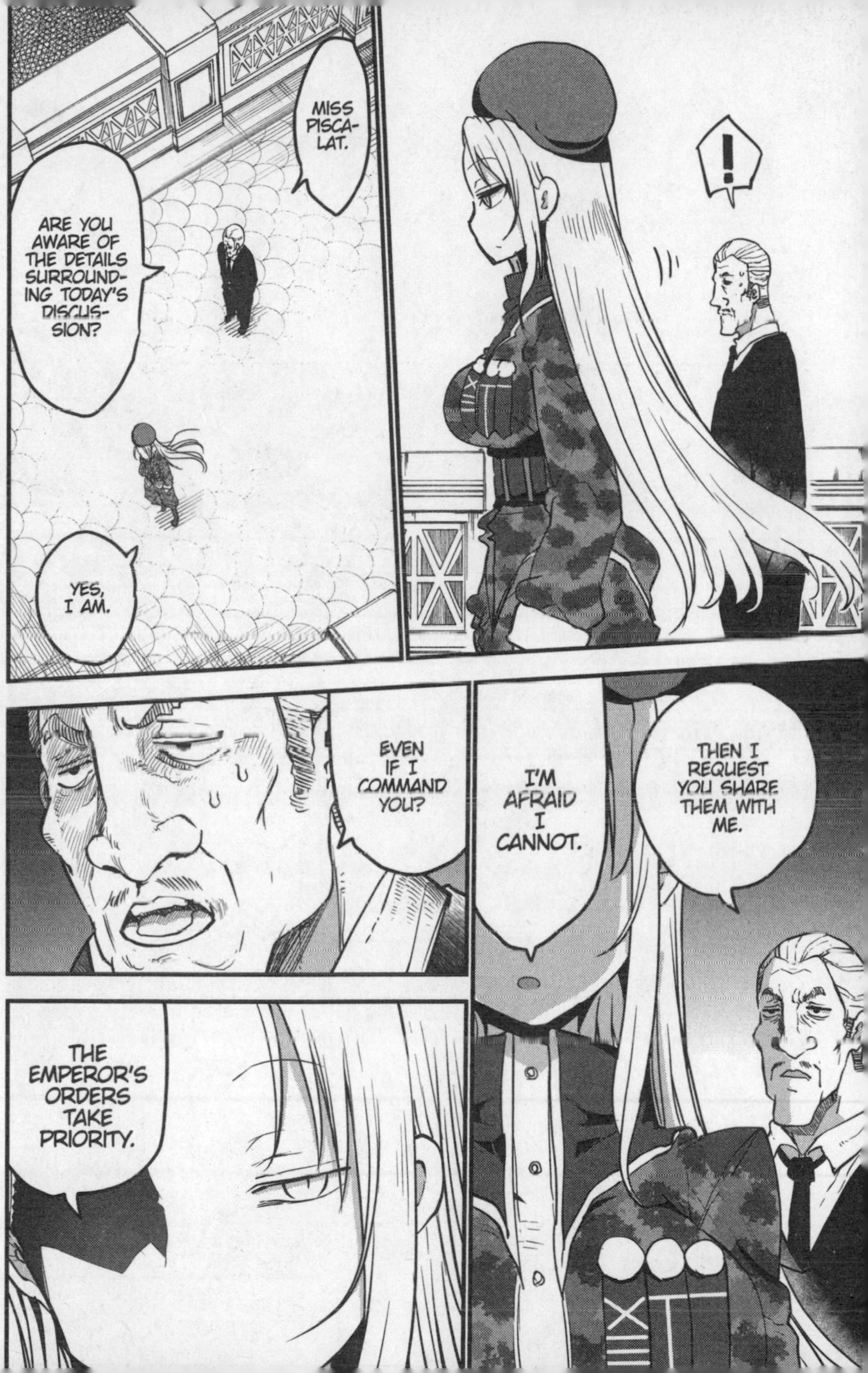
!
MISS PISCALAT.
ARE YOU AWARE OF THE DETAILS SURROUNDING TODAY'S DISCUSSION?
YES, I AM.
THEN I REQUEST YOU SHARE THEM WITH ME.
I'M AFRAID I CANNOT.
EVEN IF I COMMAND YOU?
THE EMPEROR'S ORDERS TAKE PRIORITY.

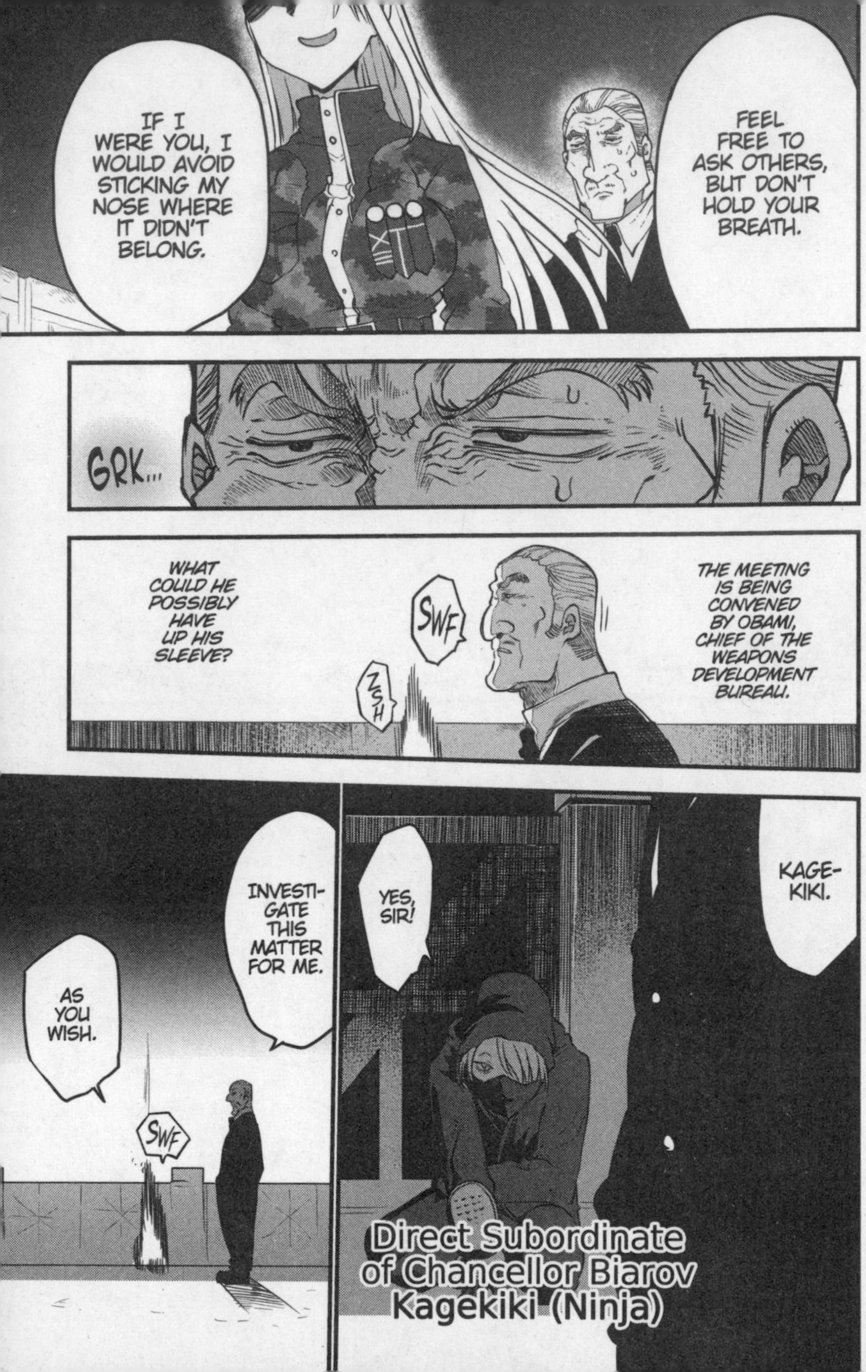
FEEL FREE TO ASK OTHERS, BUT DON'T HOLD YOUR BREATH.
IF I WERE YOU, I WOULD AVOID STICKING MY NOSE WHERE IT DIDN'T BELONG.
GRK...
THE MEETING IS BEING CONVENED BY OBAMI, CHIEF OF THE WEAPONS DEVELOPMENT BUREAU.
SWF
ZSH
WHAT COULD HE POSSIBLY HAVE UP HIS SLEEVE?
KAGE-KIKI.
YES, SIR!
Direct Subordinate of Chancellor Biarov
Kagekiki (Ninja)
INVESTI-GATE THIS MATTER FOR ME.
AS YOU WISH.
SWF

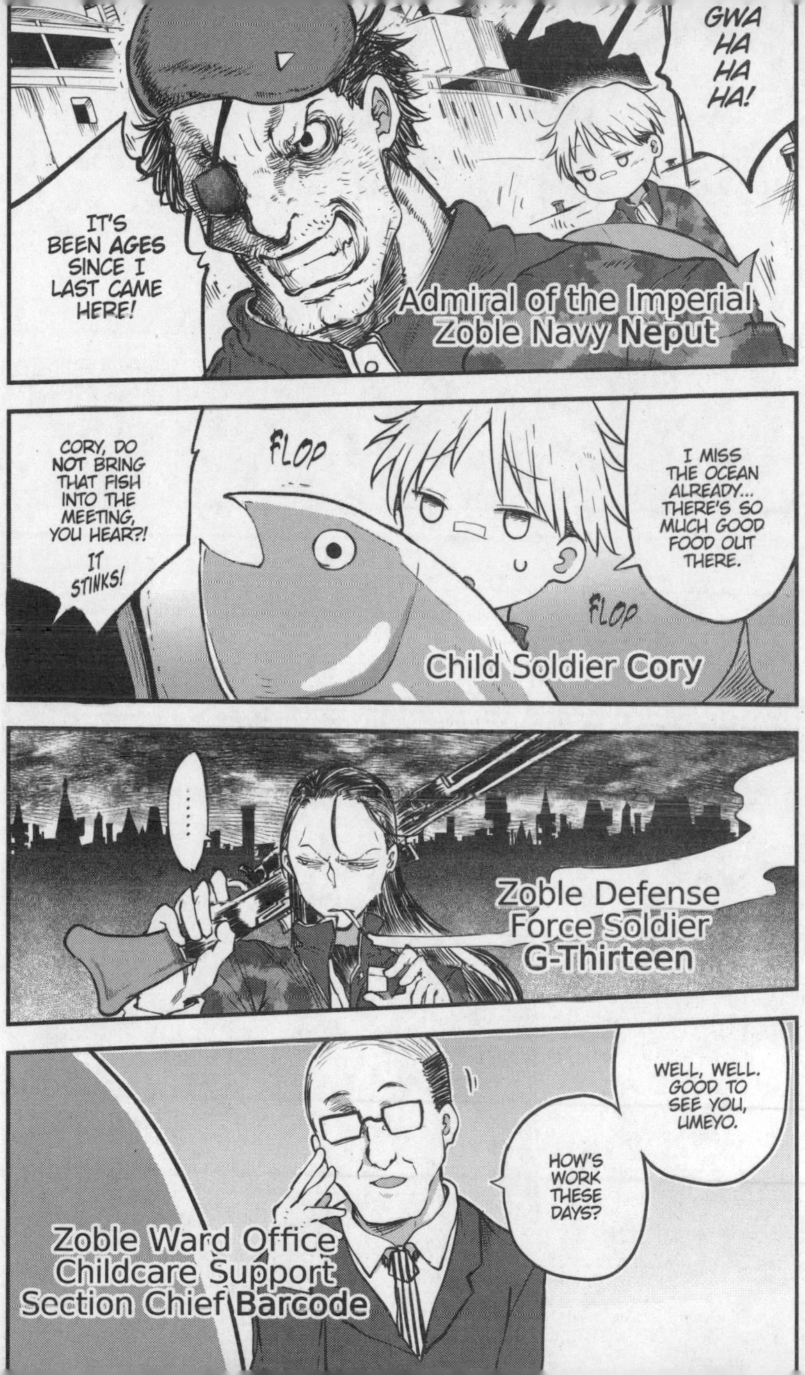
GWA HA HA HA!
IT'S BEEN AGES SINCE I LAST CAME HERE!
Admiral of the Imperial Zoble Navy Neput
I MISS THE OCEAN ALREADY... THERE'S SO MUCH GOOD FOOD OUT THERE.
FLOP
CORY, DO NOT BRING THAT FISH INTO THE MEETING, YOU HEAR?!
IT STINKS!
FLOP
Child Soldier Cory
......
Zoble Defense Force Soldier G-Thirteen
WELL, WELL. GOOD TO SEE YOU, UMEYO.
HOW'S WORK THESE DAYS?
Zoble Ward Office Childcare Support Section Chief Barcode

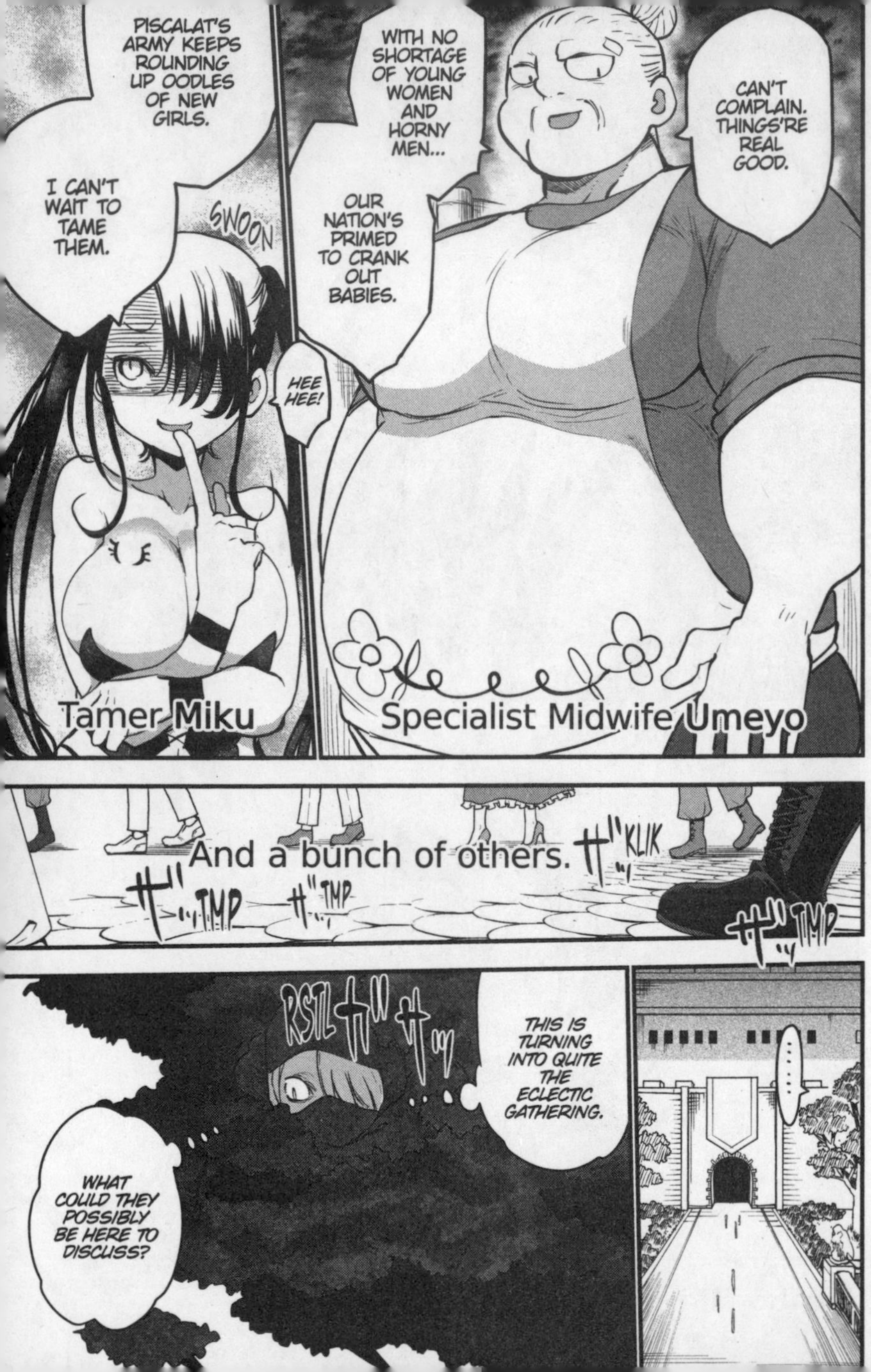

CAN'T COMPLAIN. THINGS'RE REAL GOOD.
WITH NO SHORTAGE OF YOUNG WOMEN AND HORNY MEN...
OUR NATION'S PRIMED TO CRANK OUT BABIES.
Specialist Midwife Umeyo
PISCALAT'S ARMY KEEPS ROUNDING UP OODLES OF NEW GIRLS.
SWOON
I CAN'T WAIT TO TAME THEM.
HEE HEE!
Tamer Miku
KLIK
TMP
And a bunch of others.
TMP
TMP
......
THIS IS TURNING INTO QUITE THE ECLECTIC GATHERING.
RSTL
...
WHAT COULD THEY POSSIBLY BE HERE TO DISCUSS?

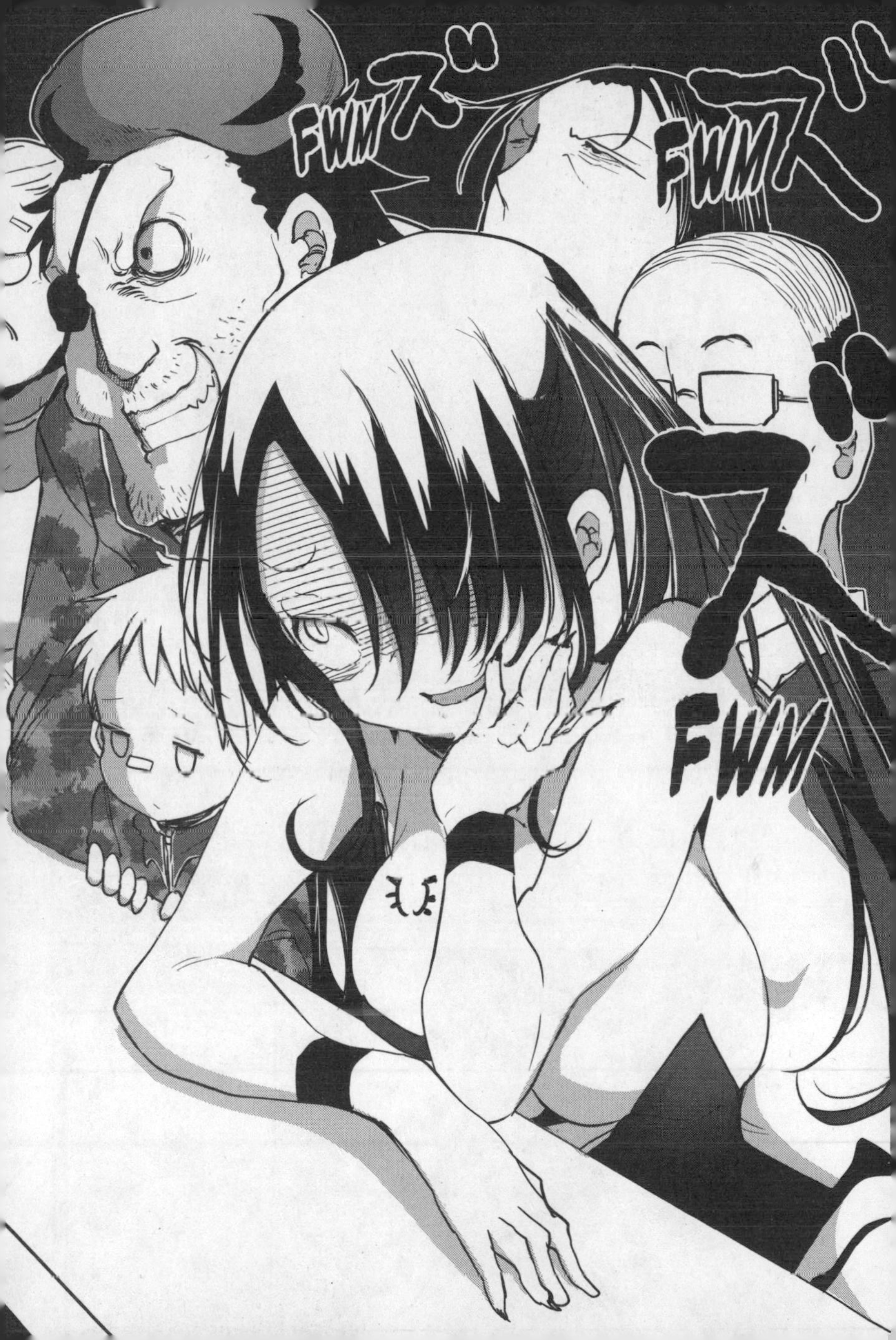
FWM
FWM
FWM

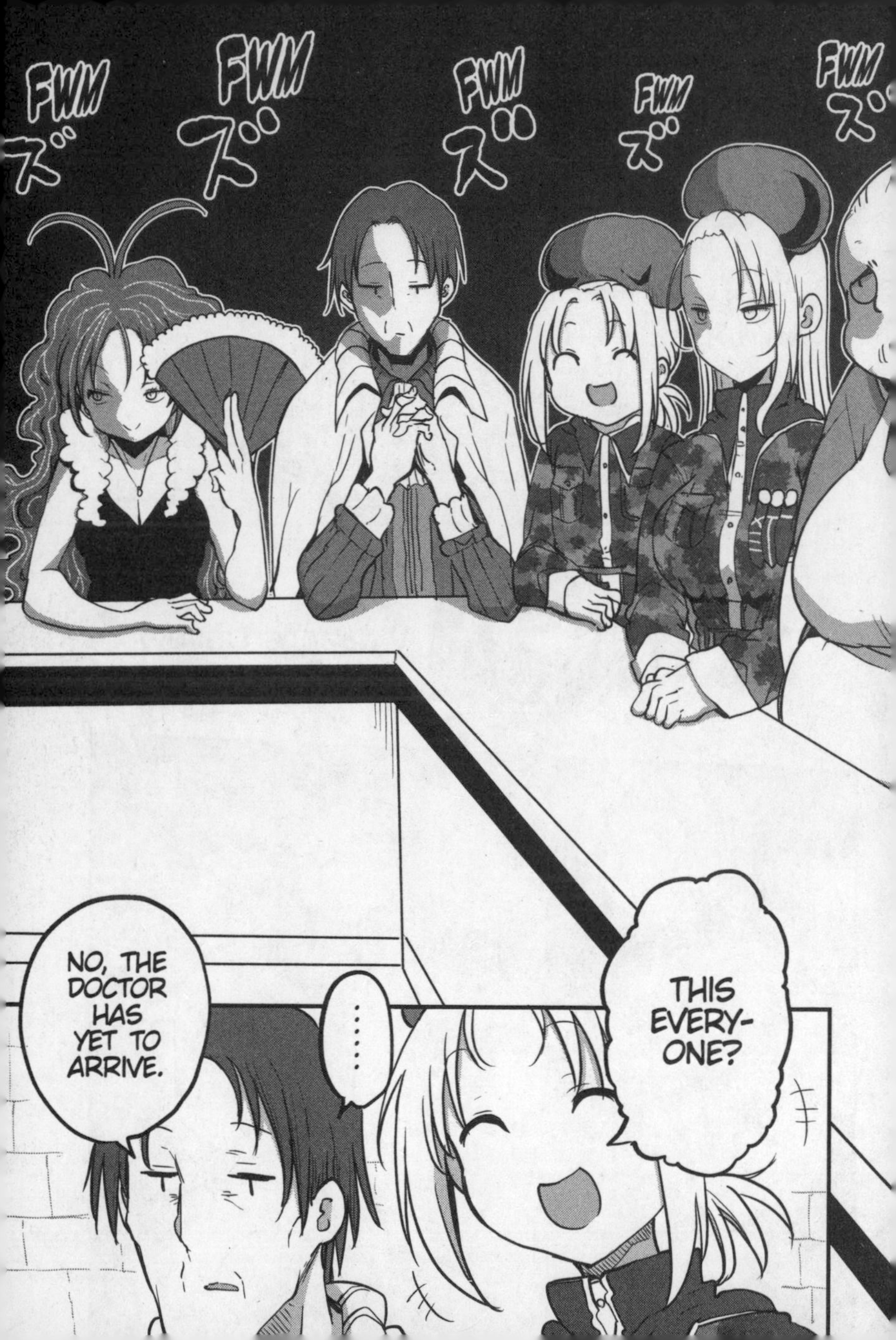
FWM ズ
FWM ズ
FWM ズ
FWM ズ
FWM ズ
THIS EVERY-ONE?
......
NO, THE DOCTOR HAS YET TO ARRIVE.

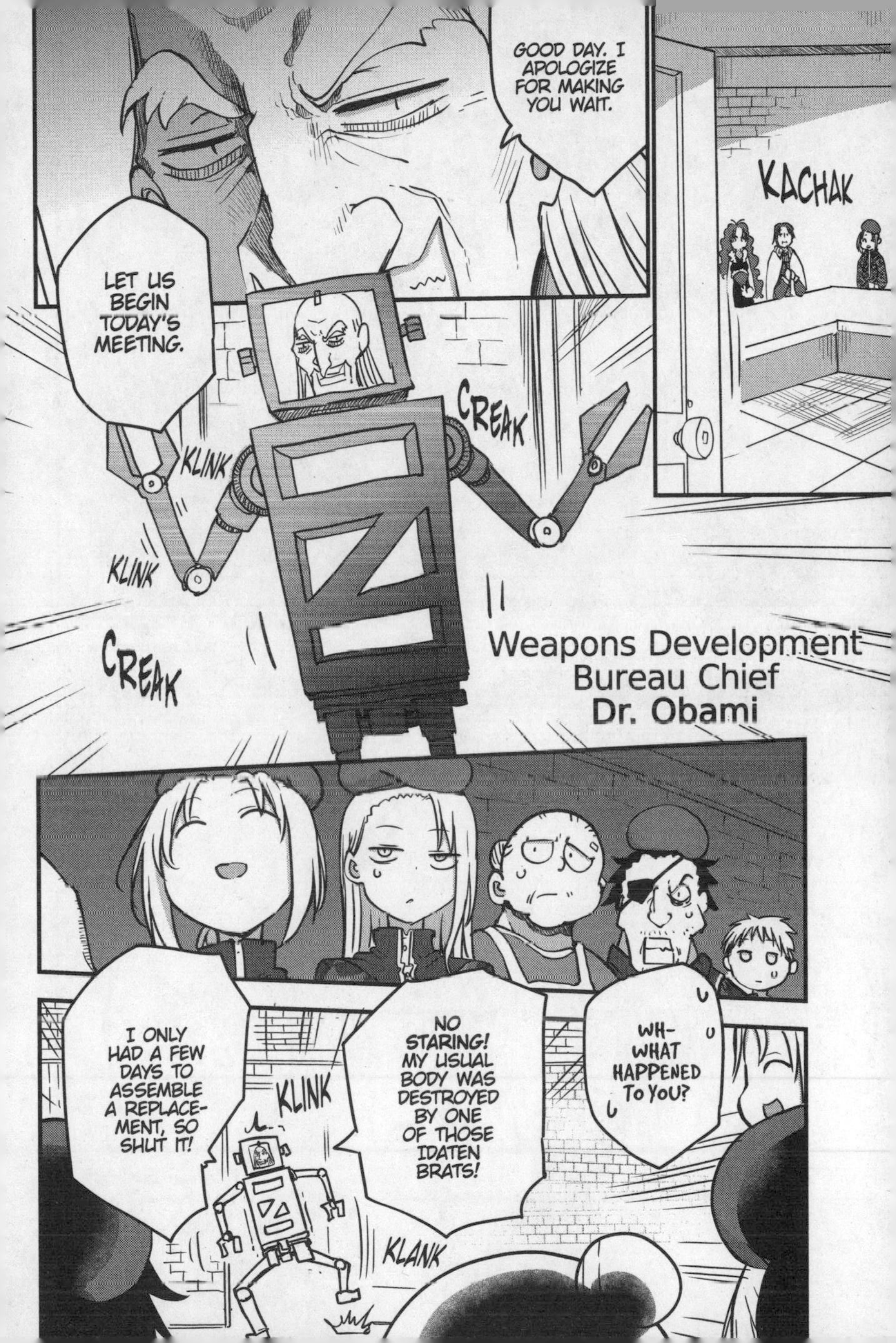
KACHAK
GOOD DAY. I APOLOGIZE FOR MAKING YOU WAIT.
LET US BEGIN TODAY'S MEETING.
CREAK
KLINK
KLINK
CREAK
Weapons Development Bureau Chief Dr. Obami
WH-WHAT HAPPENED TO YOU?
NO STARING! MY USUAL BODY WAS DESTROYED BY ONE OF THOSE IDATEN BRATS!
KLINK
I ONLY HAD A FEW DAYS TO ASSEMBLE A REPLACEMENT, SO SHUT IT!
KLANK

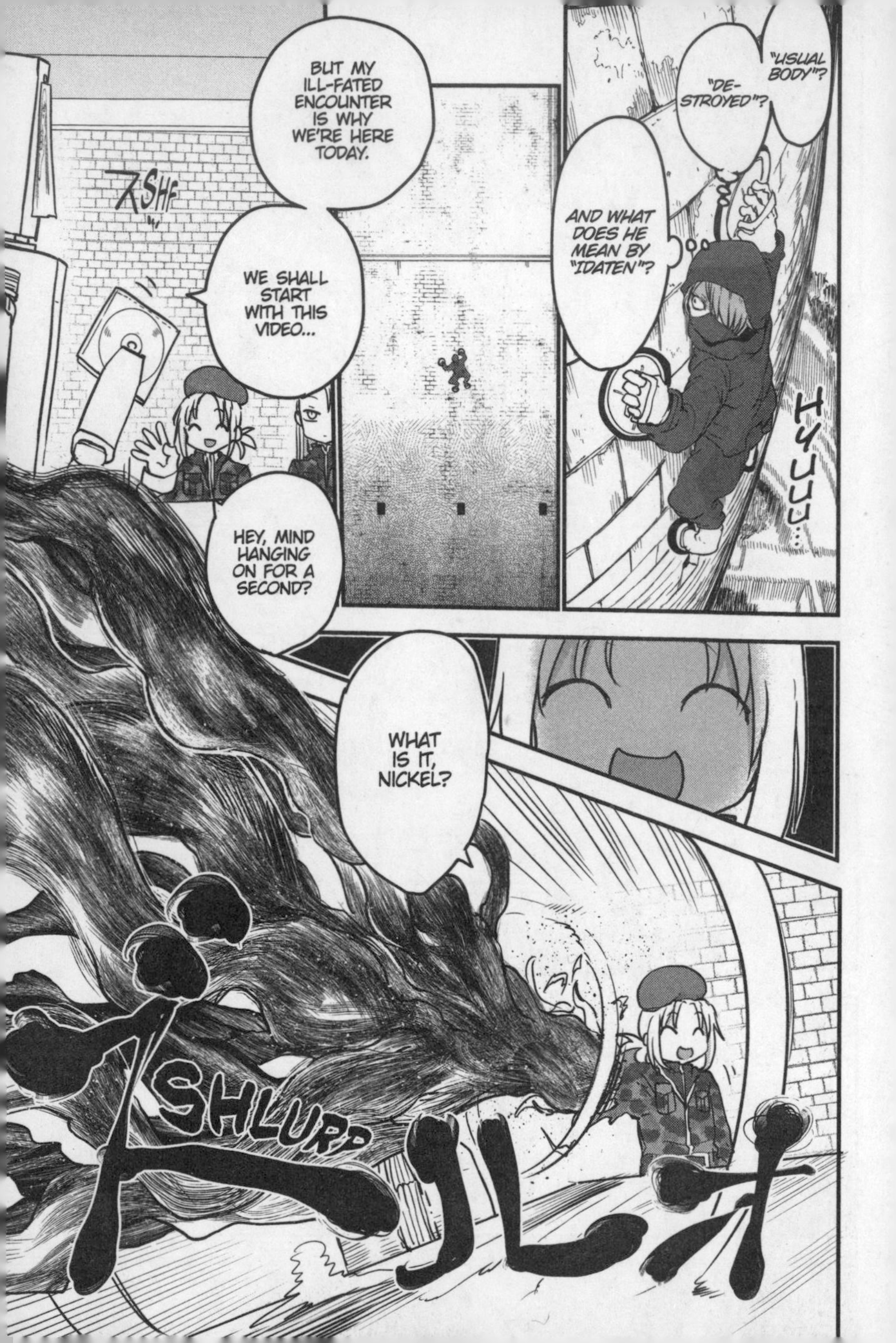
"USUAL BODY"?
"DE-STROYED"?
AND WHAT DOES HE MEAN BY "IDATEN"?
HYUUUU...
BUT MY ILL-FATED ENCOUNTER IS WHY WE'RE HERE TODAY.
SHF
WE SHALL START WITH THIS VIDEO...
HEY, MIND HANGING ON FOR A SECOND?
WHAT IS IT, NICKEL?
SHLURP

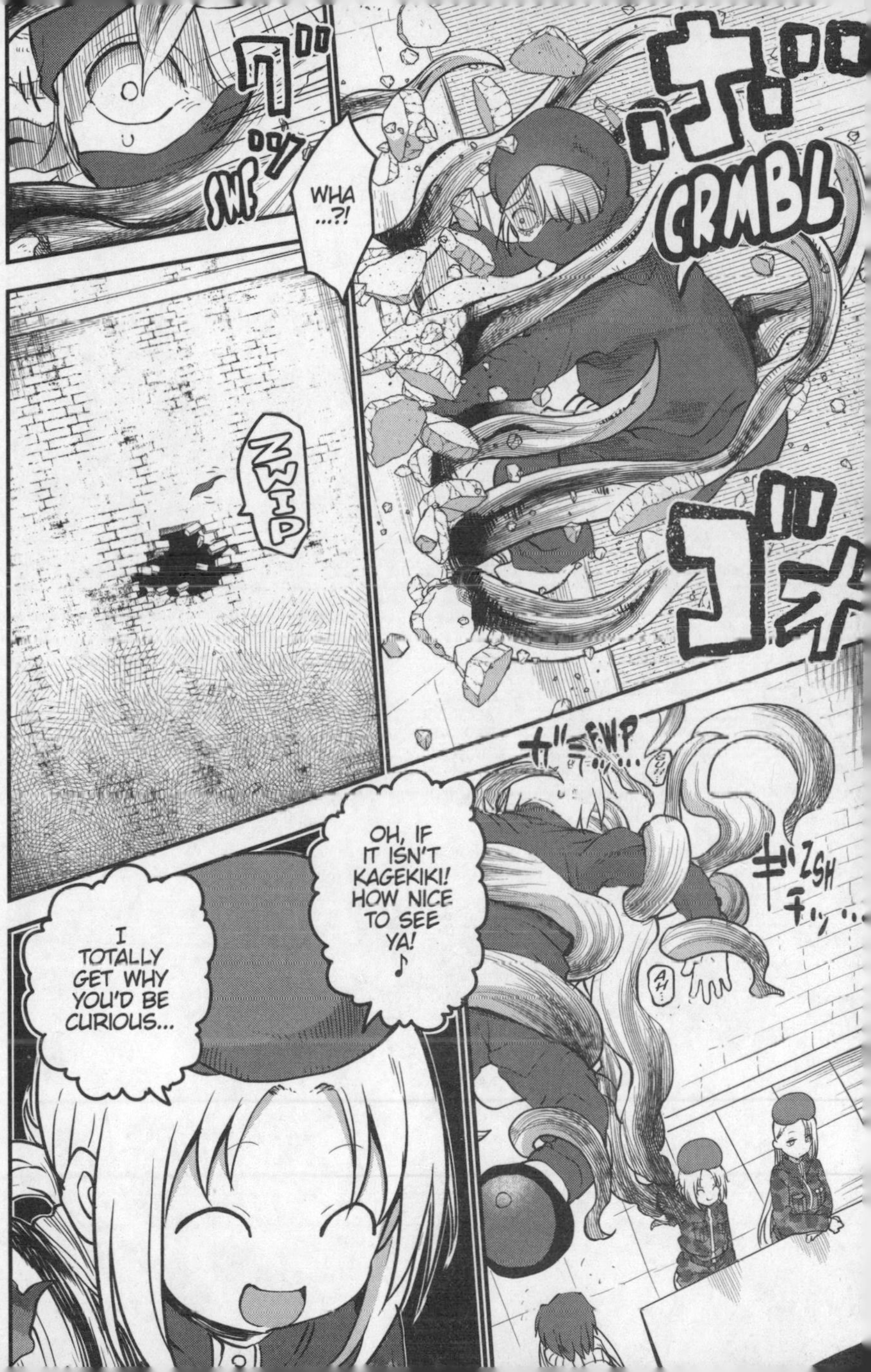
WHA ...?!
CRMBL
SWF
ZWIP
FWP...
ZSH
AH...
OH, IF IT ISN'T KAGEKIKI! HOW NICE TO SEE YA! ♪
I TOTALLY GET WHY YOU'D BE CURIOUS...

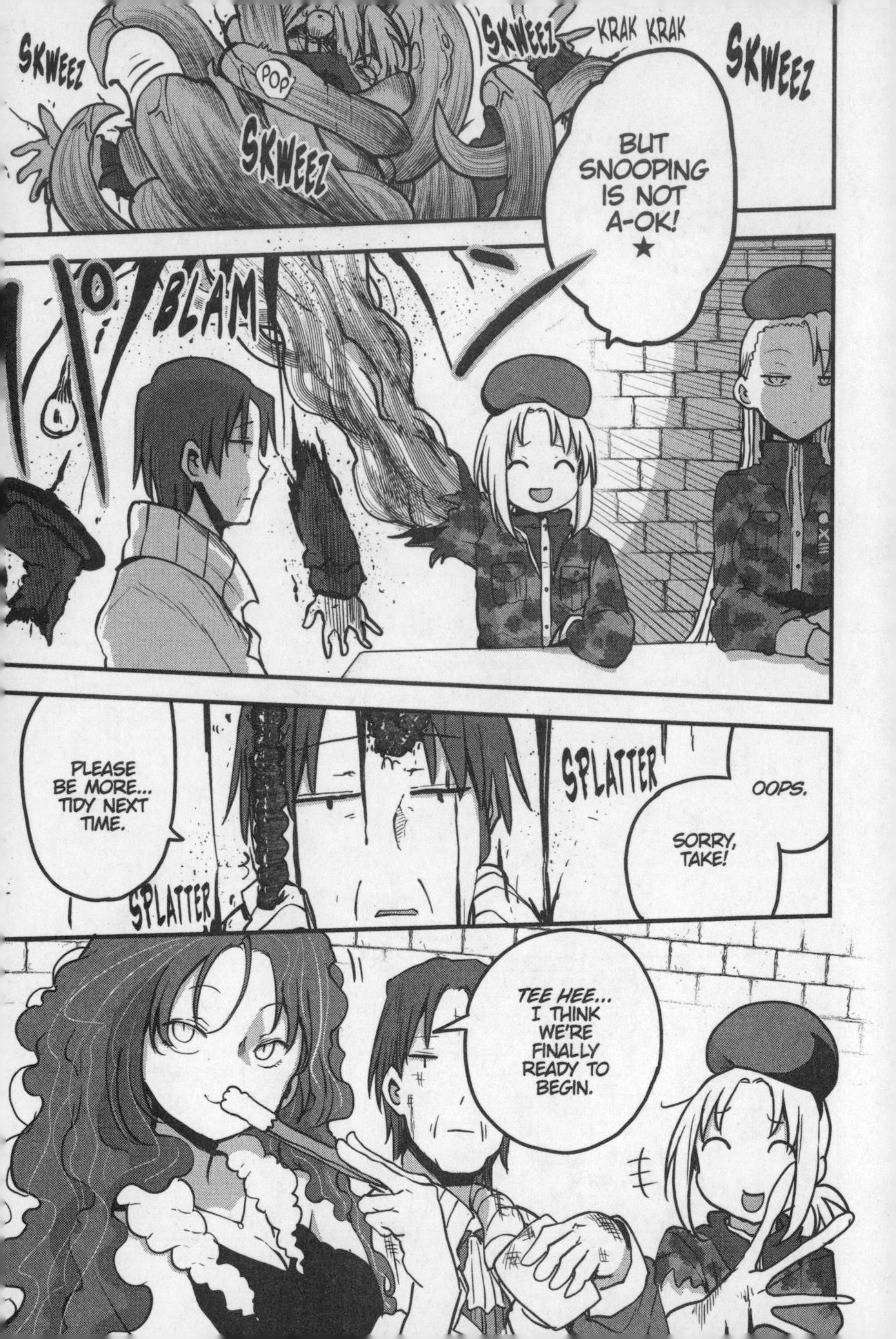
SKWEEZ
KRAK KRAK
SKWEEZ
POP
SKWEEZ
SKWEEZ
BUT SNOOPING IS NOT A-OK! ★
BLAM
O
OOPS.
SORRY, TAKE!
SPLATTER
PLEASE BE MORE... TIDY NEXT TIME.
SPLATTER
TEE HEE... I THINK WE'RE FINALLY READY TO BEGIN.

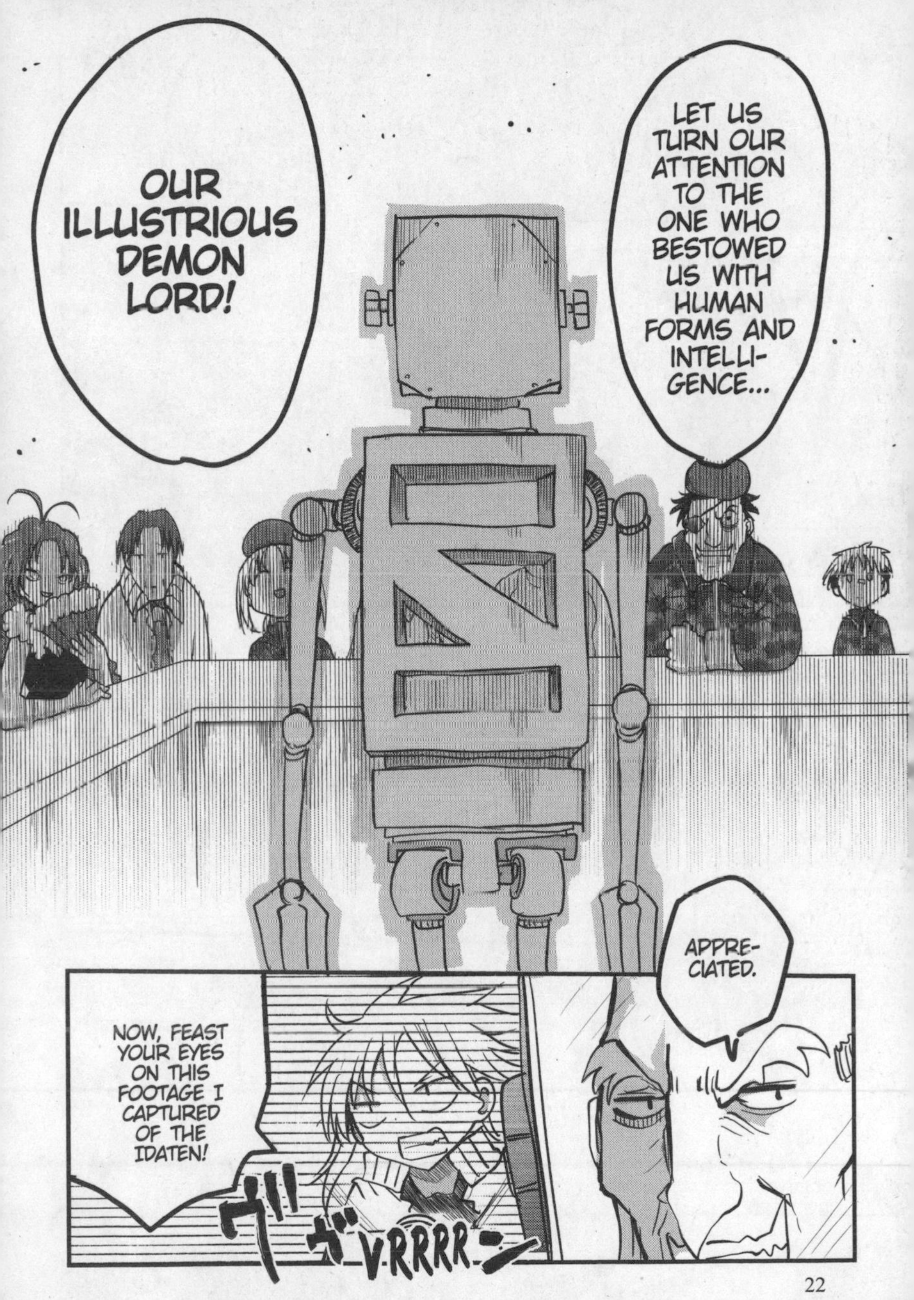
LET US TURN OUR ATTENTION TO THE ONE WHO BESTOWED US WITH HUMAN FORMS AND INTELLI-GENCE...
OUR ILLUSTRIOUS DEMON LORD!
APPRE-CIATED.
NOW, FEAST YOUR EYES ON THIS FOOTAGE I CAPTURED OF THE IDATEN!
ヴゥゥ
V-RRRR

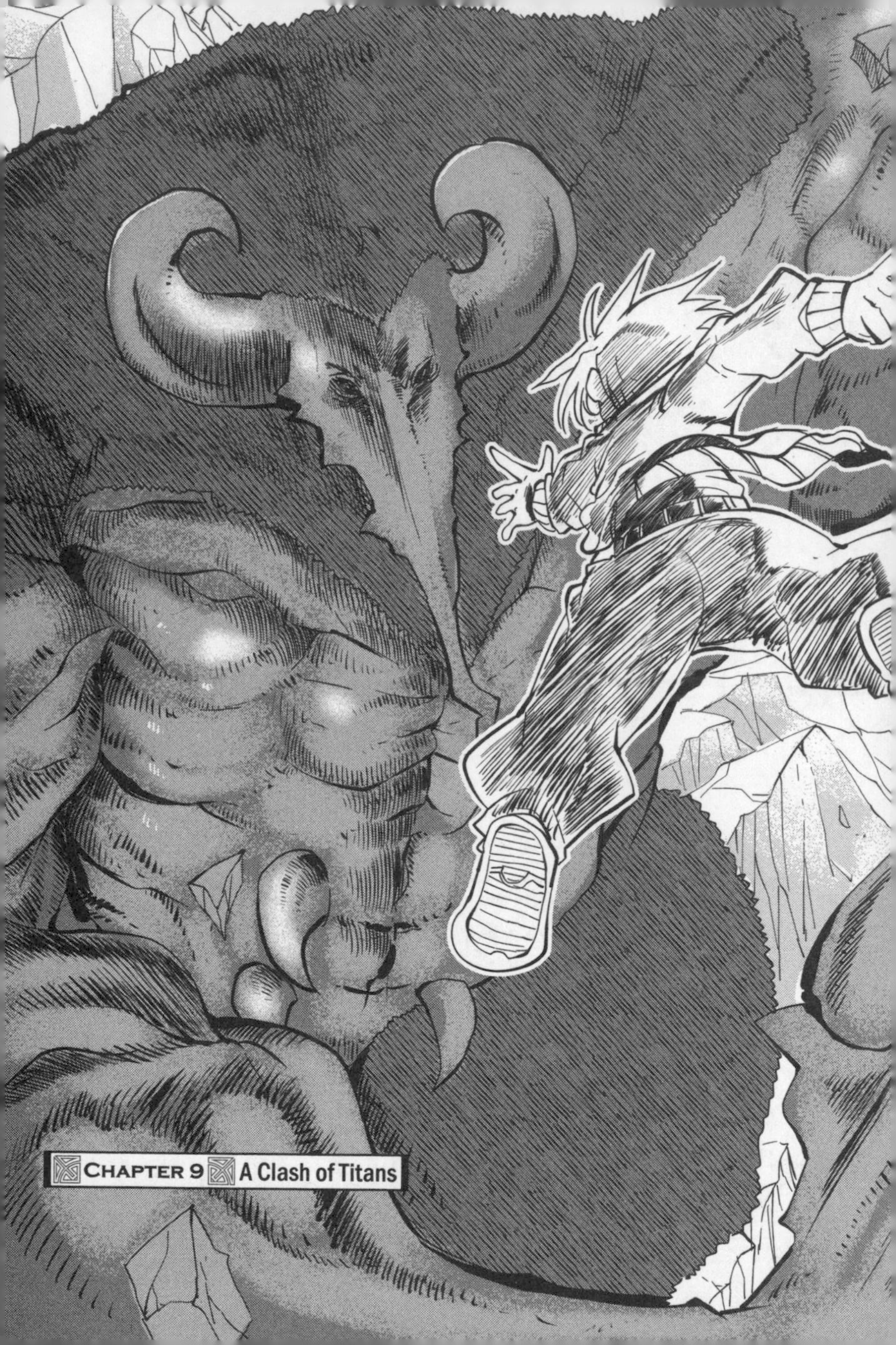
CHAPTER 9 A Clash of Titans

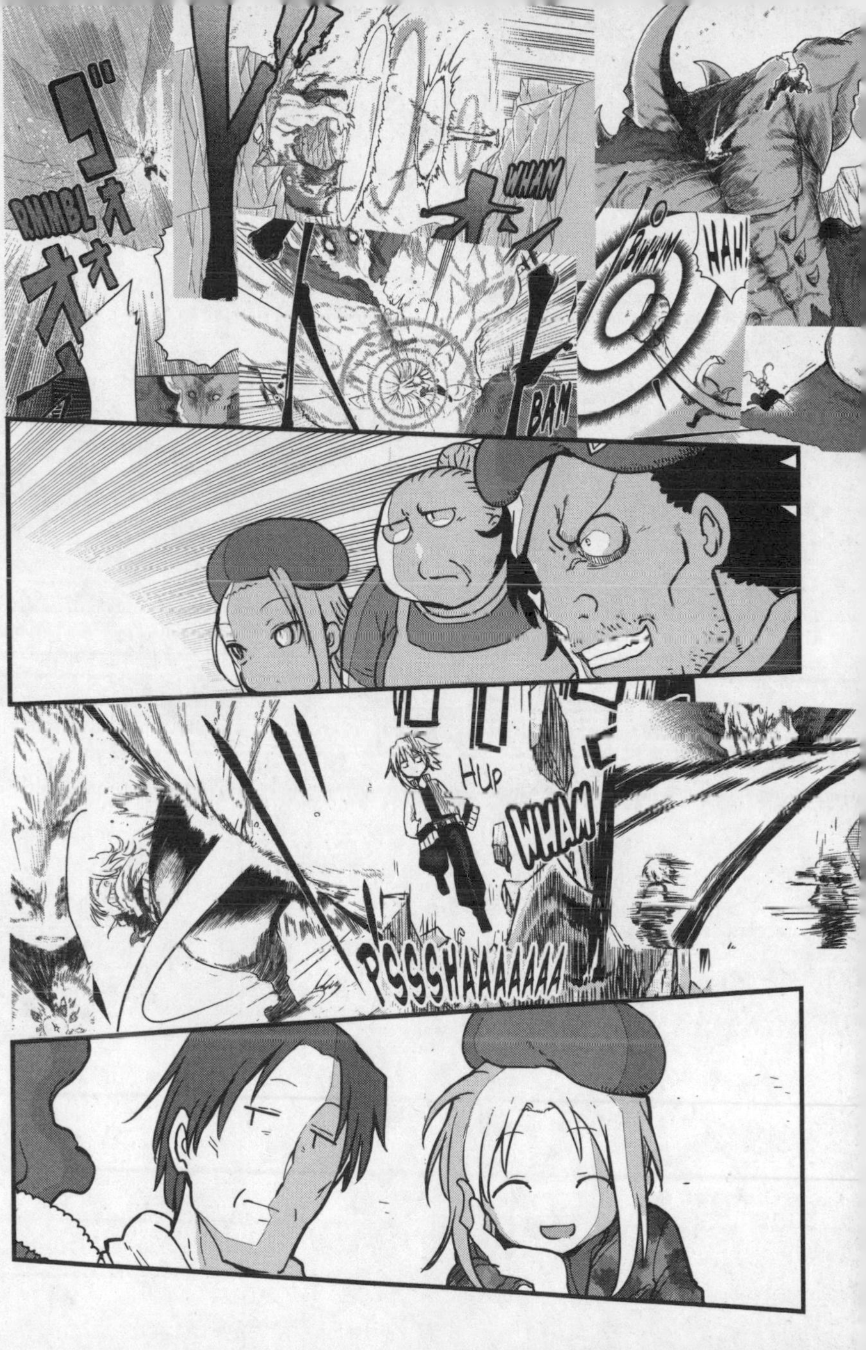
HAH!
BWAM
WHAM
BAM
RMMBL
HUP
WHAM
PSSSHAAAAAAA

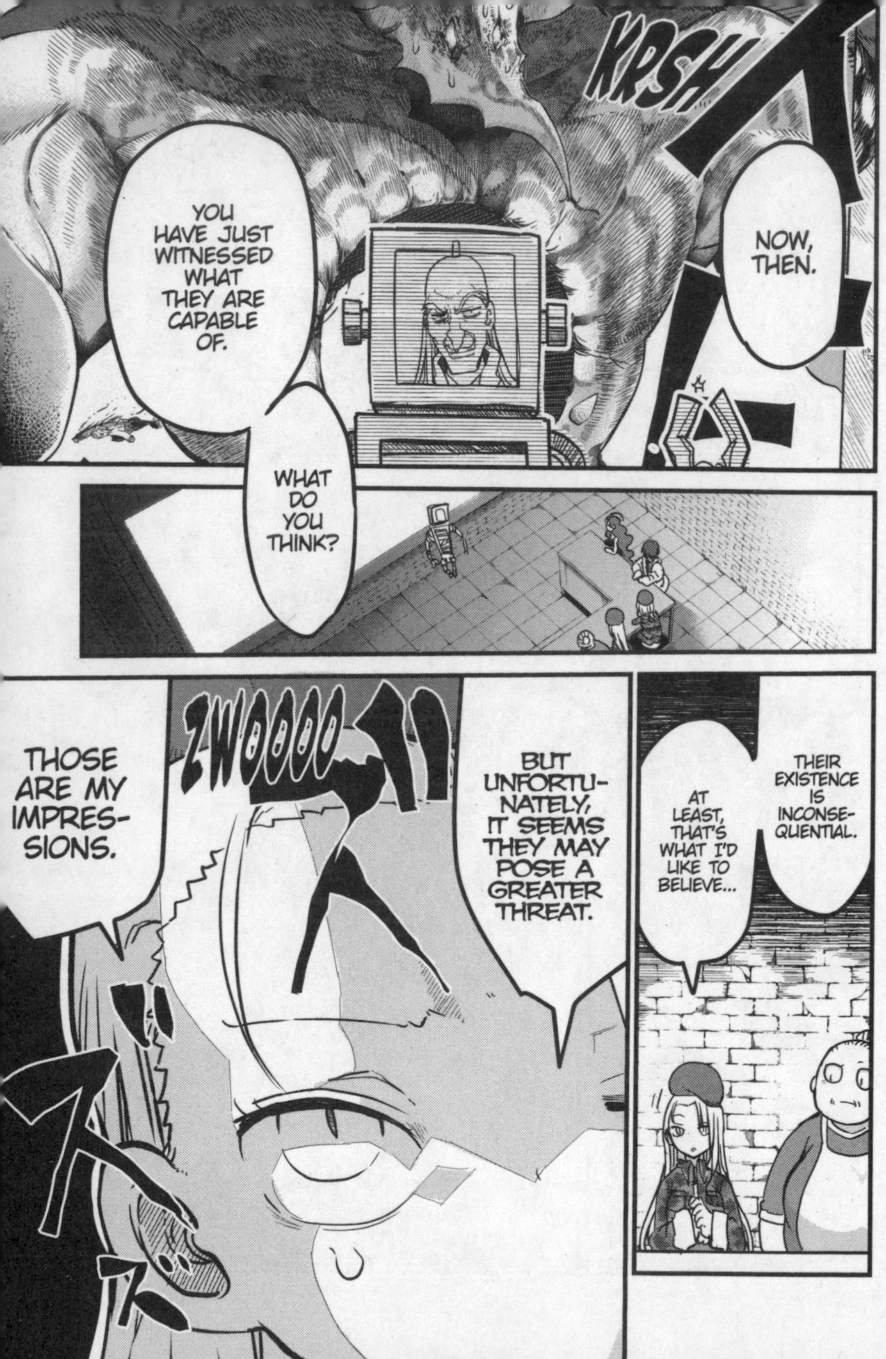
KRSH
NOW, THEN.
YOU HAVE JUST WITNESSED WHAT THEY ARE CAPABLE OF.
WHAT DO YOU THINK?
THEIR EXISTENCE IS INCONSEQUENTIAL.
AT LEAST, THAT'S WHAT I'D LIKE TO BELIEVE...
BUT UNFORTUNATELY, IT SEEMS THEY MAY POSE A GREATER THREAT.
ZWOOOO
THOSE ARE MY IMPRESSIONS.

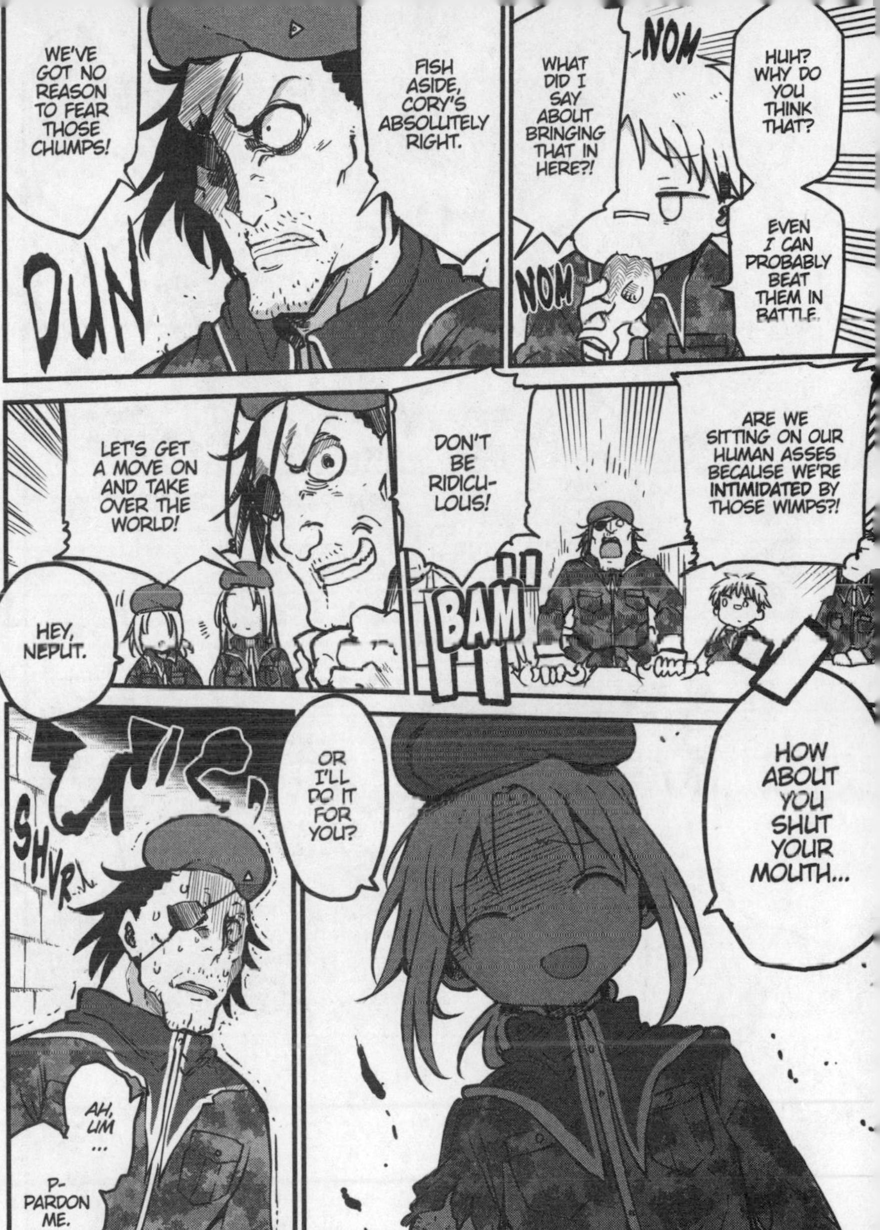

NOM
HUH? WHY DO YOU THINK THAT?
WHAT DID I SAY ABOUT BRINGING THAT IN HERE?!
EVEN I CAN PROBABLY BEAT THEM IN BATTLE.
NOM
FISH ASIDE, CORY'S ABSOLUTELY RIGHT.
WE'VE GOT NO REASON TO FEAR THOSE CHUMPS!
DUN
ARE WE SITTING ON OUR HUMAN ASSES BECAUSE WE'RE INTIMIDATED BY THOSE WIMPS?!
DON'T BE RIDICULOUS!
BAM
LET'S GET A MOVE ON AND TAKE OVER THE WORLD!
HEY, NEPUT.
HOW ABOUT YOU SHUT YOUR MOUTH...
OR I'LL DO IT FOR YOU?
SHVR
AH, UM ...
P-PARDON ME.

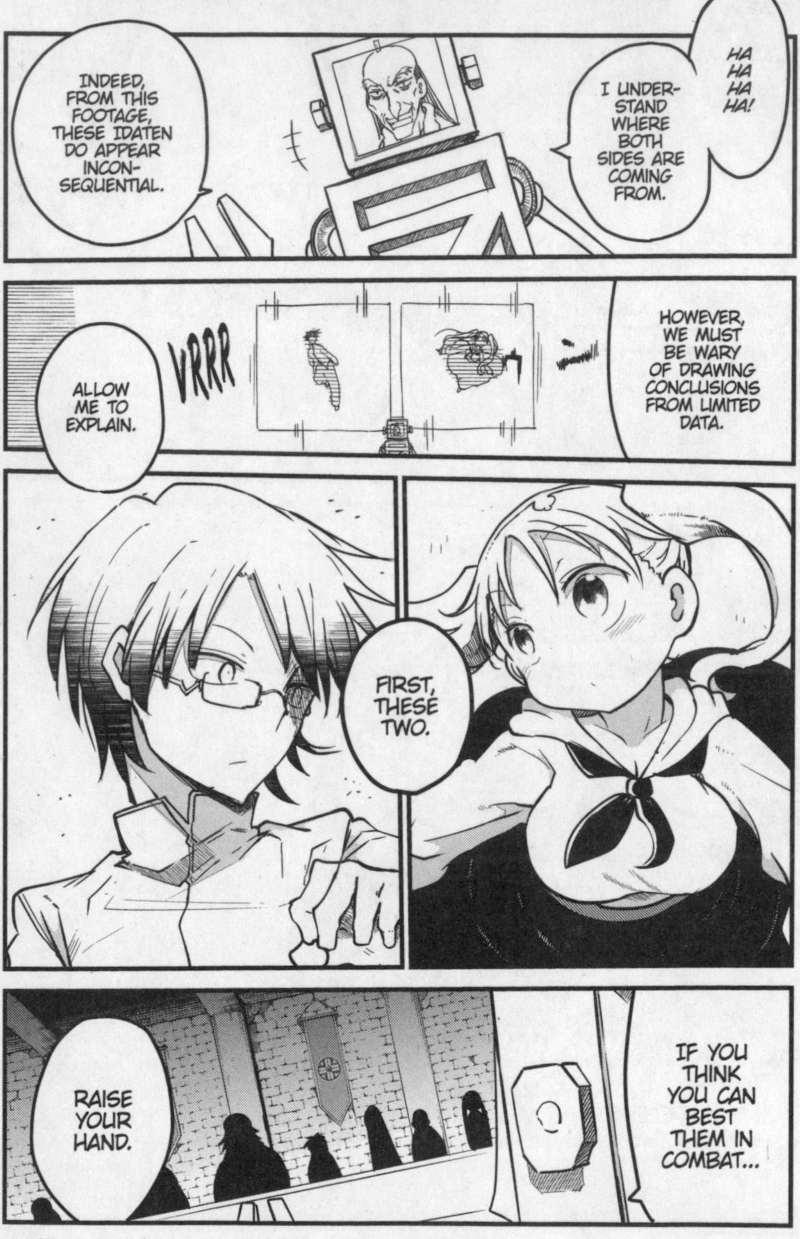
HA HA HA HA!
I UNDER-STAND WHERE BOTH SIDES ARE COMING FROM.
INDEED, FROM THIS FOOTAGE, THESE IDATEN DO APPEAR INCON-SEQUENTIAL.
HOWEVER, WE MUST BE WARY OF DRAWING CONCLUSIONS FROM LIMITED DATA.
VRRR
ALLOW ME TO EXPLAIN.
FIRST, THESE TWO.
IF YOU THINK YOU CAN BEST THEM IN COMBAT...
RAISE YOUR HAND.

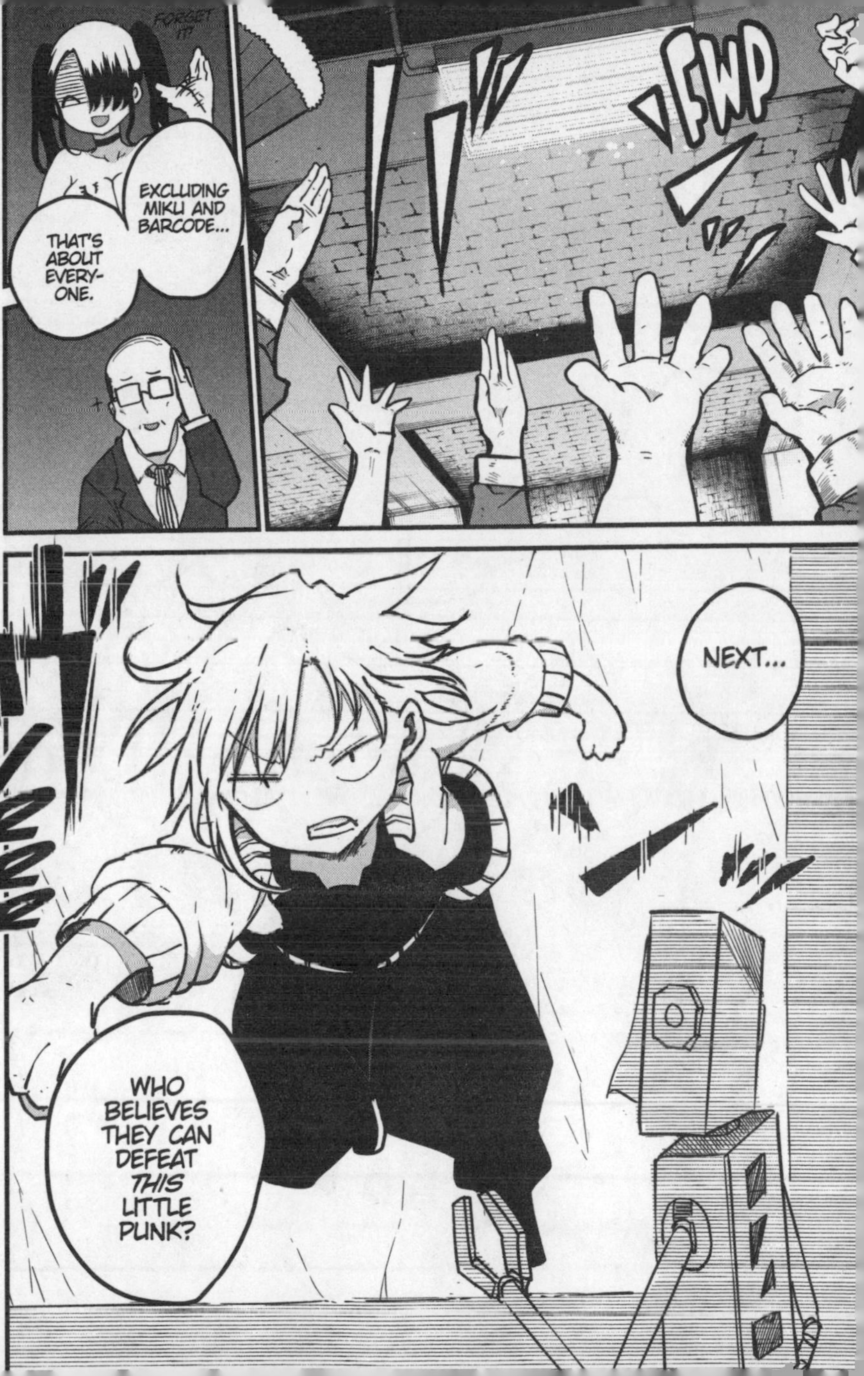
FWP
FORGET IT?
EXCLUDING MIKU AND BARCODE...
THAT'S ABOUT EVERY-ONE.
NEXT...
VZZZ
WHO BELIEVES THEY CAN DEFEAT *THIS* LITTLE PUNK?

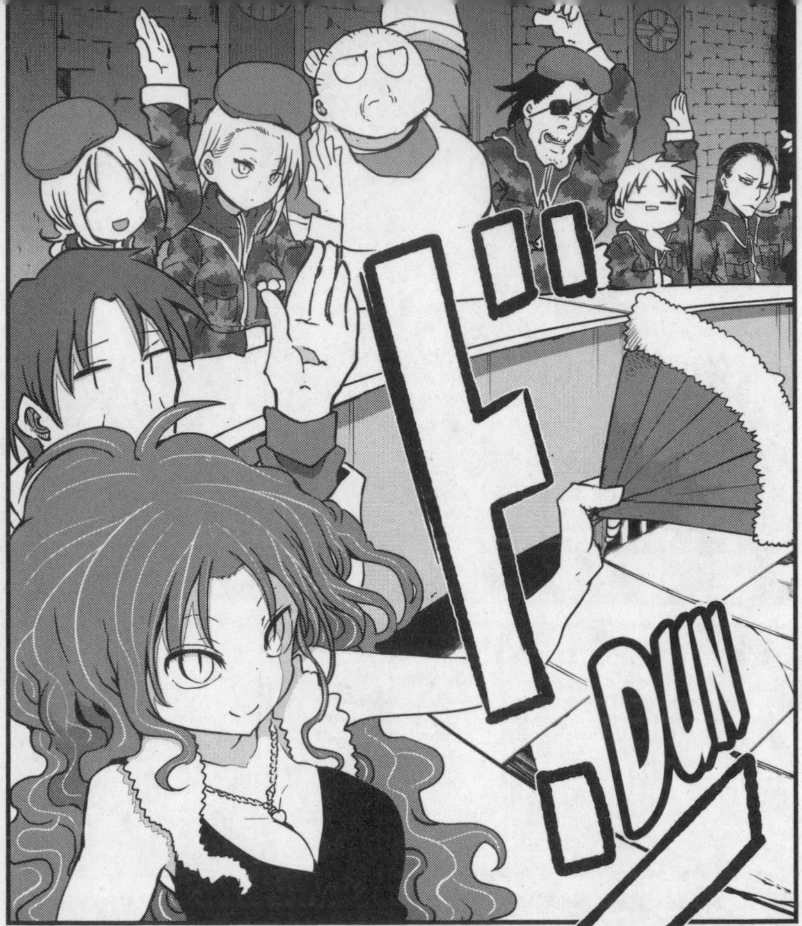
DUN

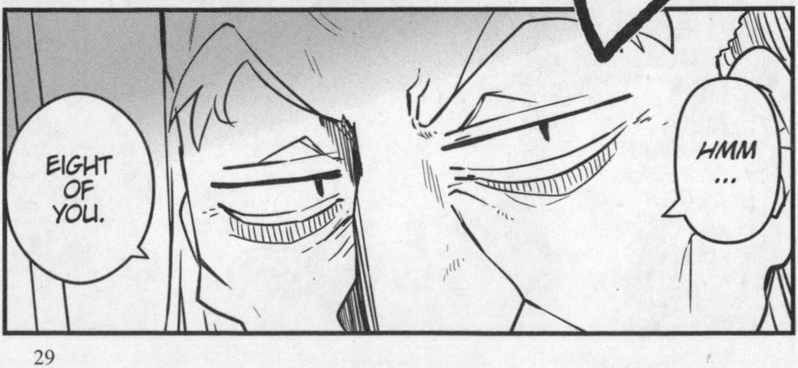
HMM ...
EIGHT OF YOU.

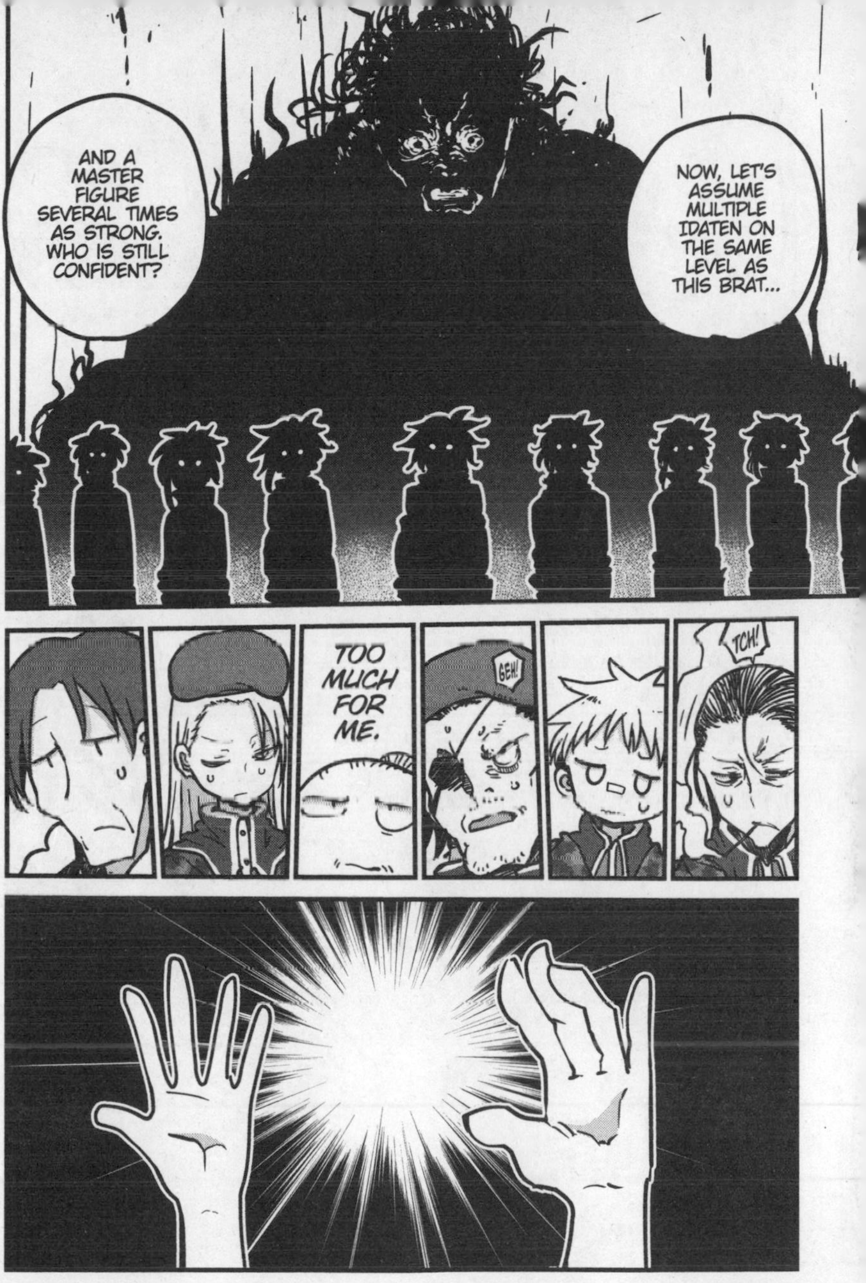
NOW, LET'S ASSUME MULTIPLE IDATEN ON THE SAME LEVEL AS THIS BRAT...
AND A MASTER FIGURE SEVERAL TIMES AS STRONG. WHO IS STILL CONFIDENT?
TCH!
GEH!
TOO MUCH FOR ME.

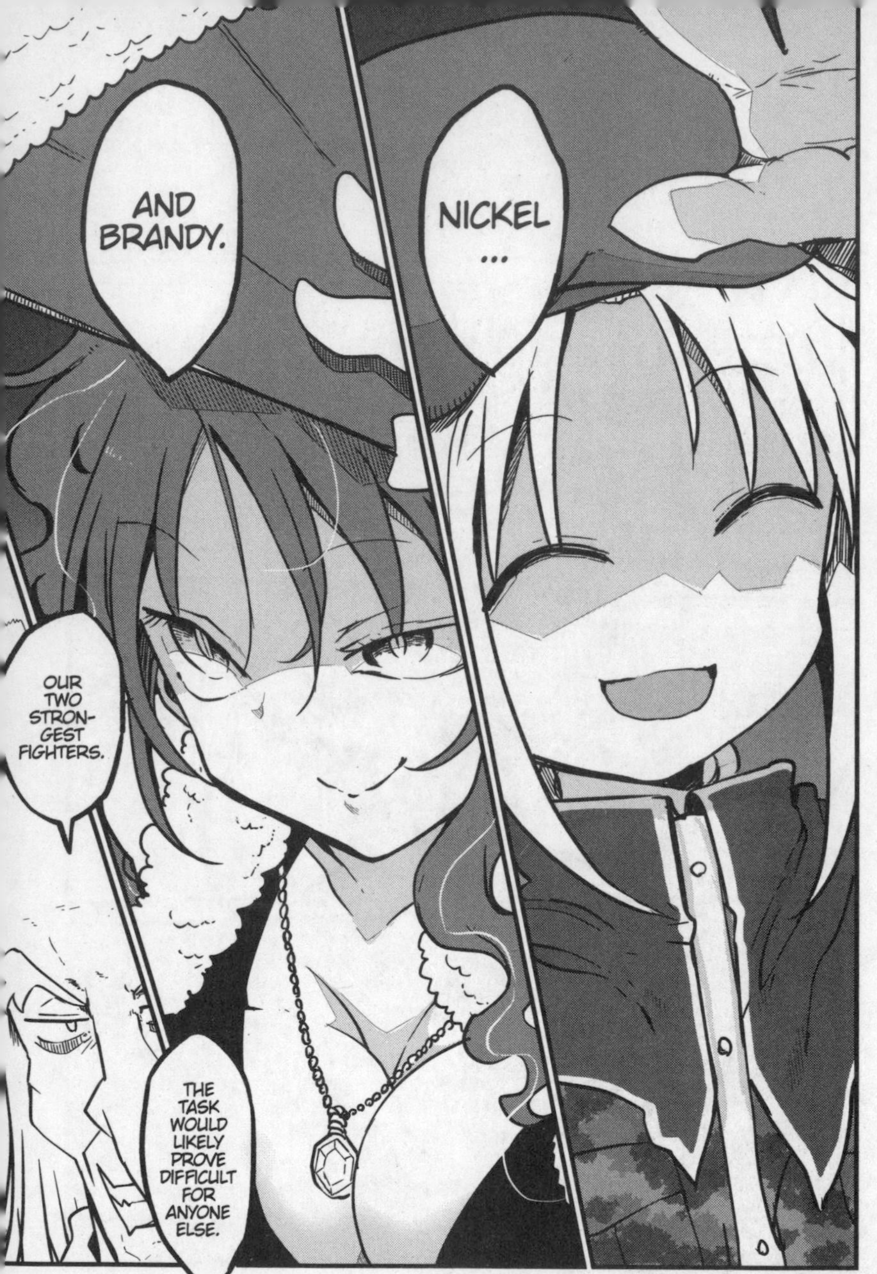
NICKEL ...
AND BRANDY.
OUR TWO STRONGEST FIGHTERS.
THE TASK WOULD LIKELY PROVE DIFFICULT FOR ANYONE ELSE.

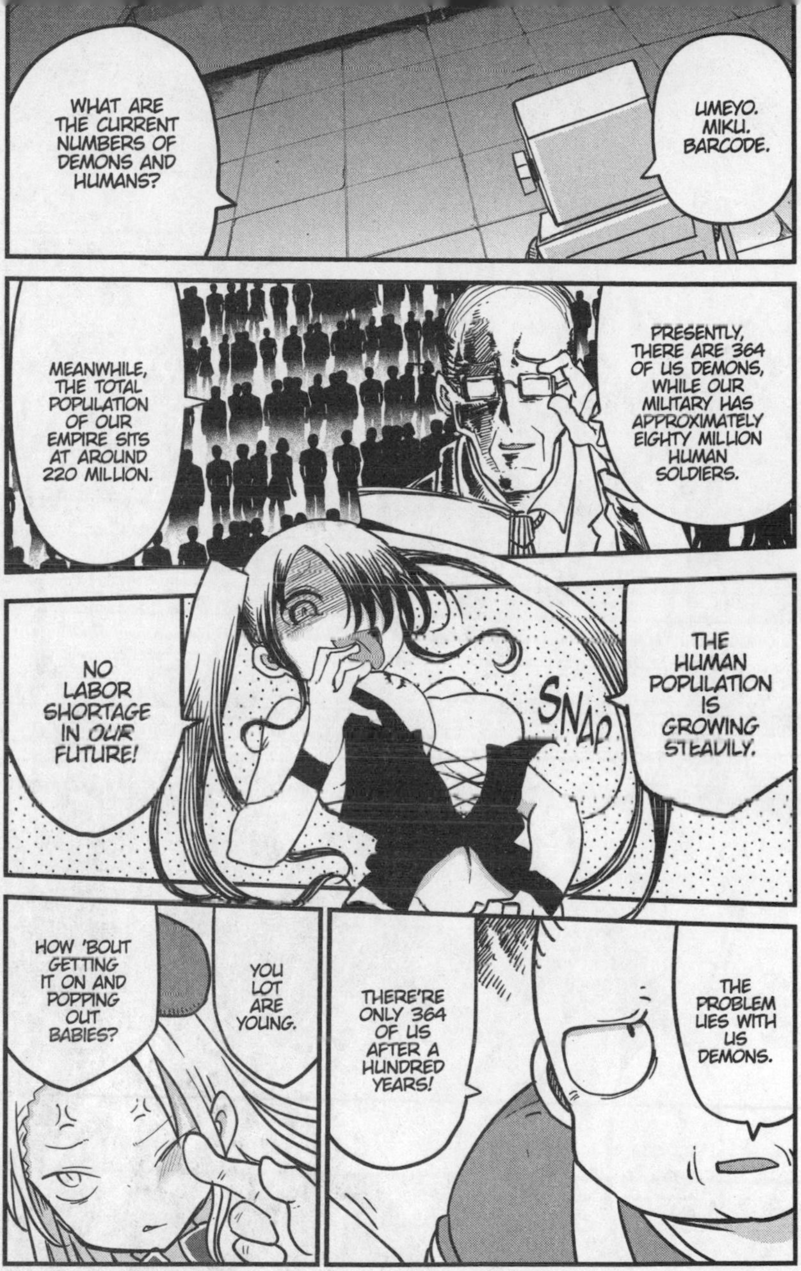
UMEYO. MIKU. BARCODE.
WHAT ARE THE CURRENT NUMBERS OF DEMONS AND HUMANS?
PRESENTLY, THERE ARE 364 OF US DEMONS, WHILE OUR MILITARY HAS APPROXIMATELY EIGHTY MILLION HUMAN SOLDIERS.
MEANWHILE, THE TOTAL POPULATION OF OUR EMPIRE SITS AT AROUND 220 MILLION.
THE HUMAN POPULATION IS GROWING STEADILY.
SNAP
NO LABOR SHORTAGE IN OUR FUTURE!
THE PROBLEM LIES WITH US DEMONS.
THERE'RE ONLY 364 OF US AFTER A HUNDRED YEARS!
YOU LOT ARE YOUNG.
HOW 'BOUT GETTING IT ON AND POPPING OUT BABIES?

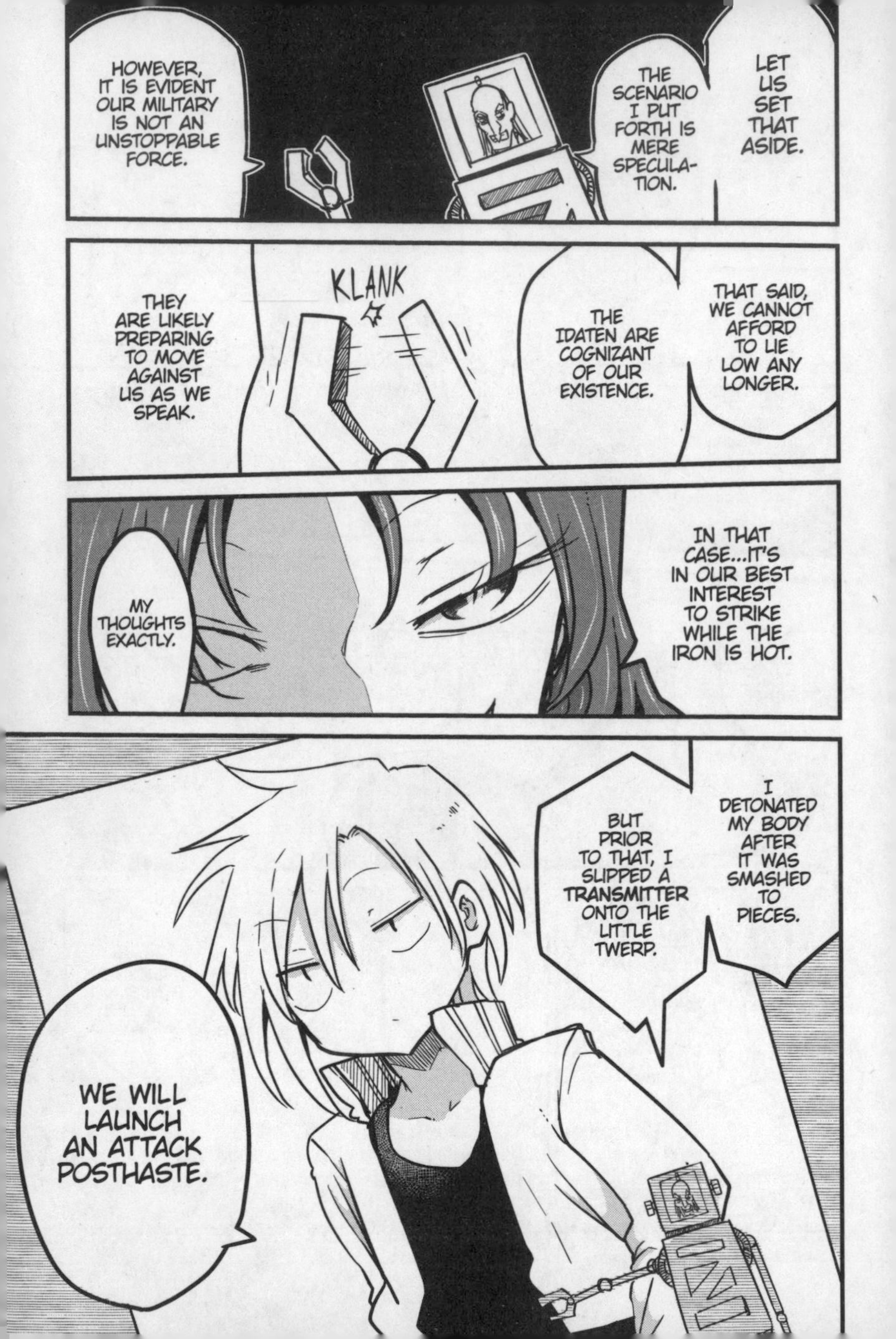
LET US SET THAT ASIDE.
THE SCENARIO I PUT FORTH IS MERE SPECULA-TION.
HOWEVER, IT IS EVIDENT OUR MILITARY IS NOT AN UNSTOPPABLE FORCE.
THAT SAID, WE CANNOT AFFORD TO LIE LOW ANY LONGER.
THE IDATEN ARE COGNIZANT OF OUR EXISTENCE.
KLANK
THEY ARE LIKELY PREPARING TO MOVE AGAINST US AS WE SPEAK.
IN THAT CASE...IT'S IN OUR BEST INTEREST TO STRIKE WHILE THE IRON IS HOT.
MY THOUGHTS EXACTLY.
I DETONATED MY BODY AFTER IT WAS SMASHED TO PIECES.
BUT PRIOR TO THAT, I SLIPPED A TRANSMITTER ONTO THE LITTLE TWERP.
WE WILL LAUNCH AN ATTACK POSTHASTE.

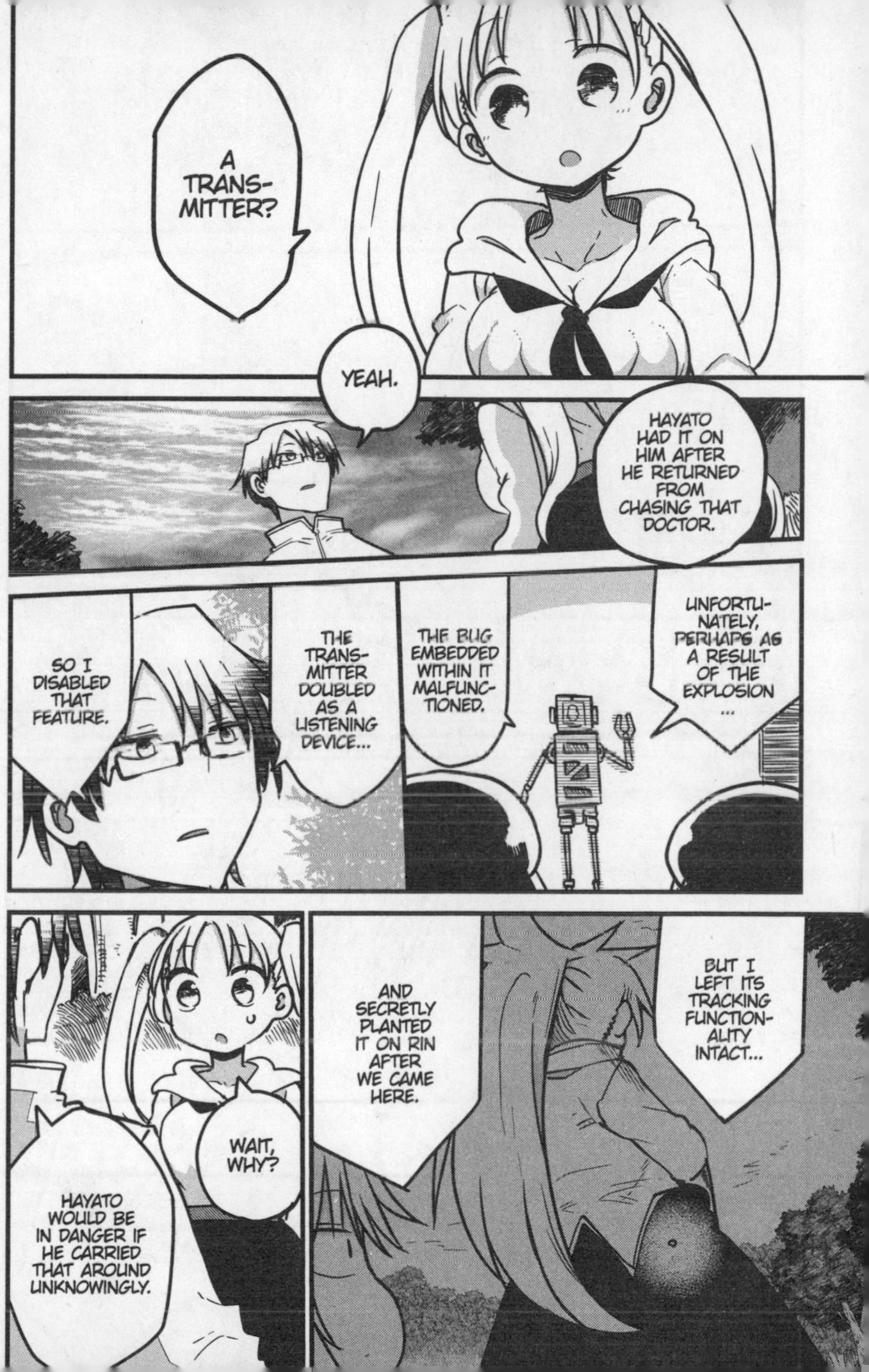
A TRANS-MITTER?
YEAH.
HAYATO HAD IT ON HIM AFTER HE RETURNED FROM CHASING THAT DOCTOR.
UNFORTUNATELY, PERHAPS AS A RESULT OF THE EXPLOSION ...
THE BUG EMBEDDED WITHIN IT MALFUNCTIONED.
THE TRANS-MITTER DOUBLED AS A LISTENING DEVICE...
SO I DISABLED THAT FEATURE.
BUT I LEFT ITS TRACKING FUNCTION-ALITY INTACT...
AND SECRETLY PLANTED IT ON RIN AFTER WE CAME HERE.
WAIT, WHY?
HAYATO WOULD BE IN DANGER IF HE CARRIED THAT AROUND UNKNOWINGLY.

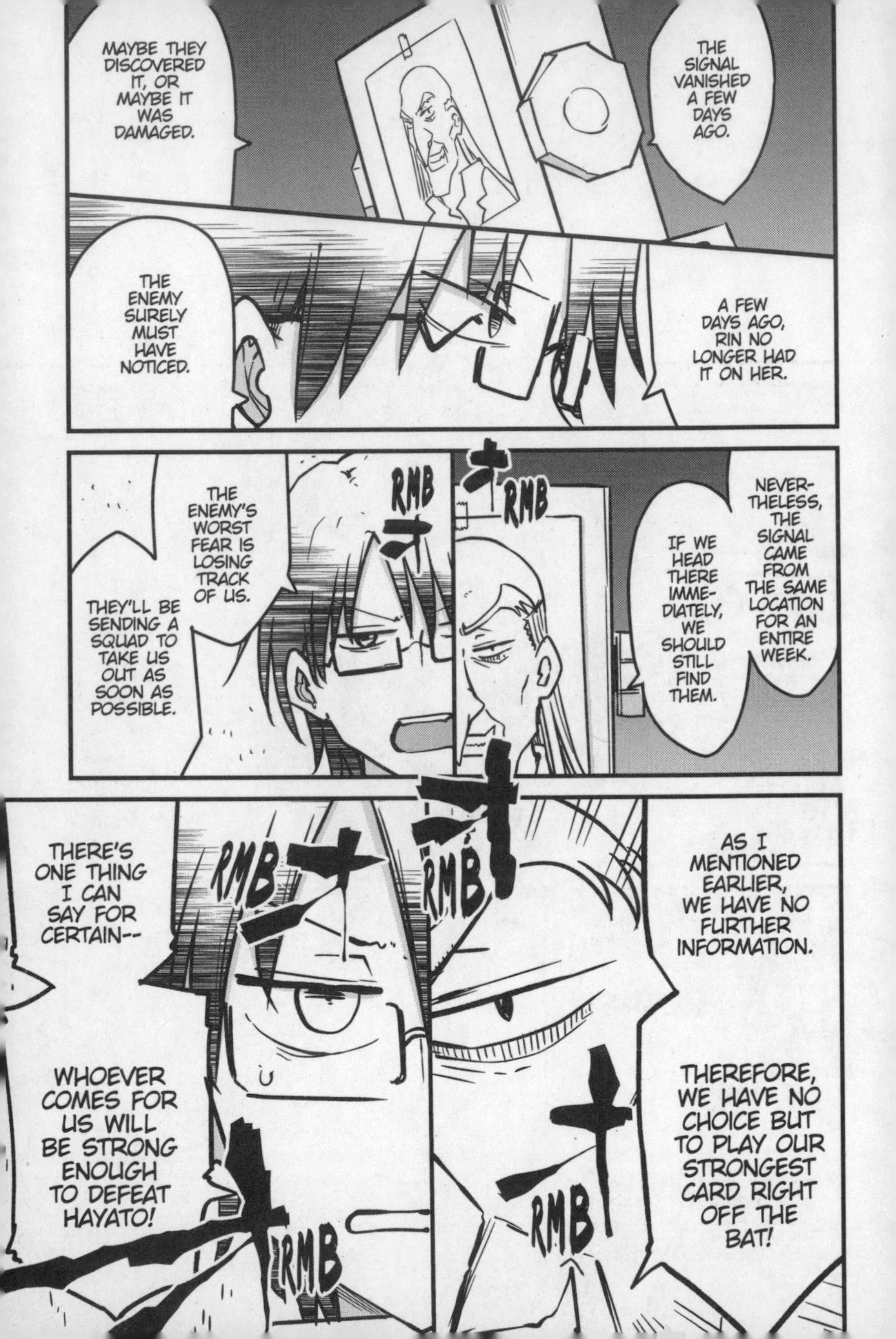
THE SIGNAL VANISHED A FEW DAYS AGO.
MAYBE THEY DISCOVERED IT, OR MAYBE IT WAS DAMAGED.
A FEW DAYS AGO, RIN NO LONGER HAD IT ON HER.
THE ENEMY SURELY MUST HAVE NOTICED.
RMB
NEVER-THELESS, THE SIGNAL CAME FROM THE SAME LOCATION FOR AN ENTIRE WEEK.
IF WE HEAD THERE IMME-DIATELY, WE SHOULD STILL FIND THEM.
RMB
THE ENEMY'S WORST FEAR IS LOSING TRACK OF US.
THEY'LL BE SENDING A SQUAD TO TAKE US OUT AS SOON AS POSSIBLE.
RMB
AS I MENTIONED EARLIER, WE HAVE NO FURTHER INFORMATION.
THEREFORE, WE HAVE NO CHOICE BUT TO PLAY OUR STRONGEST CARD RIGHT OFF THE BAT!
RMB
RMB
THERE'S ONE THING I CAN SAY FOR CERTAIN--
WHOEVER COMES FOR US WILL BE STRONG ENOUGH TO DEFEAT HAYATO!
RMB

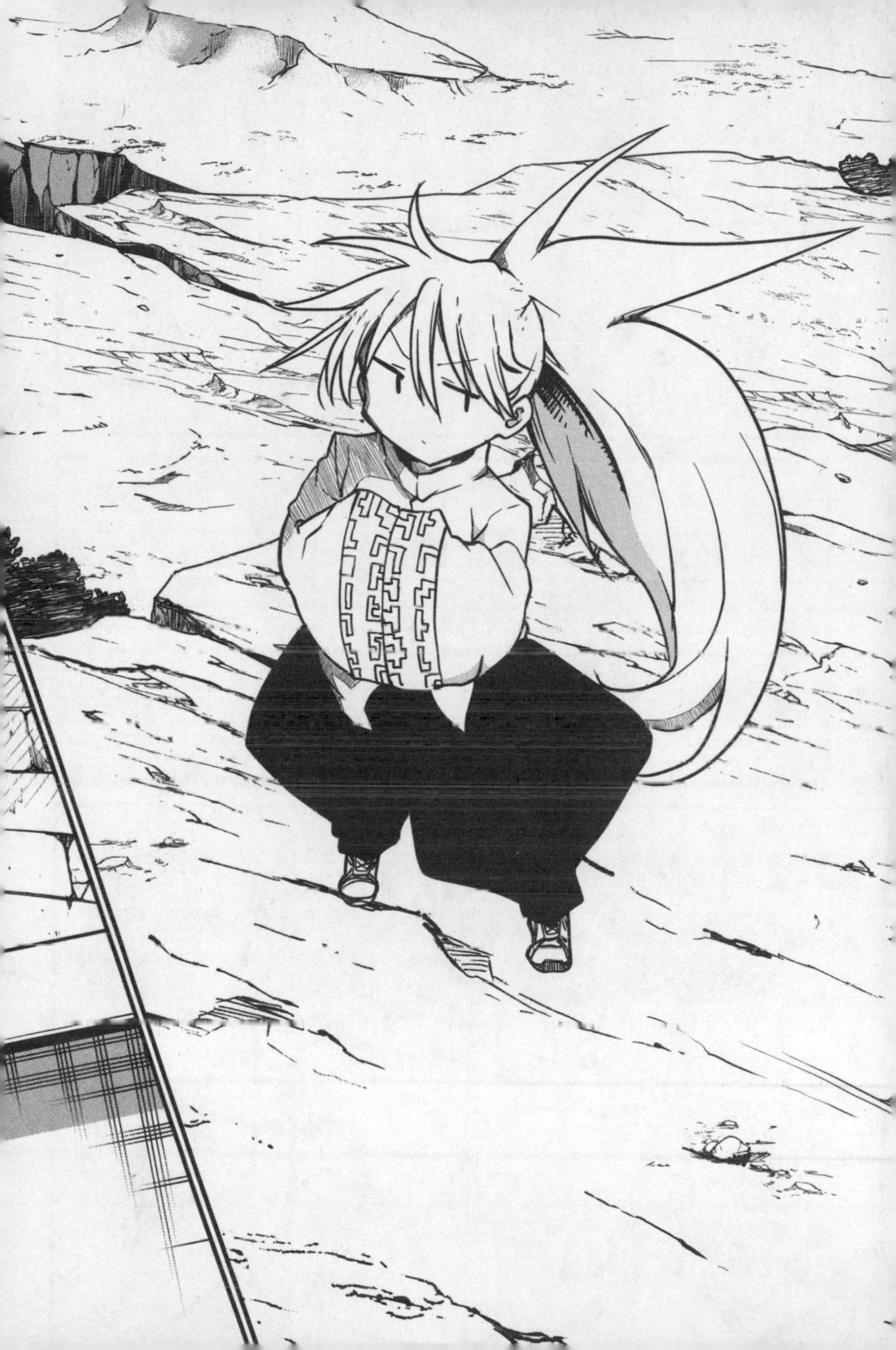

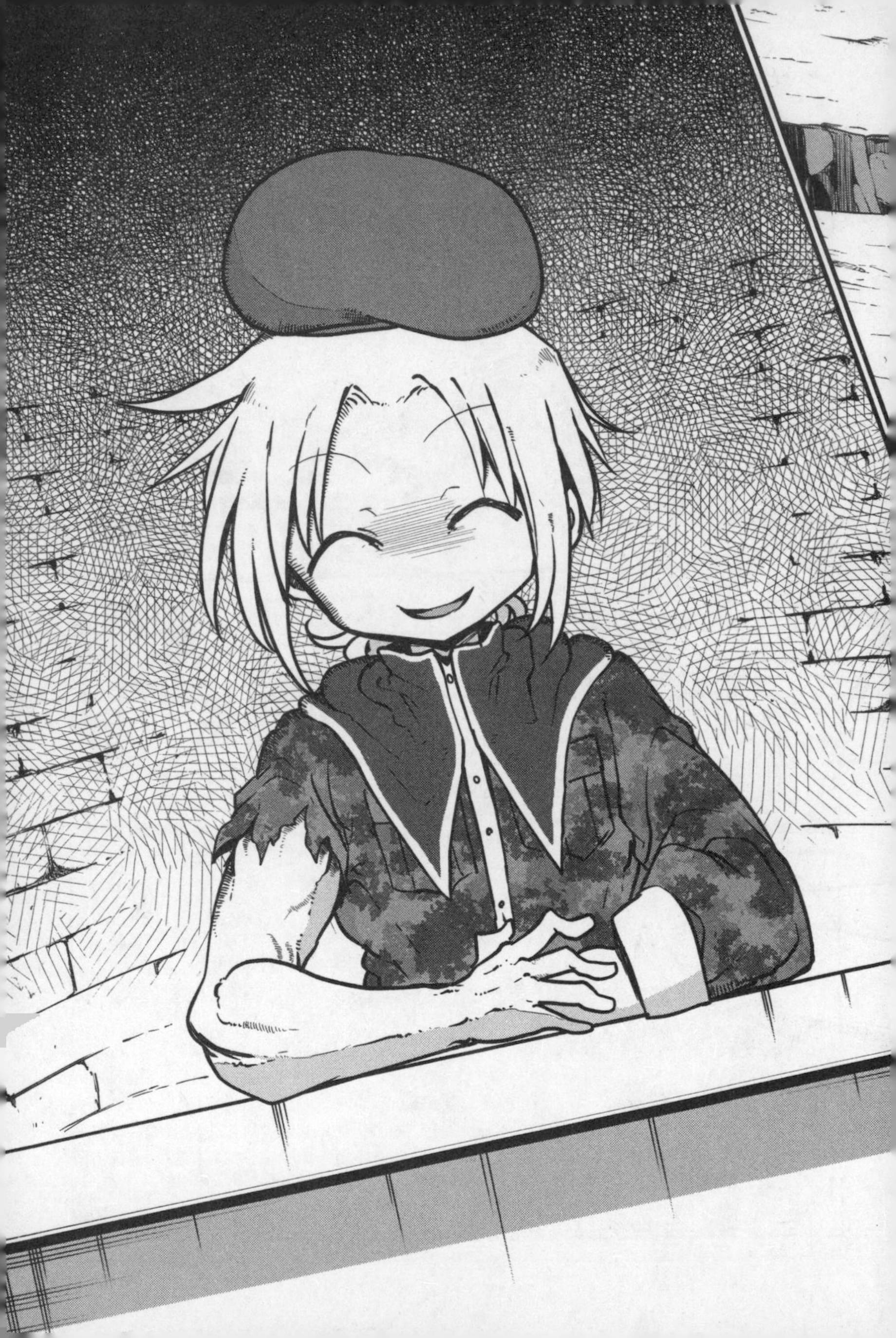

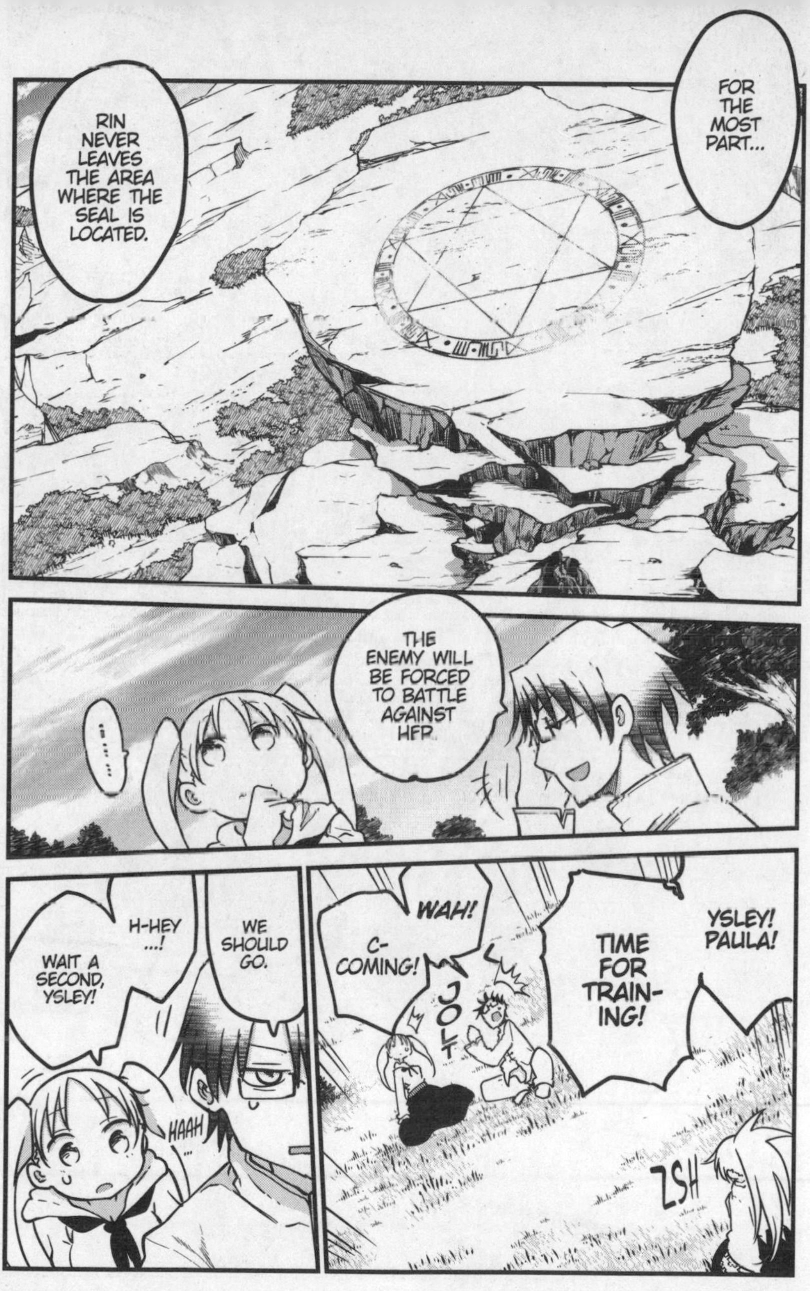
FOR THE MOST PART...
RIN NEVER LEAVES THE AREA WHERE THE SEAL IS LOCATED.
THE ENEMY WILL BE FORCED TO BATTLE AGAINST HER.
......
YSLEY! PAULA!
TIME FOR TRAINING!
ZSH
WAH!
JOLT
C-COMING!
WE SHOULD GO.
H-HEY ...!
WAIT A SECOND, YSLEY!
HAAH ...

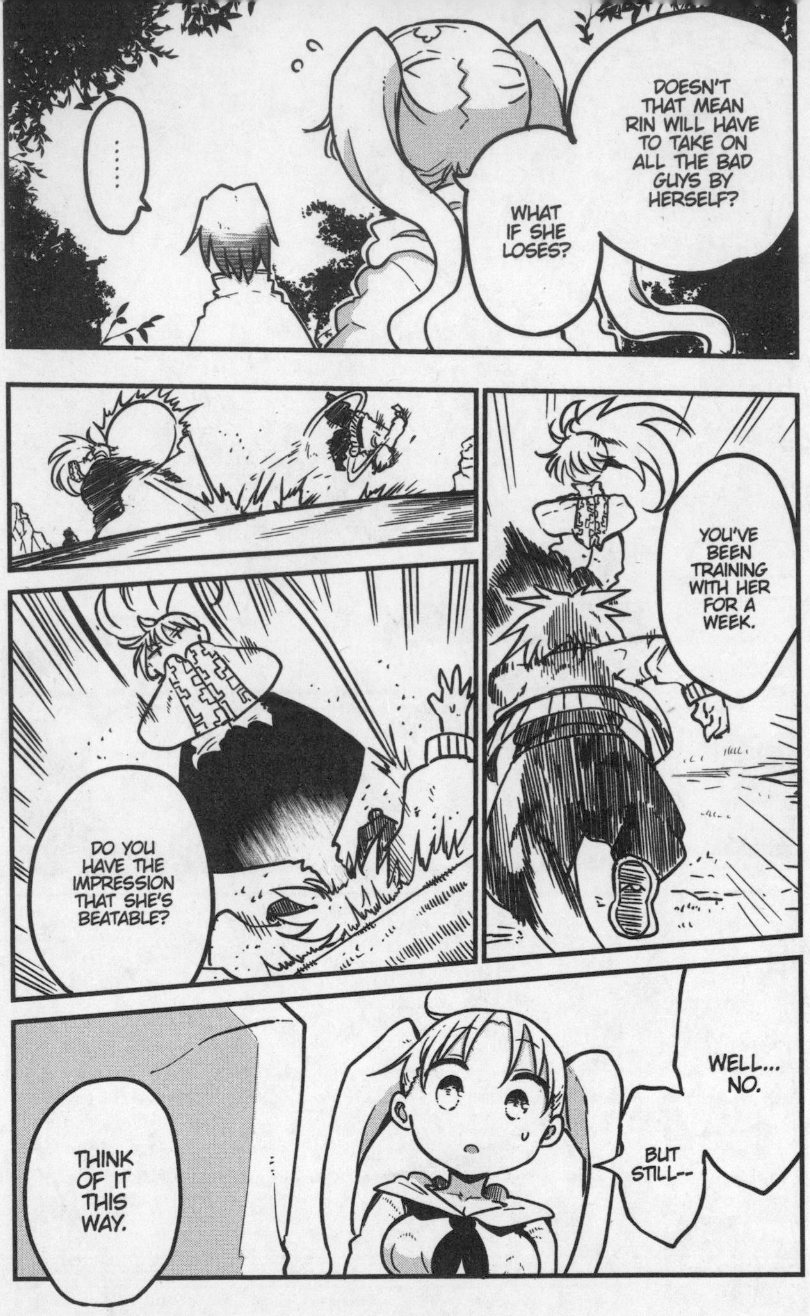
DOESN'T THAT MEAN RIN WILL HAVE TO TAKE ON ALL THE BAD GUYS BY HERSELF?
WHAT IF SHE LOSES?
......
YOU'VE BEEN TRAINING WITH HER FOR A WEEK.
DO YOU HAVE THE IMPRESSION THAT SHE'S BEATABLE?
WELL... NO.
BUT STILL--
THINK OF IT THIS WAY.

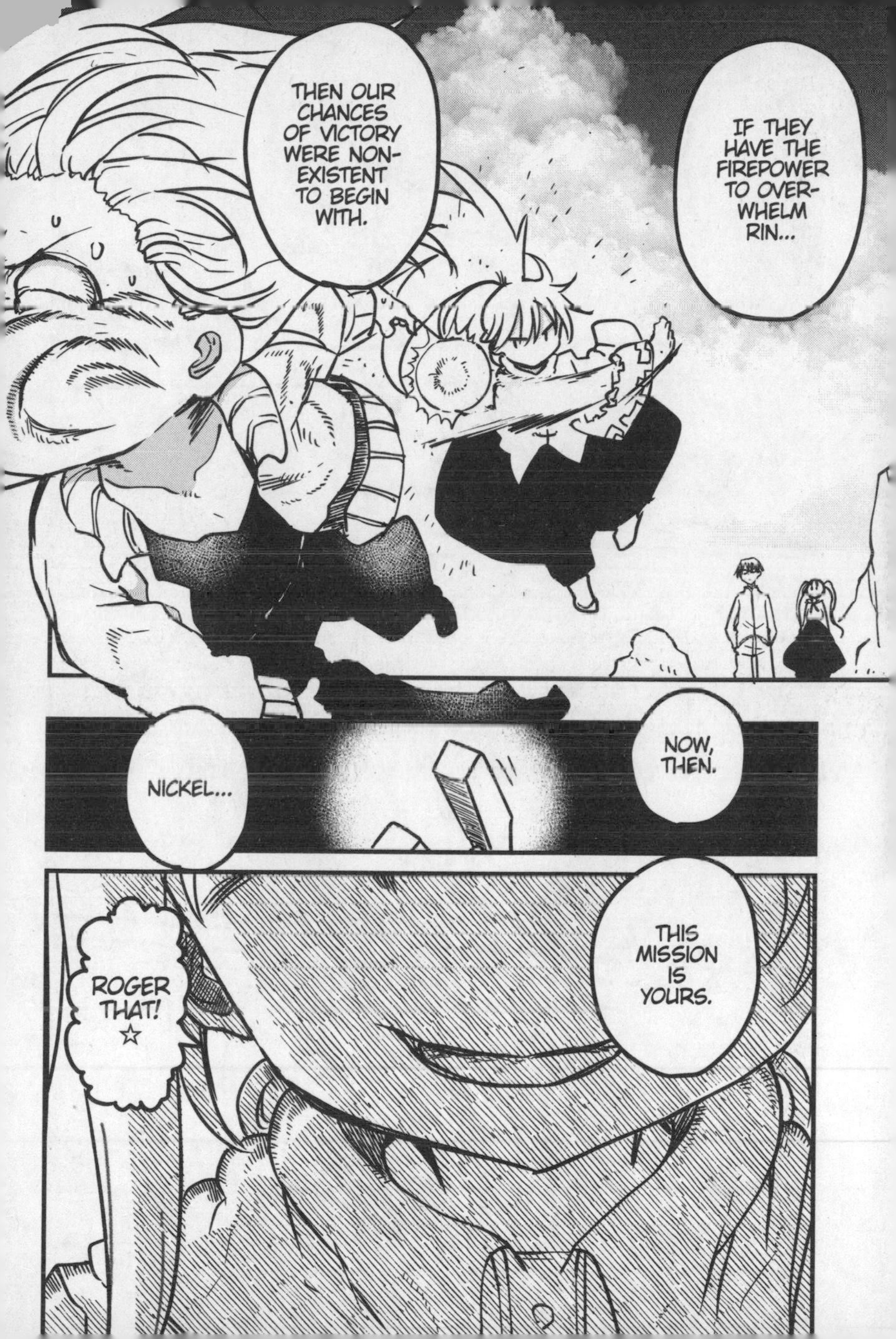
IF THEY HAVE THE FIREPOWER TO OVER-WHELM RIN...
THEN OUR CHANCES OF VICTORY WERE NON-EXISTENT TO BEGIN WITH.
NOW, THEN.
NICKEL...
THIS MISSION IS YOURS.
ROGER THAT! ☆

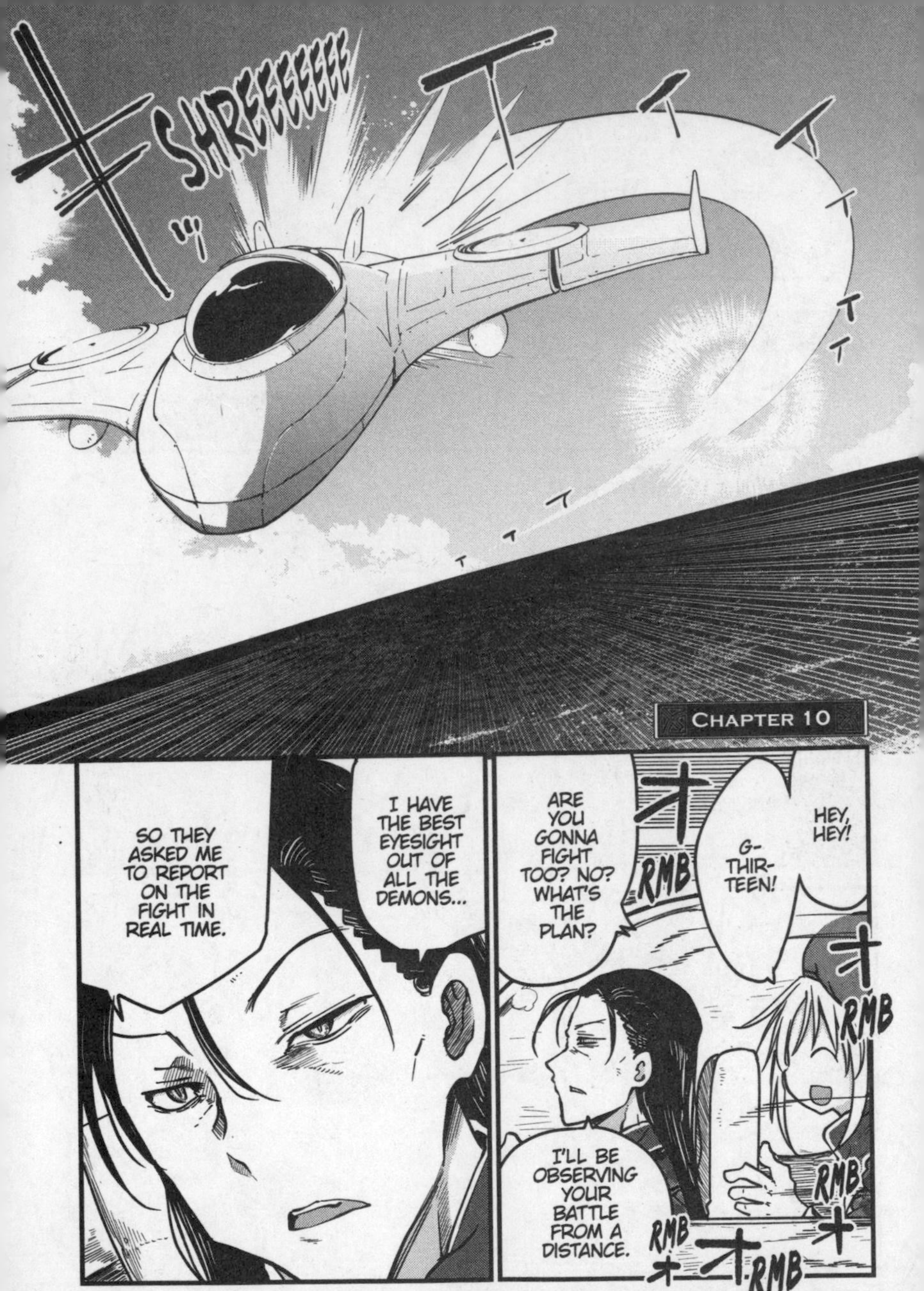
SHREEEEEEE
CHAPTER 10
HEY, HEY!
G-THIRTEEN!
ARE YOU GONNA FIGHT TOO? NO? WHAT'S THE PLAN?
RMB
RMB
I'LL BE OBSERVING YOUR BATTLE FROM A DISTANCE.
RMB
RMB
RMB
I HAVE THE BEST EYESIGHT OUT OF ALL THE DEMONS...
SO THEY ASKED ME TO REPORT ON THE FIGHT IN REAL TIME.

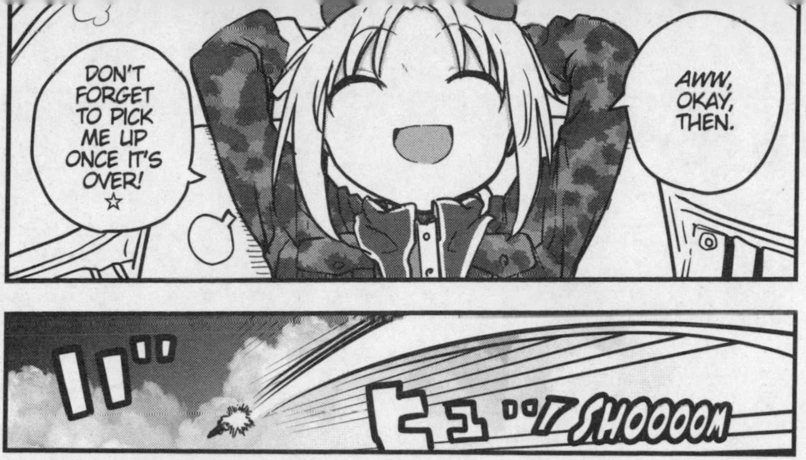
AWW, OKAY, THEN.
DON'T FORGET TO PICK ME UP ONCE IT'S OVER! ☆
SHOOOOM

CHAPTER 10 First Hit in Two Centuries

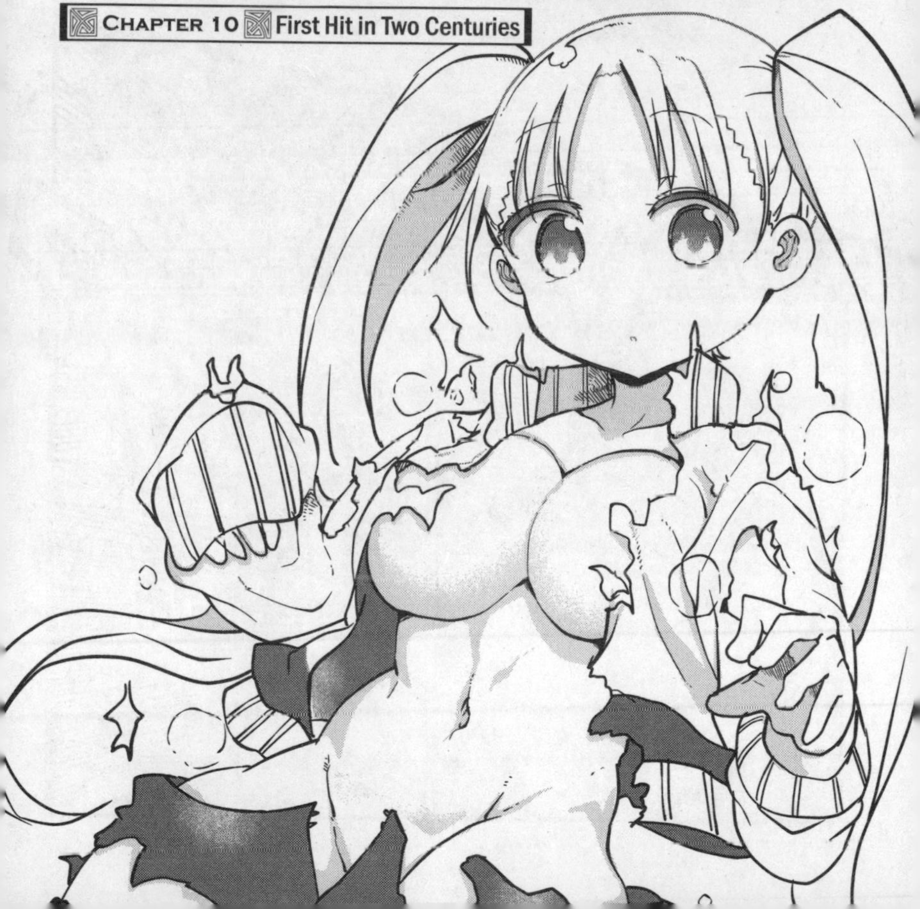

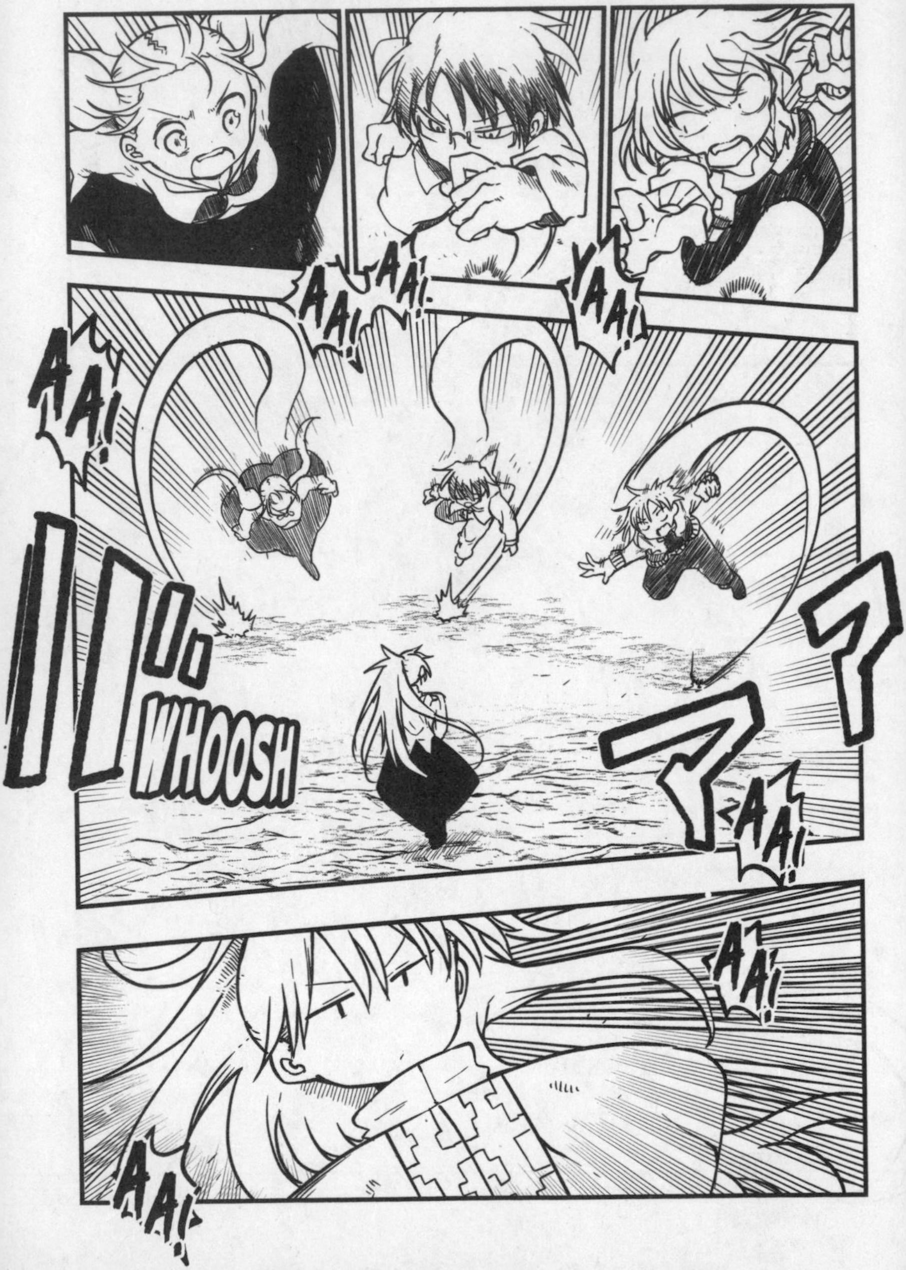
YAA!
AA!
AA!
?
AA!
AA!
WHOOSH
AA!
AA!

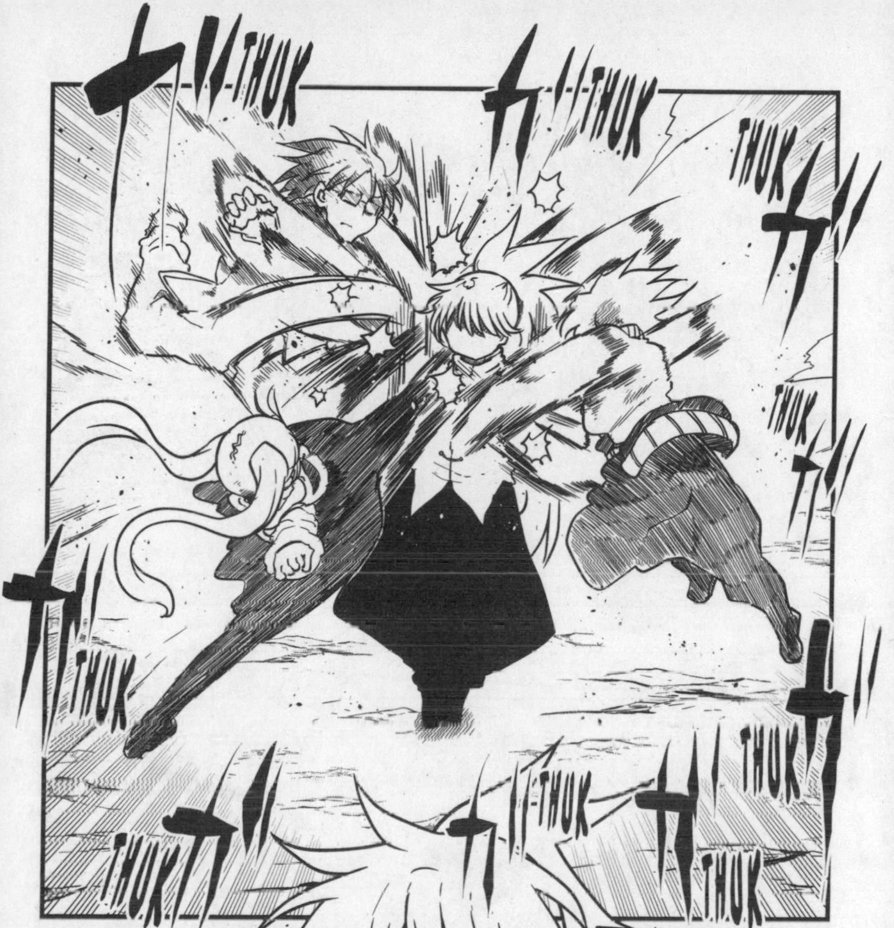
THUK
THUK
THUK
THUK
THUK
THUK
THUK
THUK
THUK

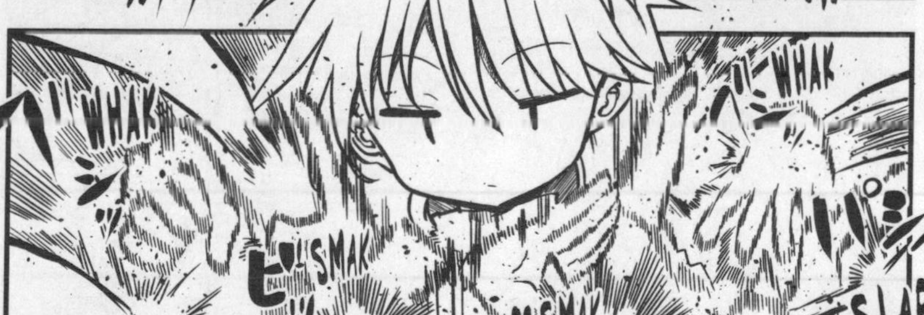
WHAK
SLAP
WHAK
SMAK
SMAK

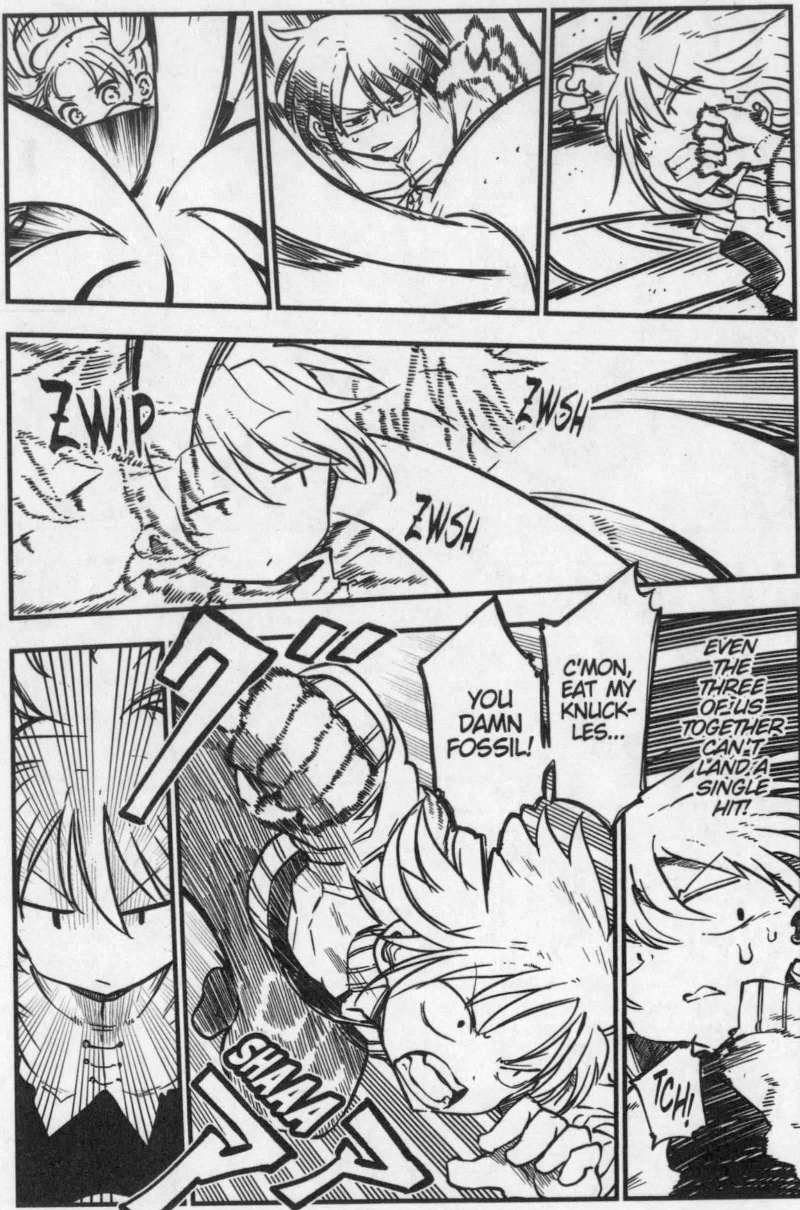
ZWSH
ZWSH
ZWIP
EVEN THE THREE OF US TOGETHER CAN'T LAND A SINGLE HIT!
TCH!
C'MON, EAT MY KNUCK-LES...
YOU DAMN FOSSIL!
SHAAA

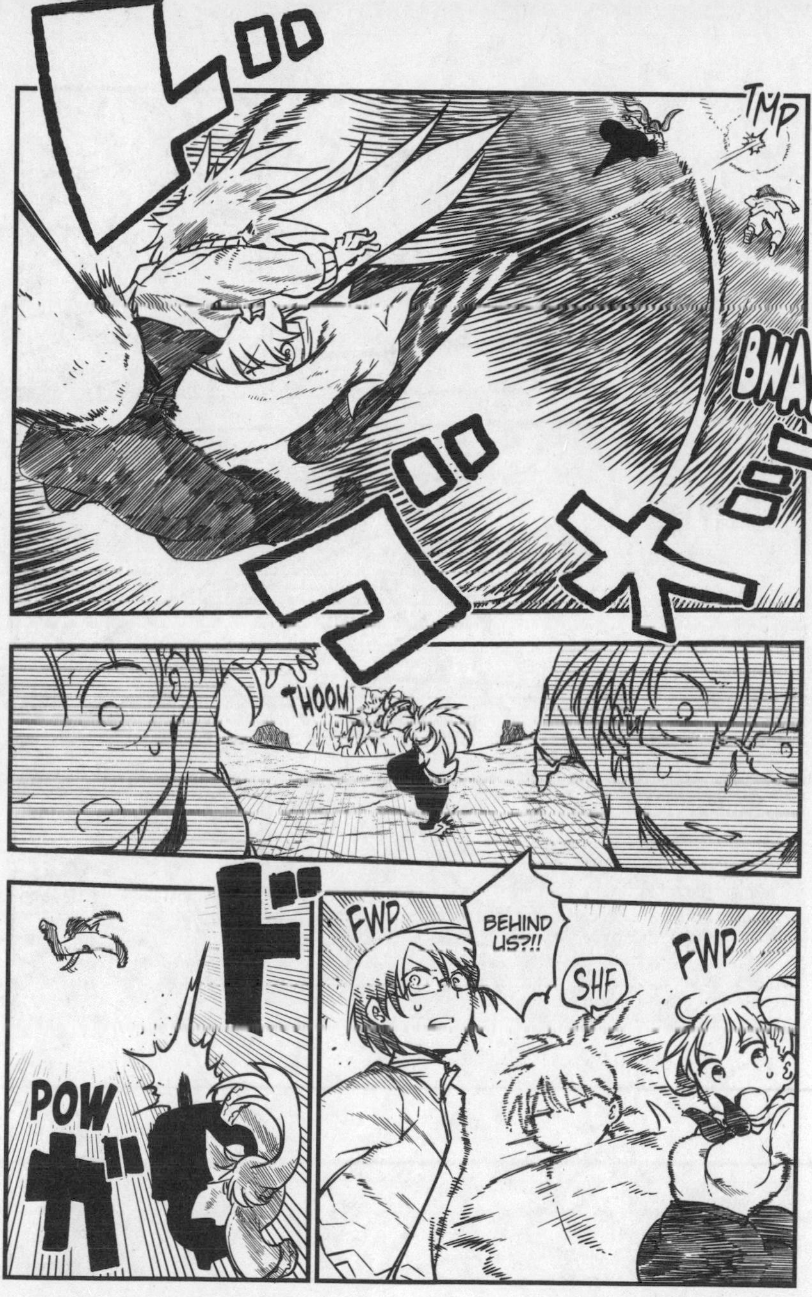

TMP
BWAM
THOOM
FWP
BEHIND US?!!
SHF
FWP
ド
POW
ガ

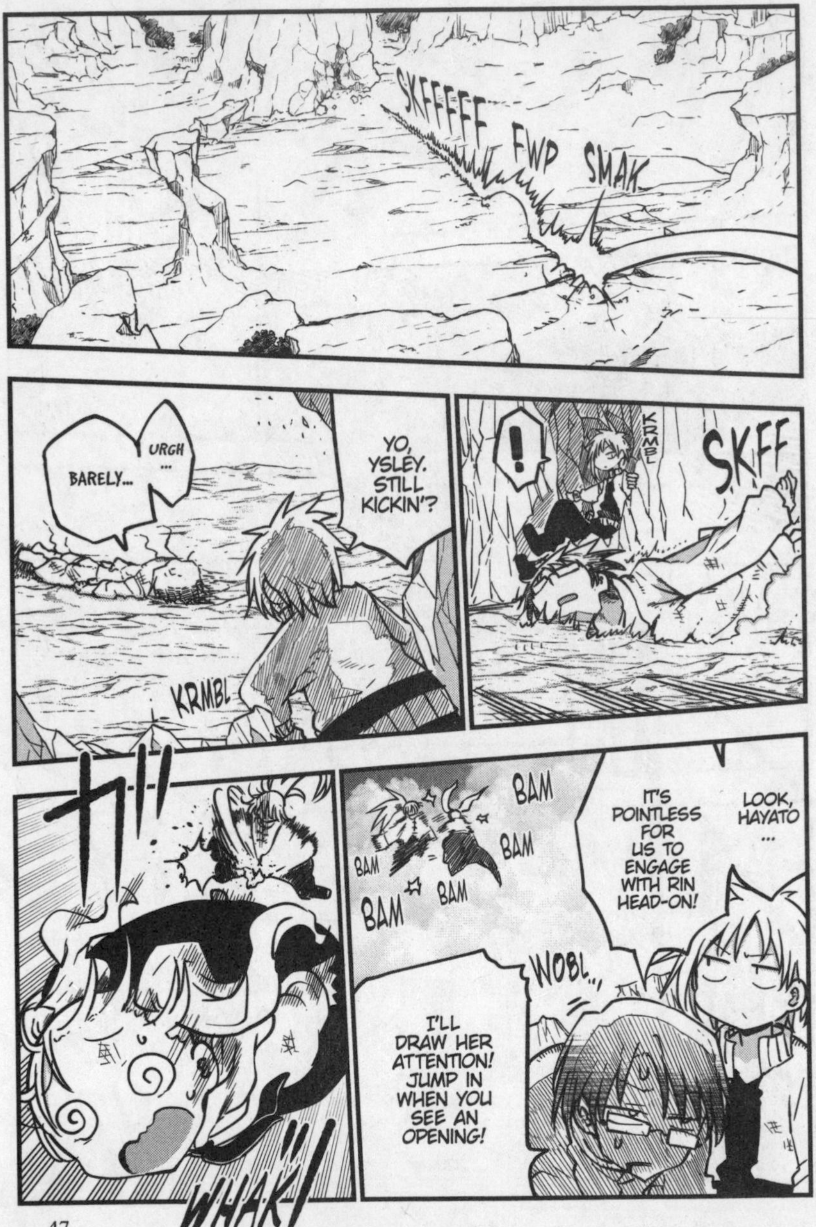
SKFFFFF
FWP
SMAK
!
KRMBL
SKFF
YO, YSLEY. STILL KICKIN'?
URGH ...
BARELY...
KRMBL
LOOK, HAYATO ...
IT'S POINTLESS FOR US TO ENGAGE WITH RIN HEAD-ON!
BAM
BAM
BAM
BAM
BAM
WOBL..
I'LL DRAW HER ATTENTION! JUMP IN WHEN YOU SEE AN OPENING!
WHAK!

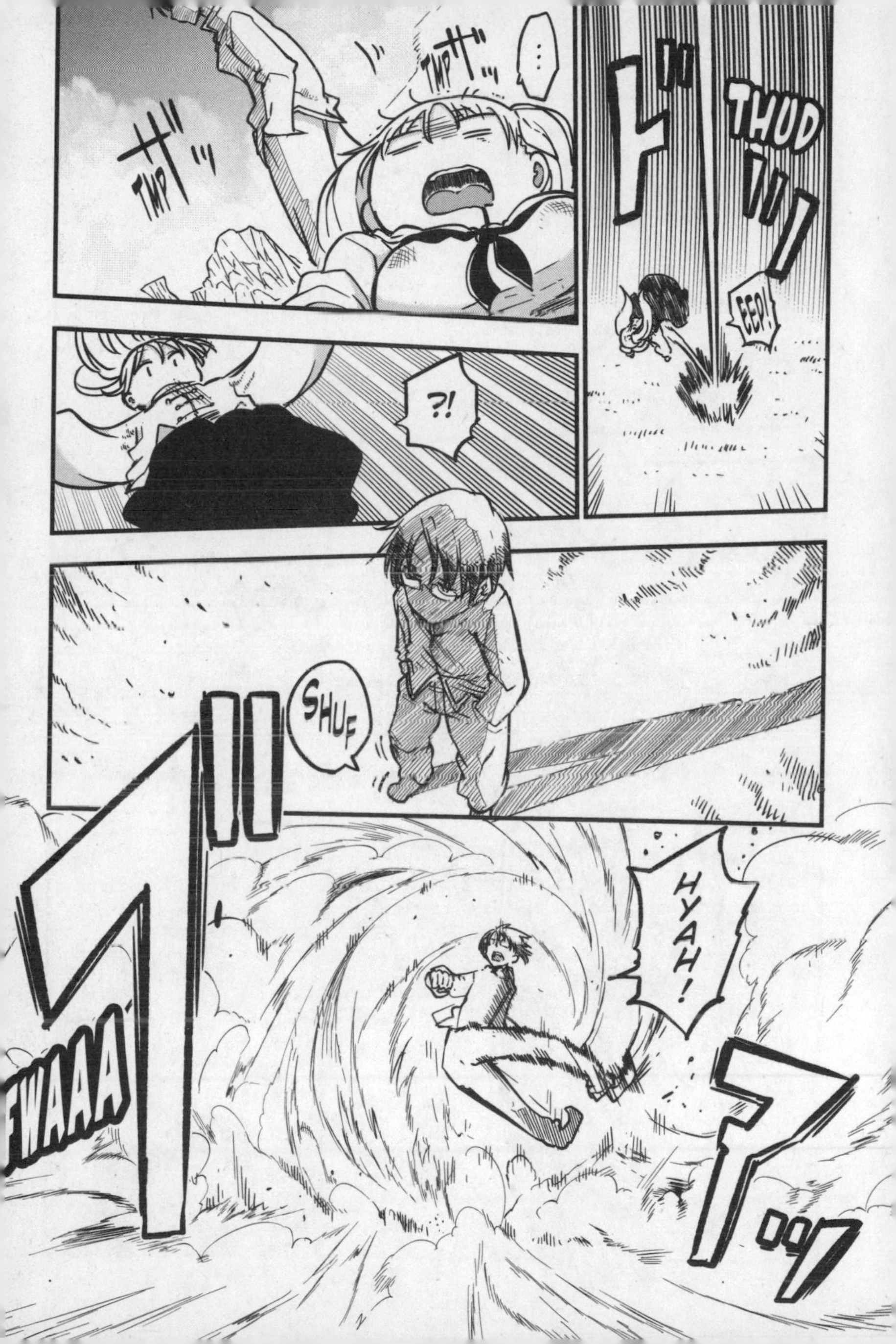
THUD
EEP!
...
TMP
TMP
?!
SHUF
HYAH!
FWAAA

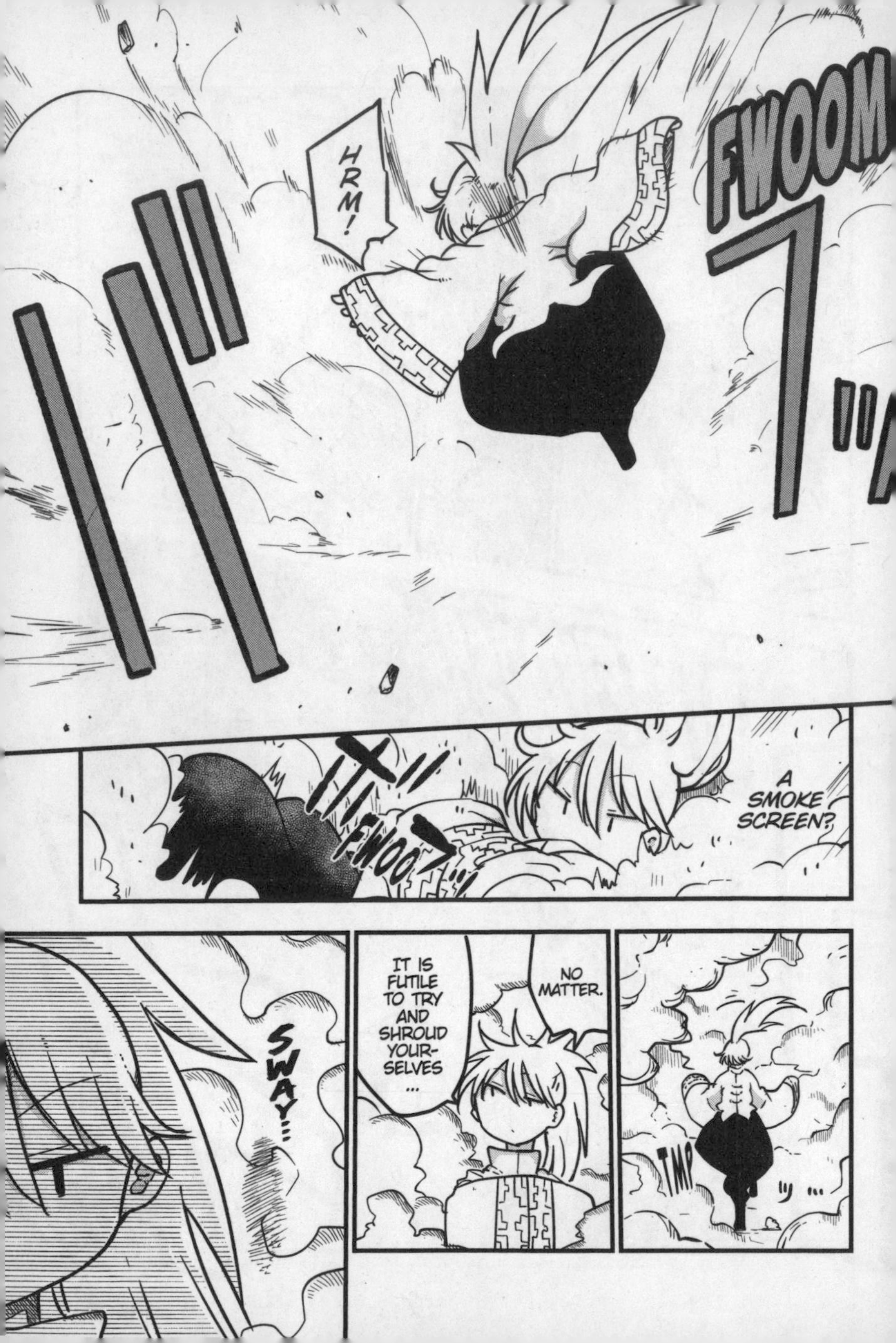
FWOOM
HRM!
FWOO
A SMOKE SCREEN?
TMP
NO MATTER.
IT IS FUTILE TO TRY AND SHROUD YOUR-SELVES ...
SWAY...

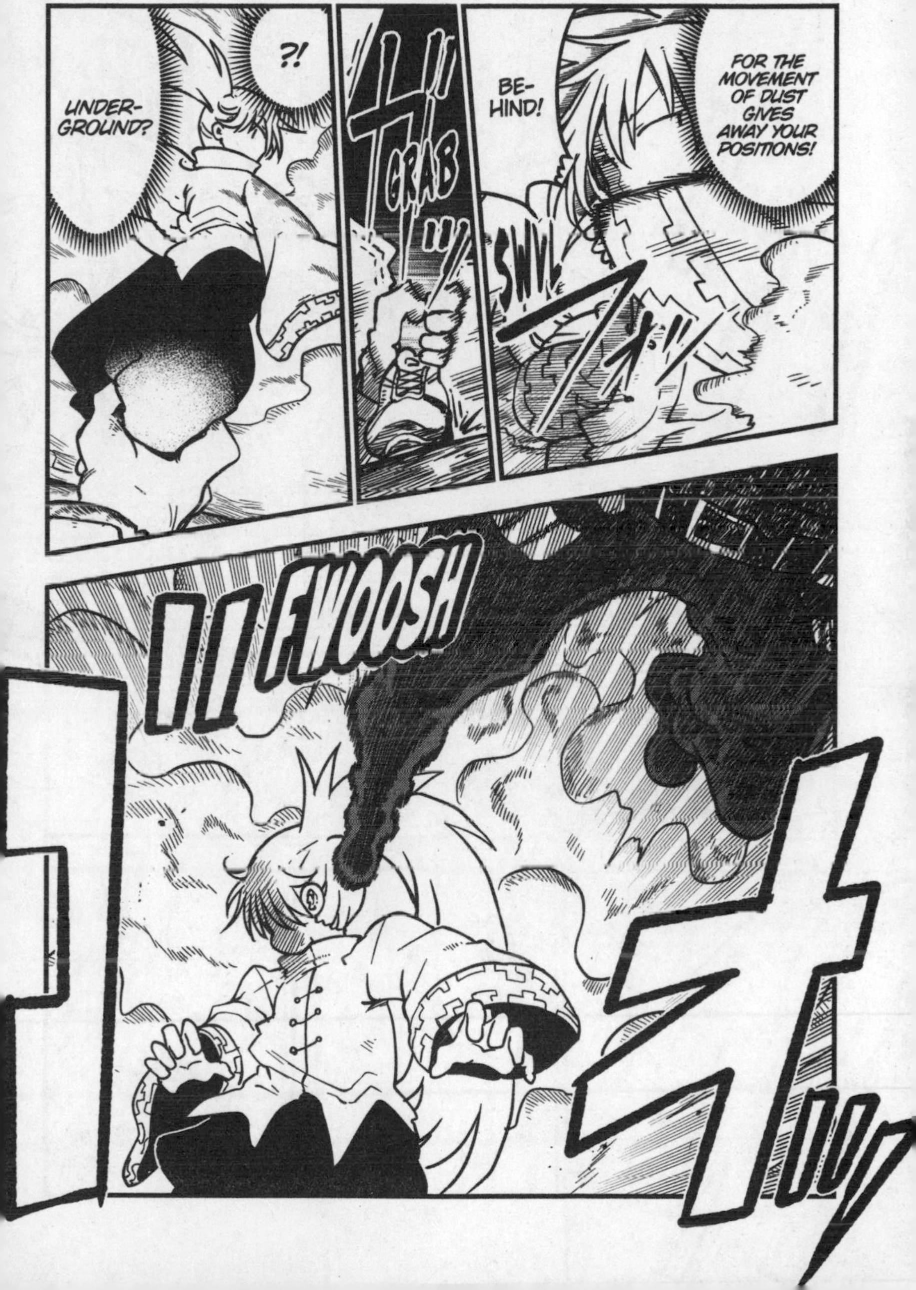
FOR THE MOVEMENT OF DUST GIVES AWAY YOUR POSITIONS!
BE-HIND!
SWVL
GRAB
?!
UNDER-GROUND?
FWOOSH

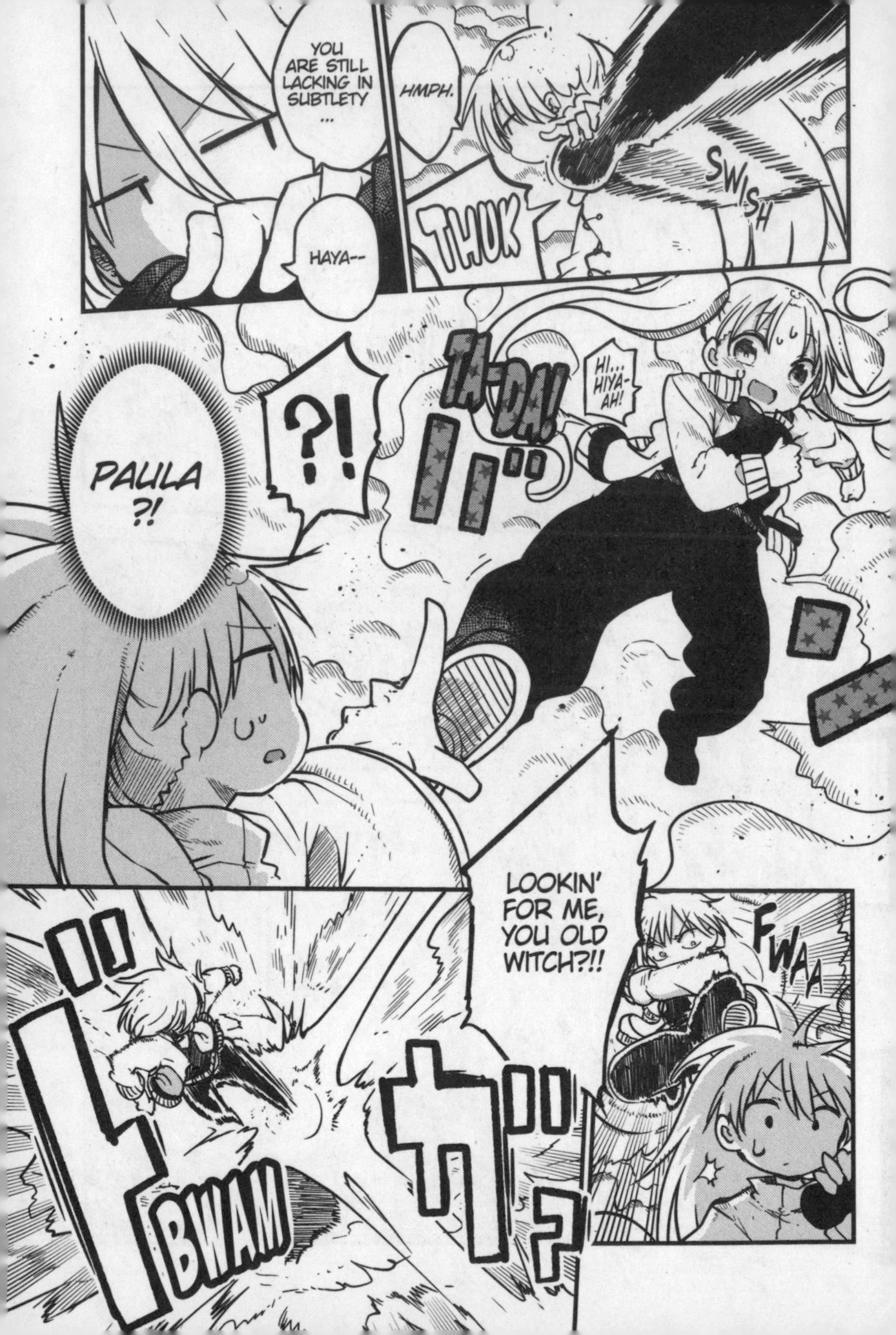
HMPH.
SWISH
THUK
YOU ARE STILL LACKING IN SUBTLETY ...
HAYA--
HI... HIYA-AH!
TA-DA!
?!
PAULA ?!
LOOKIN' FOR ME, YOU OLD WITCH?!!
FWAA
BWAM

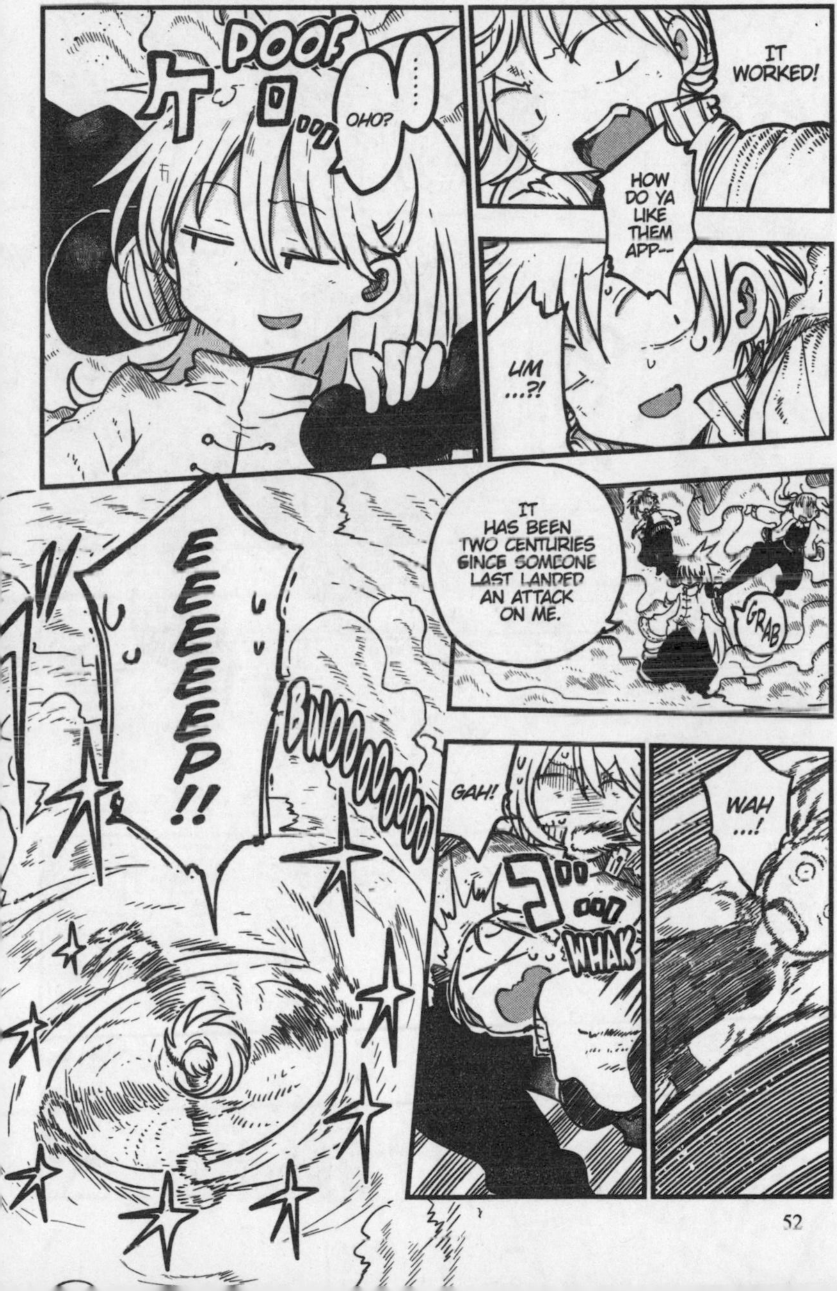
IT WORKED!
HOW DO YA LIKE THEM APP--
UM ...?!
POOF
...
OHO?
IT HAS BEEN TWO CENTURIES SINCE SOMEONE LAST LANDED AN ATTACK ON ME.
GRAB
EEEEEEEP!!
BWOOOOOOOOO
WAH ...!
GAH!
WHAK

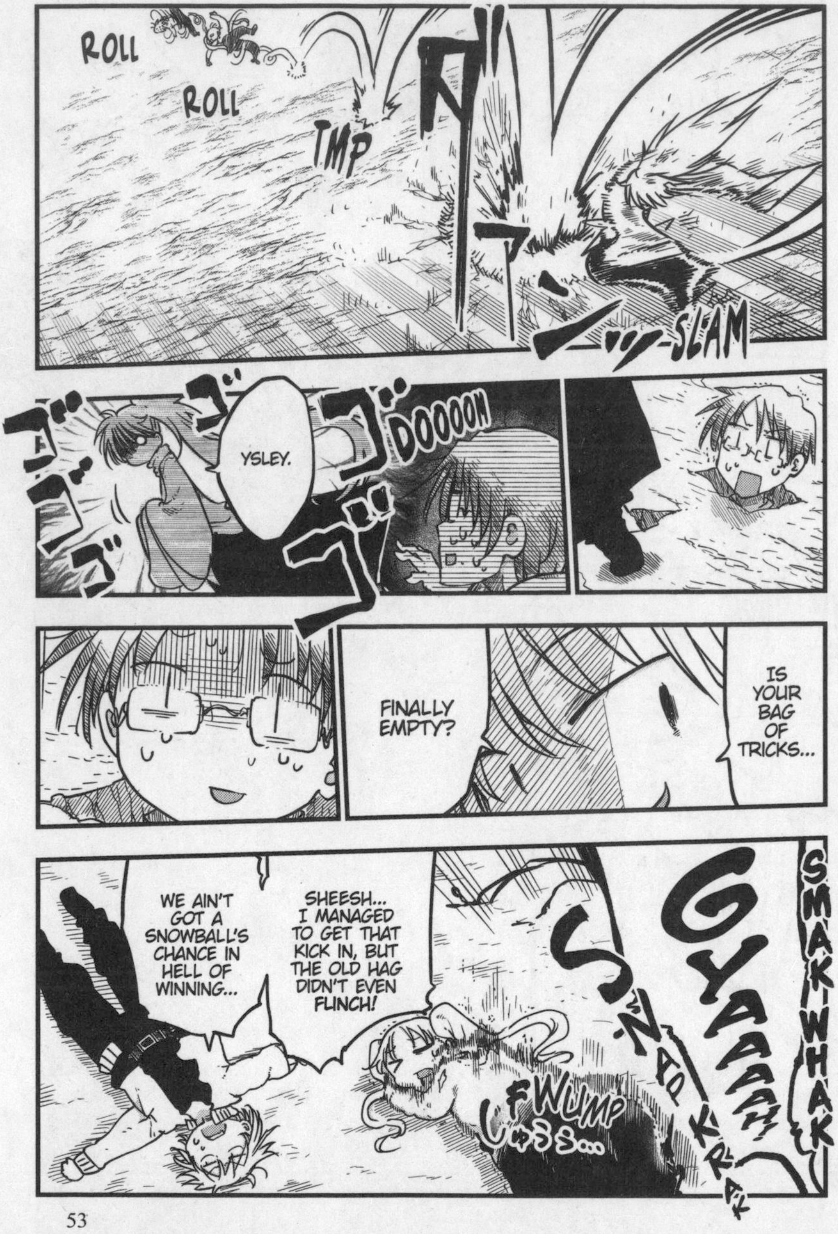
ROLL
ROLL
TMP
SLAM
DOOOON
YSLEY.
IS YOUR BAG OF TRICKS...
FINALLY EMPTY?
SMAK WHAK
GYAAAAH
KRAK
FWUMP
SHEESH... I MANAGED TO GET THAT KICK IN, BUT THE OLD HAG DIDN'T EVEN FLINCH!
WE AIN'T GOT A SNOWBALL'S CHANCE IN HELL OF WINNING...

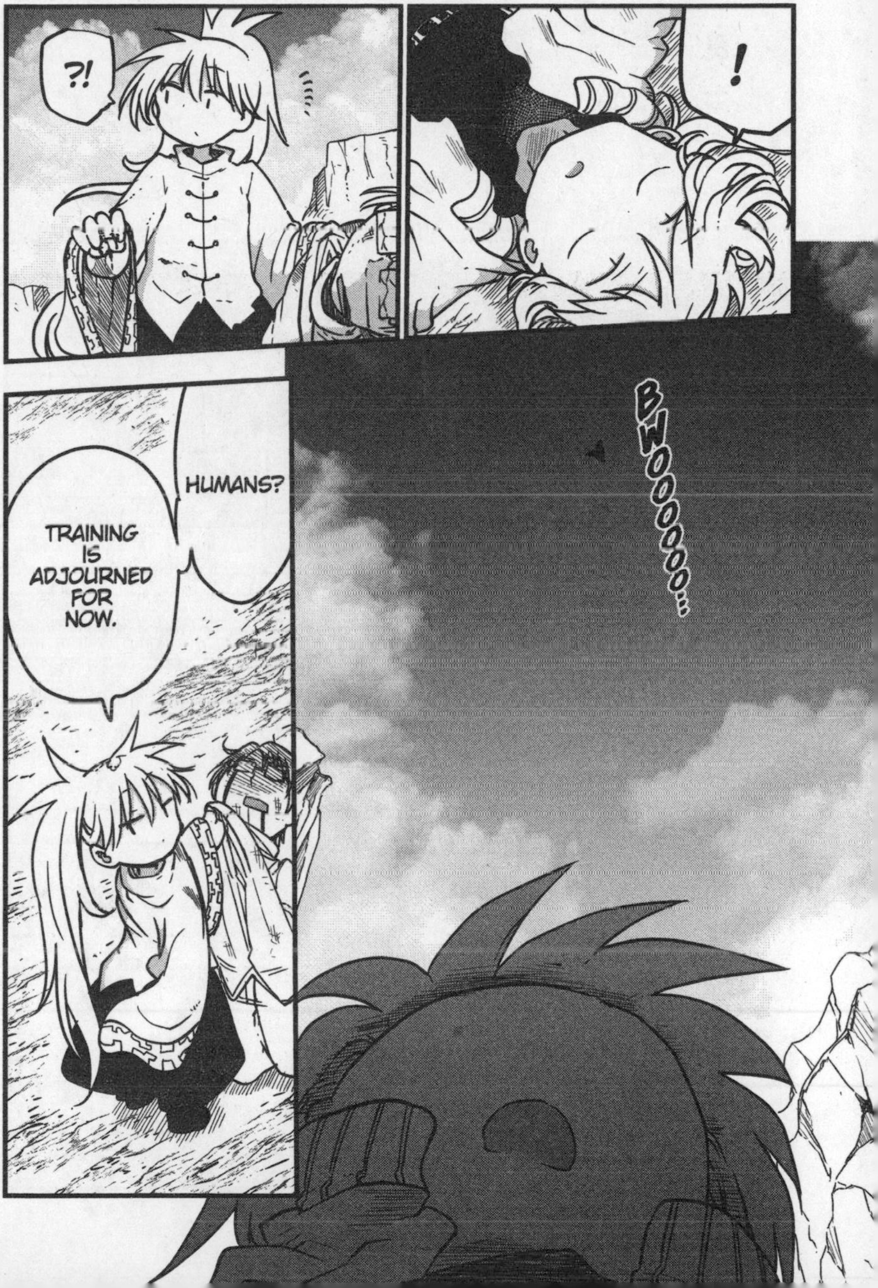
!
?!
BWOOOOOOO...
HUMANS?
TRAINING IS ADJOURNED FOR NOW.

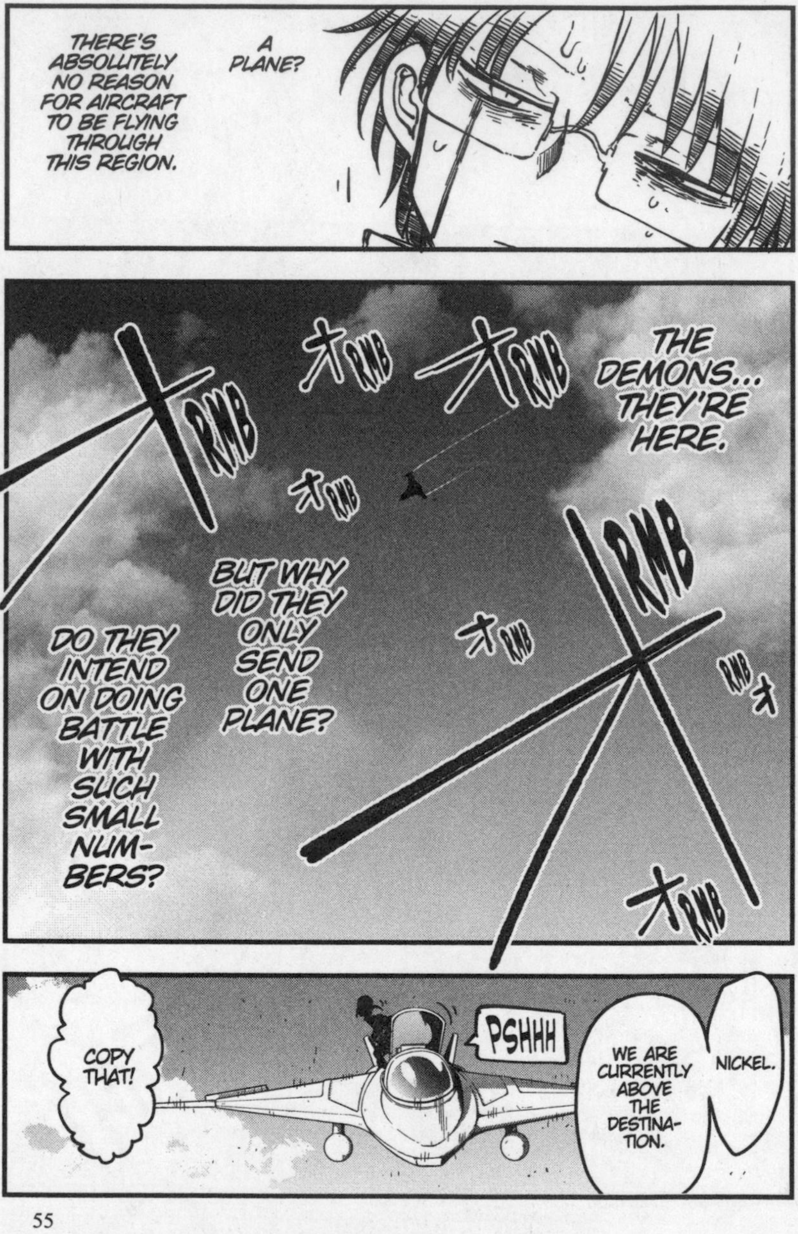
A PLANE?
THERE'S ABSOLUTELY NO REASON FOR AIRCRAFT TO BE FLYING THROUGH THIS REGION.
THE DEMONS... THEY'RE HERE.
RMB
BUT WHY DID THEY ONLY SEND ONE PLANE?
DO THEY INTEND ON DOING BATTLE WITH SUCH SMALL NUM-BERS?
NICKEL.
WE ARE CURRENTLY ABOVE THE DESTINA-TION.
PSHHH
COPY THAT!

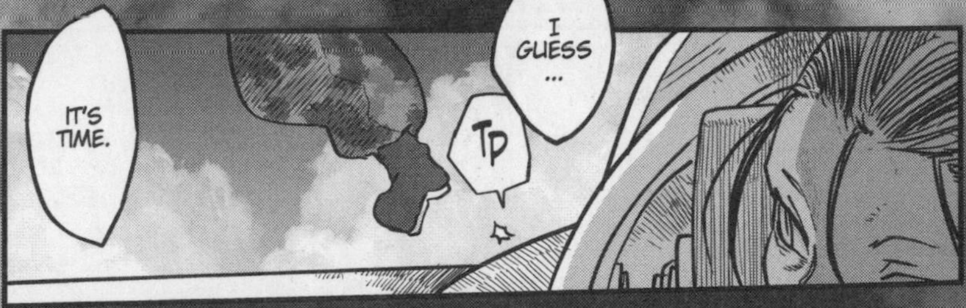
I GUESS ...
Tp
IT'S TIME.
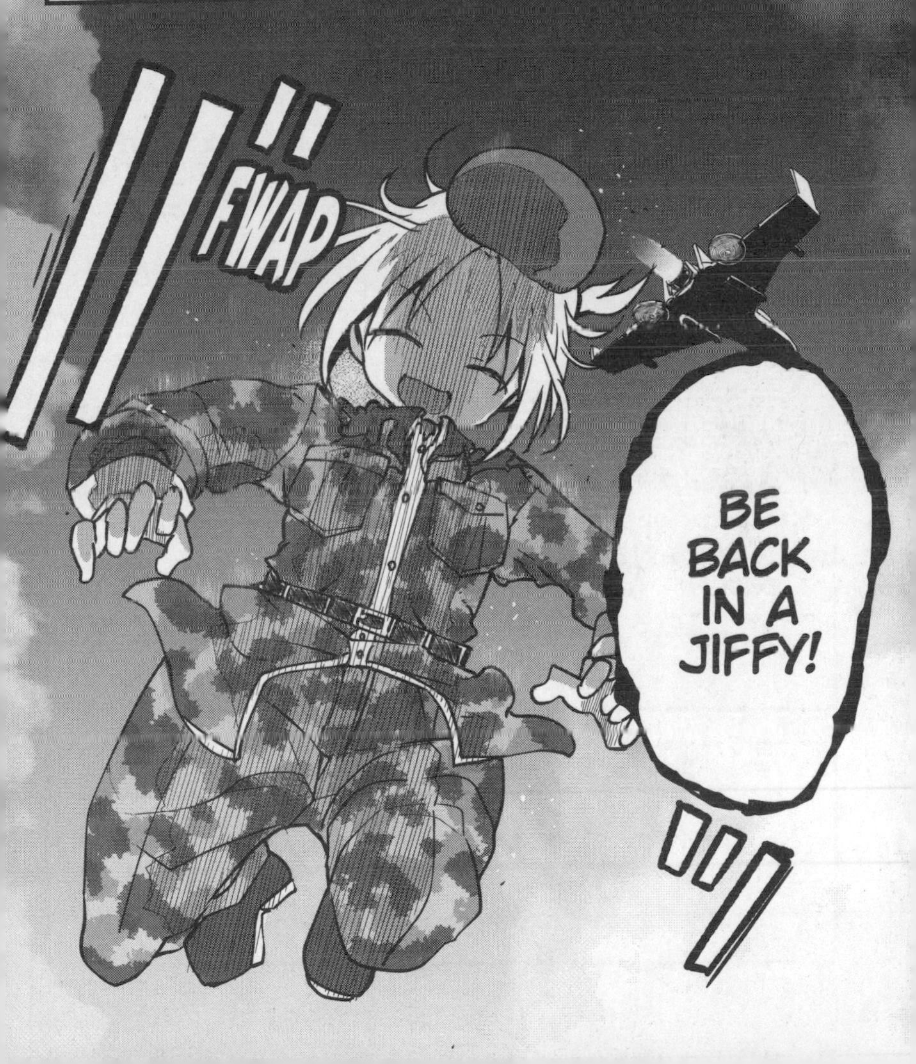
FWAP
BE BACK IN A JIFFY!

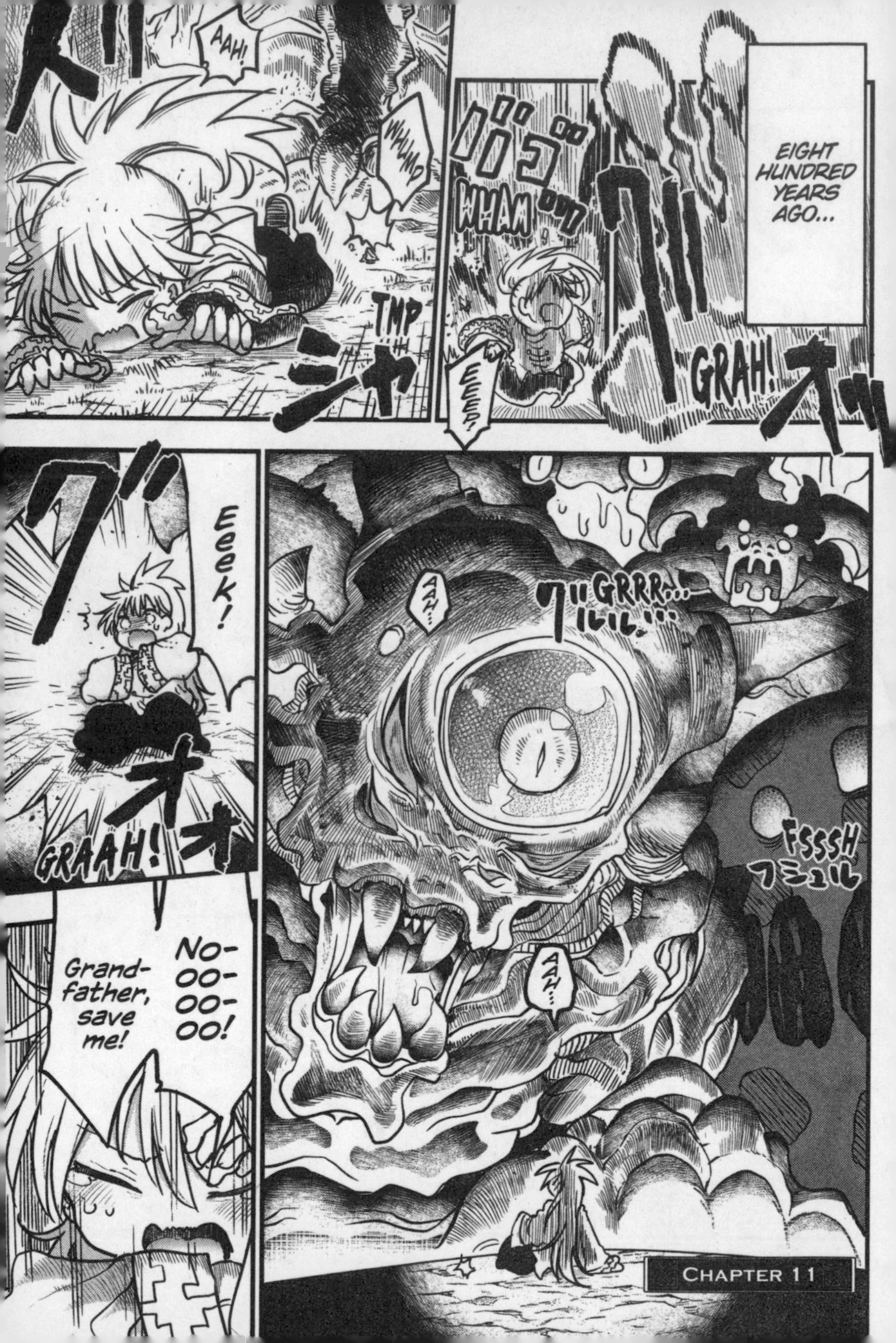
EIGHT HUNDRED YEARS AGO...
GRAH!
WHAM
EEEP!
WHUMP
AAH!
TMP
GRRR...
AAH...
AAH...
FSSSH
CHAPTER 11
Eeek!
GRAAH!
No-oo-oo-oo!
Grand-father, save me!

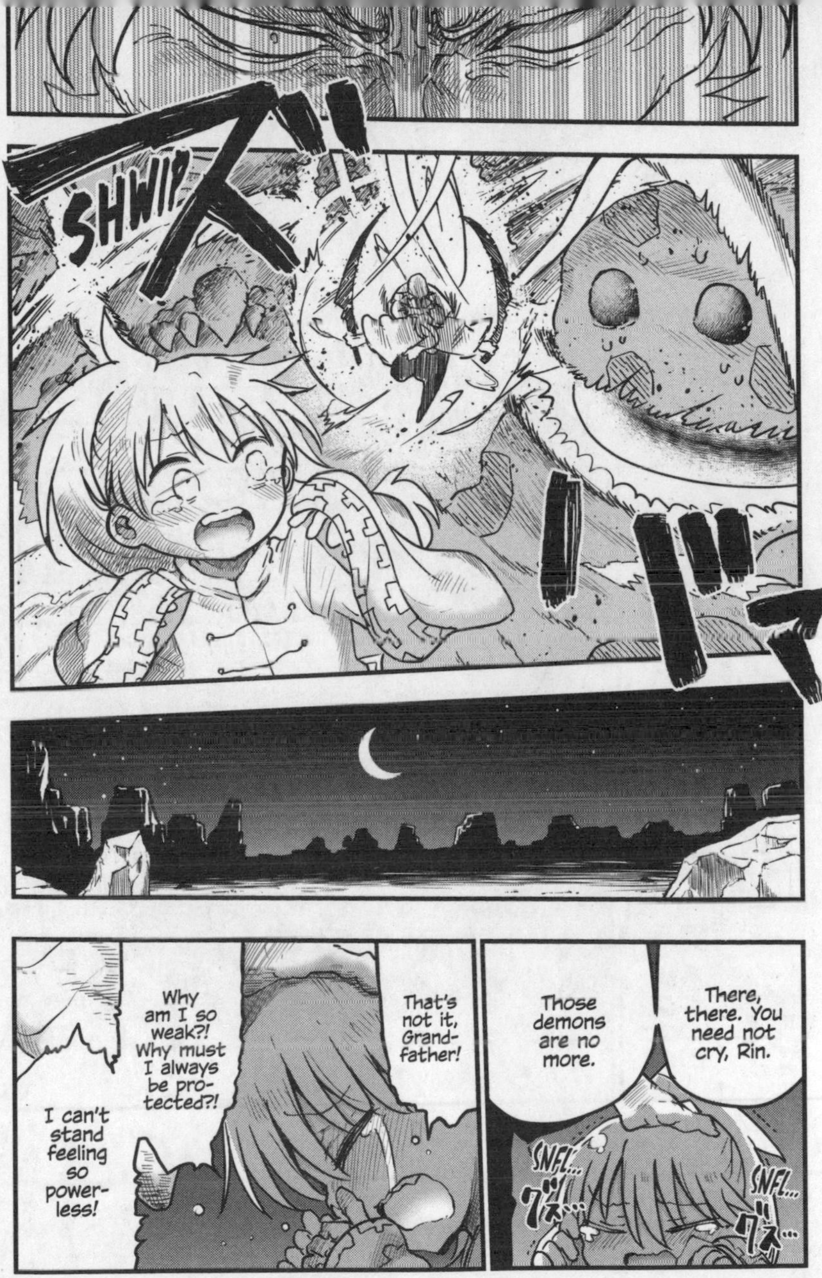
SHWIP
There, there. You need not cry, Rin.
Those demons are no more.
SNFL...
SNFL...
That's not it, Grandfather!
Why am I so weak?! Why must I always be protected?!
I can't stand feeling so powerless!

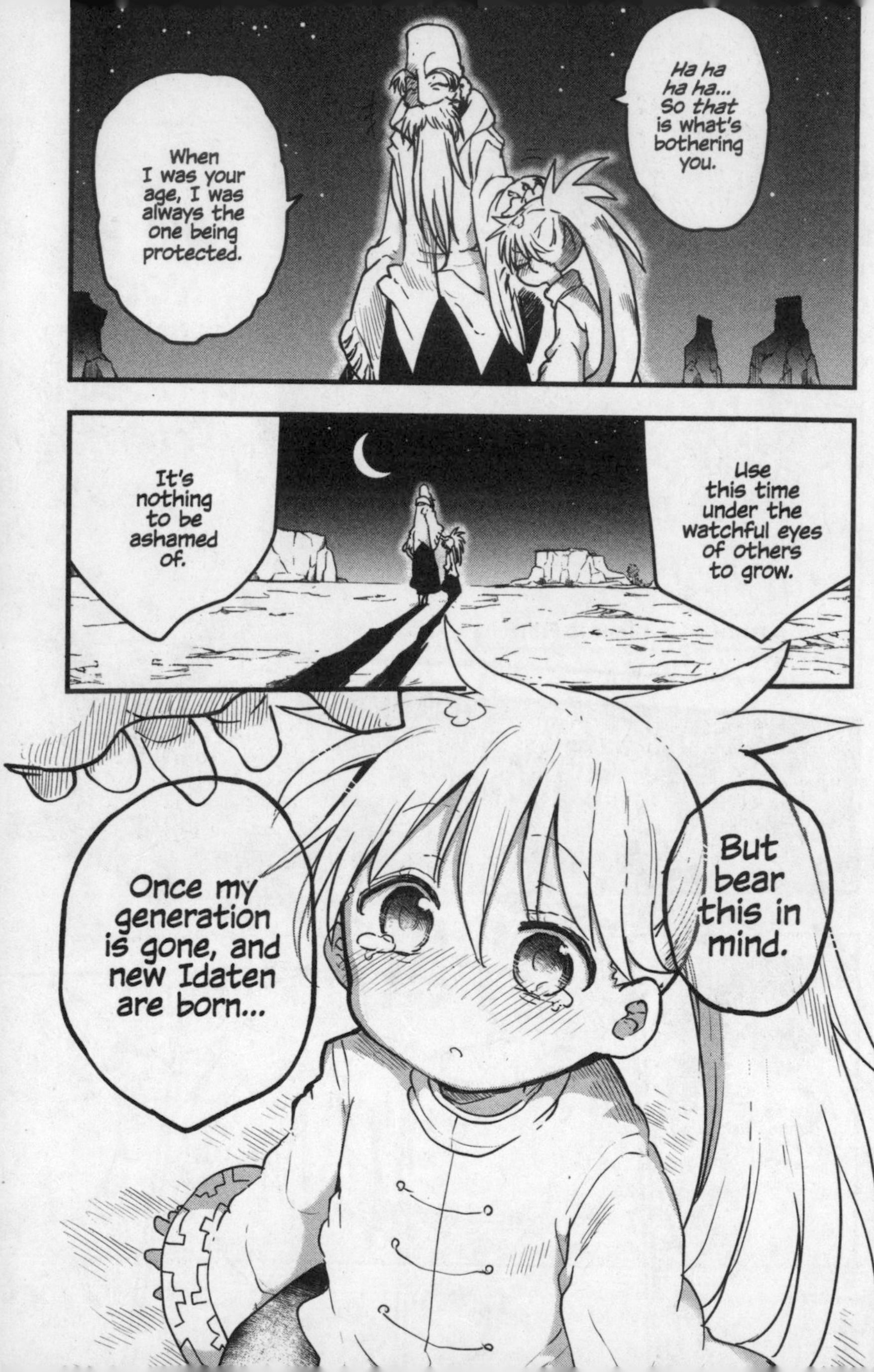
Ha ha ha ha... So that is what's bothering you.
When I was your age, I was always the one being protected.
Use this time under the watchful eyes of others to grow.
It's nothing to be ashamed of.
But bear this in mind.
Once my generation is gone, and new Idaten are born...

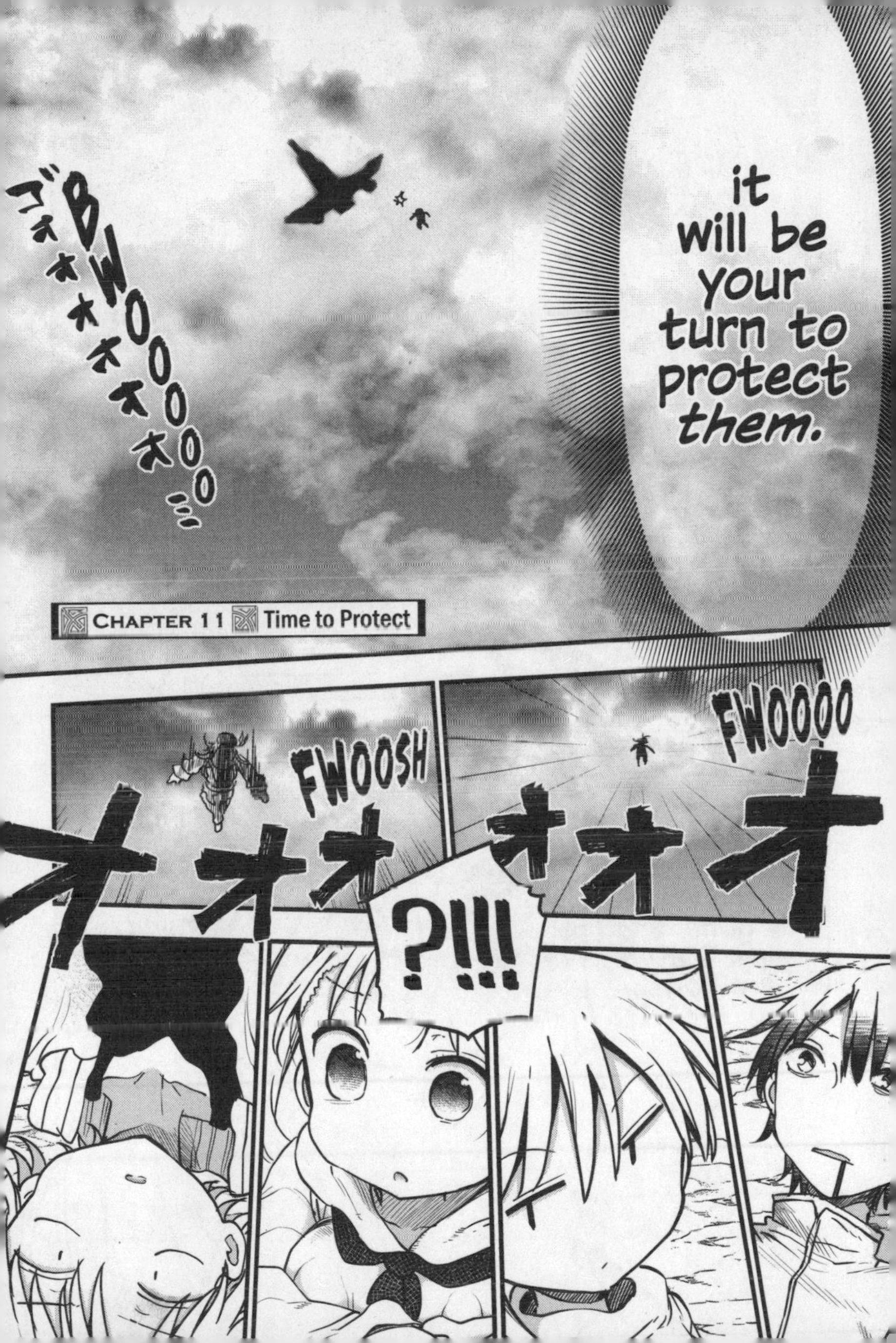
it will be your turn to protect *them.*
BWOOOOOO...
ゴォォォォォ…
CHAPTER 11 Time to Protect
FWOOOO
FWOOSH
オオオオオオ
?!!!

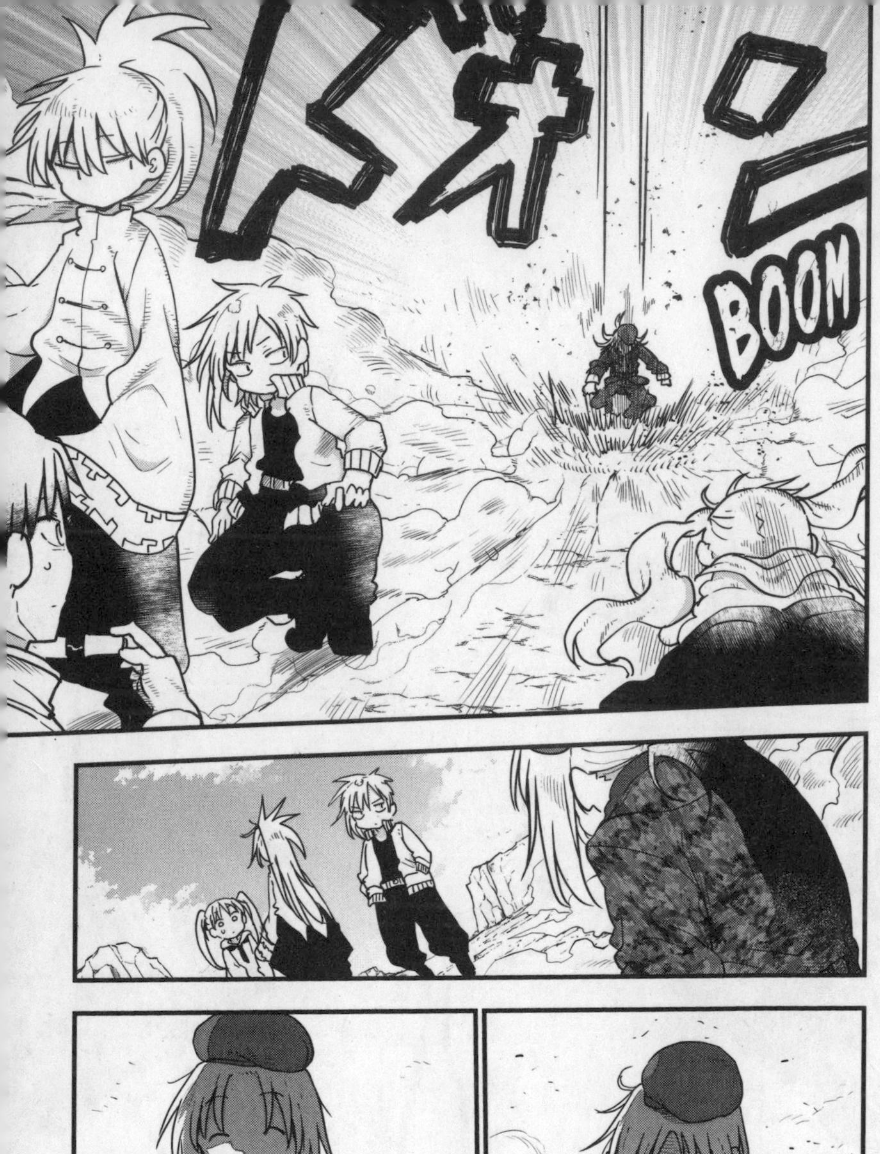
BOOM

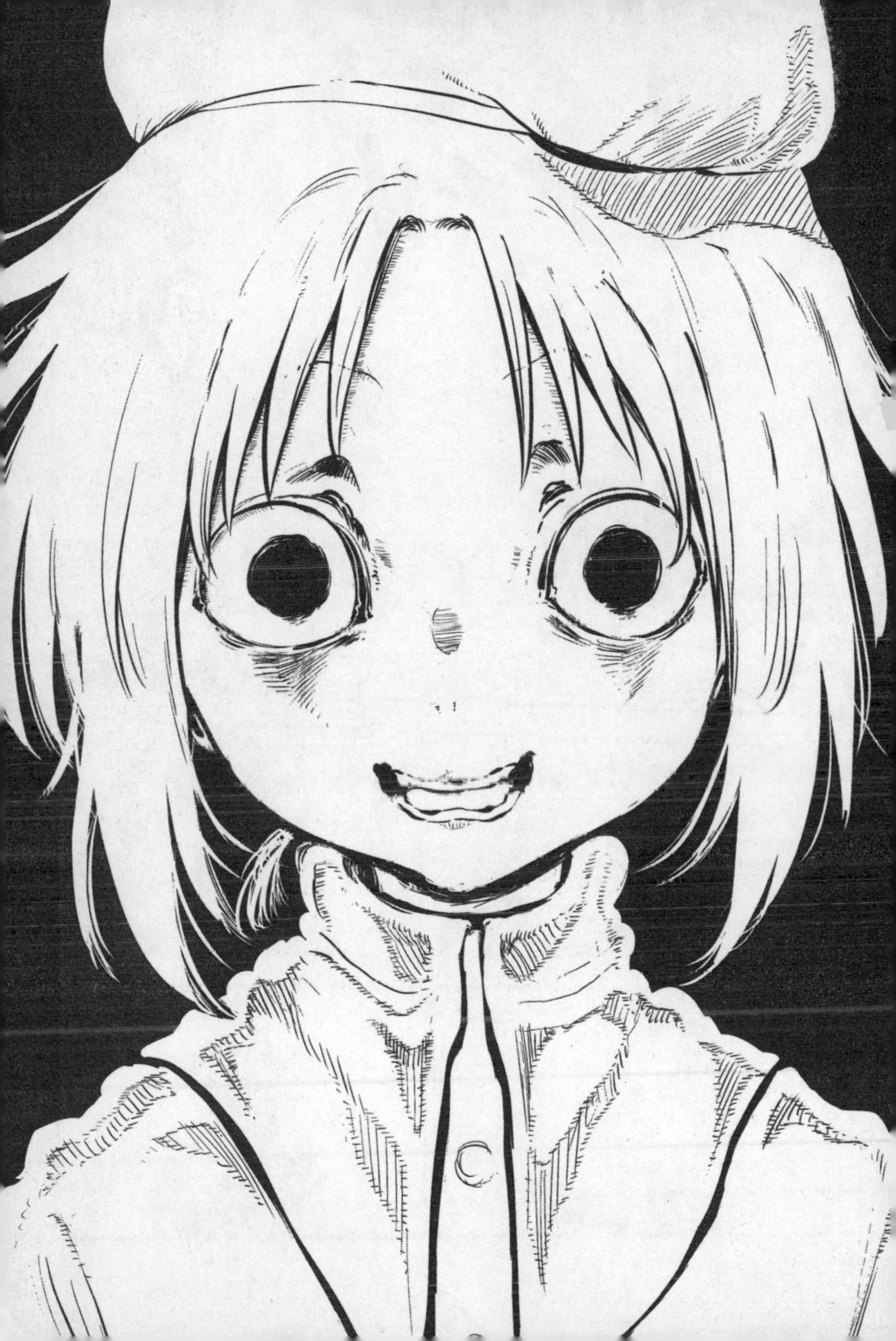

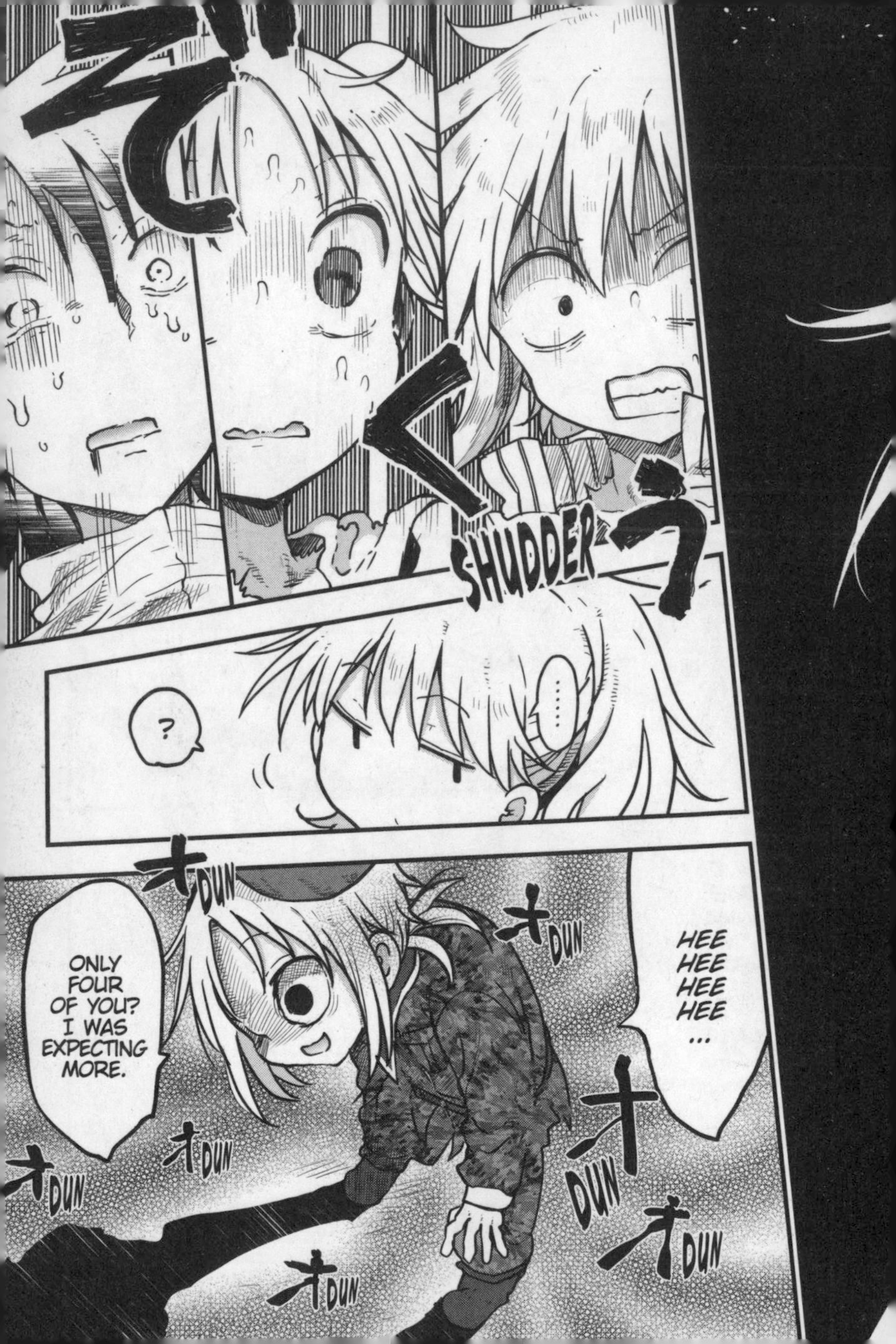
SHUDDER
...
?
DUN
HEE HEE HEE HEE ...
ONLY FOUR OF YOU? I WAS EXPECTING MORE.
DUN
DUN
DUN
DUN
DUN
DUN
DUN

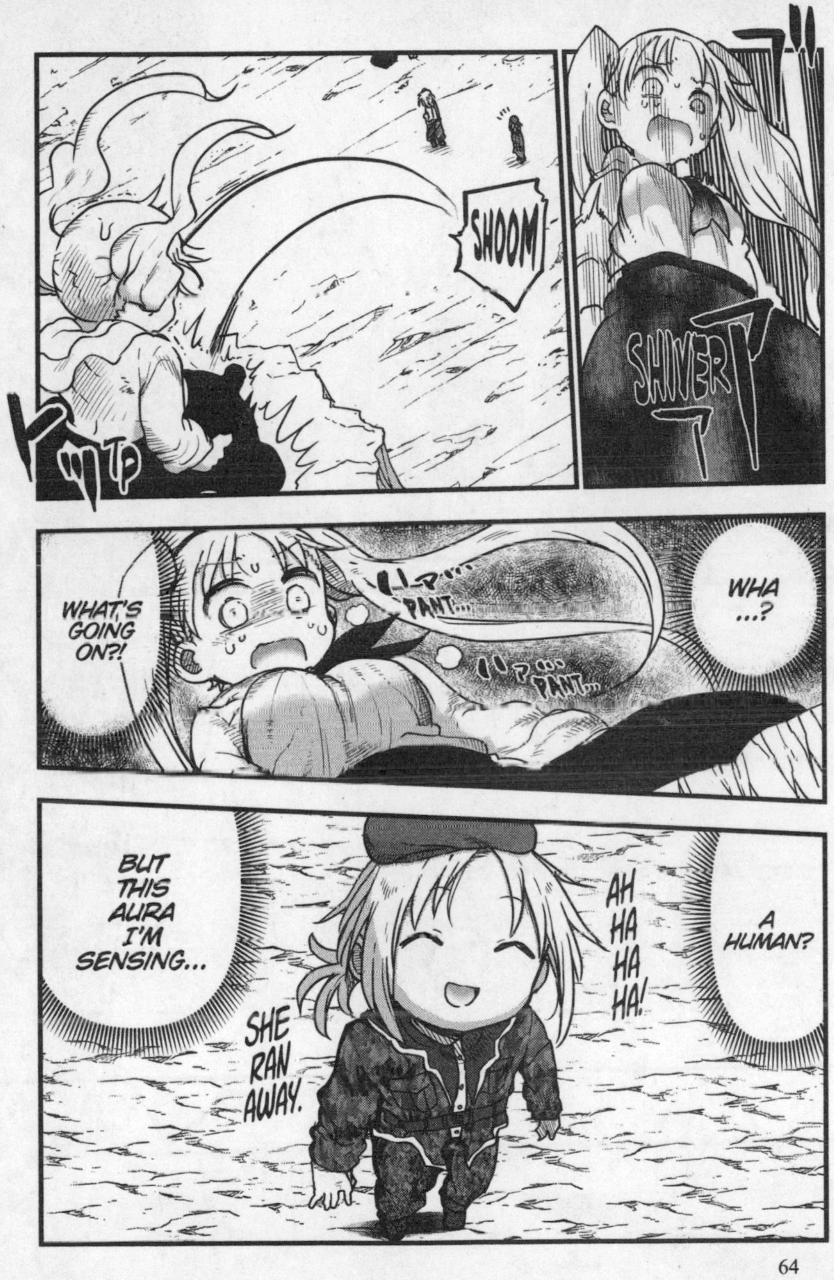
SHIVER
SHOOM
WHA ...?
PANT...
PANT...
WHAT'S GOING ON?!
A HUMAN?
AH HA HA HA!
SHE RAN AWAY.
BUT THIS AURA I'M SENSING...

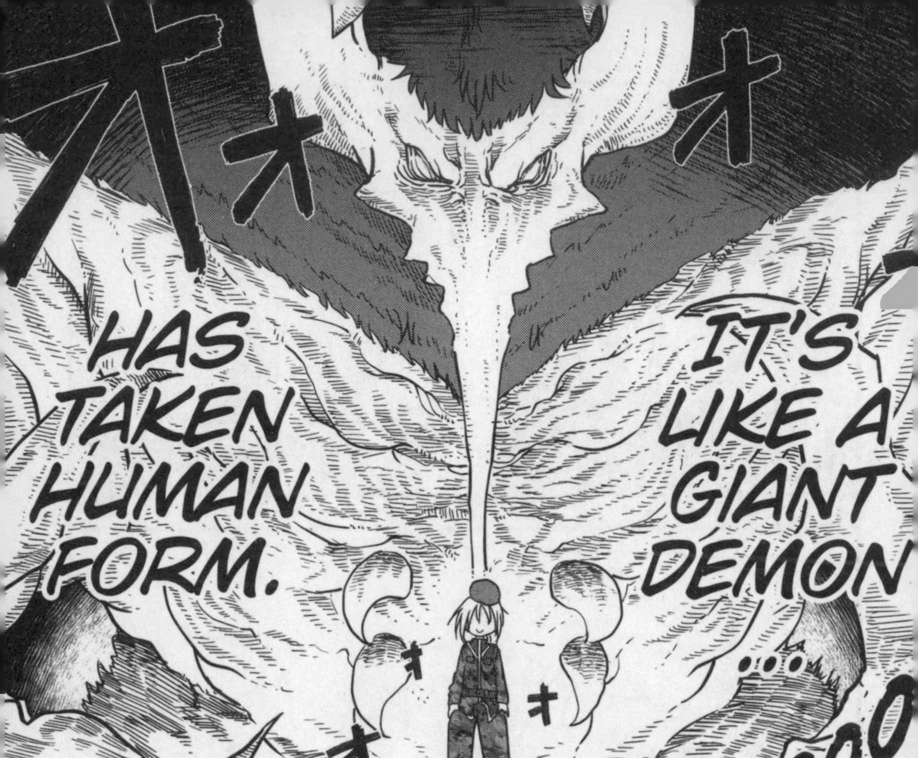
IT'S LIKE A GIANT DEMON...
HAS TAKEN HUMAN FORM.
FWOOOOOOOOO
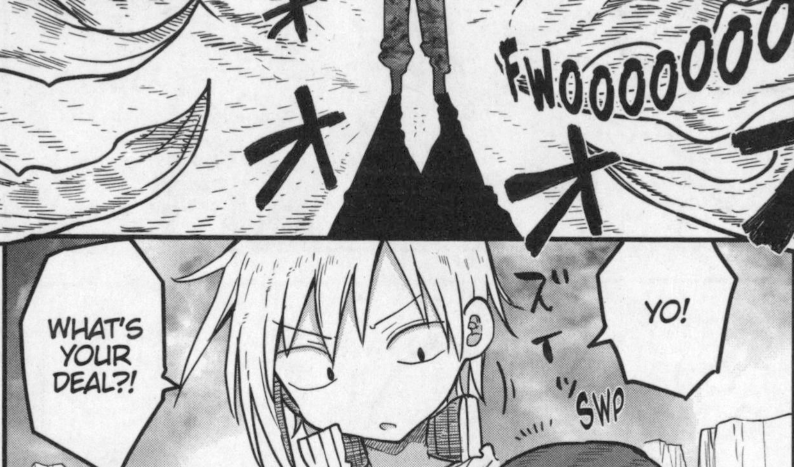
YO!
SWP
WHAT'S YOUR DEAL?!

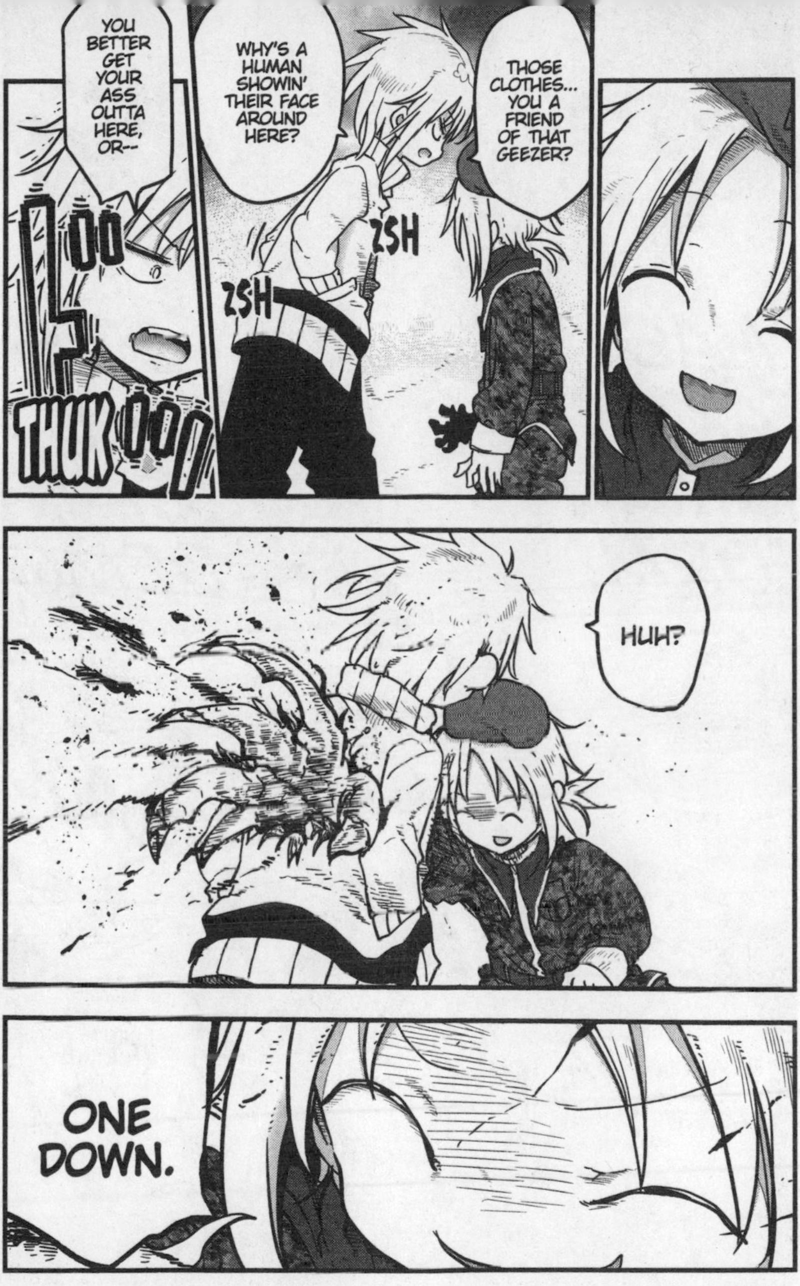
THOSE CLOTHES... YOU A FRIEND OF THAT GEEZER?
WHY'S A HUMAN SHOWIN' THEIR FACE AROUND HERE?
ZSH
ZSH
YOU BETTER GET YOUR ASS OUTTA HERE, OR--
THUK
HUH?
ONE DOWN.

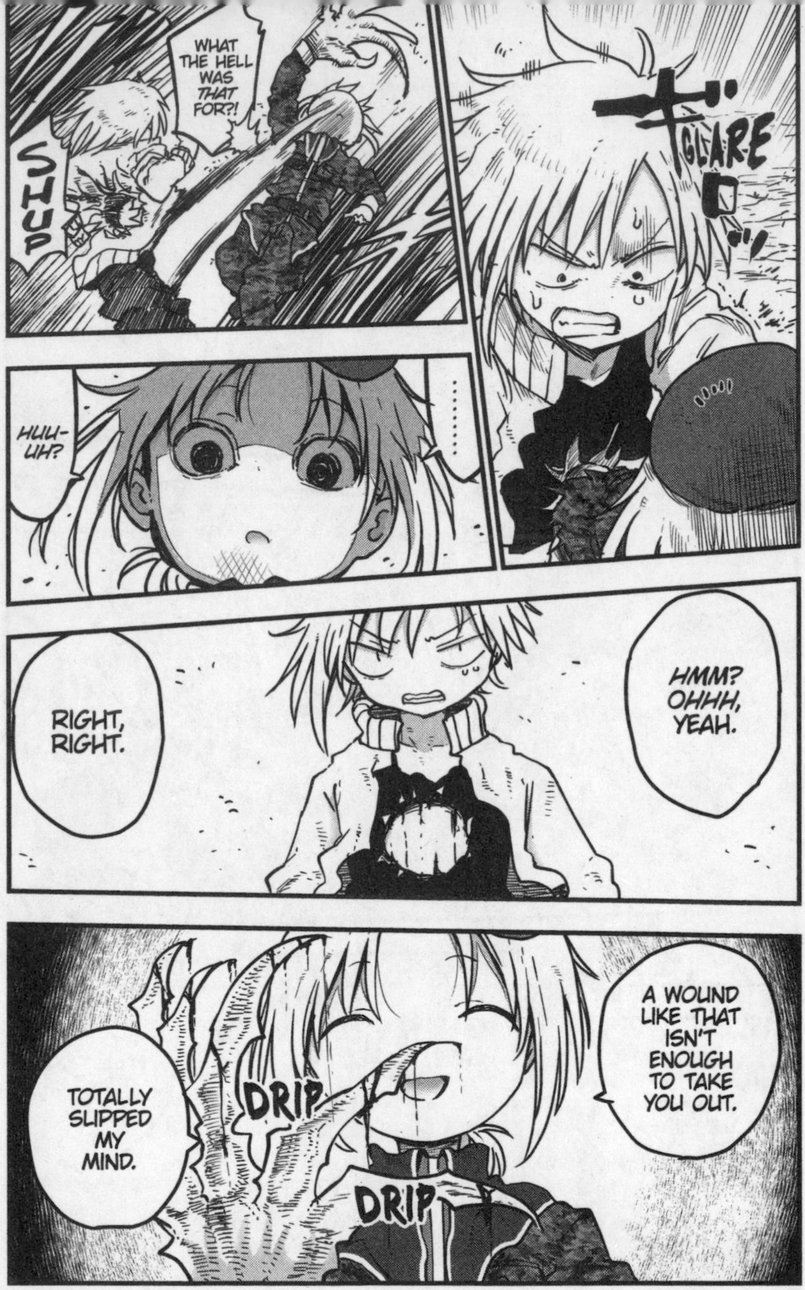
GLARE
WHAT THE HELL WAS THAT FOR?!
SHUP
HUU-UH?
HMM? OHHH, YEAH.
RIGHT, RIGHT.
A WOUND LIKE THAT ISN'T ENOUGH TO TAKE YOU OUT.
DRIP
TOTALLY SLIPPED MY MIND.
DRIP

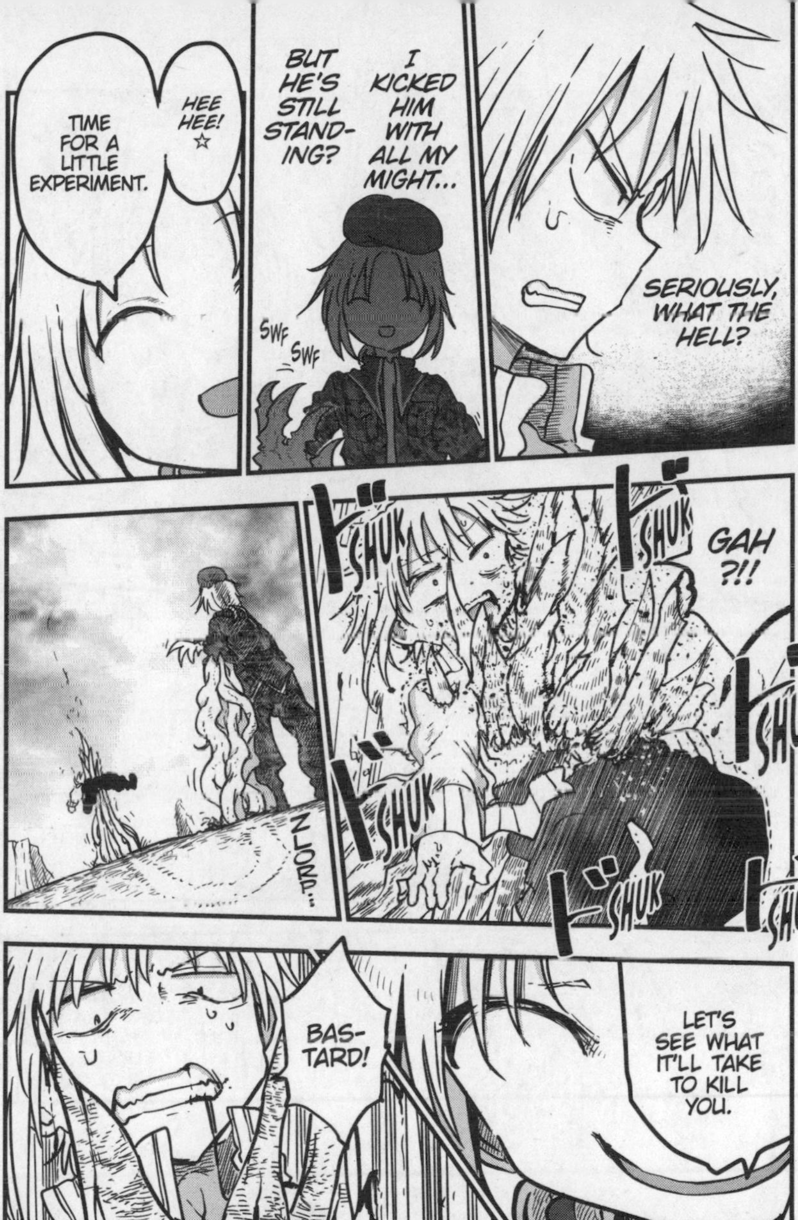
SERIOUSLY, WHAT THE HELL?
I KICKED HIM WITH ALL MY MIGHT...
BUT HE'S STILL STANDING?
SWF SWF
HEE HEE! ☆
TIME FOR A LITTLE EXPERIMENT.
SHUK
SHUK
GAH ?!!
SHUK
SHUK
SHUK
SHUK
ZLORP...
LET'S SEE WHAT IT'LL TAKE TO KILL YOU.
BAS-TARD!

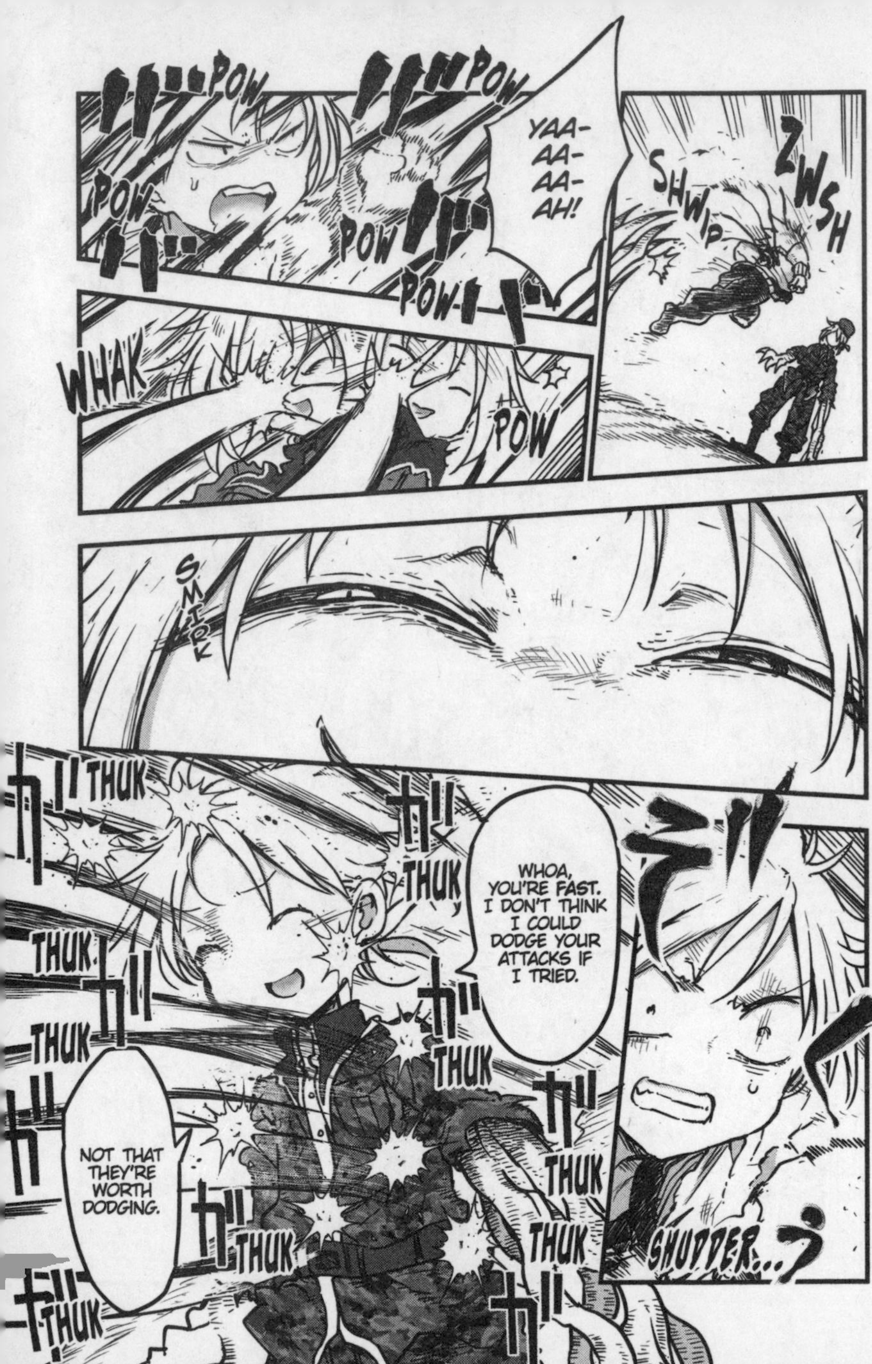
YAA-AA-AA-AH!
ZWSH
SHWIP
POW
POW
POW
POW
POW
WHAK
POW
SMIRK
SHUDDER...
WHOA, YOU'RE FAST. I DON'T THINK I COULD DODGE YOUR ATTACKS IF I TRIED.
THUK
THUK
THUK
THUK
THUK
THUK
NOT THAT THEY'RE WORTH DODGING.
THUK
THUK
THUK

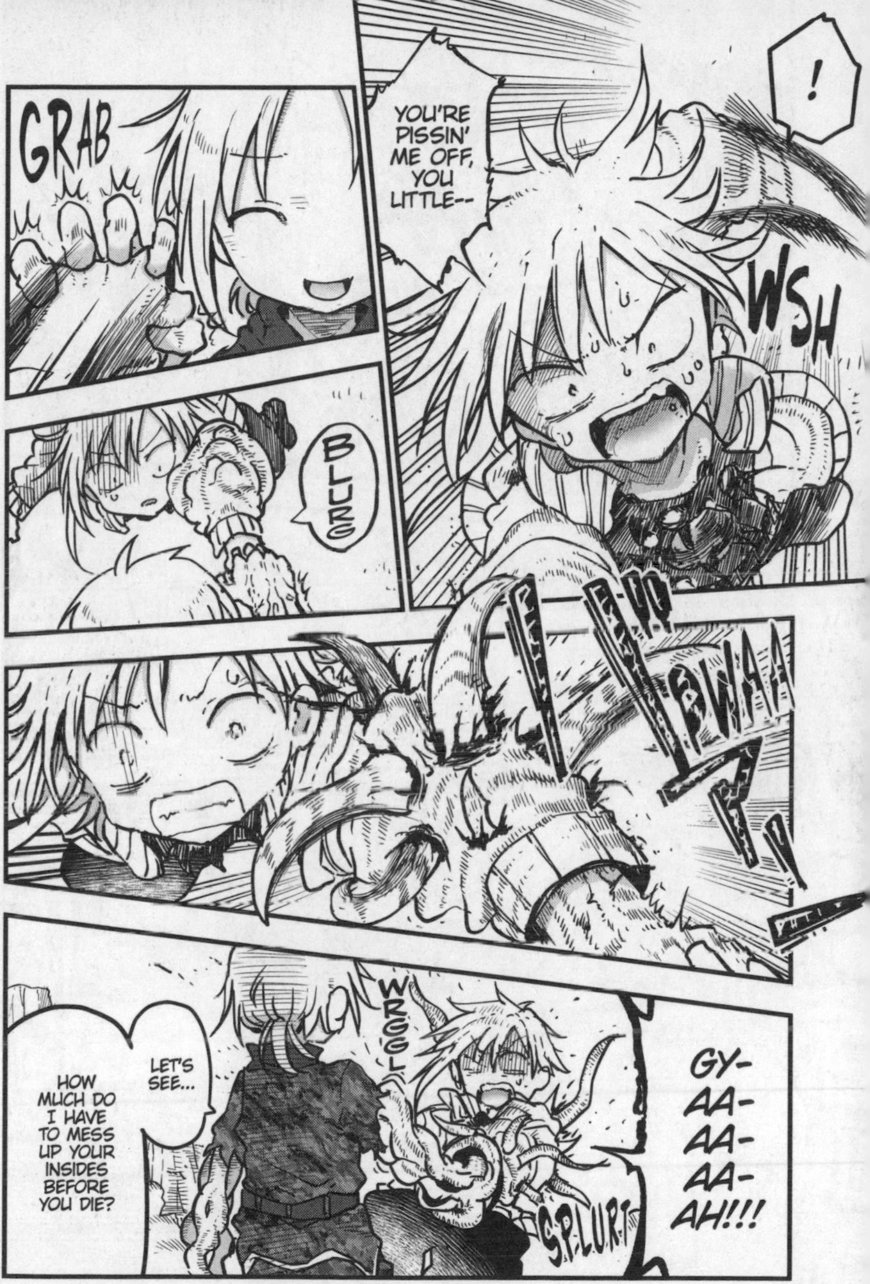
!
YOU'RE PISSIN' ME OFF, YOU LITTLE--
WSH
GRAB
BLURG
BWAA
GY-AA-AA-AA-AH!!!
S.P.L.U.R.T
WRGGL
LET'S SEE...
HOW MUCH DO I HAVE TO MESS UP YOUR INSIDES BEFORE YOU DIE?

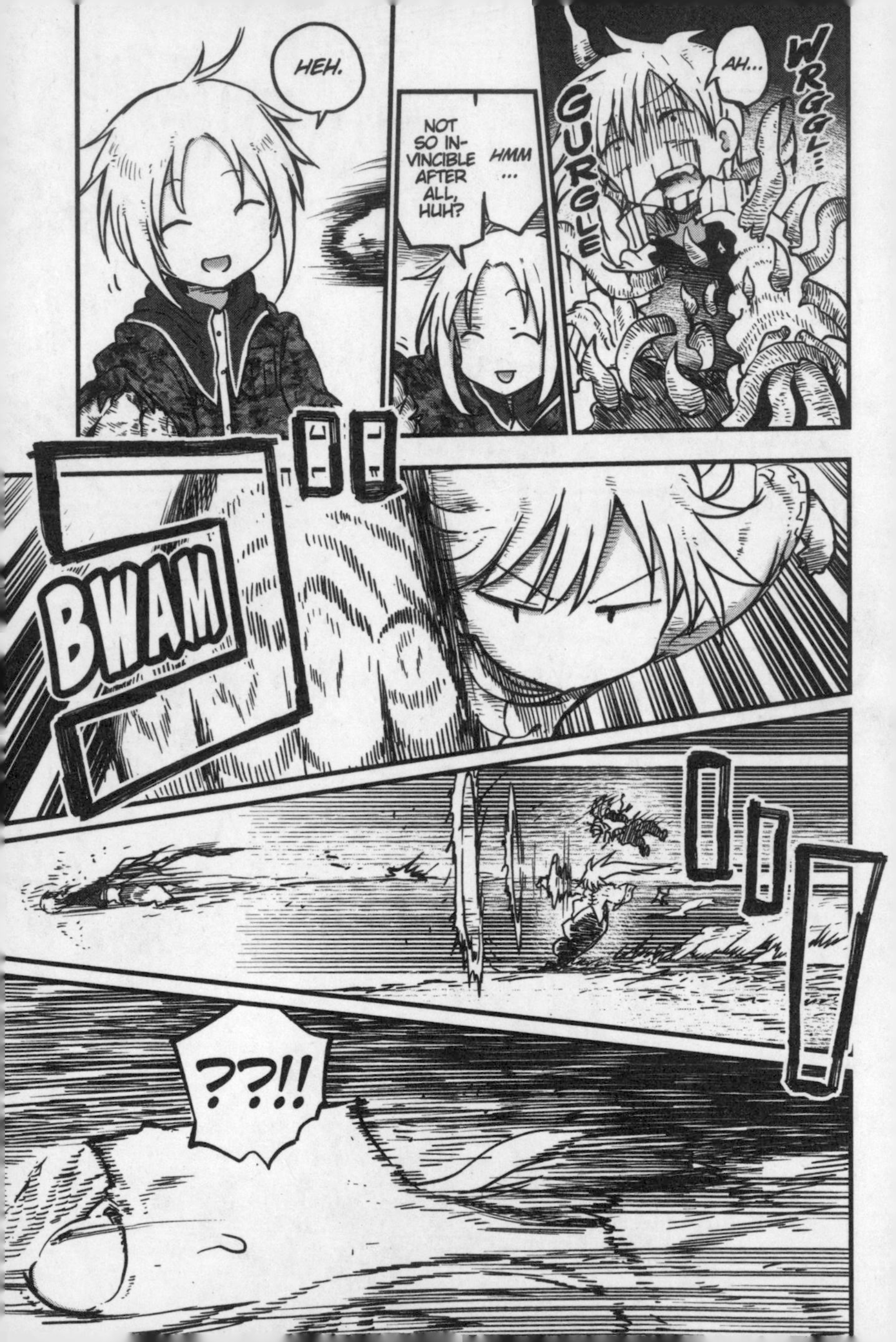
AH...
WRGGL...
GURGLE
HMM ...
NOT SO IN-VINCIBLE AFTER ALL, HUH?
HEH.
BWAM
!
??!!

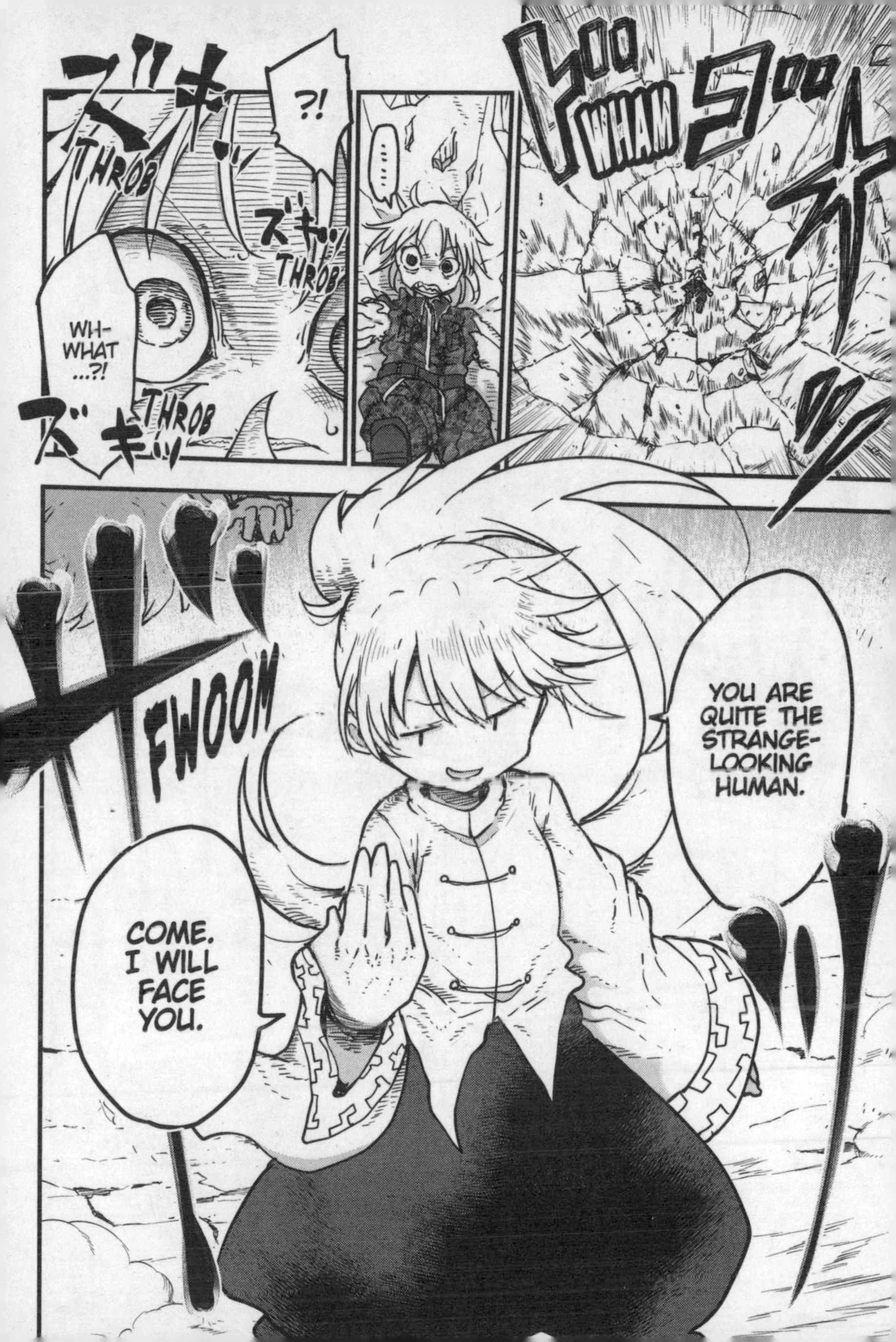
WHAM
...
?!
THROB
THROB
WH-WHAT ...?!
THROB
FWOOM
YOU ARE QUITE THE STRANGE-LOOKING HUMAN.
COME. I WILL FACE YOU.

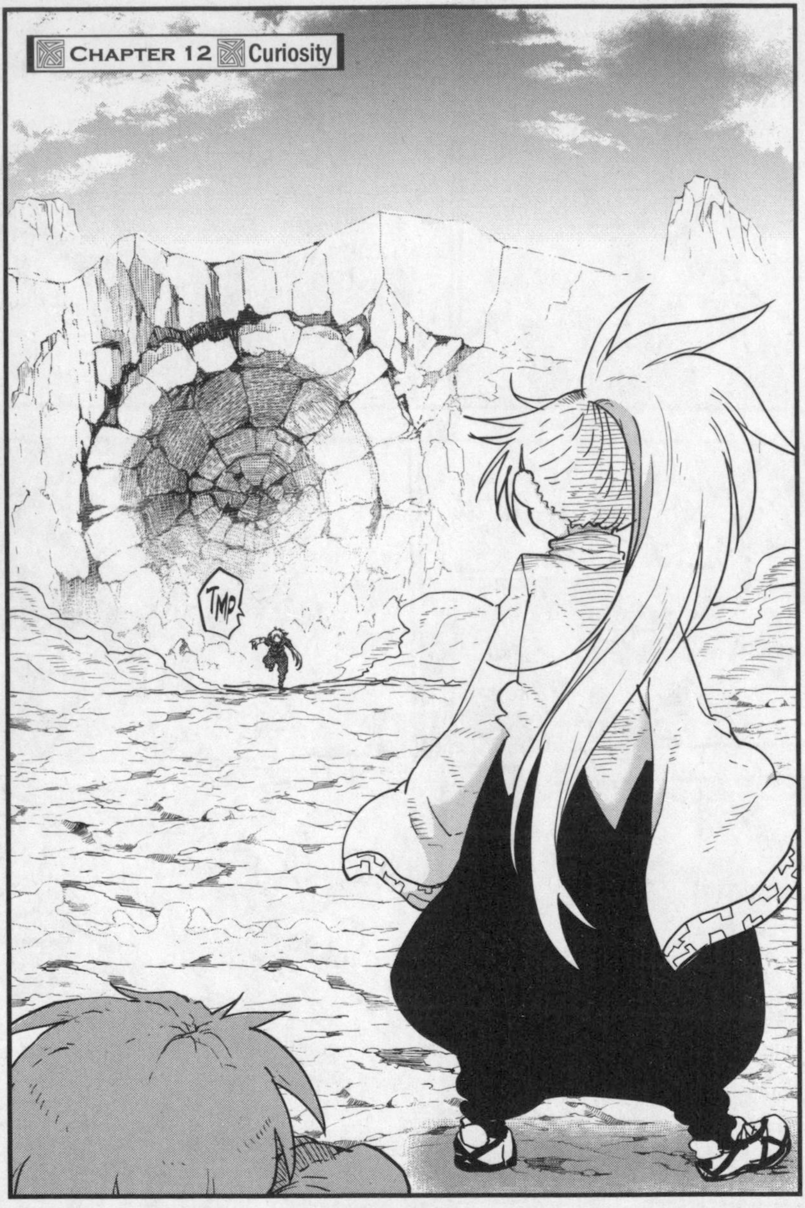
Chapter 12 Curiosity
TMP

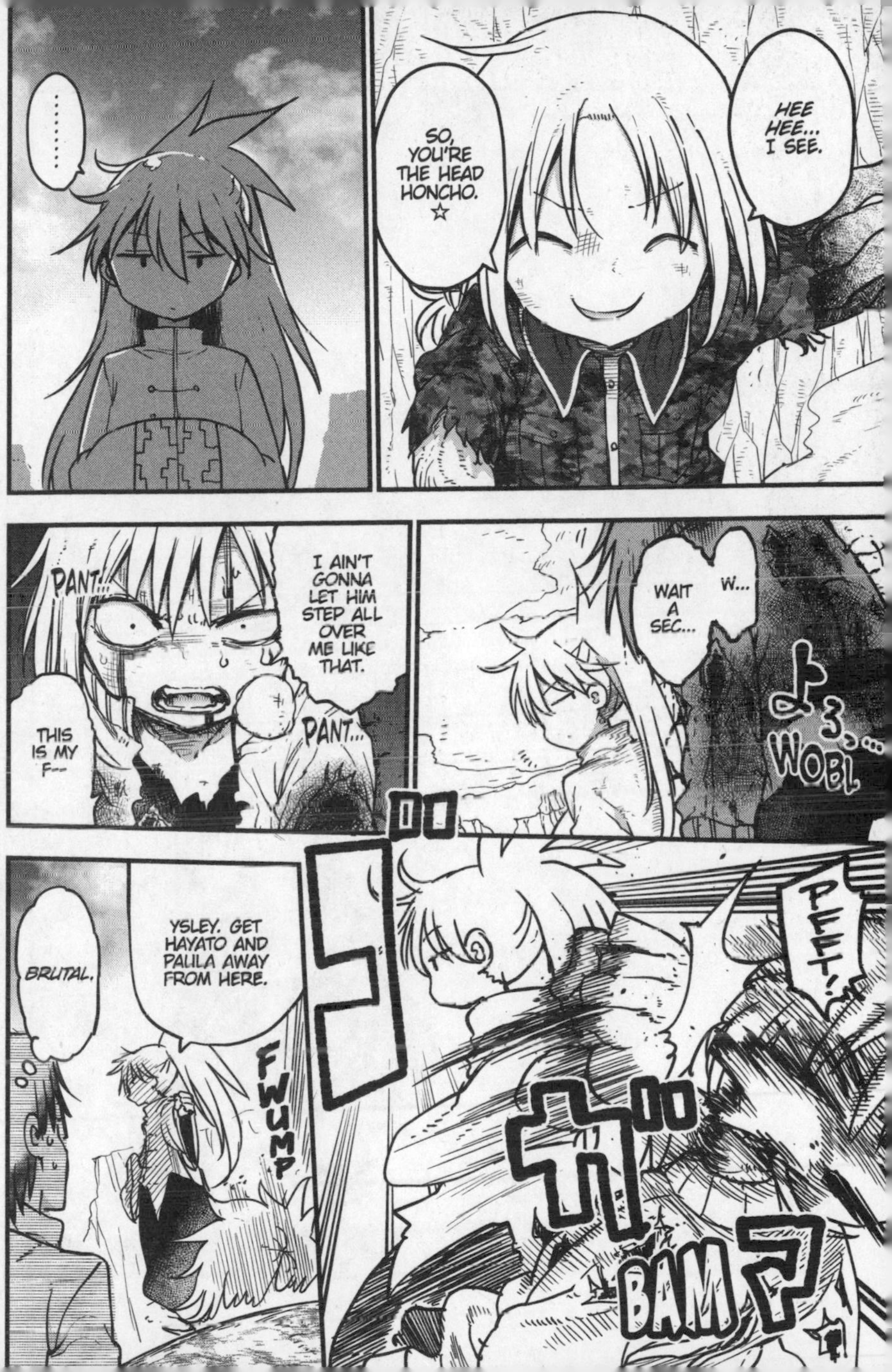

HEE HEE... I SEE.
SO, YOU'RE THE HEAD HONCHO. ☆
......
W...
WAIT A SEC...
WOBL
I AIN'T GONNA LET HIM STEP ALL OVER ME LIKE THAT.
PANT...
PANT...
THIS IS MY F--
PFFT!
BAM
YSLEY. GET HAYATO AND PAULA AWAY FROM HERE.
FWUMP
BRUTAL.

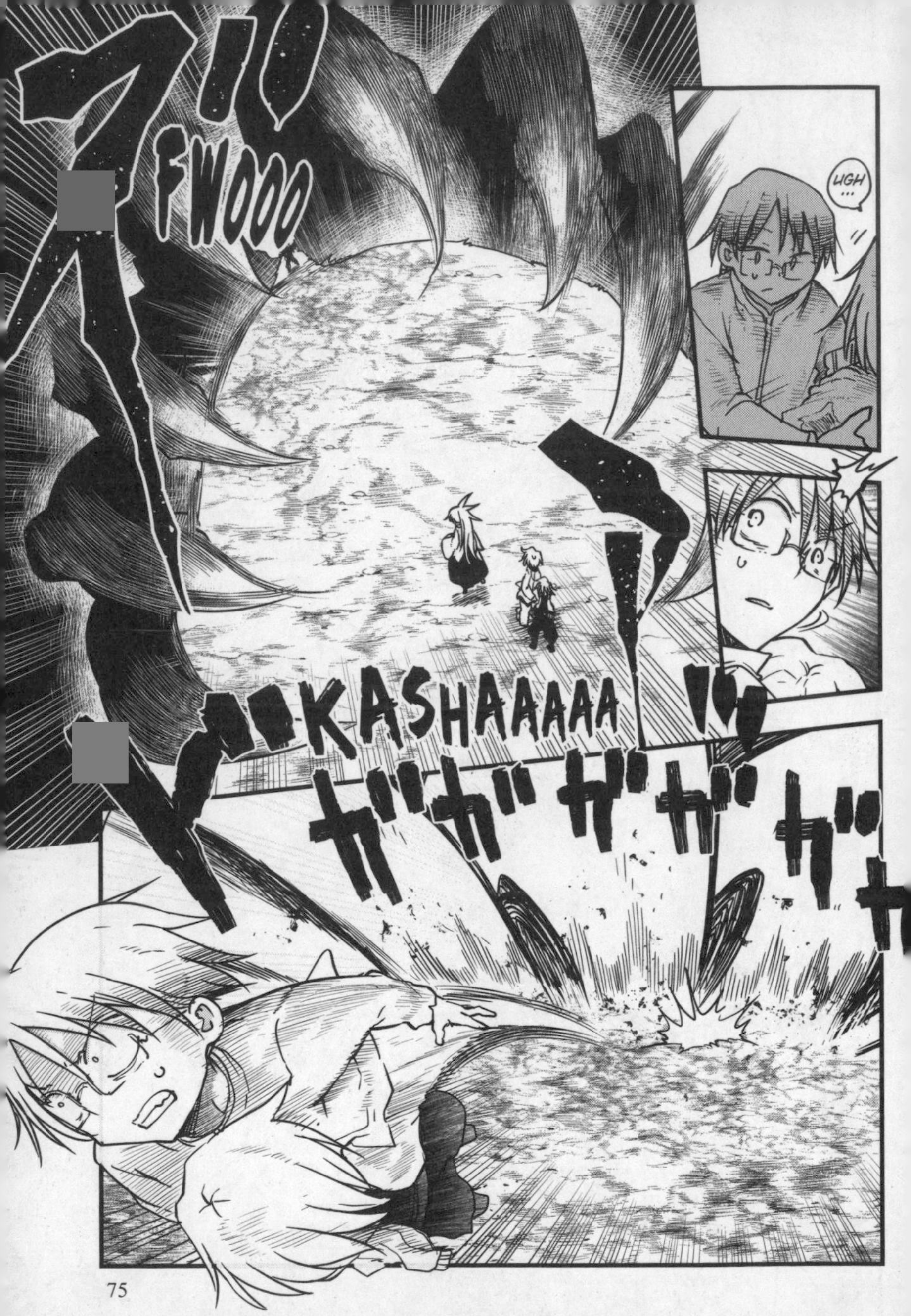
UGH ...
FWOOO
KASHAAAAA

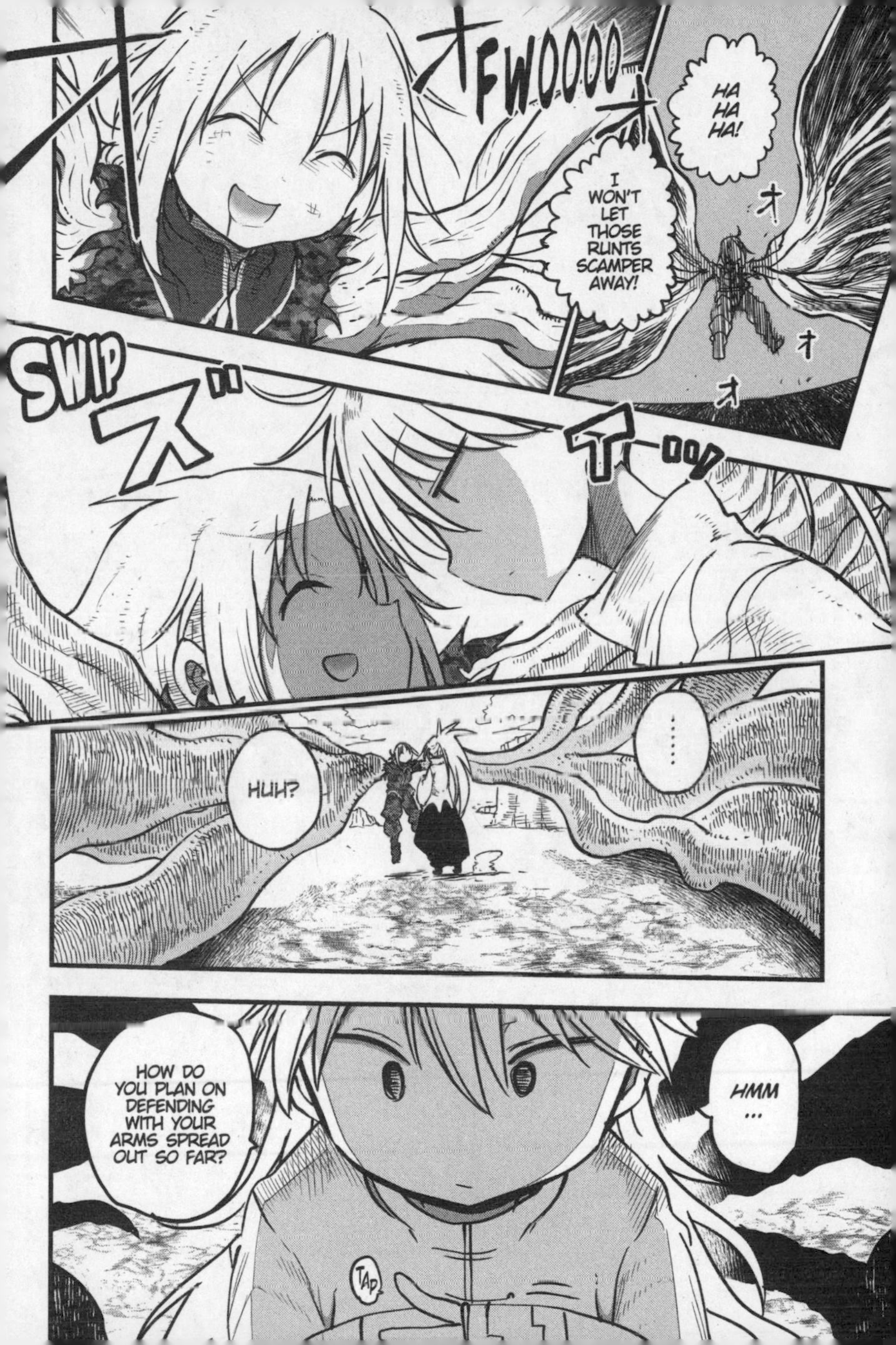
HA HA HA!
I WON'T LET THOSE RUNTS SCAMPER AWAY!
FWOOOO
SWIP
......
HUH?
HMM ...
HOW DO YOU PLAN ON DEFENDING WITH YOUR ARMS SPREAD OUT SO FAR?
TAP

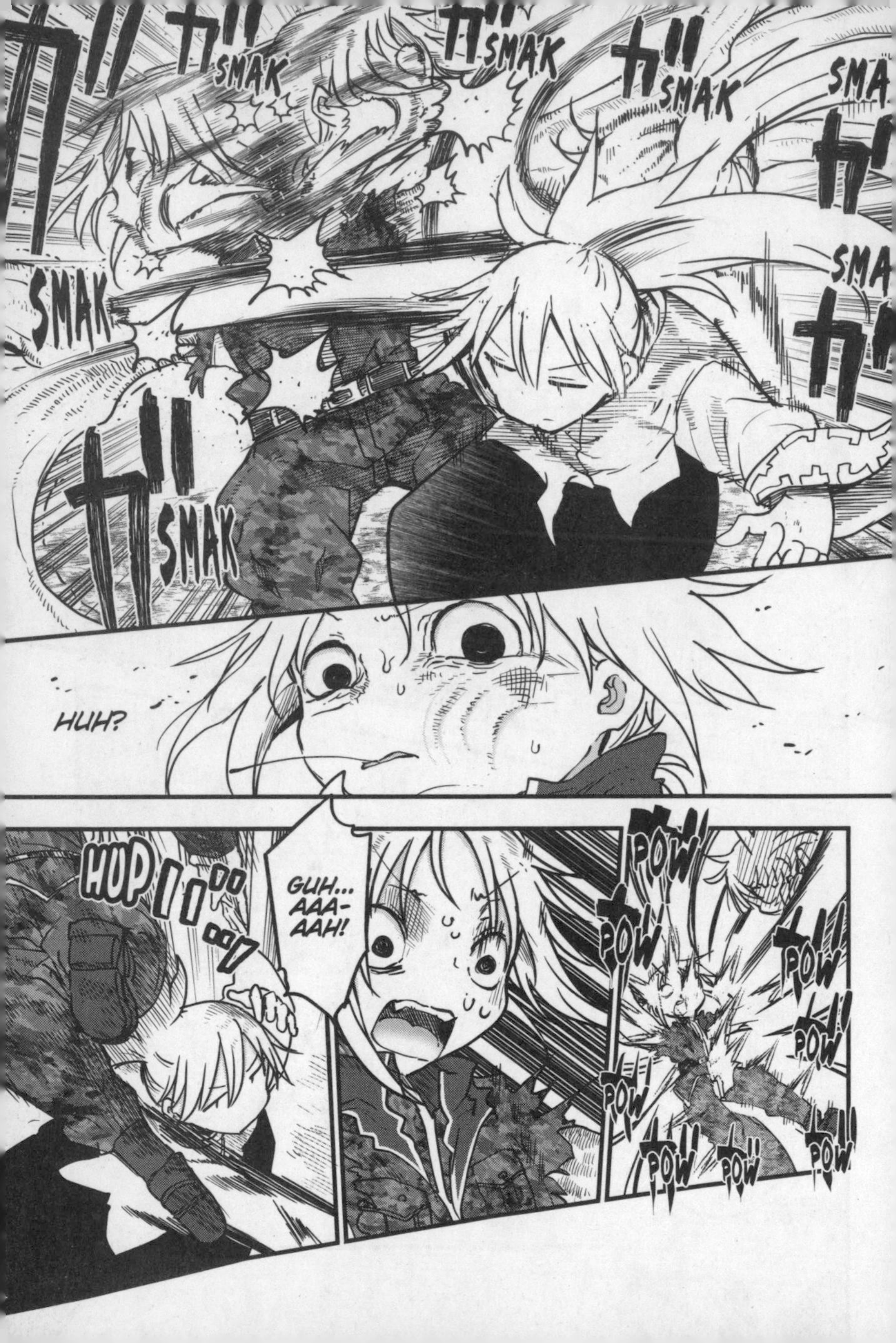
SMA
SMA
SMAK
SMAK
SMAK
SMAK
SMAK
HUH?
POW
POW
POW
POW
POW
POW
POW
POW
GUH... AAA-AAH!
HUP

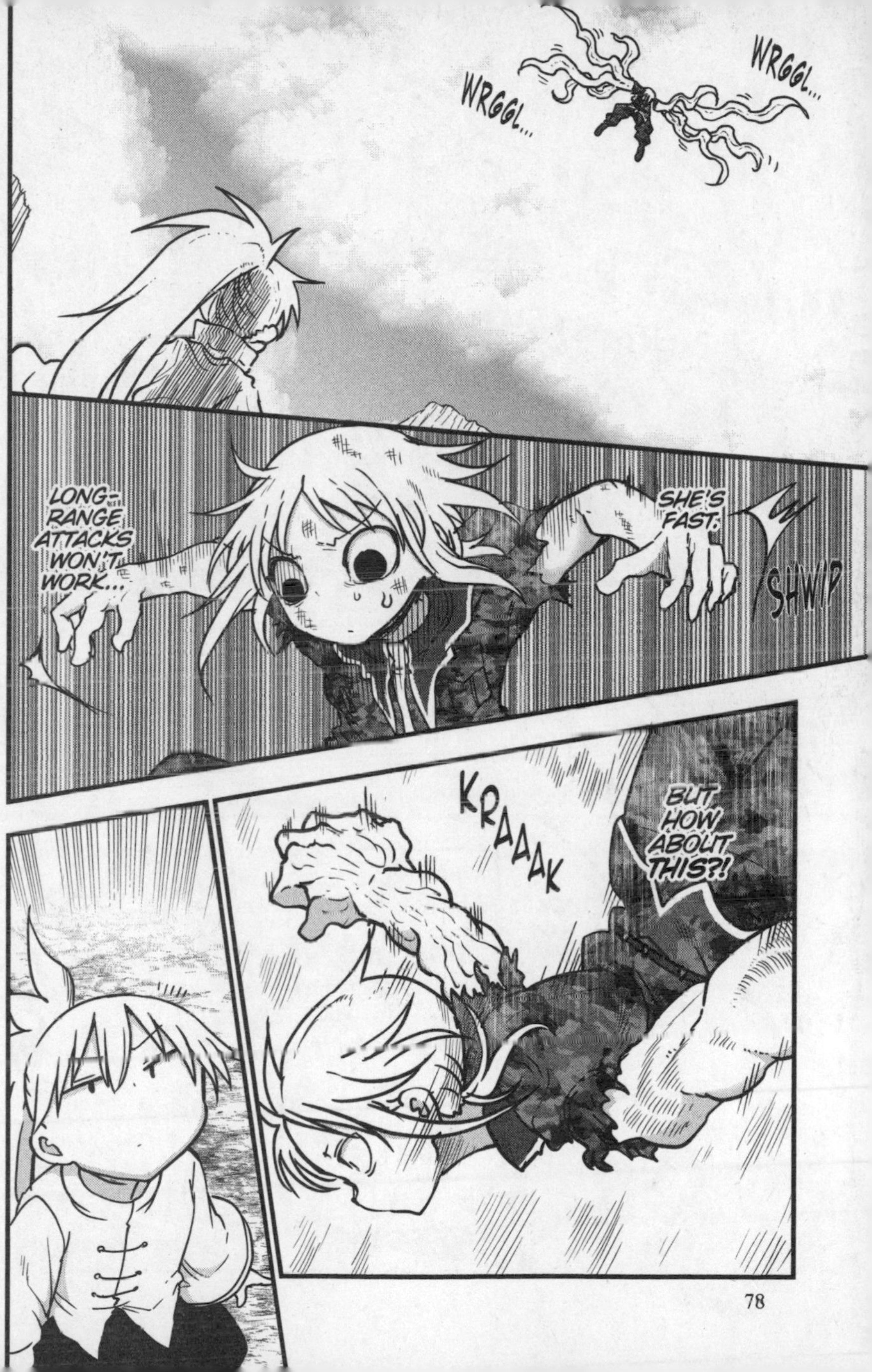
WRGGL...
WRGGL...
SHE'S FAST.
SHWIP
LONG-RANGE ATTACKS WON'T WORK...
BUT HOW ABOUT THIS?!
KRAAAK

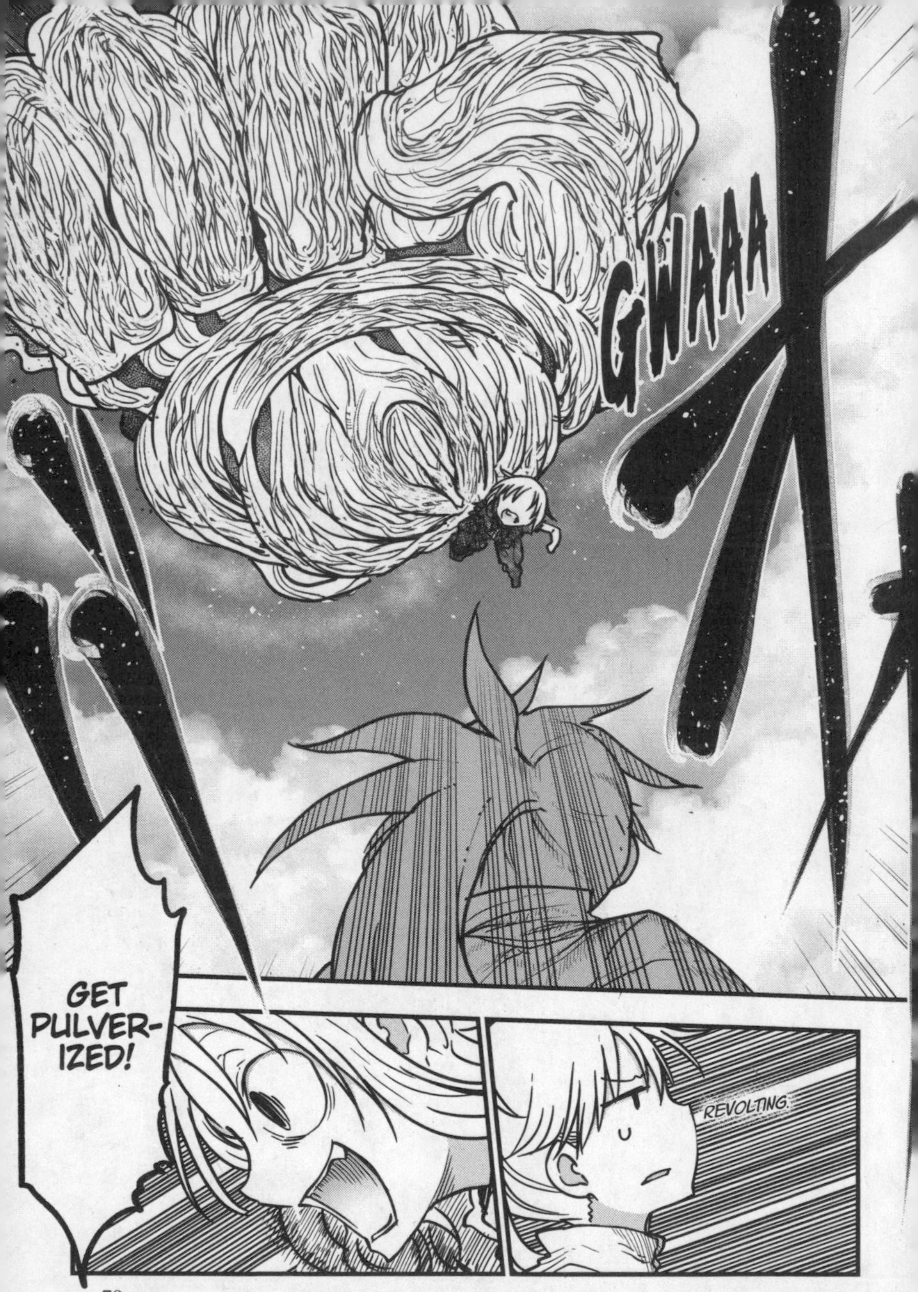
GWAAA
REVOLTING.
GET PULVER-IZED!

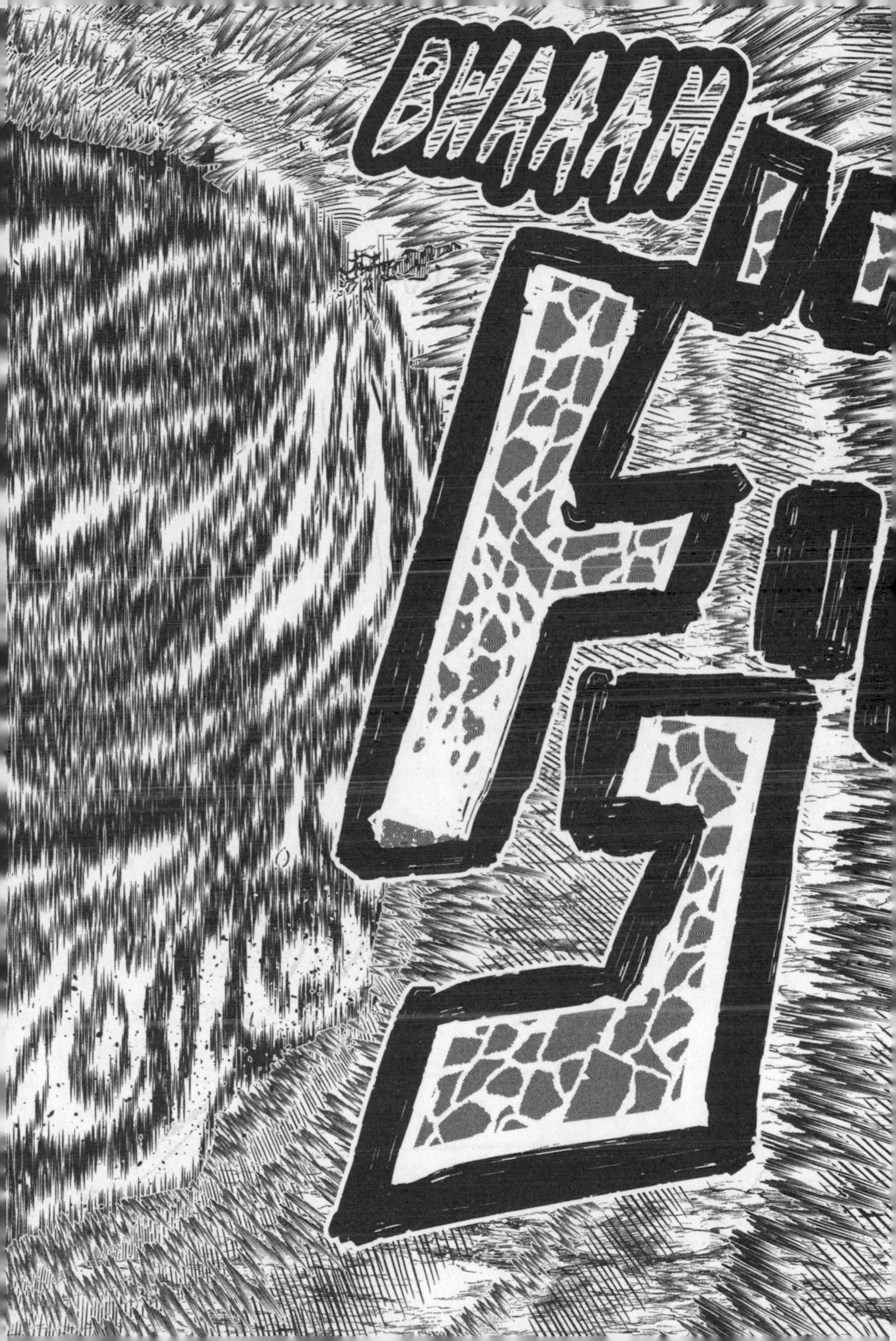
BWAAAM

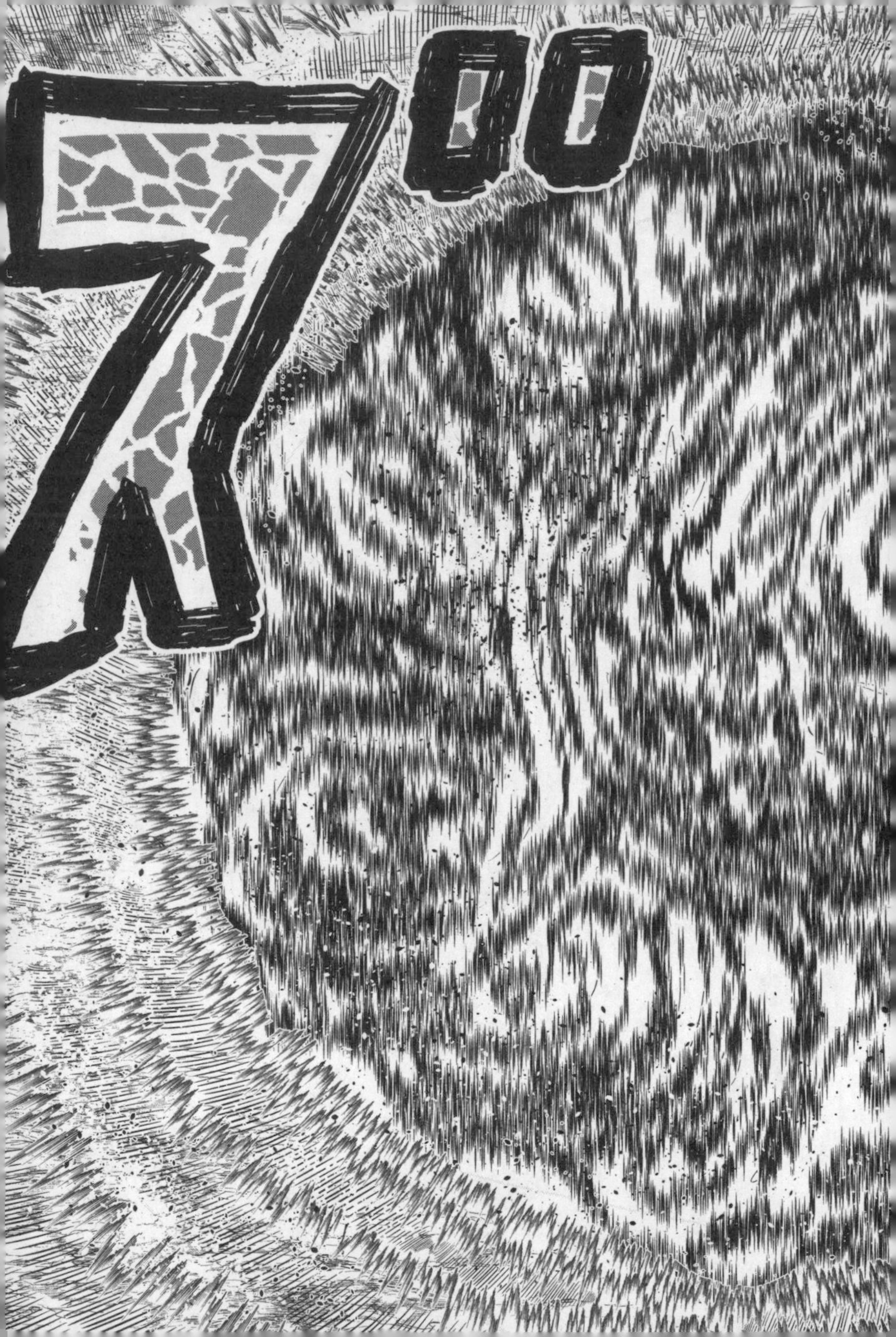
ズ

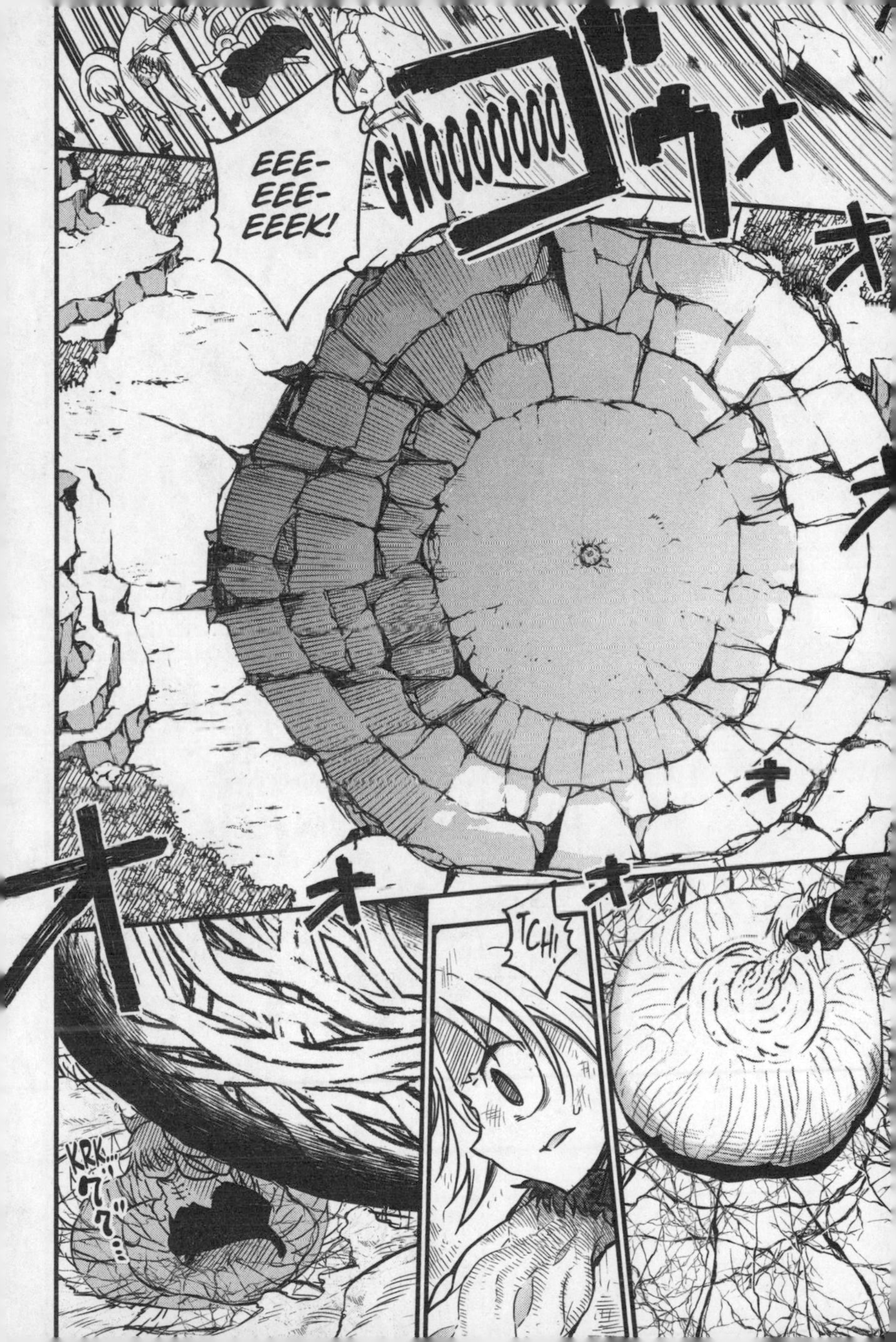
GWOOOOOO
EEE-EEE-EEEK!
TCH!
KRK...

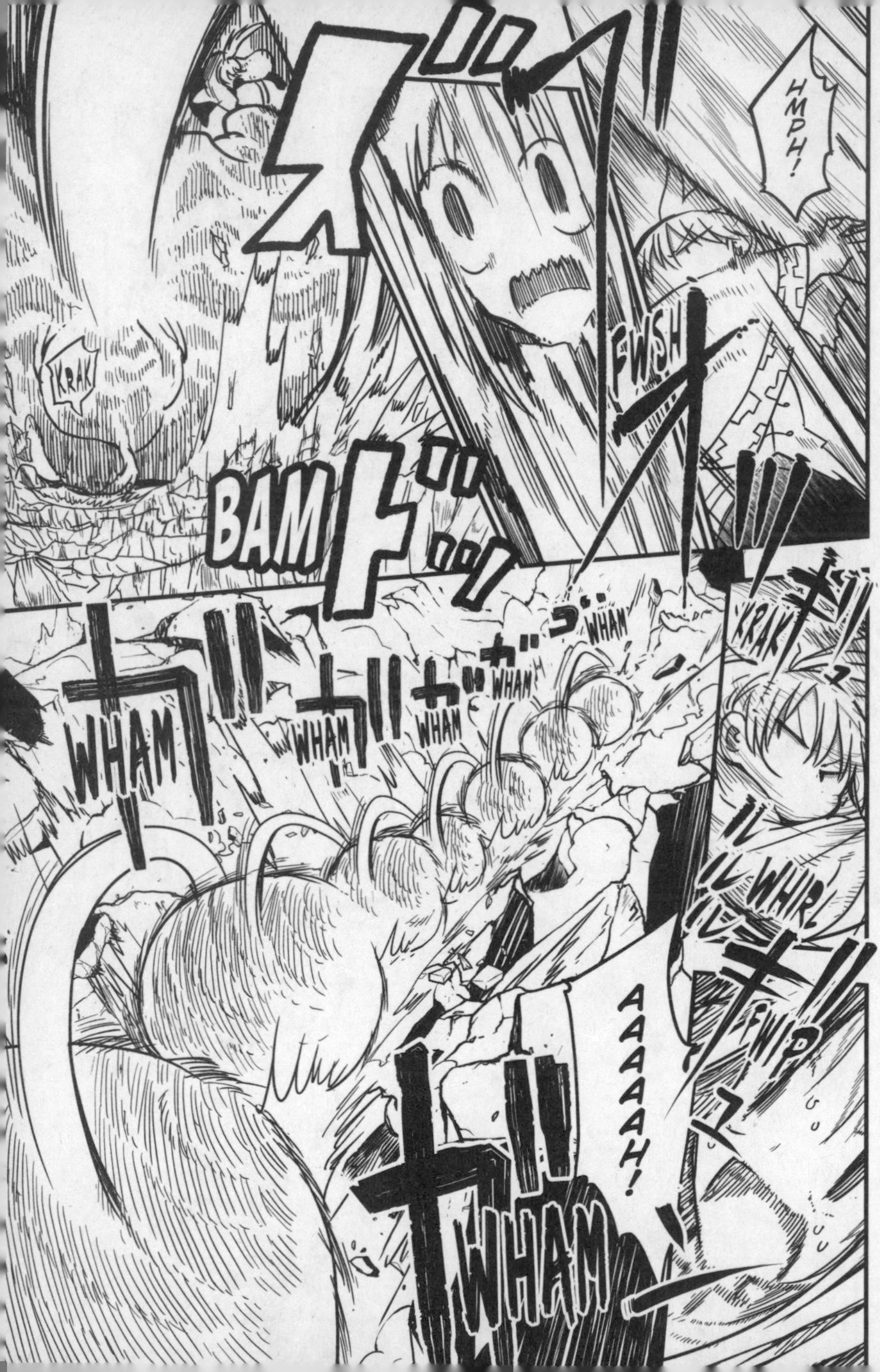
HMPH!
FWSH
BAM
KRAK
KRAK
WHRL
FWIP
WHAM
WHAM
WHAM
WHAM
WHAM
AAAAAAH!
WHAM

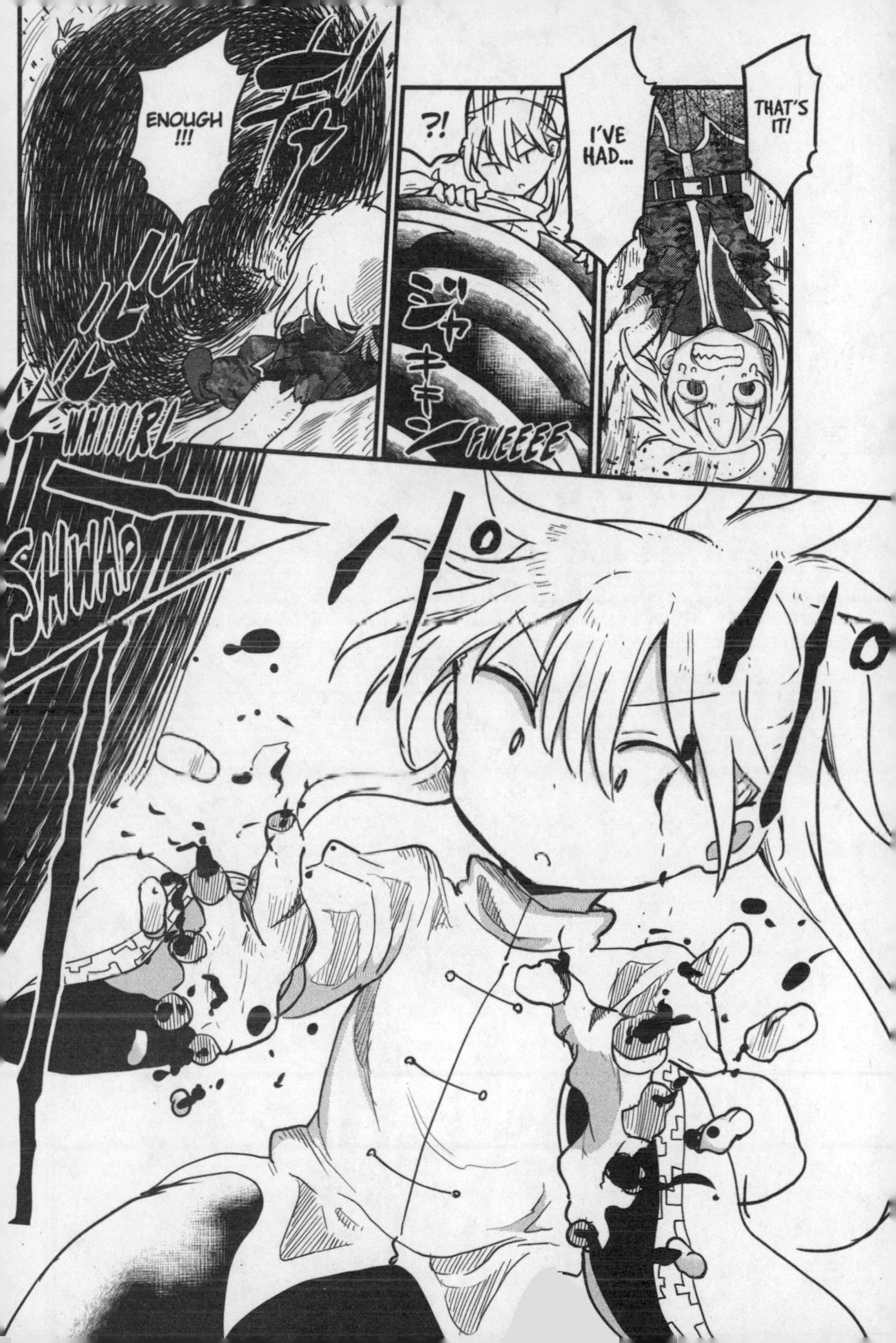
THAT'S IT!
I'VE HAD...
?!
ジャキキン
FWEEEE
ENOUGH !!!
WHIIIIRL
SHWAP

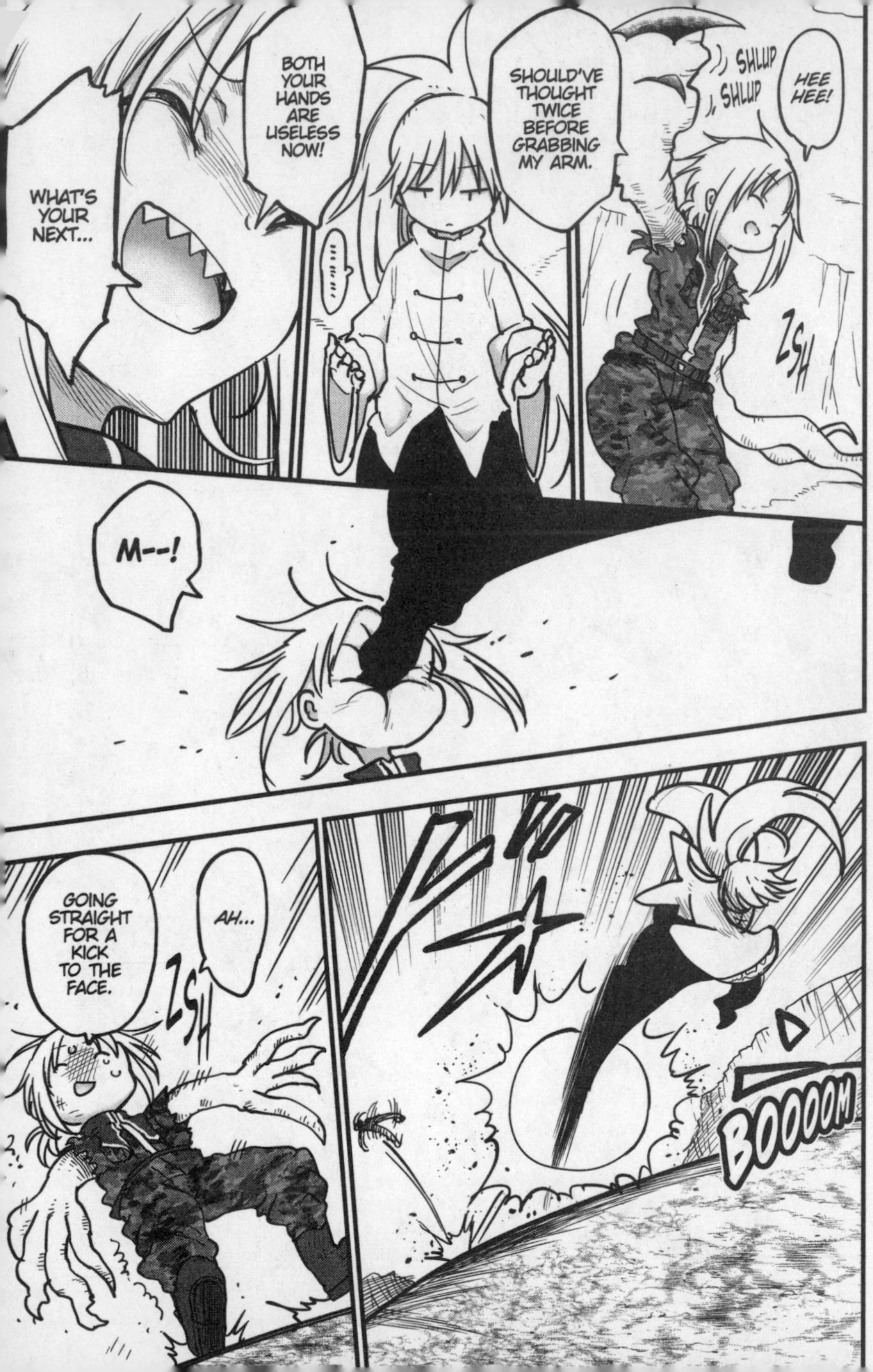

HEE HEE!
SHLUP SHLUP
ZSH
SHOULD'VE THOUGHT TWICE BEFORE GRABBING MY ARM.
BOTH YOUR HANDS ARE USELESS NOW!
...
WHAT'S YOUR NEXT...
M--!
BOOOOM
AH...
GOING STRAIGHT FOR A KICK TO THE FACE.
ZSH

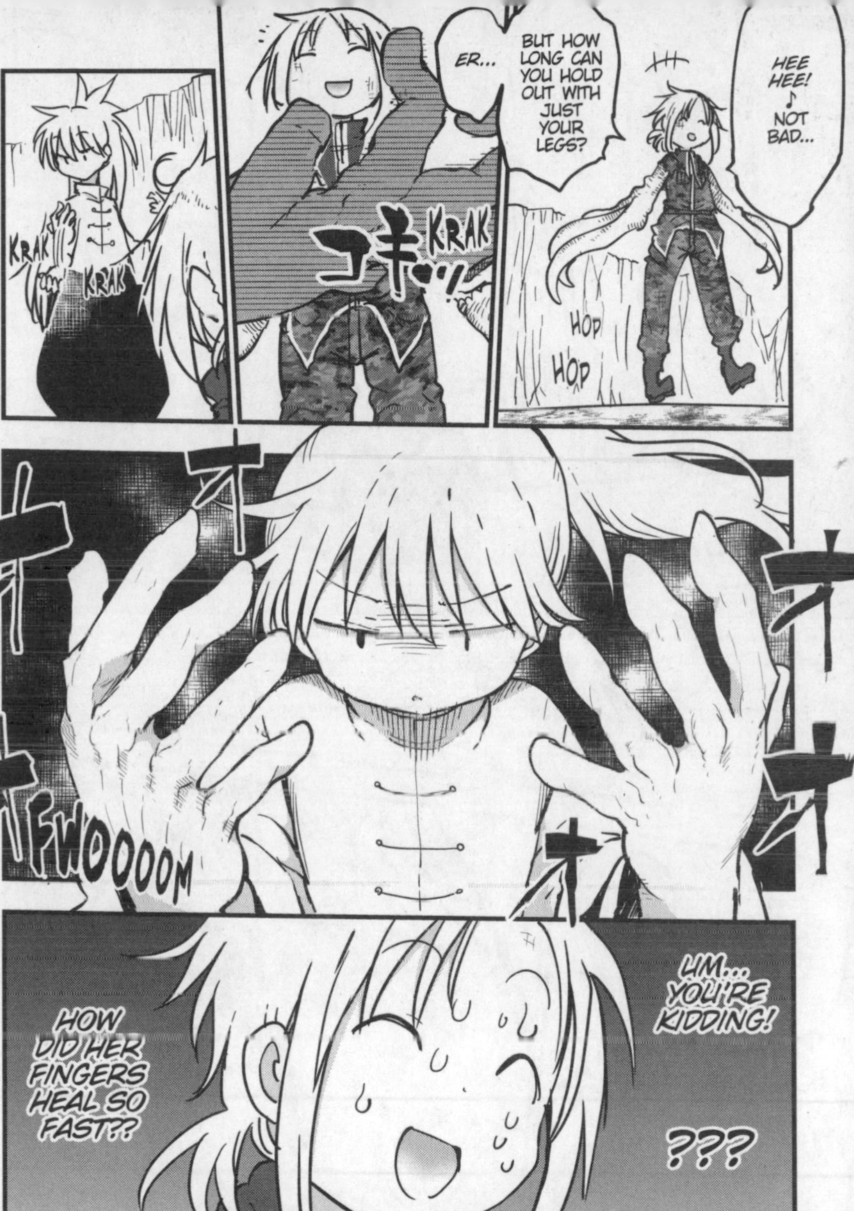
HEE HEE! ♪ NOT BAD...
HOP
HOP
ER...
BUT HOW LONG CAN YOU HOLD OUT WITH JUST YOUR LEGS?
KRAK
KRAK
KRAK
FWOOOOM
UM... YOU'RE KIDDING!
???
HOW DID HER FINGERS HEAL SO FAST??

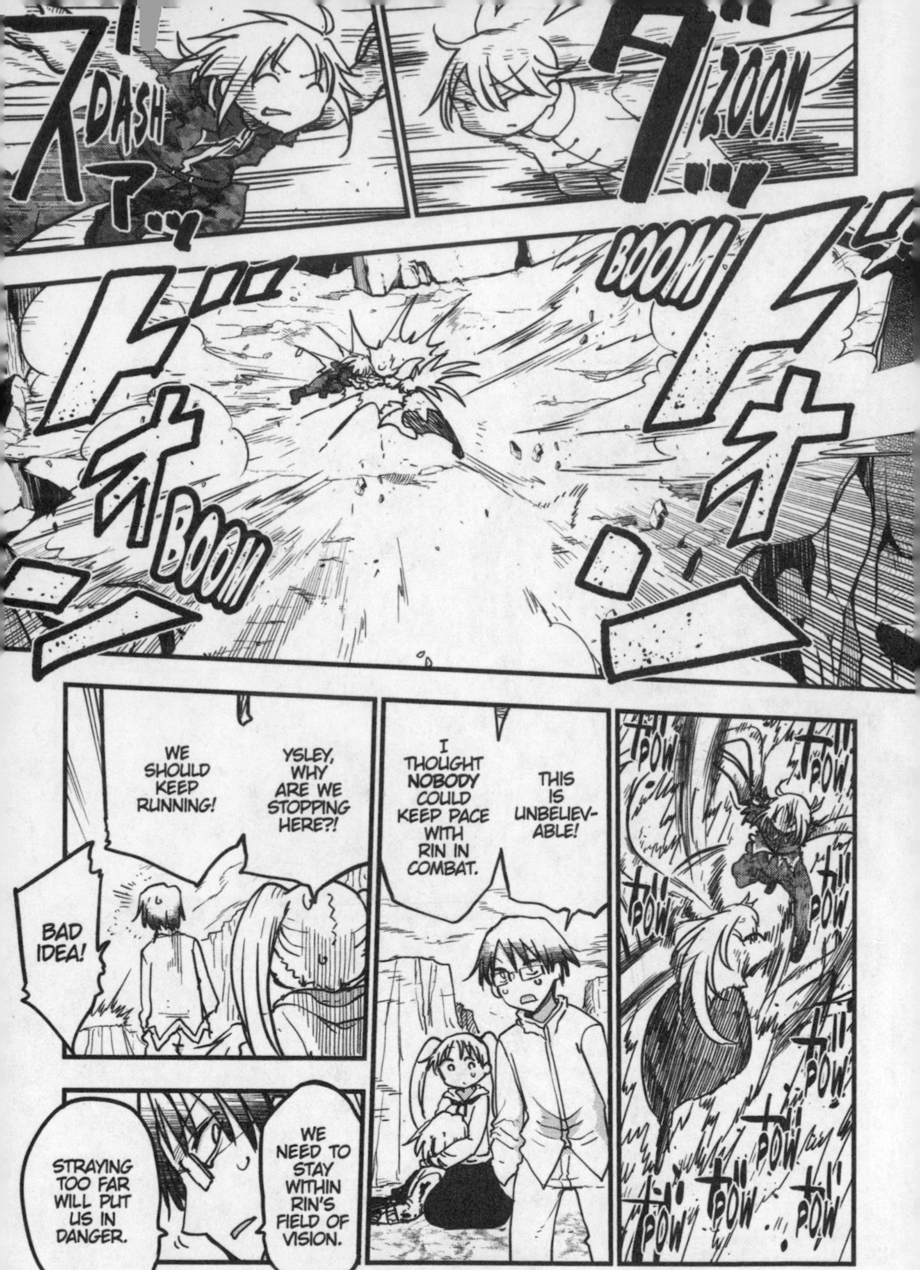
ZOOM
DASH
BOOM
BOOM
POW
POW
POW
POW
POW
POW
POW
POW
POW
THIS IS UNBELIEVABLE!
I THOUGHT NOBODY COULD KEEP PACE WITH RIN IN COMBAT.
YSLEY, WHY ARE WE STOPPING HERE?!
WE SHOULD KEEP RUNNING!
BAD IDEA!
WE NEED TO STAY WITHIN RIN'S FIELD OF VISION.
STRAYING TOO FAR WILL PUT US IN DANGER.

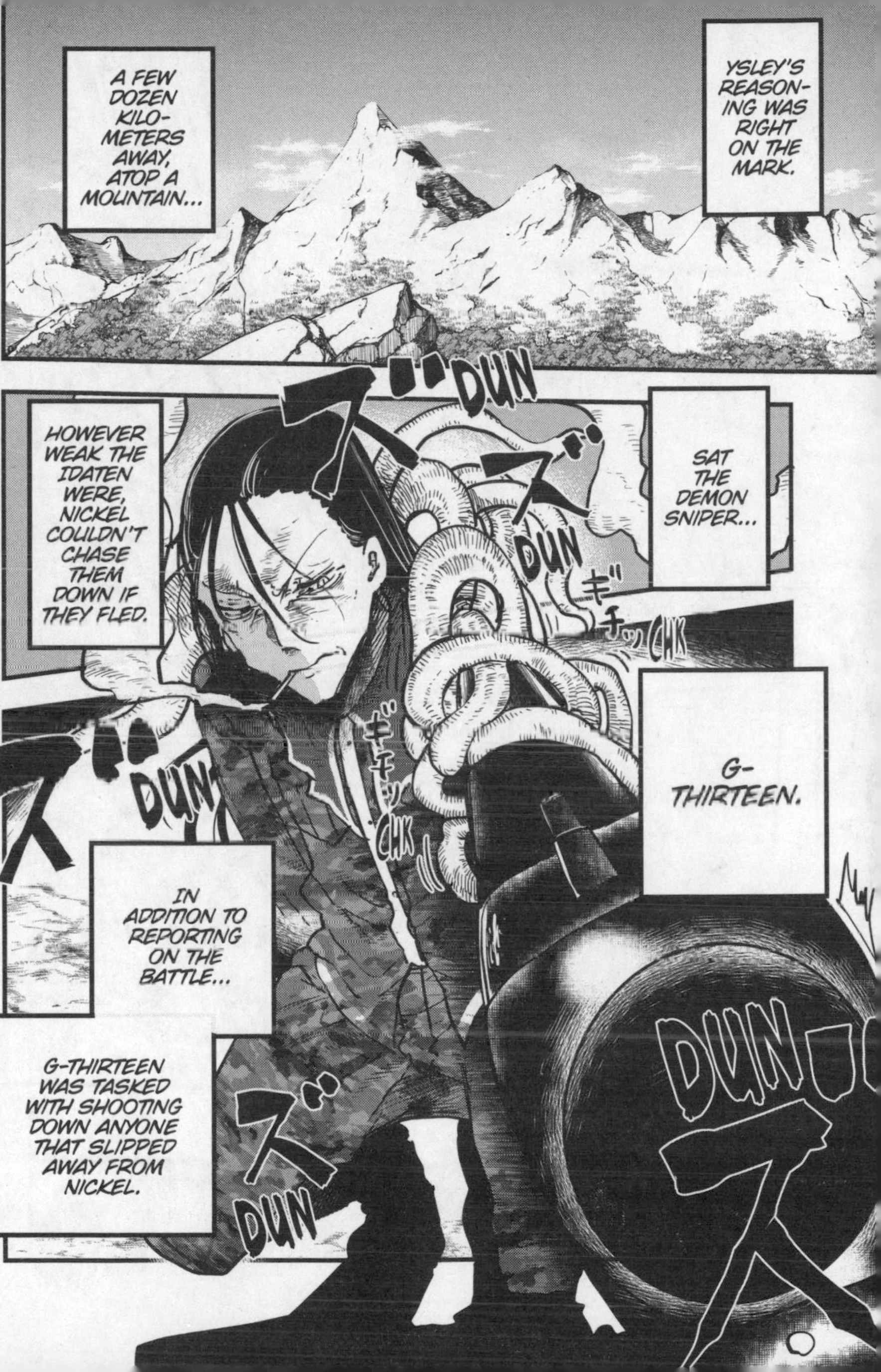

YSLEY'S REASONING WAS RIGHT ON THE MARK.
A FEW DOZEN KILOMETERS AWAY, ATOP A MOUNTAIN...
ズ DUN
SAT THE DEMON SNIPER...
ズ DUN
ギチッ CHK
HOWEVER WEAK THE IDATEN WERE, NICKEL COULDN'T CHASE THEM DOWN IF THEY FLED.
G-THIRTEEN.
ギチッ CHK
ズ DUN
IN ADDITION TO REPORTING ON THE BATTLE...
ズ DUN
G-THIRTEEN WAS TASKED WITH SHOOTING DOWN ANYONE THAT SLIPPED AWAY FROM NICKEL.
ズ DUN

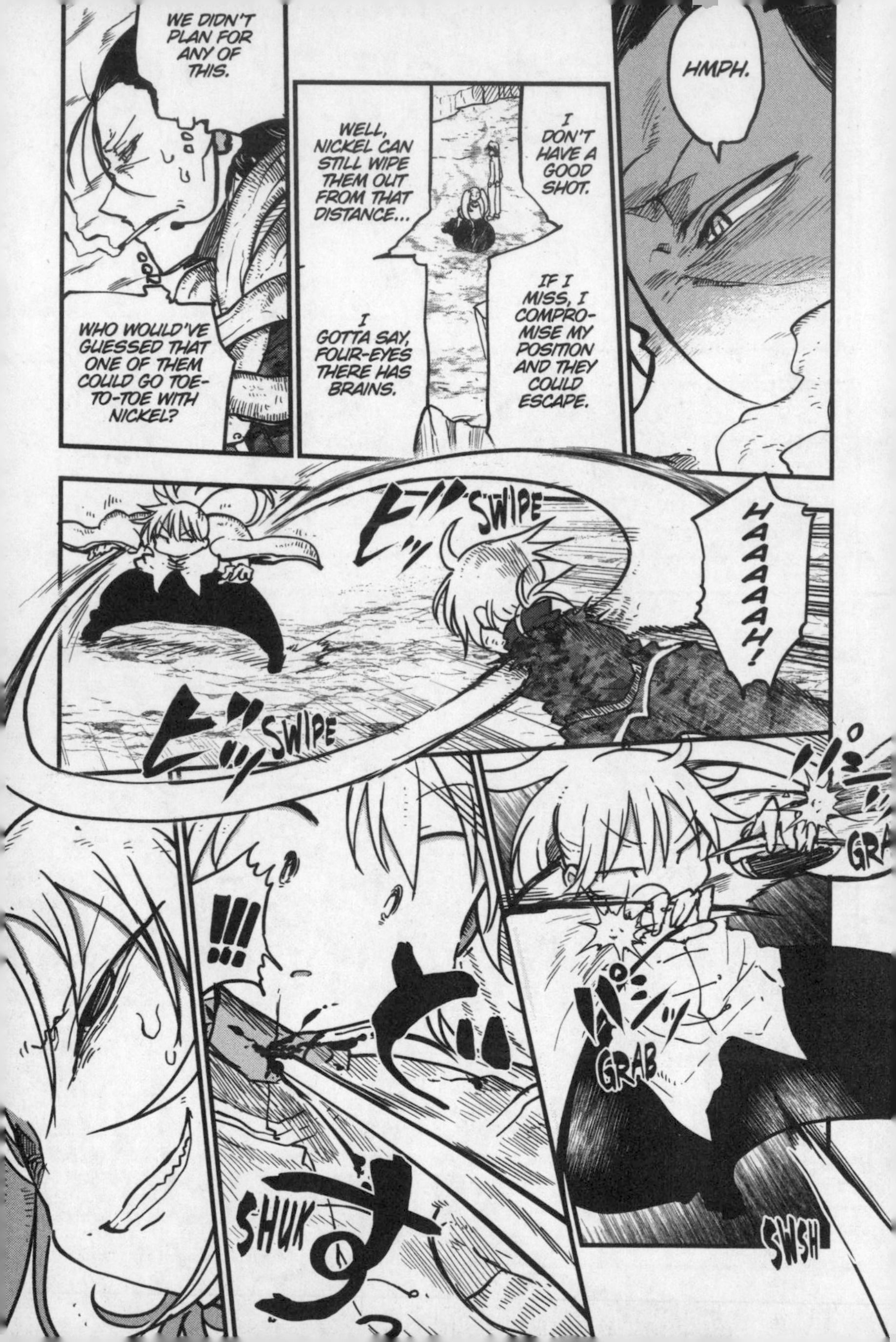
HMPH.
I DON'T HAVE A GOOD SHOT.
IF I MISS, I COMPROMISE MY POSITION AND THEY COULD ESCAPE.
WELL, NICKEL CAN STILL WIPE THEM OUT FROM THAT DISTANCE...
I GOTTA SAY, FOUR-EYES THERE HAS BRAINS.
WE DIDN'T PLAN FOR ANY OF THIS.
WHO WOULD'VE GUESSED THAT ONE OF THEM COULD GO TOE-TO-TOE WITH NICKEL?
HAAAAAAH!
SWIPE
SWIPE
GRAB
GRAB
SWSH
!!!
SHUK

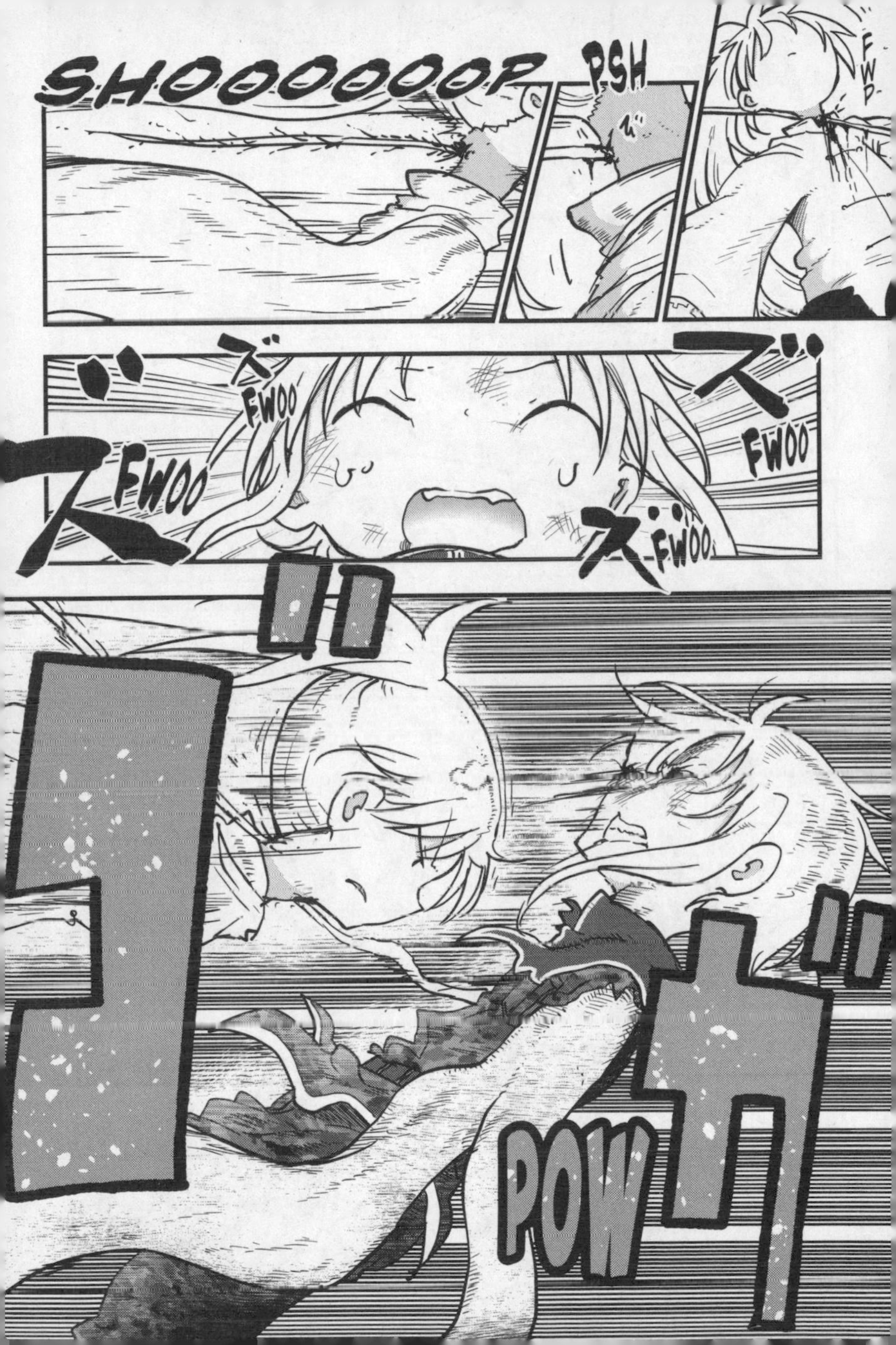
FWP
PSH
SHOOOOOOP
FWOO
FWOO
FWOO
FWOO
POW

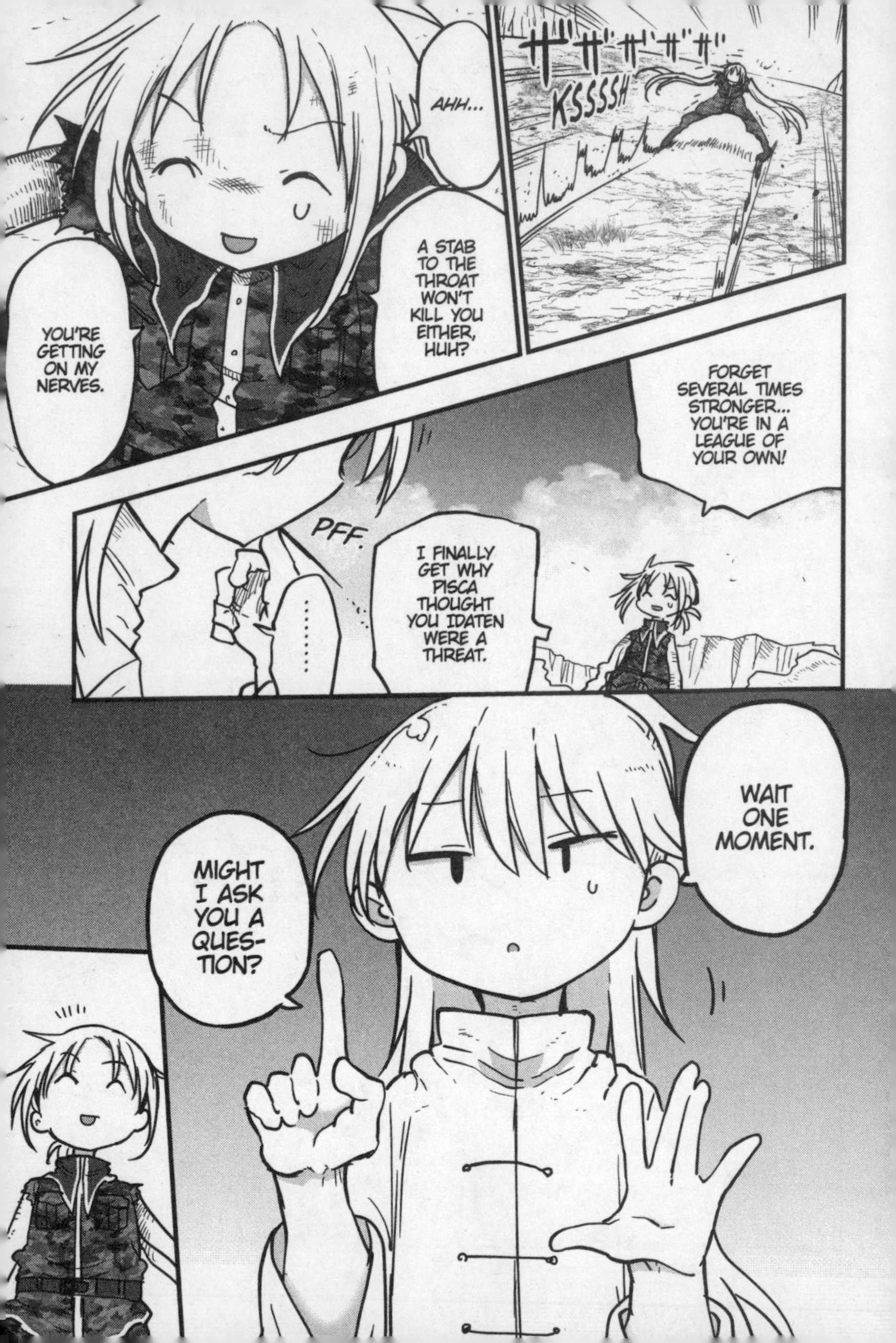
KSSSSH
AHH...
A STAB TO THE THROAT WON'T KILL YOU EITHER, HUH?
YOU'RE GETTING ON MY NERVES.
FORGET SEVERAL TIMES STRONGER... YOU'RE IN A LEAGUE OF YOUR OWN!
I FINALLY GET WHY PISCA THOUGHT YOU IDATEN WERE A THREAT.
PFF.
WAIT ONE MOMENT.
MIGHT I ASK YOU A QUES-TION?

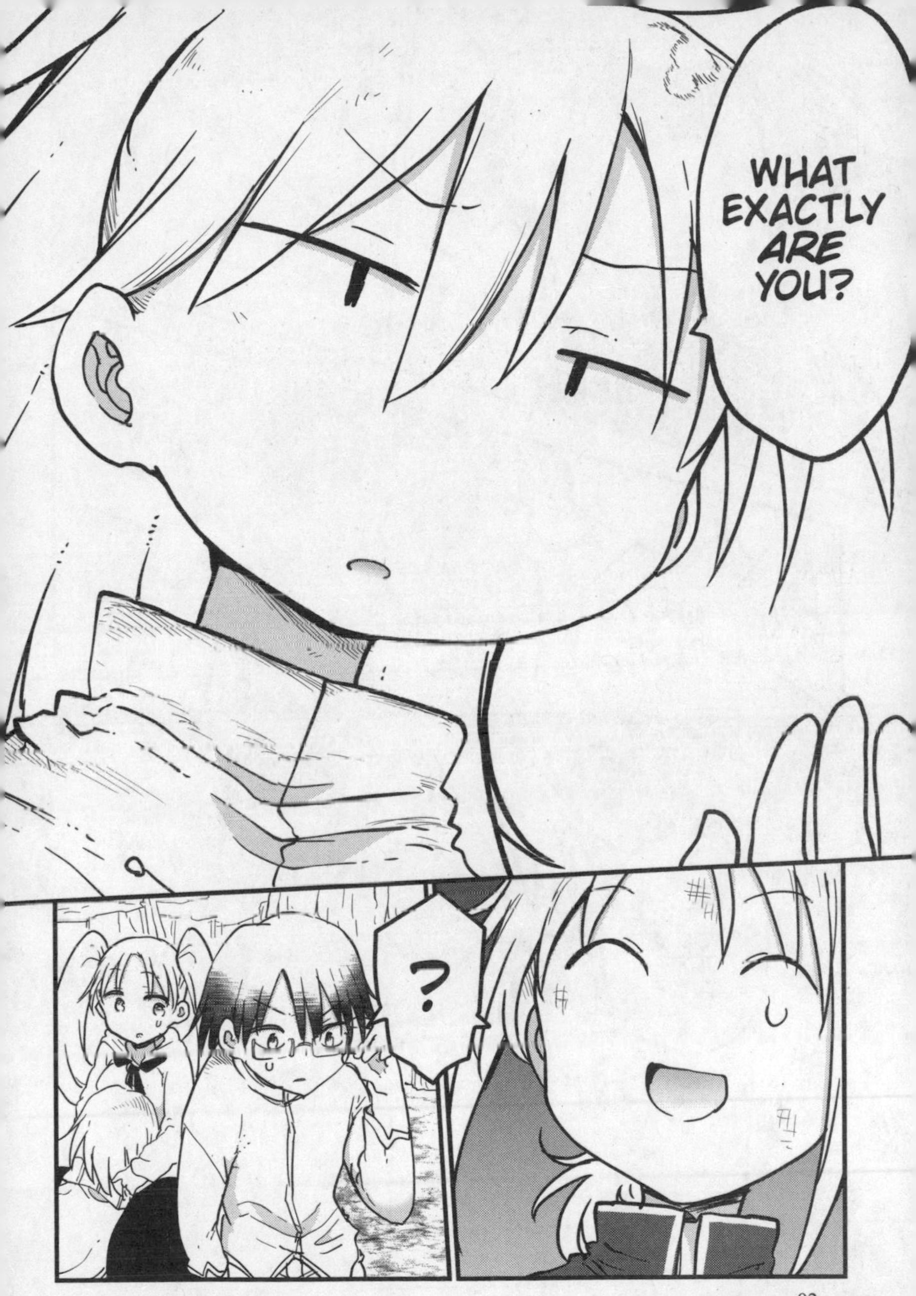
WHAT EXACTLY ARE YOU?
?

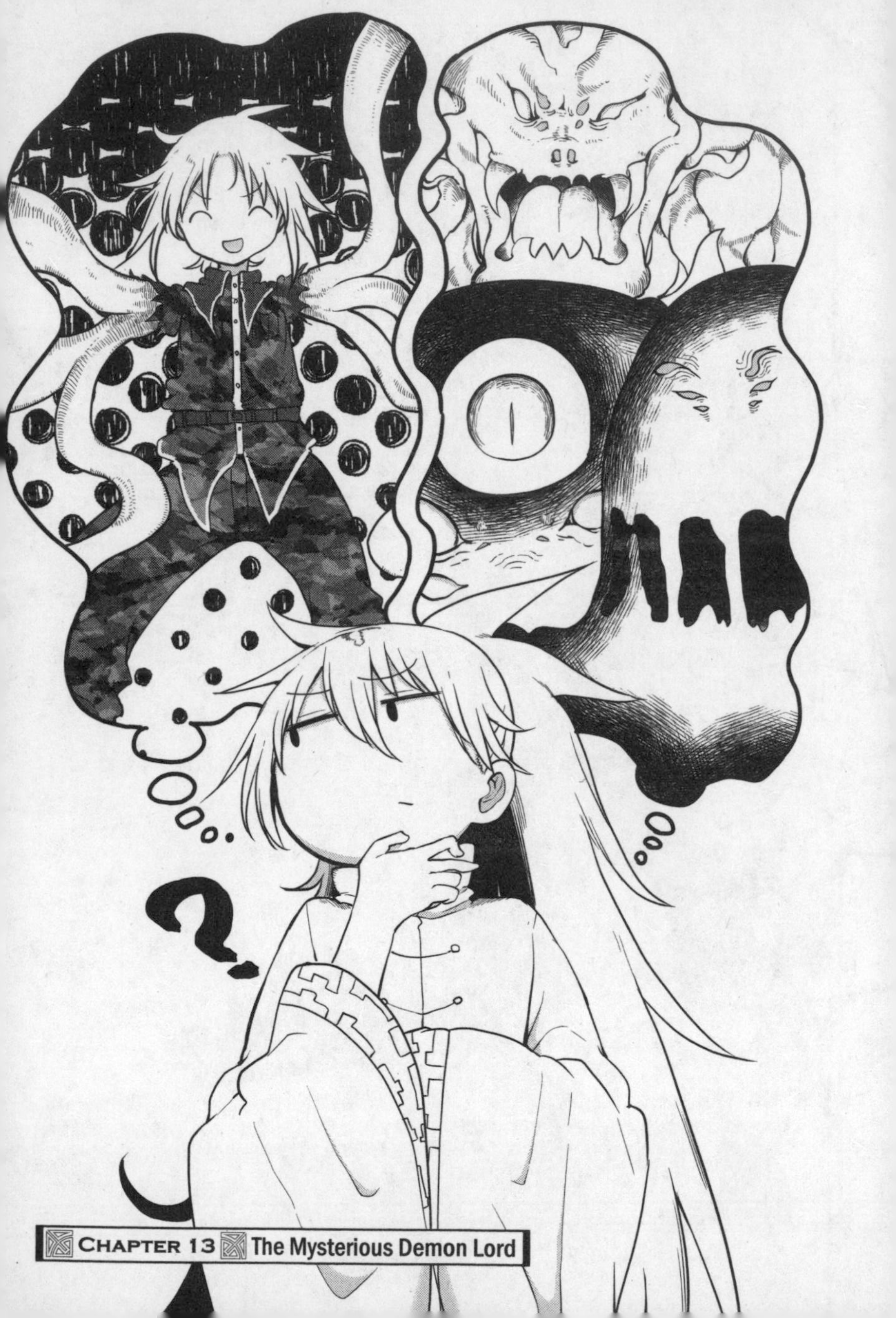
?

CHAPTER 13 The Mysterious Demon Lord

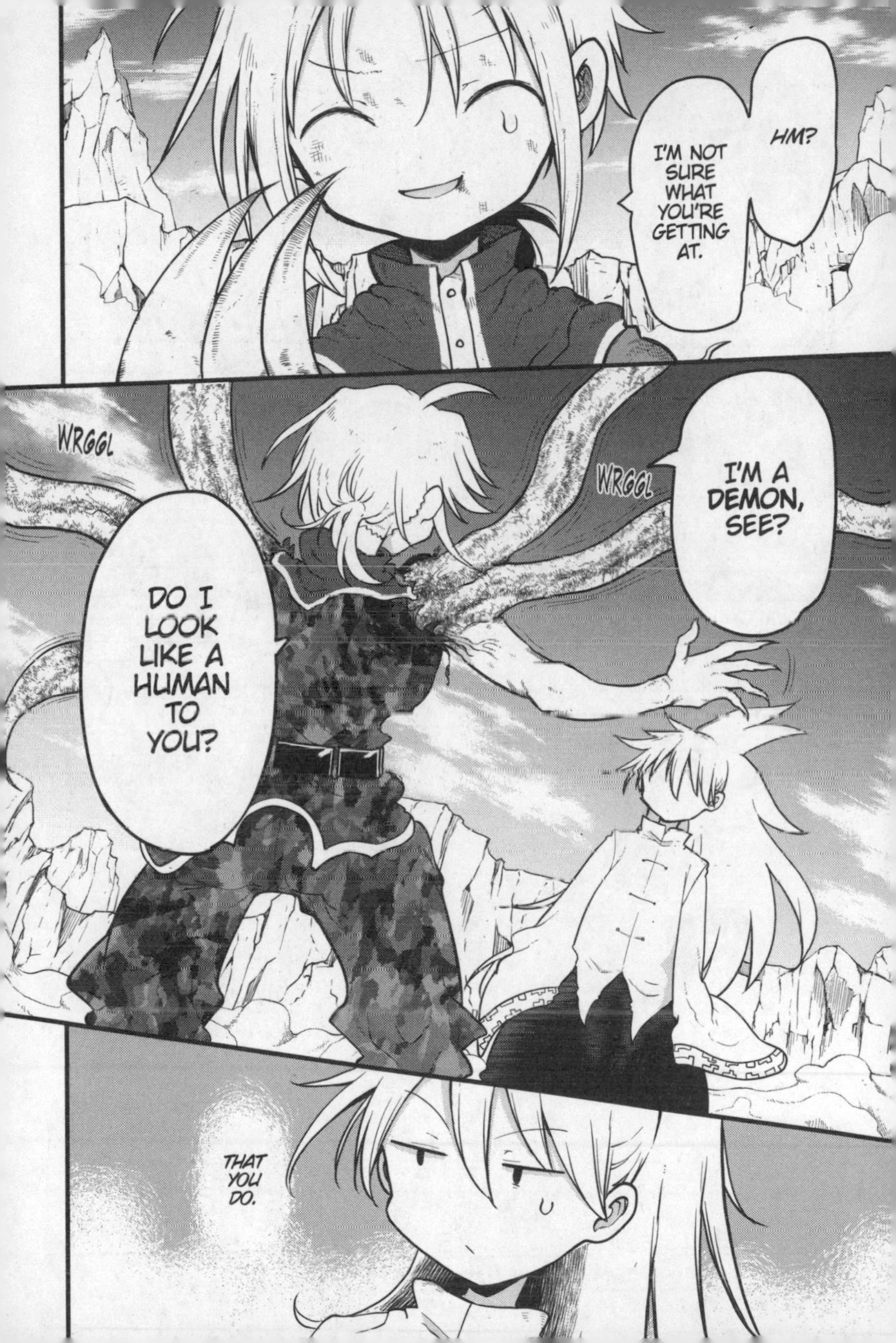
HM?
I'M NOT SURE WHAT YOU'RE GETTING AT.
I'M A DEMON, SEE?
WRGGL
WRGGL
DO I LOOK LIKE A HUMAN TO YOU?
THAT YOU DO.

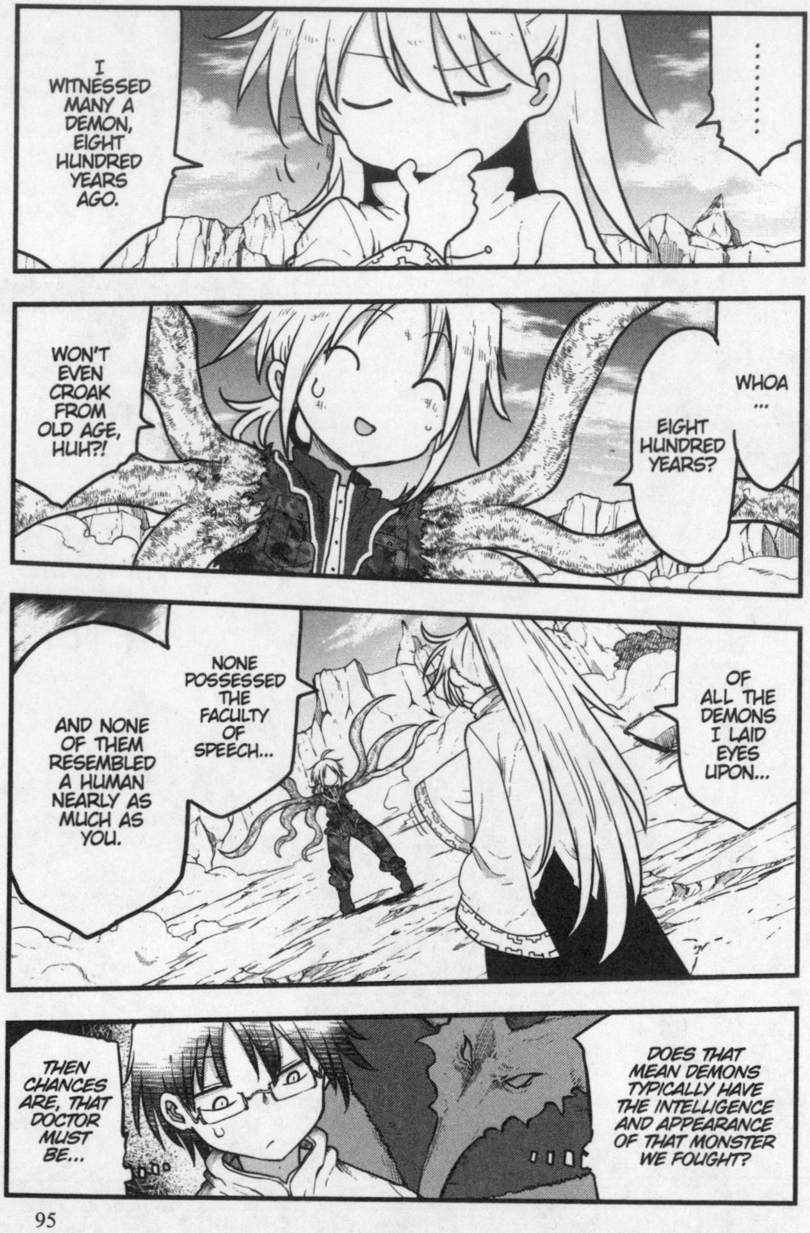
......
I WITNESSED MANY A DEMON, EIGHT HUNDRED YEARS AGO.
WHOA ...
EIGHT HUNDRED YEARS?
WON'T EVEN CROAK FROM OLD AGE, HUH?!
OF ALL THE DEMONS I LAID EYES UPON...
NONE POSSESSED THE FACULTY OF SPEECH...
AND NONE OF THEM RESEMBLED A HUMAN NEARLY AS MUCH AS YOU.
DOES THAT MEAN DEMONS TYPICALLY HAVE THE INTELLIGENCE AND APPEARANCE OF THAT MONSTER WE FOUGHT?
THEN CHANCES ARE, THAT DOCTOR MUST BE...

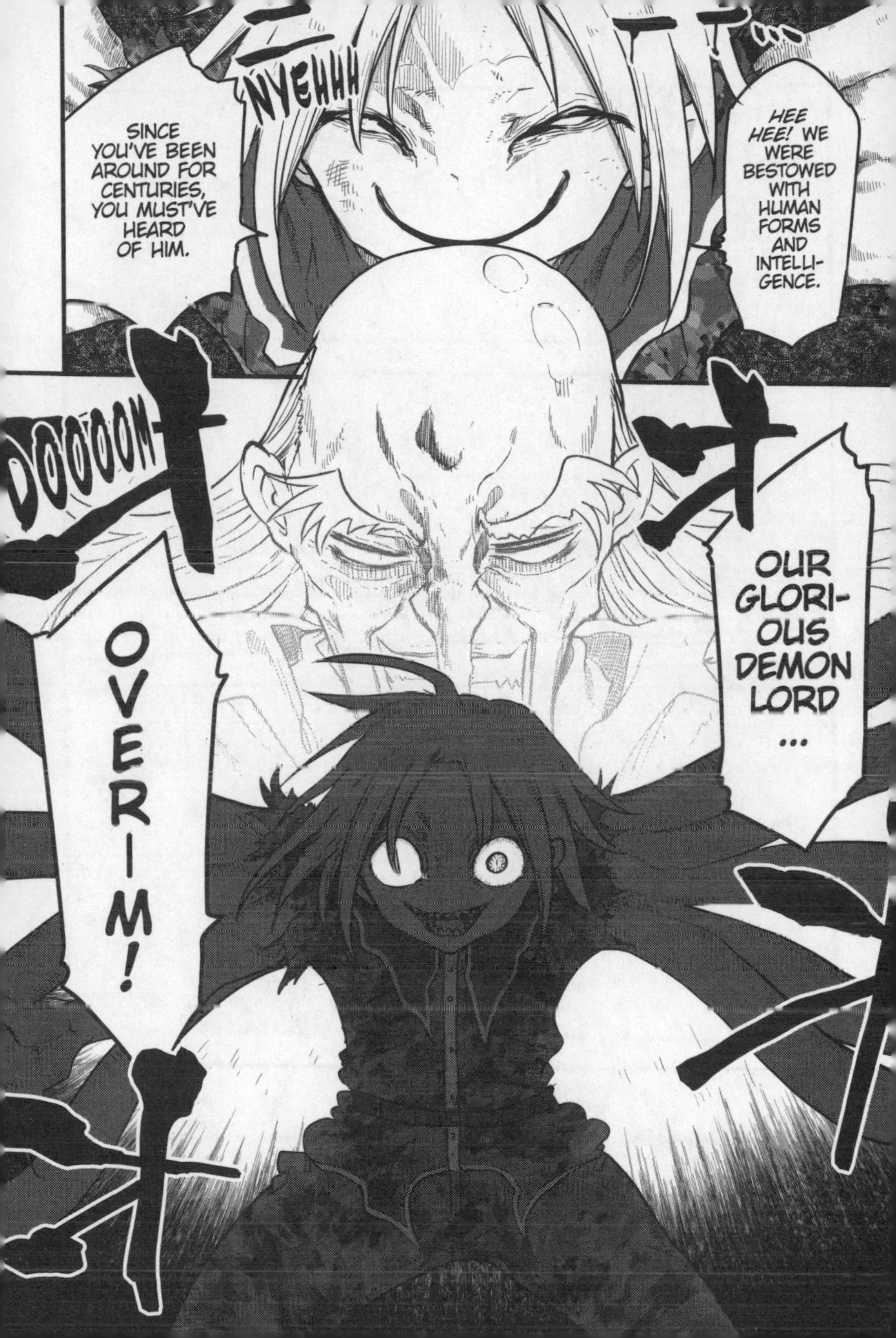
HEE HEE! WE WERE BESTOWED WITH HUMAN FORMS AND INTELLI-GENCE.
NYEHHH
SINCE YOU'VE BEEN AROUND FOR CENTURIES, YOU MUST'VE HEARD OF HIM.
OUR GLORI-OUS DEMON LORD...
DOOOOM
OVER-I-M!

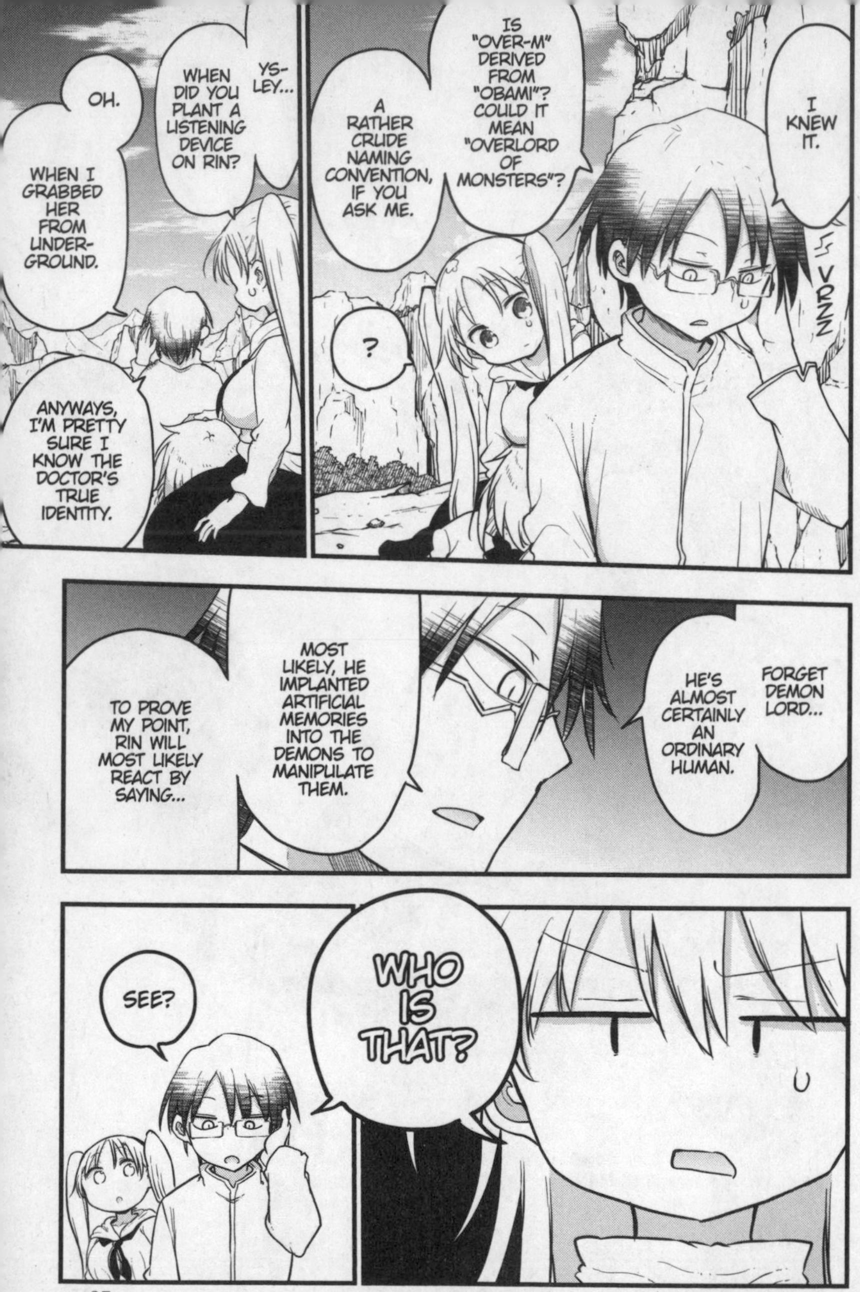
I KNEW IT.
VRZZ
IS "OVER-M" DERIVED FROM "OBAMI"? COULD IT MEAN "OVERLORD OF MONSTERS"?
A RATHER CRUDE NAMING CONVENTION, IF YOU ASK ME.
?
YS-LEY... WHEN DID YOU PLANT A LISTENING DEVICE ON RIN?
OH.
WHEN I GRABBED HER FROM UNDER-GROUND.
ANYWAYS, I'M PRETTY SURE I KNOW THE DOCTOR'S TRUE IDENTITY.
FORGET DEMON LORD...
HE'S ALMOST CERTAINLY AN ORDINARY HUMAN.
MOST LIKELY, HE IMPLANTED ARTIFICIAL MEMORIES INTO THE DEMONS TO MANIPULATE THEM.
TO PROVE MY POINT, RIN WILL MOST LIKELY REACT BY SAYING...
WHO IS THAT?
SEE?

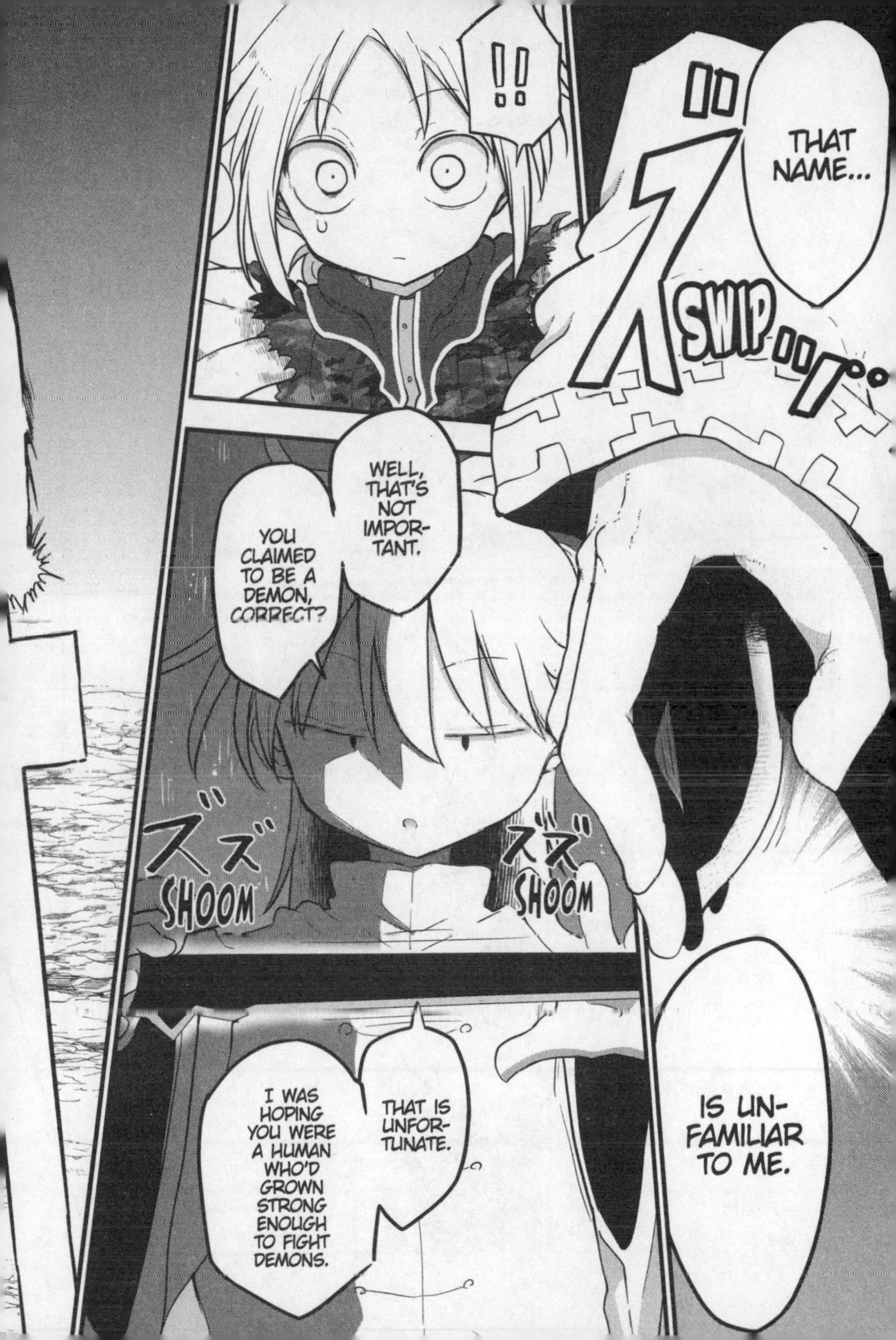

THAT NAME...
SWIP
IS UN-FAMILIAR TO ME.
!!
WELL, THAT'S NOT IMPOR-TANT.
YOU CLAIMED TO BE A DEMON, CORRECT?
ズズ SHOOM
ズズ SHOOM
THAT IS UNFOR-TUNATE.
I WAS HOPING YOU WERE A HUMAN WHO'D GROWN STRONG ENOUGH TO FIGHT DEMONS.

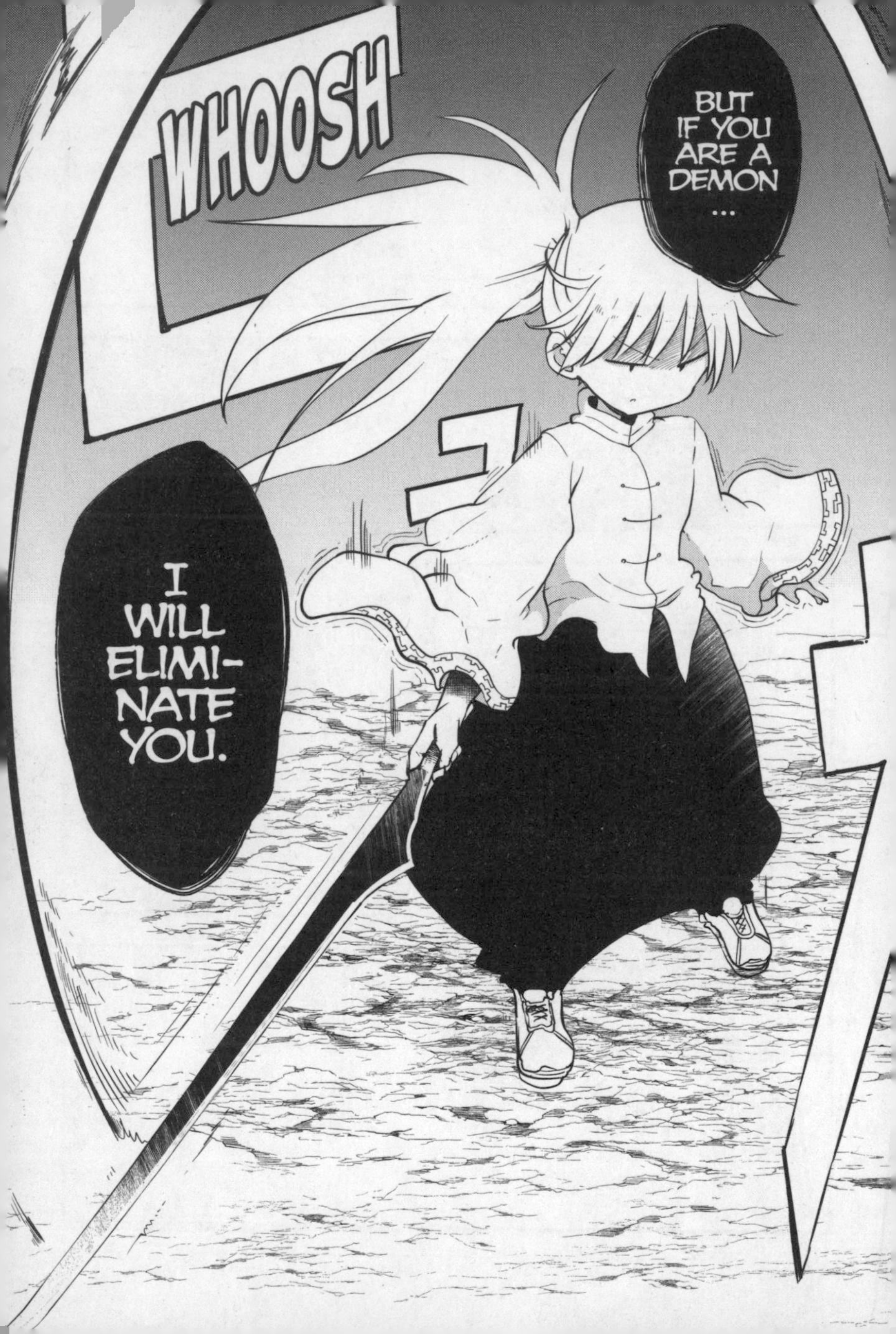
BUT IF YOU ARE A DEMON ...
WHOOSH
I WILL ELIMI-NATE YOU.

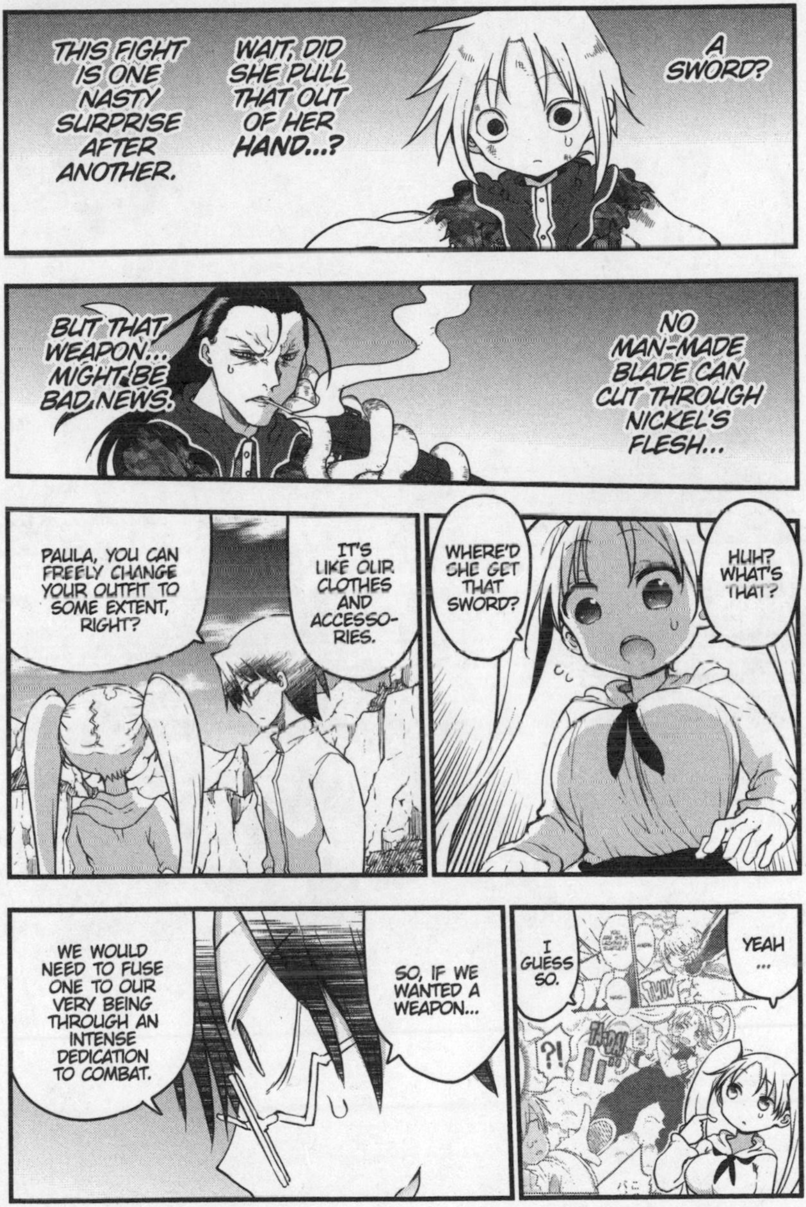
A SWORD?
WAIT, DID SHE PULL THAT OUT OF HER HAND...?
THIS FIGHT IS ONE NASTY SURPRISE AFTER ANOTHER.
NO MAN-MADE BLADE CAN CUT THROUGH NICKEL'S FLESH...
BUT THAT WEAPON... MIGHT BE BAD NEWS.
HUH? WHAT'S THAT?
WHERE'D SHE GET THAT SWORD?
IT'S LIKE OUR CLOTHES AND ACCESSORIES.
PAULA, YOU CAN FREELY CHANGE YOUR OUTFIT TO SOME EXTENT, RIGHT?
YEAH ...
I GUESS SO.
?!
SO, IF WE WANTED A WEAPON...
WE WOULD NEED TO FUSE ONE TO OUR VERY BEING THROUGH AN INTENSE DEDICATION TO COMBAT.

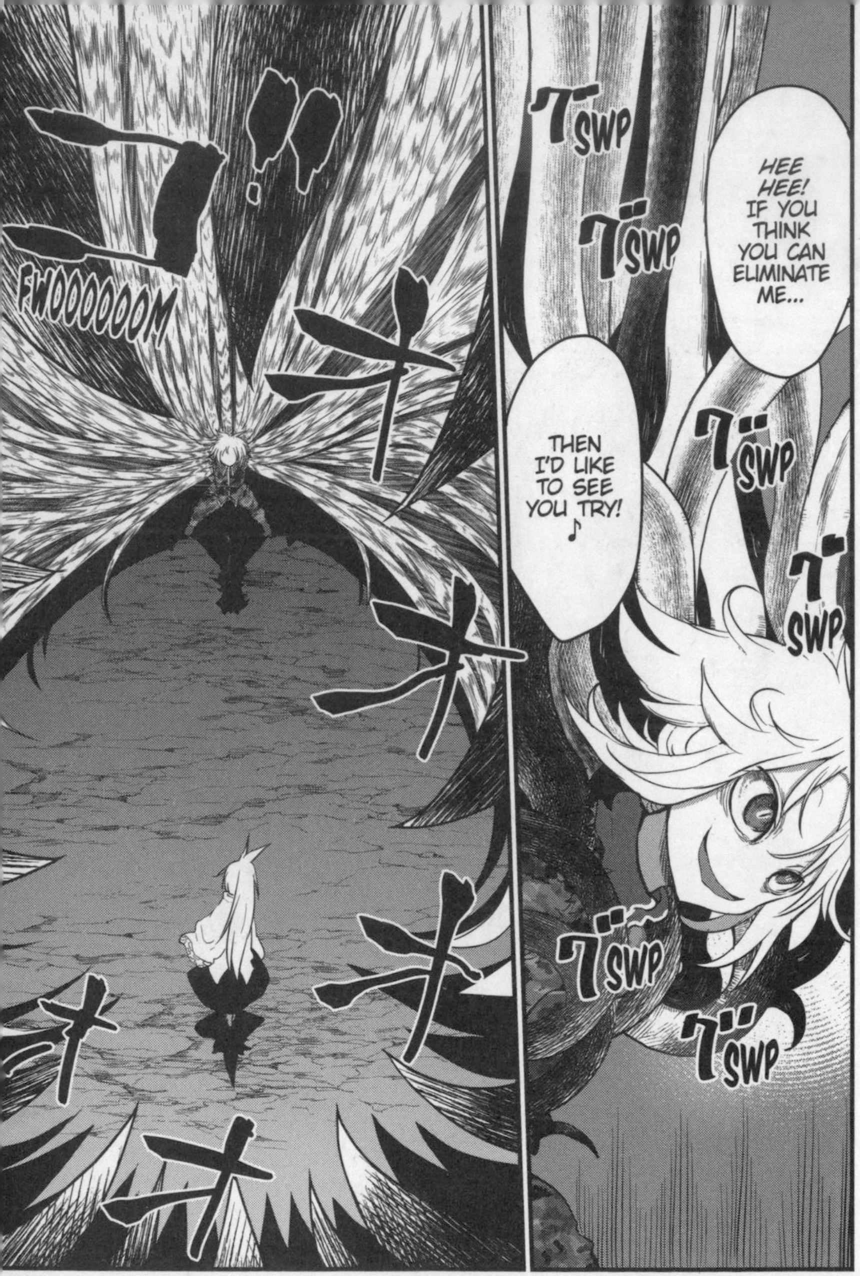
SWP
SWP
HEE HEE! IF YOU THINK YOU CAN ELIMINATE ME...
SWP
THEN I'D LIKE TO SEE YOU TRY! ♪
SWP
SWP
SWP
FWOOOOOOM

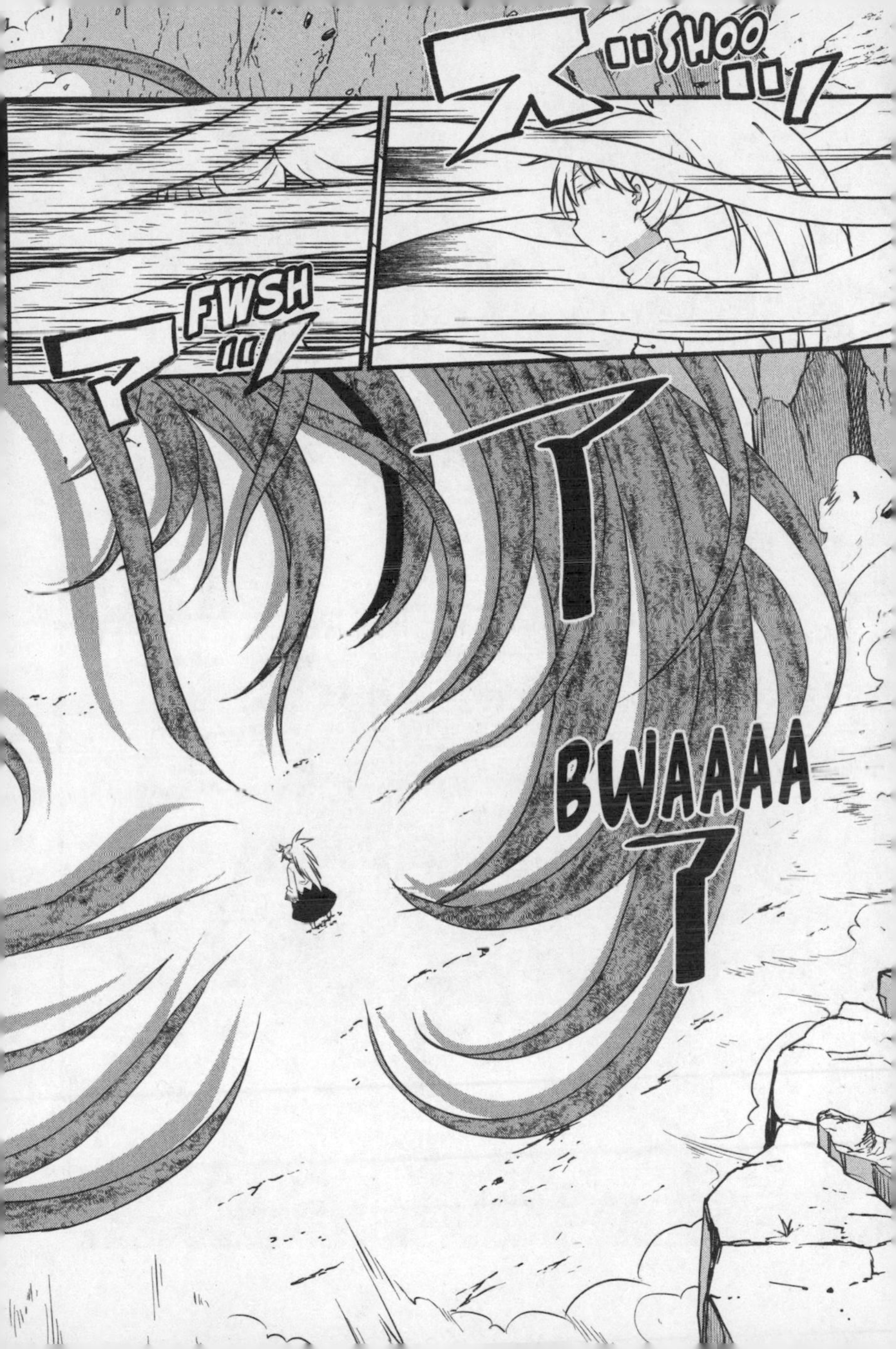
..SHOO..!
FWSH..!
BWAAAA

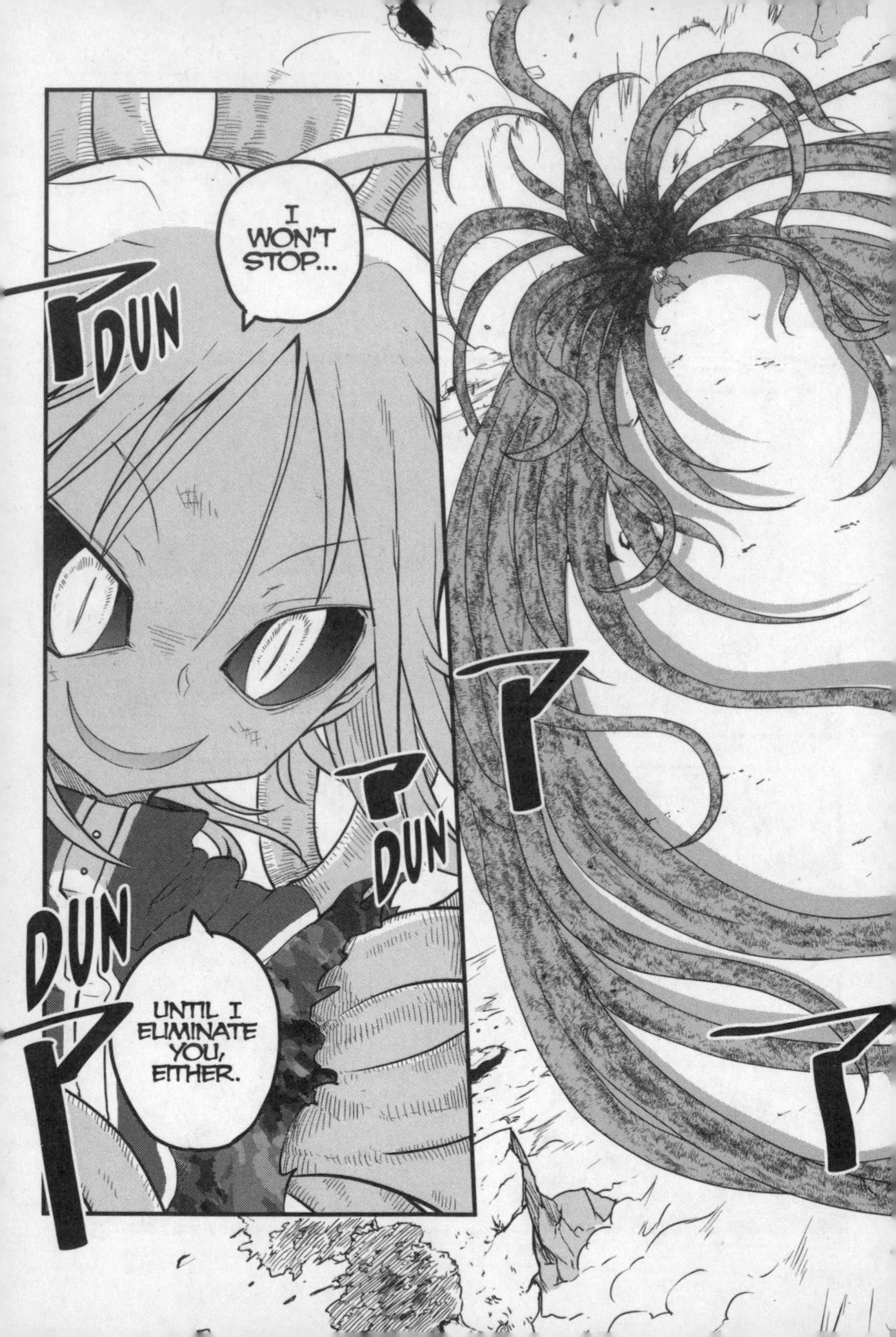
I WON'T STOP...
DUN
DUN
DUN
UNTIL I ELIMINATE YOU, EITHER.

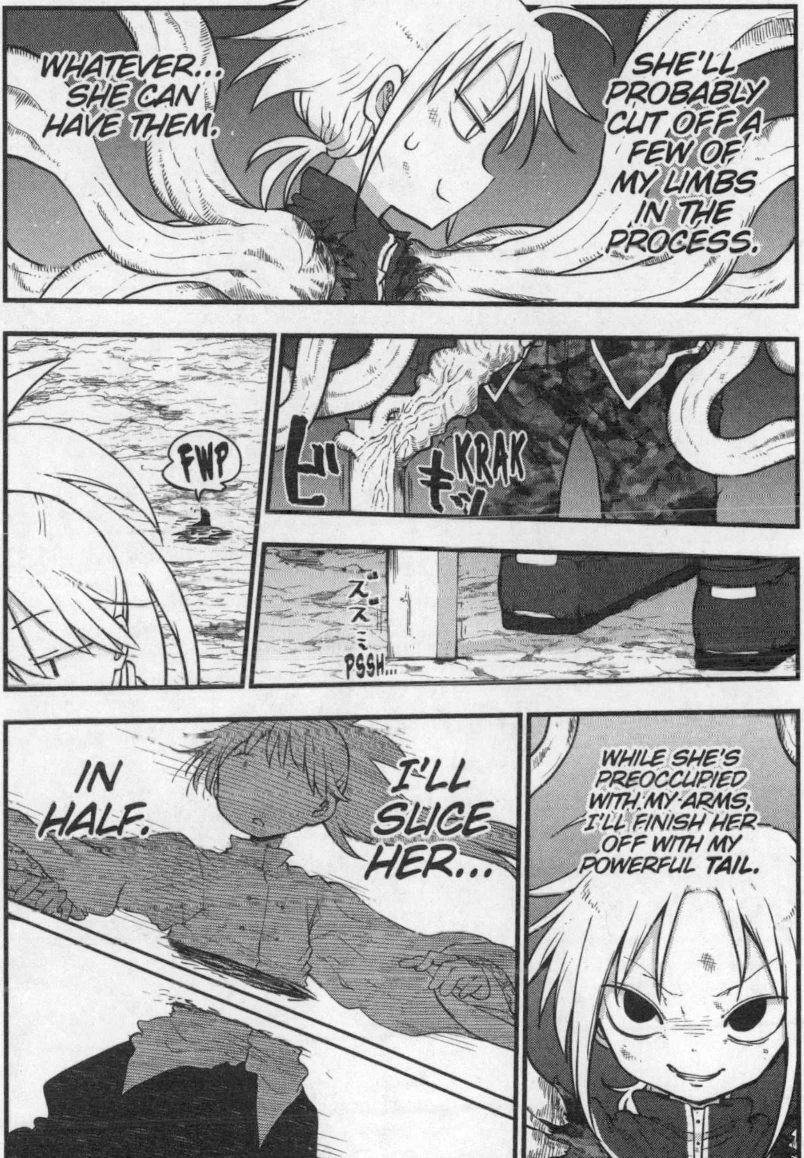
SHE'LL PROBABLY CUT OFF A FEW OF MY LIMBS IN THE PROCESS.
WHATEVER... SHE CAN HAVE THEM.
ビキッ
KRAK
ズズ
PSSH...
FWP
WHILE SHE'S PREOCCUPIED WITH MY ARMS, I'LL FINISH HER OFF WITH MY POWERFUL TAIL.
I'LL SLICE HER...
IN HALF.

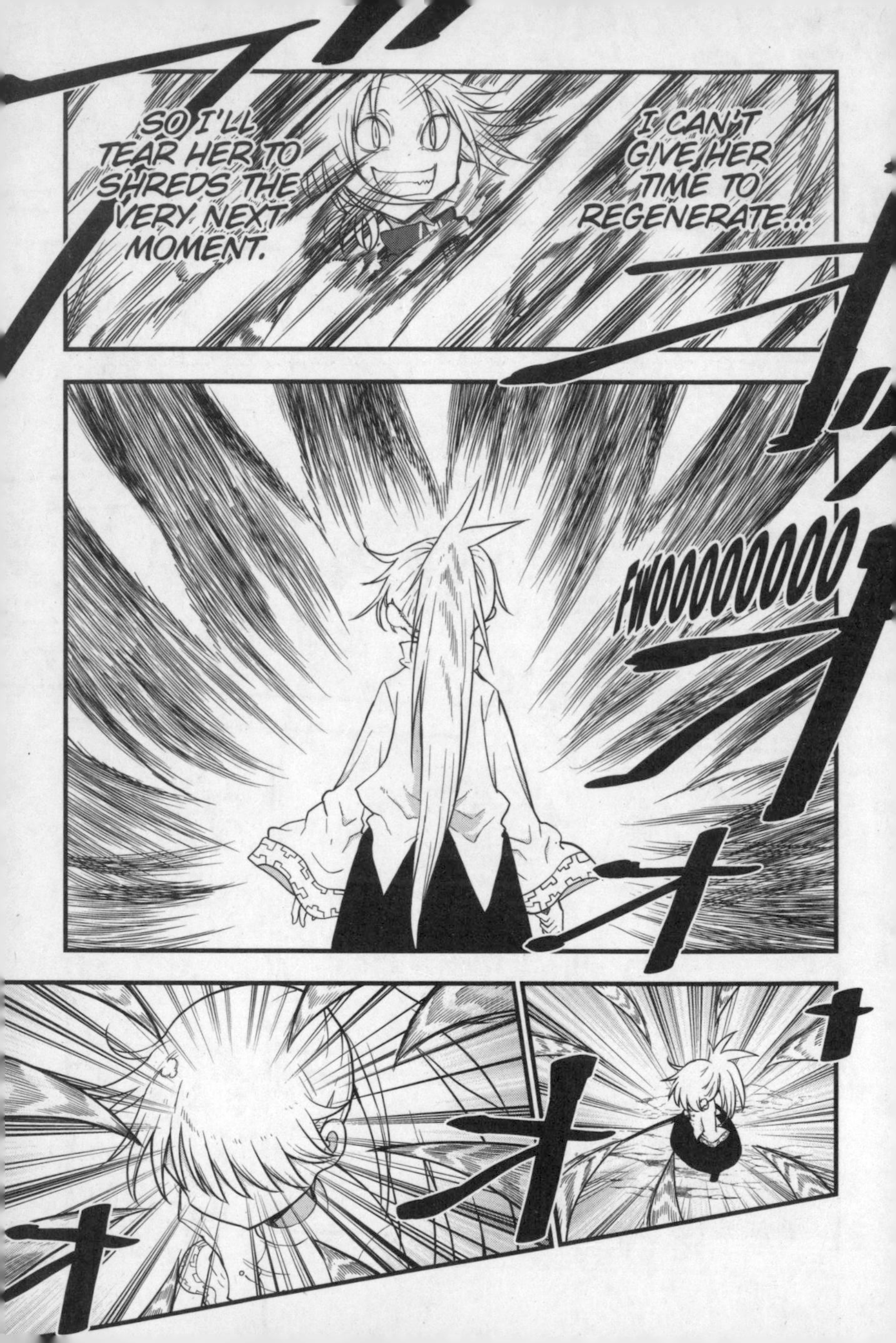
I CAN'T GIVE HER TIME TO REGENERATE...
SO I'LL TEAR HER TO SHREDS THE VERY NEXT MOMENT.
FWOOOOOOOO

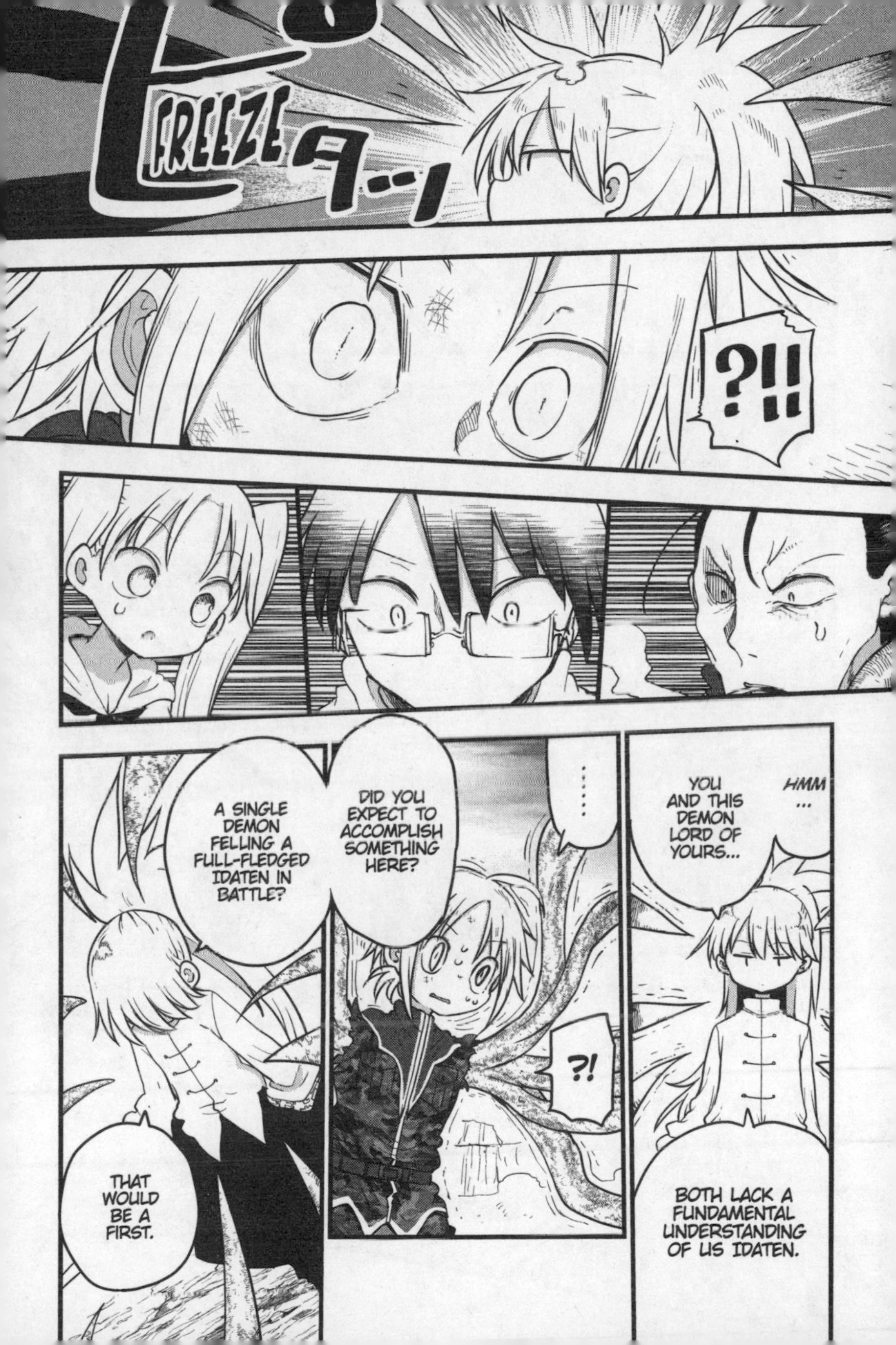
FREEZE
?!!
HMM ...
YOU AND THIS DEMON LORD OF YOURS...
BOTH LACK A FUNDAMENTAL UNDERSTANDING OF US IDATEN.
......
DID YOU EXPECT TO ACCOMPLISH SOMETHING HERE?
?!
A SINGLE DEMON FELLING A FULL-FLEDGED IDATEN IN BATTLE?
THAT WOULD BE A FIRST.

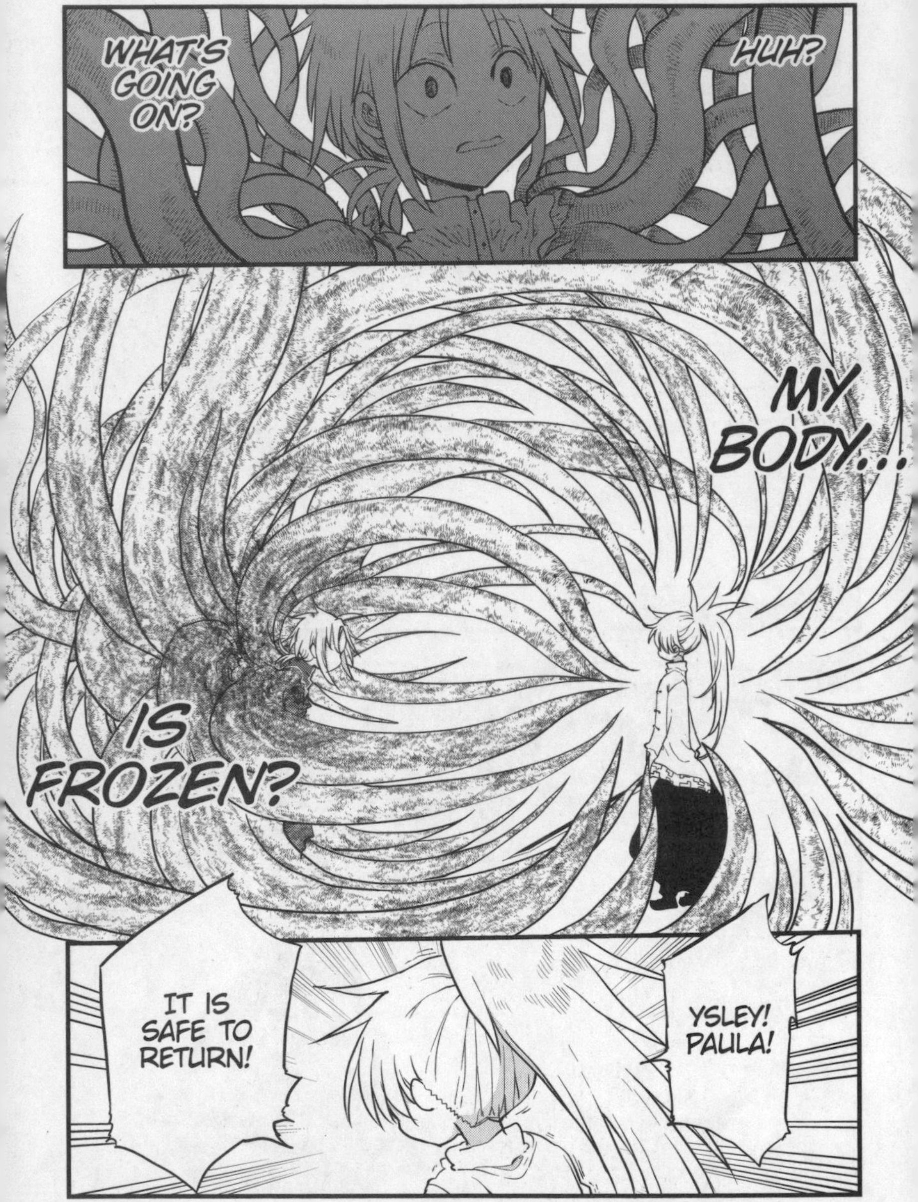
HUH?
WHAT'S GOING ON?
MY BODY...
IS FROZEN?
YSLEY! PAULA!
IT IS SAFE TO RETURN!

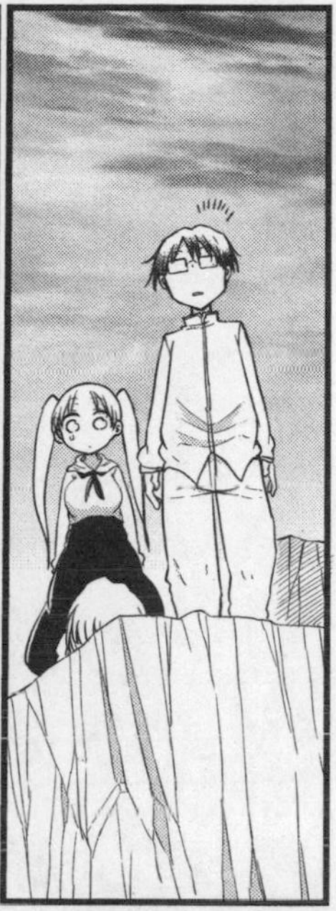

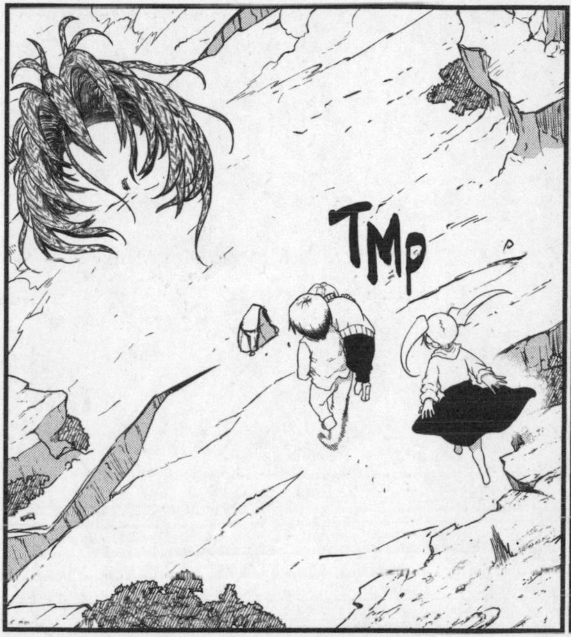
TMp

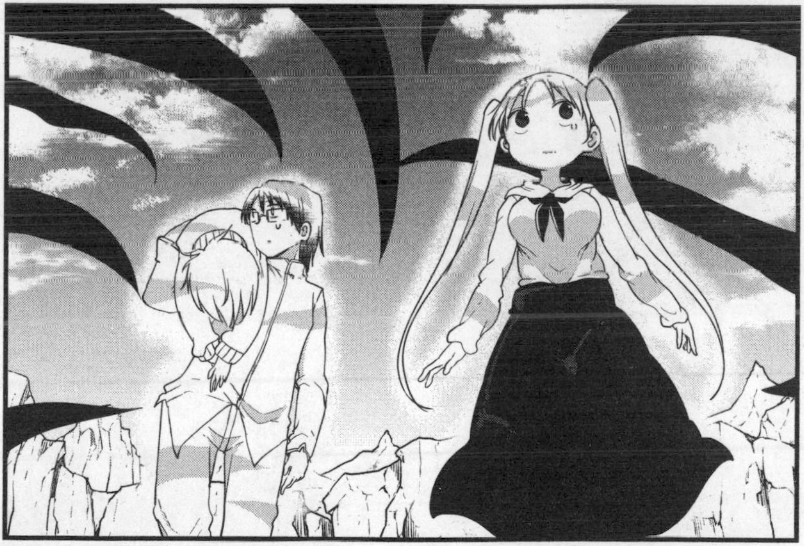

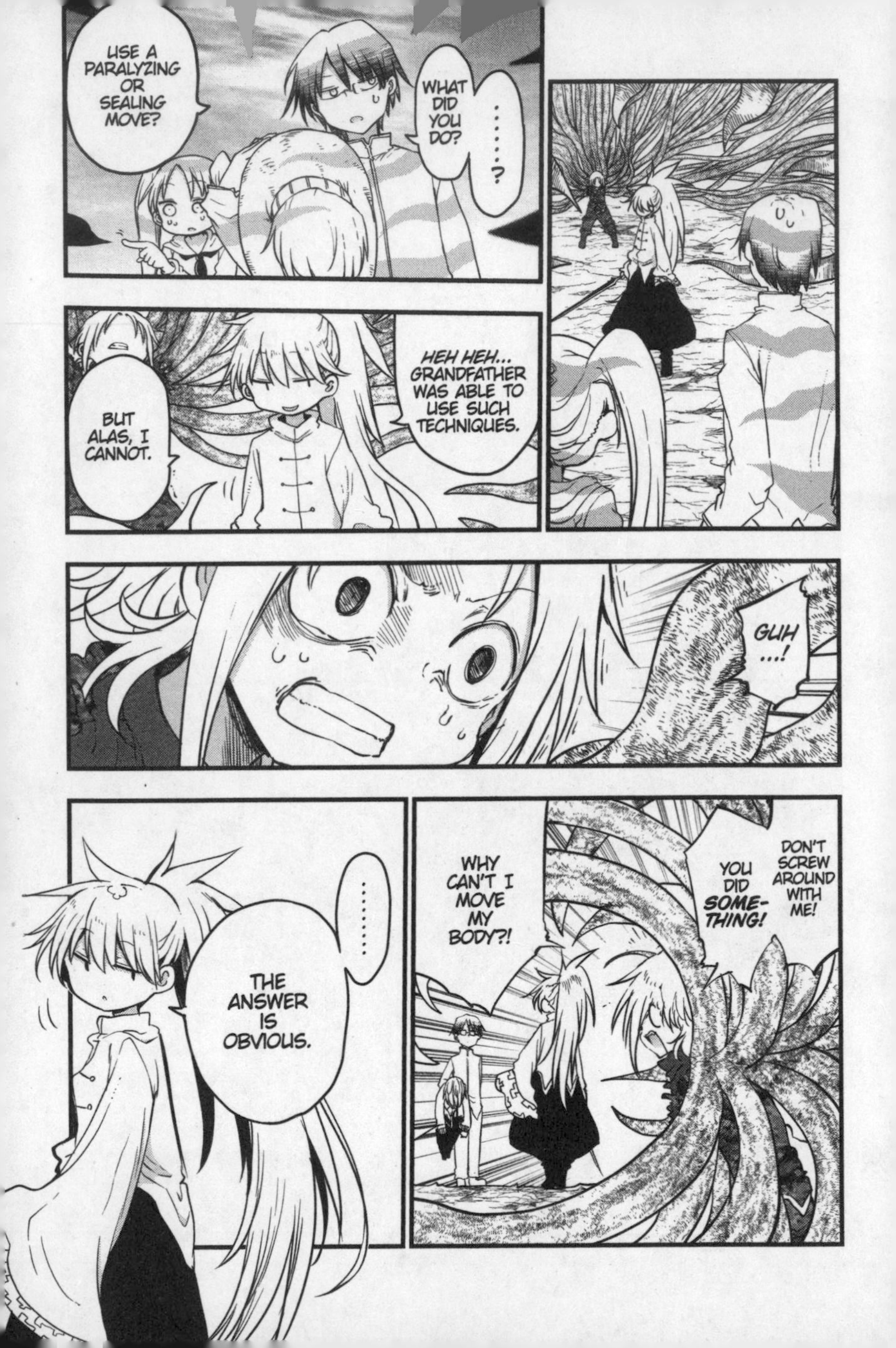
WHAT DID YOU DO?
......?
USE A PARALYZING OR SEALING MOVE?
HEH HEH... GRANDFATHER WAS ABLE TO USE SUCH TECHNIQUES.
BUT ALAS, I CANNOT.
GUH ...!
DON'T SCREW AROUND WITH ME!
YOU DID **SOMETHING!**
WHY CAN'T I MOVE MY BODY?!
......
THE ANSWER IS OBVIOUS.

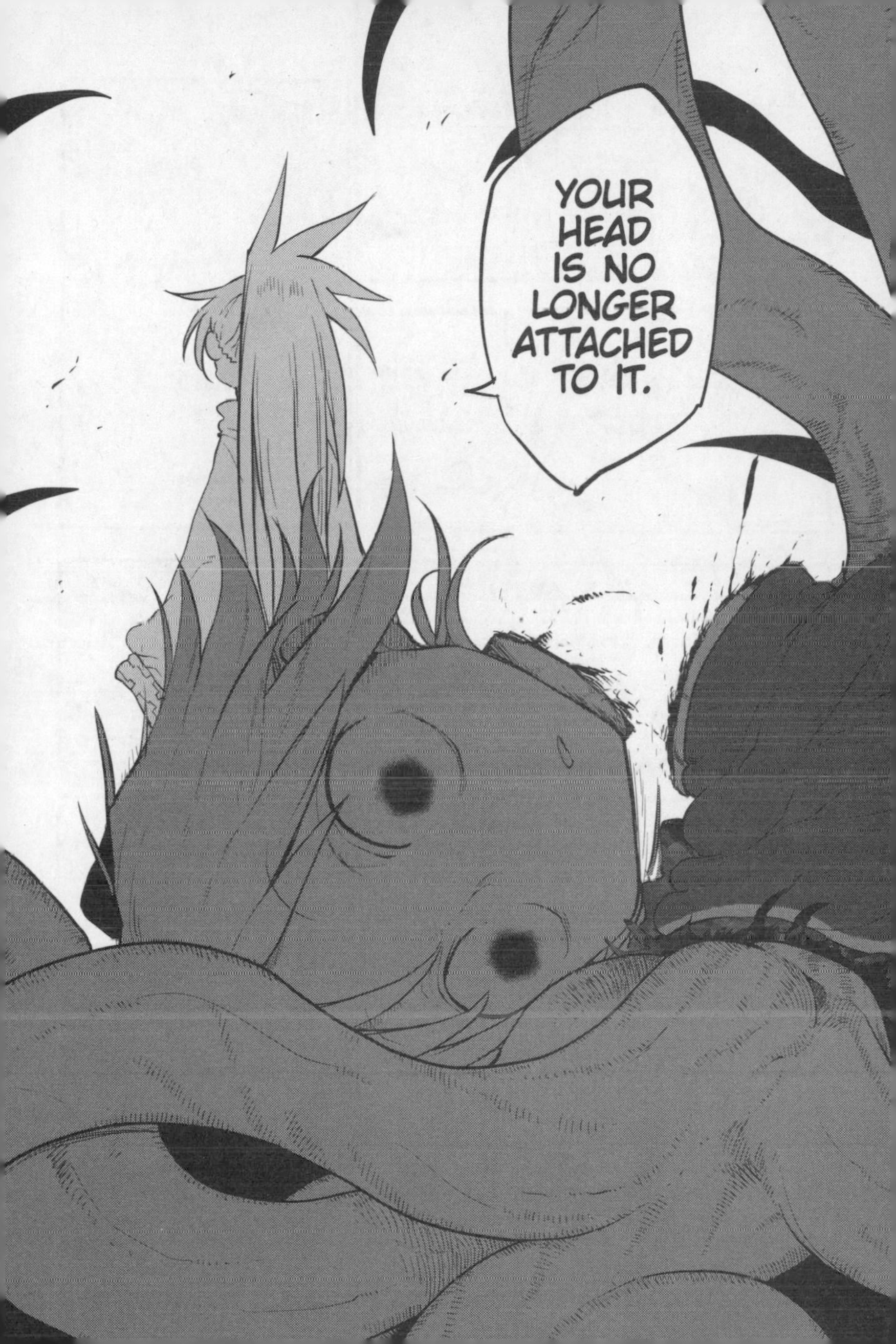
YOUR HEAD IS NO LONGER ATTACHED TO IT.

CHAPTER 14 Turning the Tide of Battle

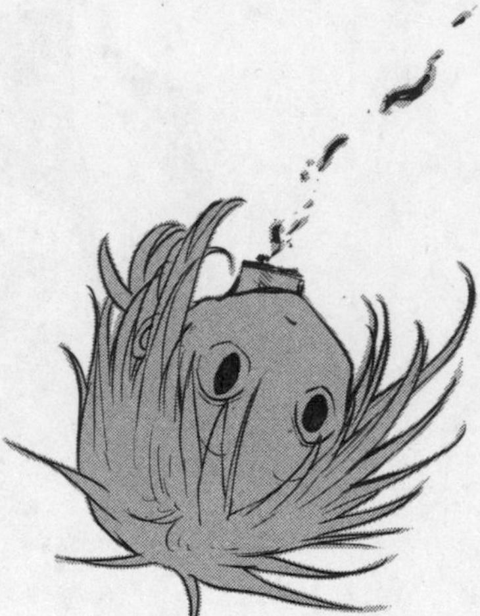

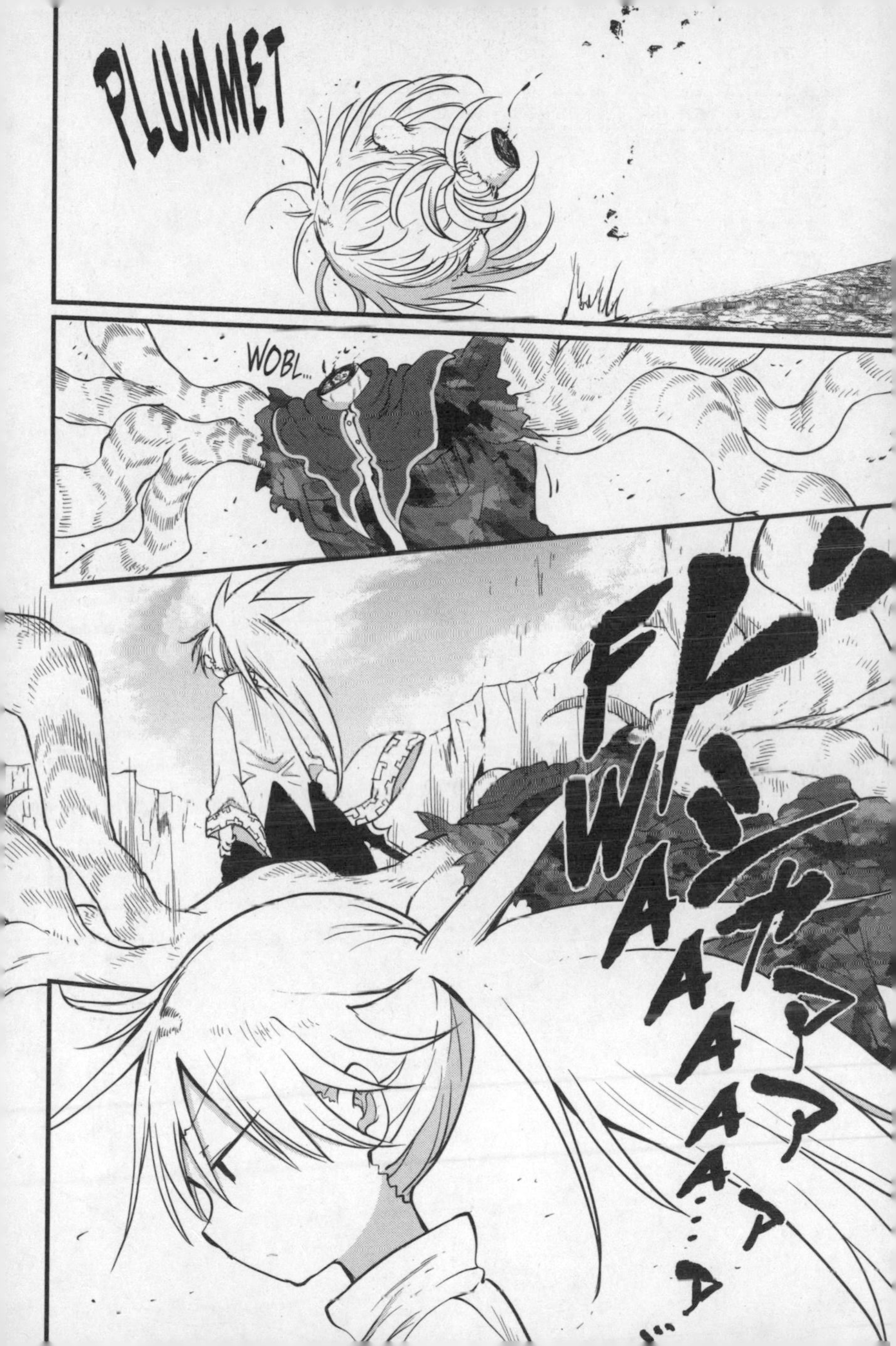
PLUMMET
WOBL...
FWAAAAA...

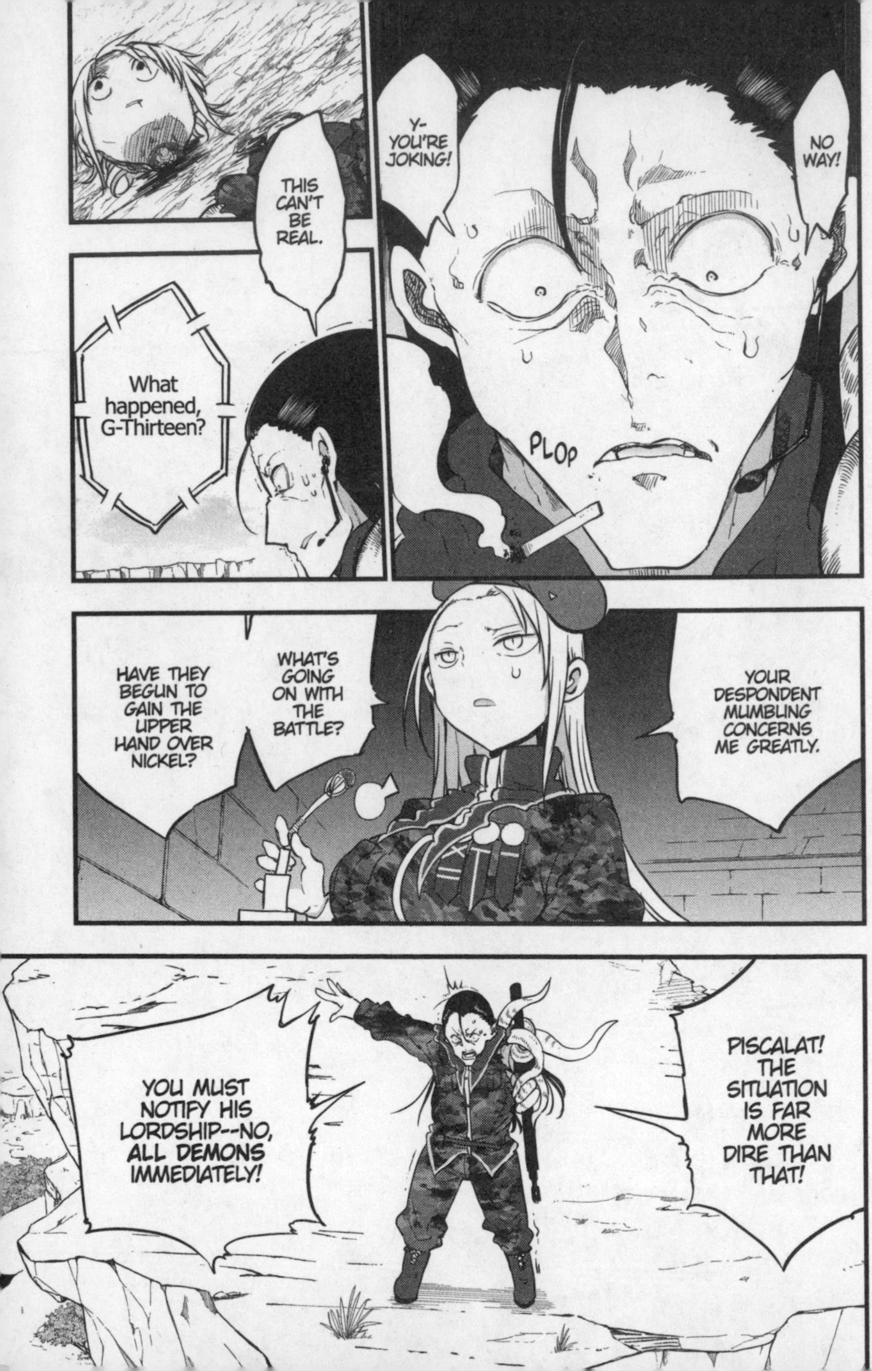
NO WAY!
Y- YOU'RE JOKING!
PLOP
THIS CAN'T BE REAL.
What happened, G-Thirteen?
YOUR DESPONDENT MUMBLING CONCERNS ME GREATLY.
WHAT'S GOING ON WITH THE BATTLE?
HAVE THEY BEGUN TO GAIN THE UPPER HAND OVER NICKEL?
PISCALAT! THE SITUATION IS FAR MORE DIRE THAN THAT!
YOU MUST NOTIFY HIS LORDSHIP--NO, ALL DEMONS IMMEDIATELY!

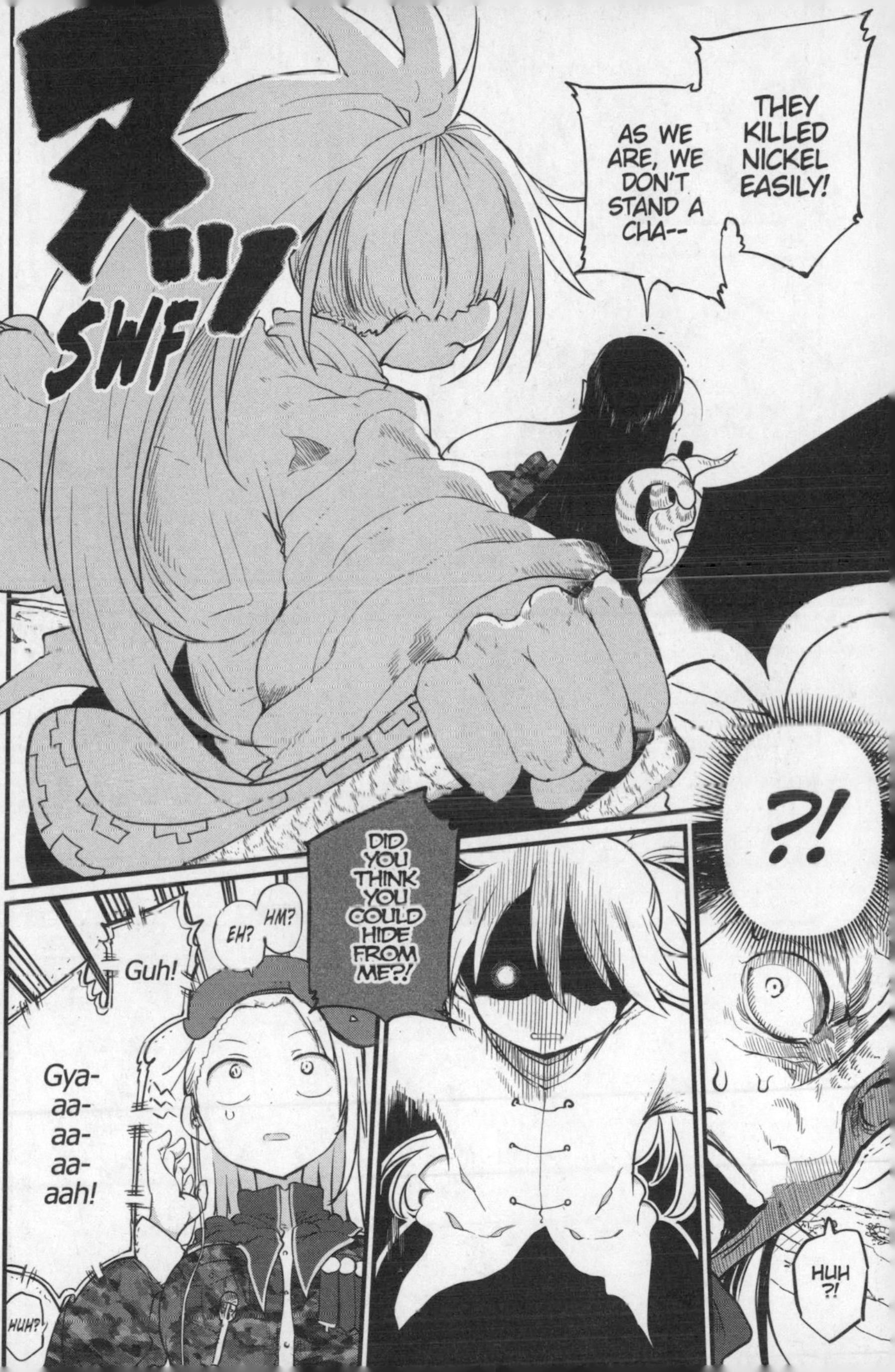
THEY KILLED NICKEL EASILY!
AS WE ARE, WE DON'T STAND A CHA--
SWF
?!
HUH ?!
DID YOU THINK YOU COULD HIDE FROM ME?!
HM?
EH?
Guh!
Gya-aa-aa-aa-aah!
HUH?

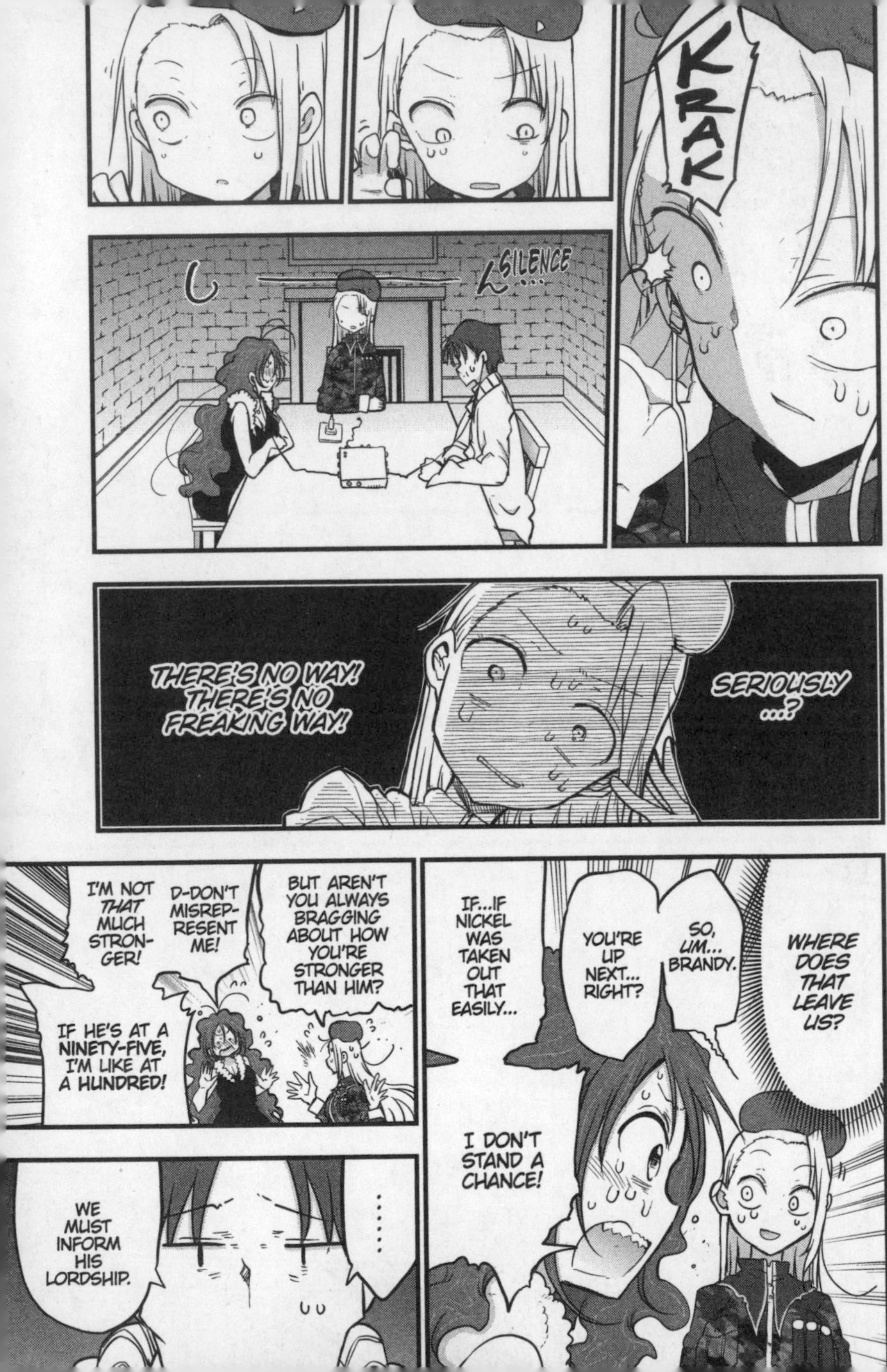
KRAK
SILENCE...
SERIOUSLY ...?
THERE'S NO WAY! THERE'S NO FREAKING WAY!
WHERE DOES THAT LEAVE US?
SO, UM... BRANDY.
YOU'RE UP NEXT... RIGHT?
IF...IF NICKEL WAS TAKEN OUT THAT EASILY...
I DON'T STAND A CHANCE!
BUT AREN'T YOU ALWAYS BRAGGING ABOUT HOW YOU'RE STRONGER THAN HIM?
D-DON'T MISREP- RESENT ME!
I'M NOT *THAT* MUCH STRON- GER!
IF HE'S AT A NINETY-FIVE, I'M LIKE AT A HUNDRED!
......
WE MUST INFORM HIS LORDSHIP.

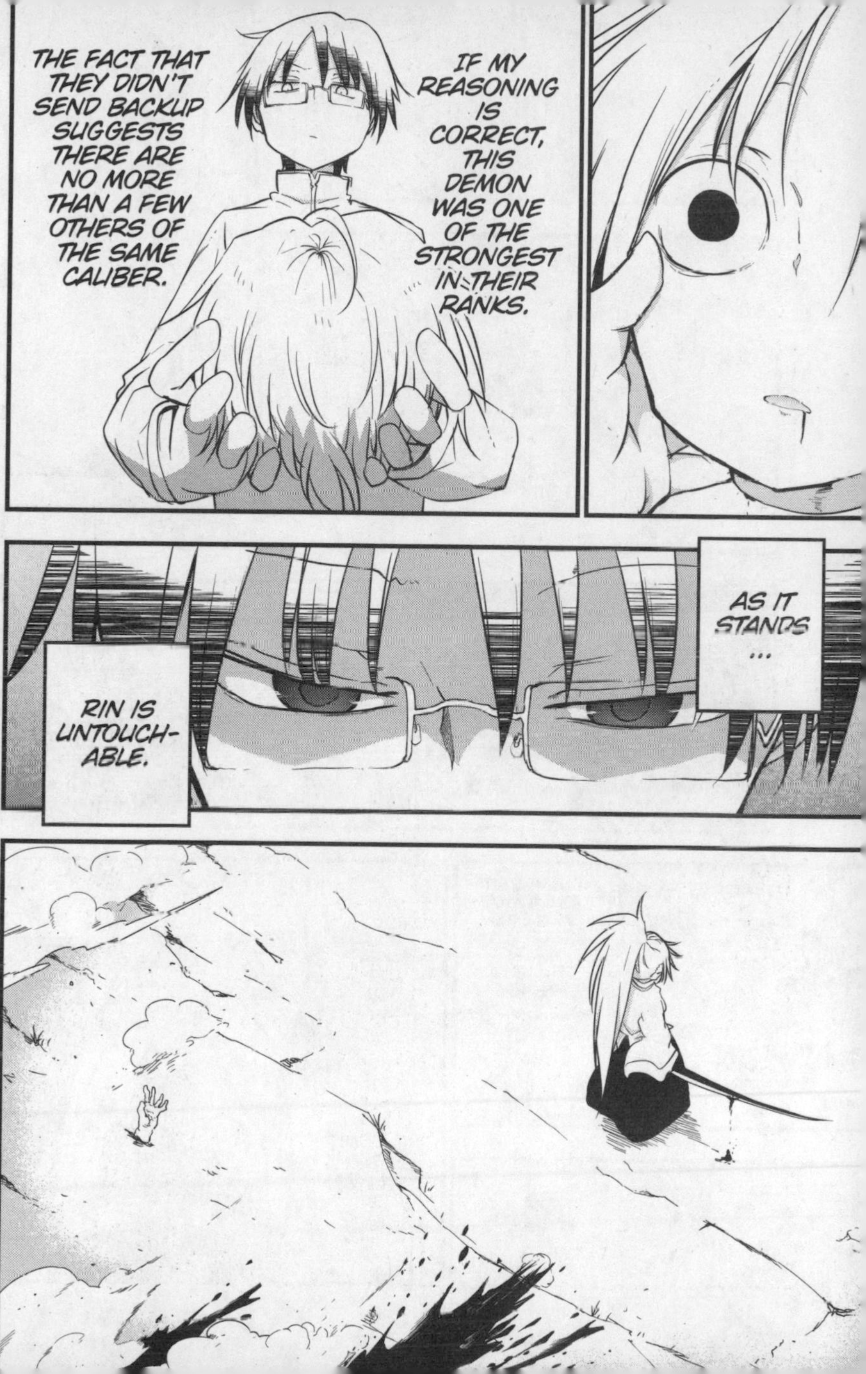
IF MY REASONING IS CORRECT, THIS DEMON WAS ONE OF THE STRONGEST IN THEIR RANKS.
THE FACT THAT THEY DIDN'T SEND BACKUP SUGGESTS THERE ARE NO MORE THAN A FEW OTHERS OF THE SAME CALIBER.
AS IT STANDS...
RIN IS UNTOUCHABLE.

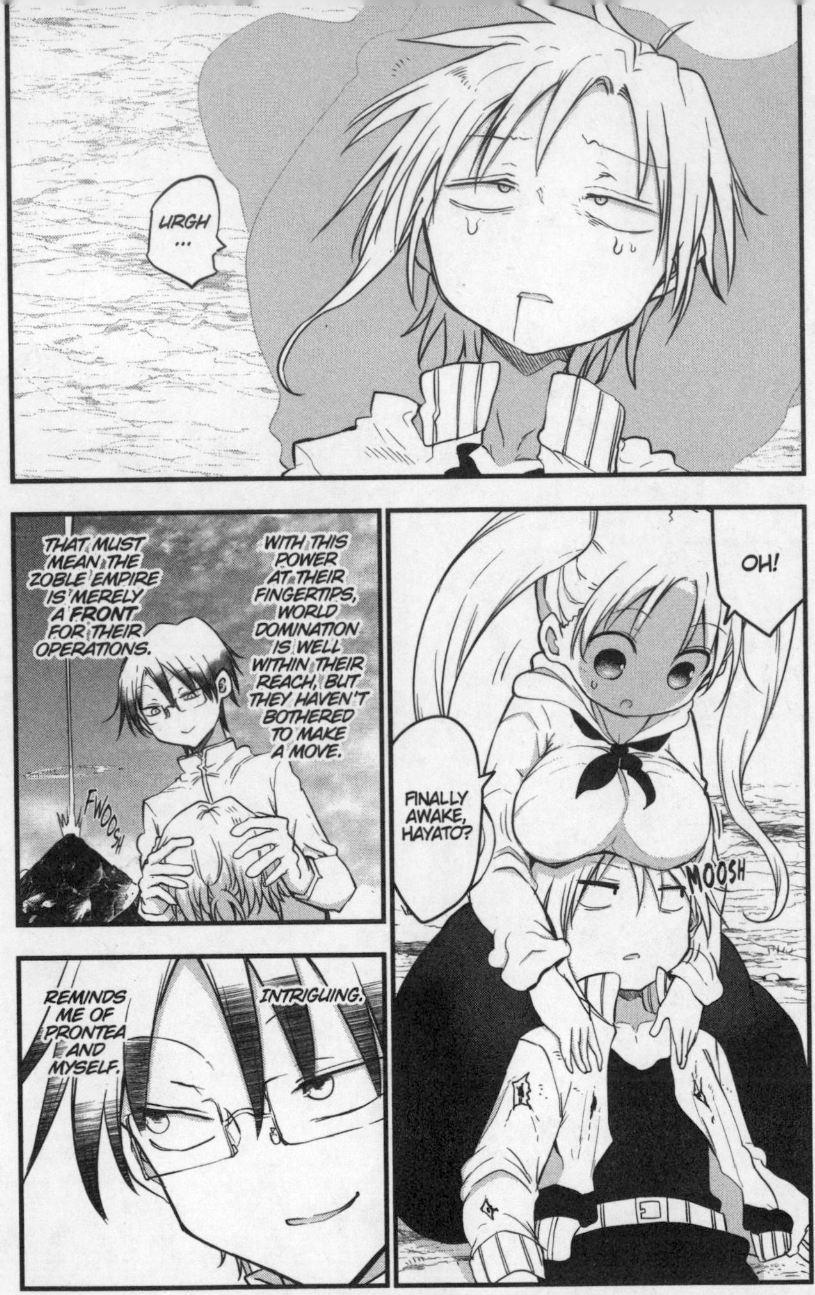
URGH ...
OH!
FINALLY AWAKE, HAYATO?
MOOSH
WITH THIS POWER AT THEIR FINGERTIPS, WORLD DOMINATION IS WELL WITHIN THEIR REACH, BUT THEY HAVEN'T BOTHERED TO MAKE A MOVE.
THAT MUST MEAN THE ZOBLE EMPIRE IS MERELY A FRONT FOR THEIR OPERATIONS.
FWOOSH
INTRIGUING.
REMINDS ME OF PRONTEA AND MYSELF.

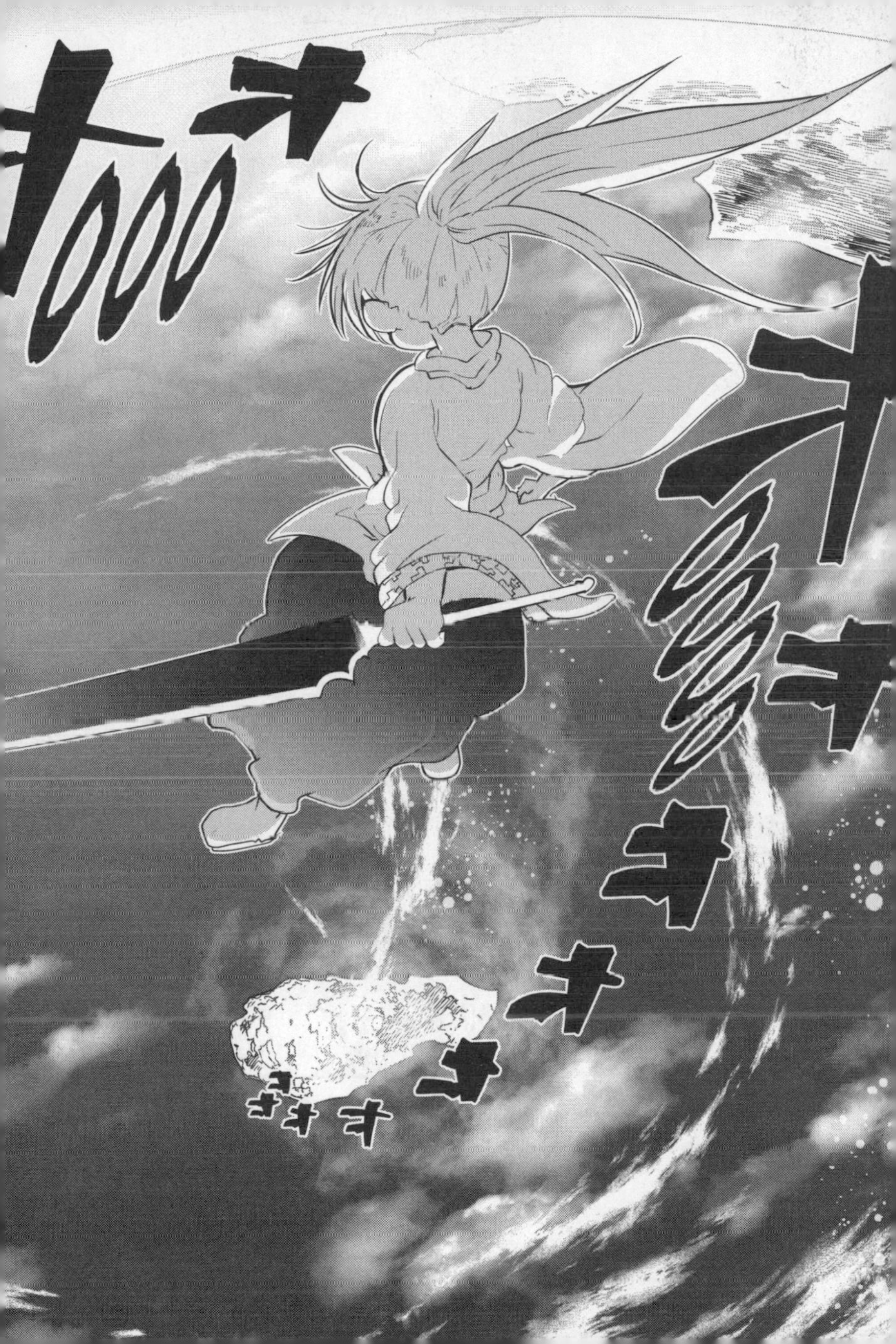

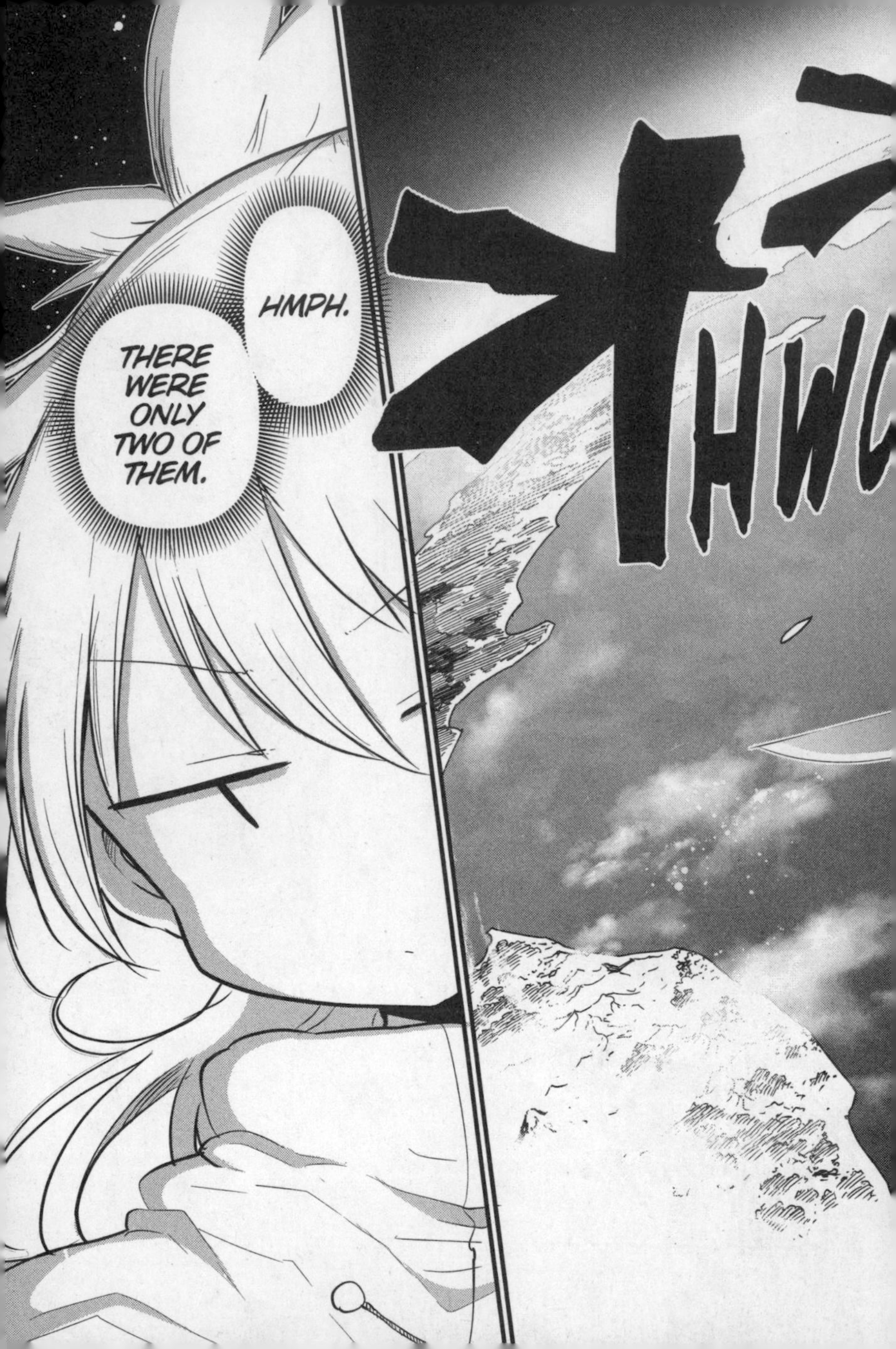
HMPH.
THERE WERE ONLY TWO OF THEM.

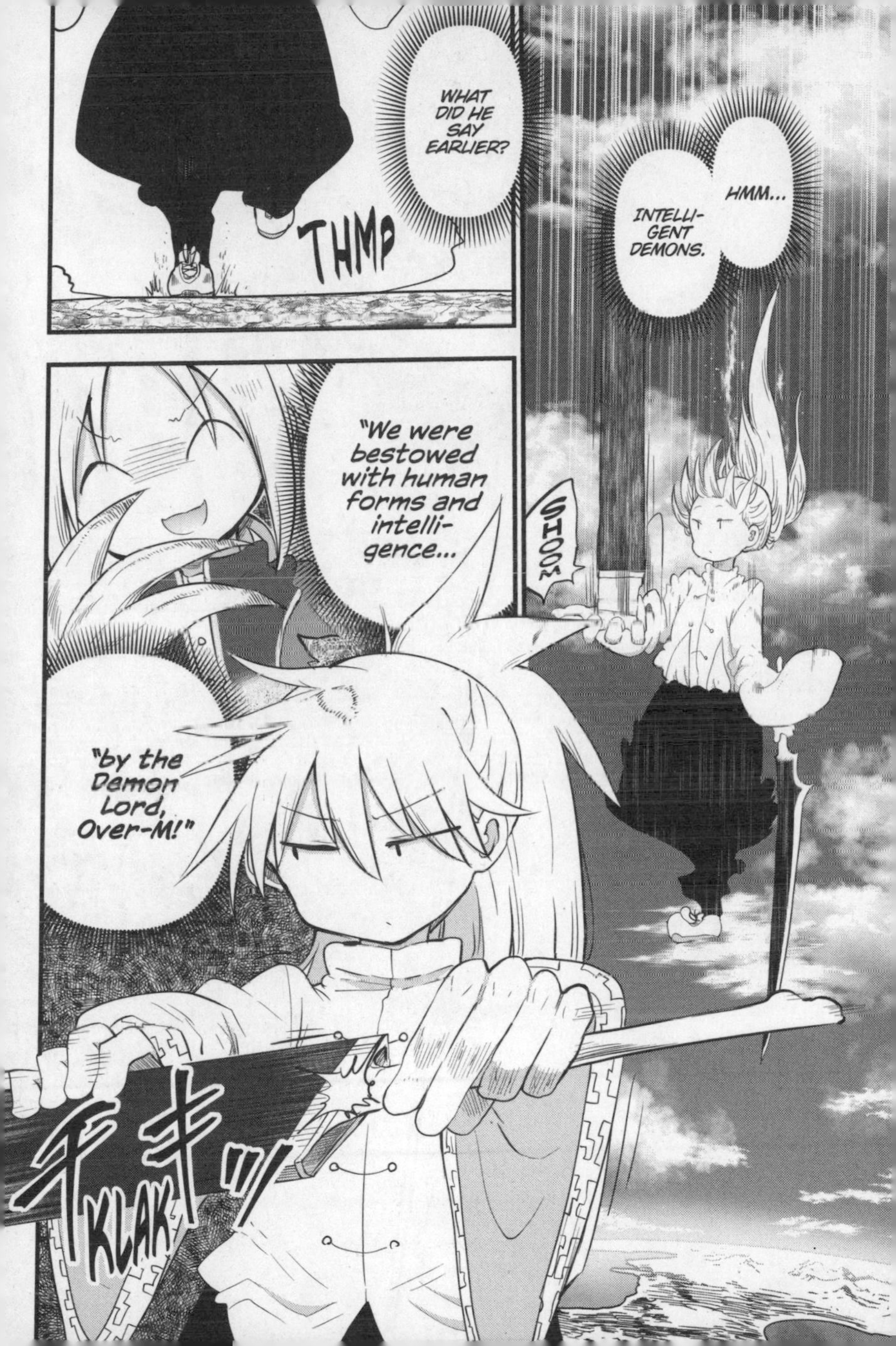
HMM...
INTELLI-GENT DEMONS.
WHAT DID HE SAY EARLIER?
THMP
"We were bestowed with human forms and intelli-gence...
"by the Demon Lord, Over-M!"
SHOOM
KLAK

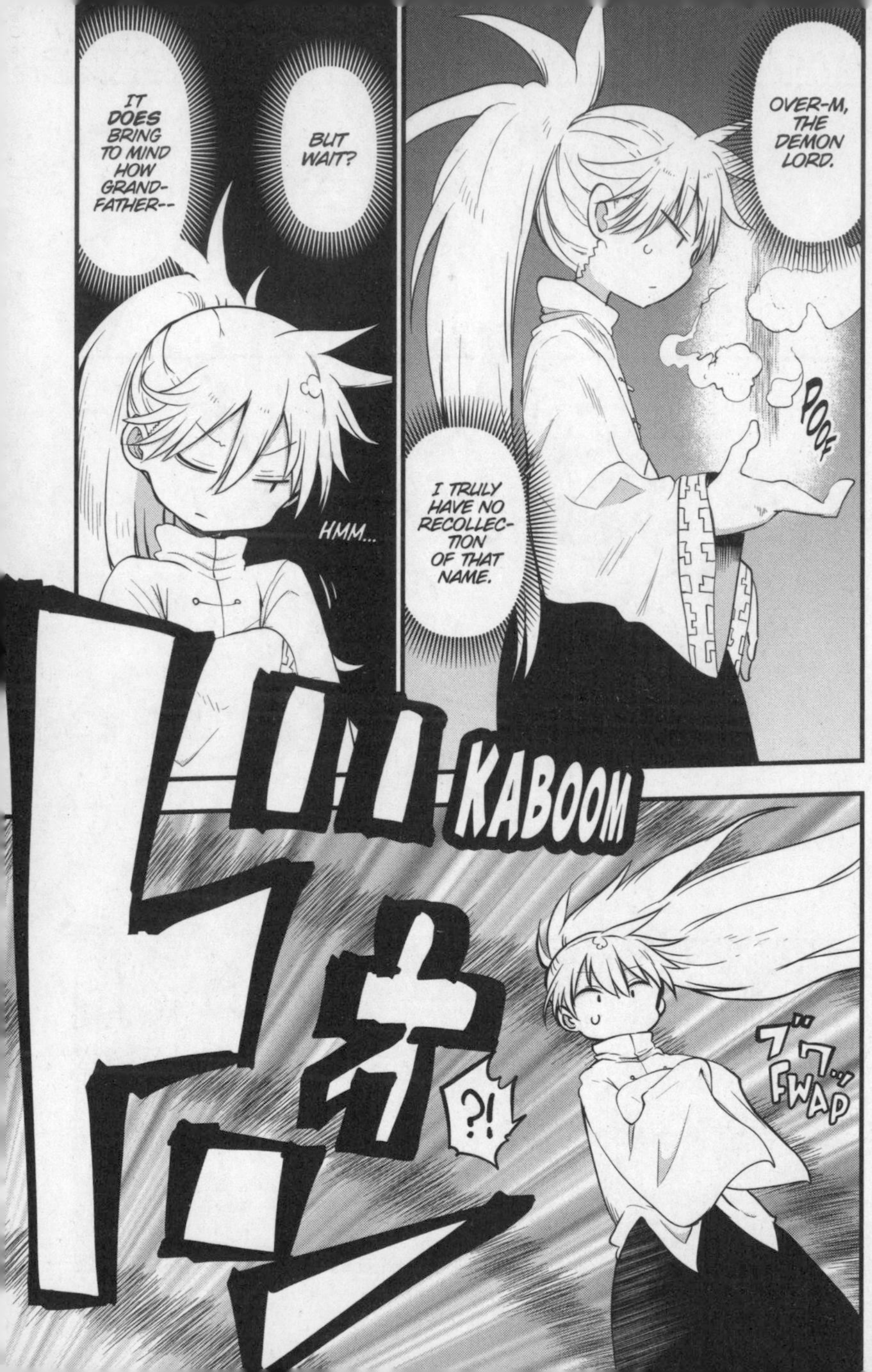
OVER-M, THE DEMON LORD.
POOF
I TRULY HAVE NO RECOLLEC-TION OF THAT NAME.
BUT WAIT?
IT DOES BRING TO MIND HOW GRAND-FATHER--
HMM...
KABOOM
?!
FWAP

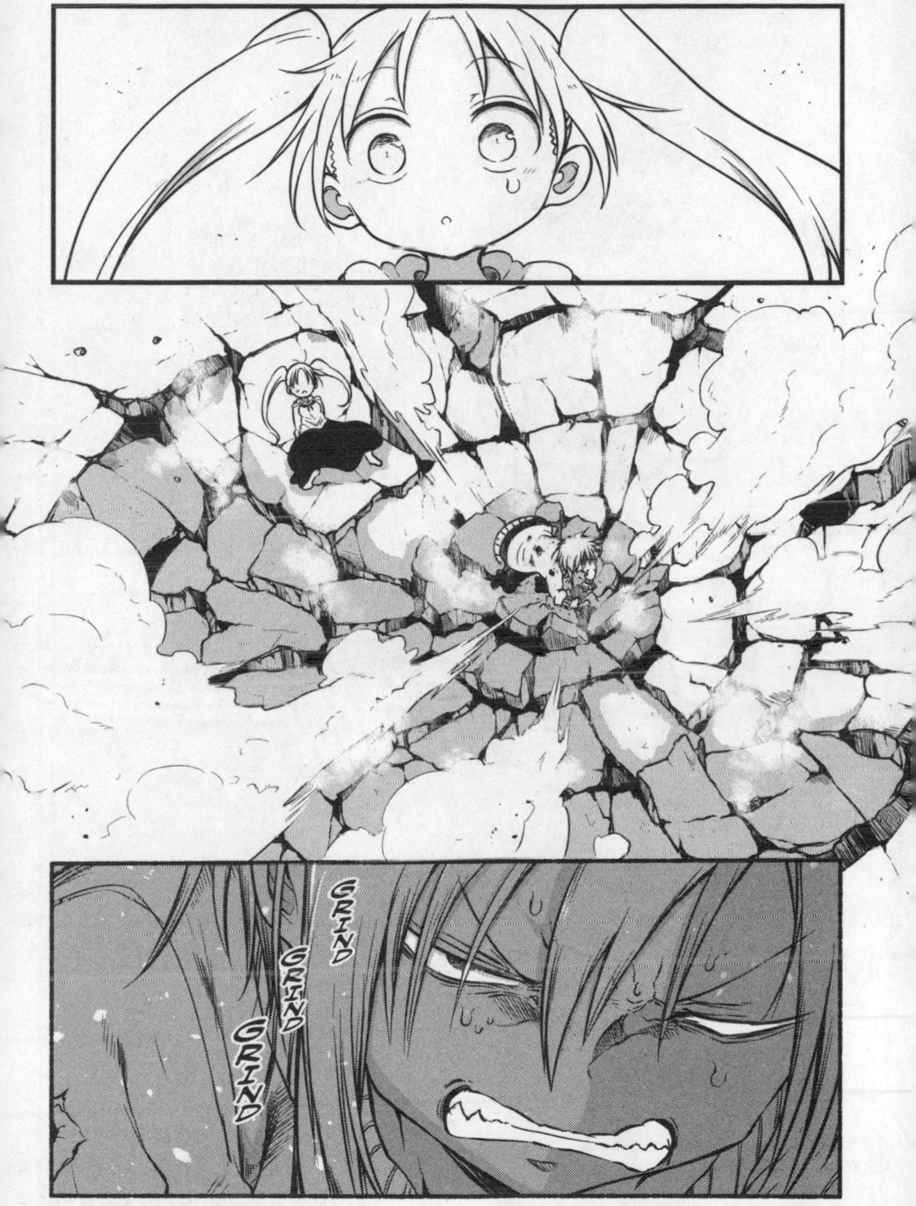
GRIND
GRIND
GRIND

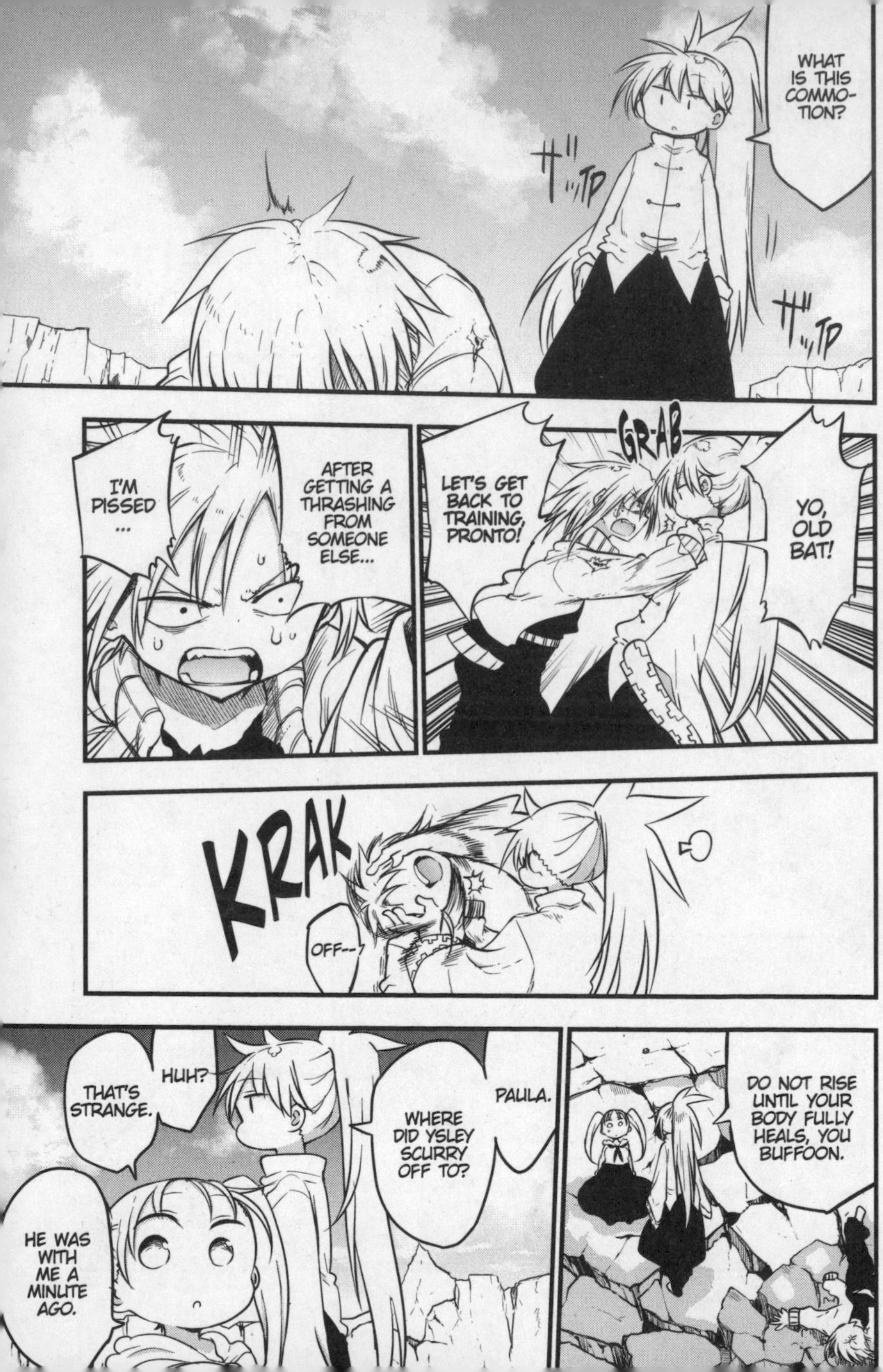
WHAT IS THIS COMMOTION?
TP
TP
YO, OLD BAT!
GRAB
LET'S GET BACK TO TRAINING, PRONTO!
AFTER GETTING A THRASHING FROM SOMEONE ELSE...
I'M PISSED ...
KRAK
OFF--
DO NOT RISE UNTIL YOUR BODY FULLY HEALS, YOU BUFFOON.
PAULA.
WHERE DID YSLEY SCURRY OFF TO?
HUH?
THAT'S STRANGE.
HE WAS WITH ME A MINUTE AGO.

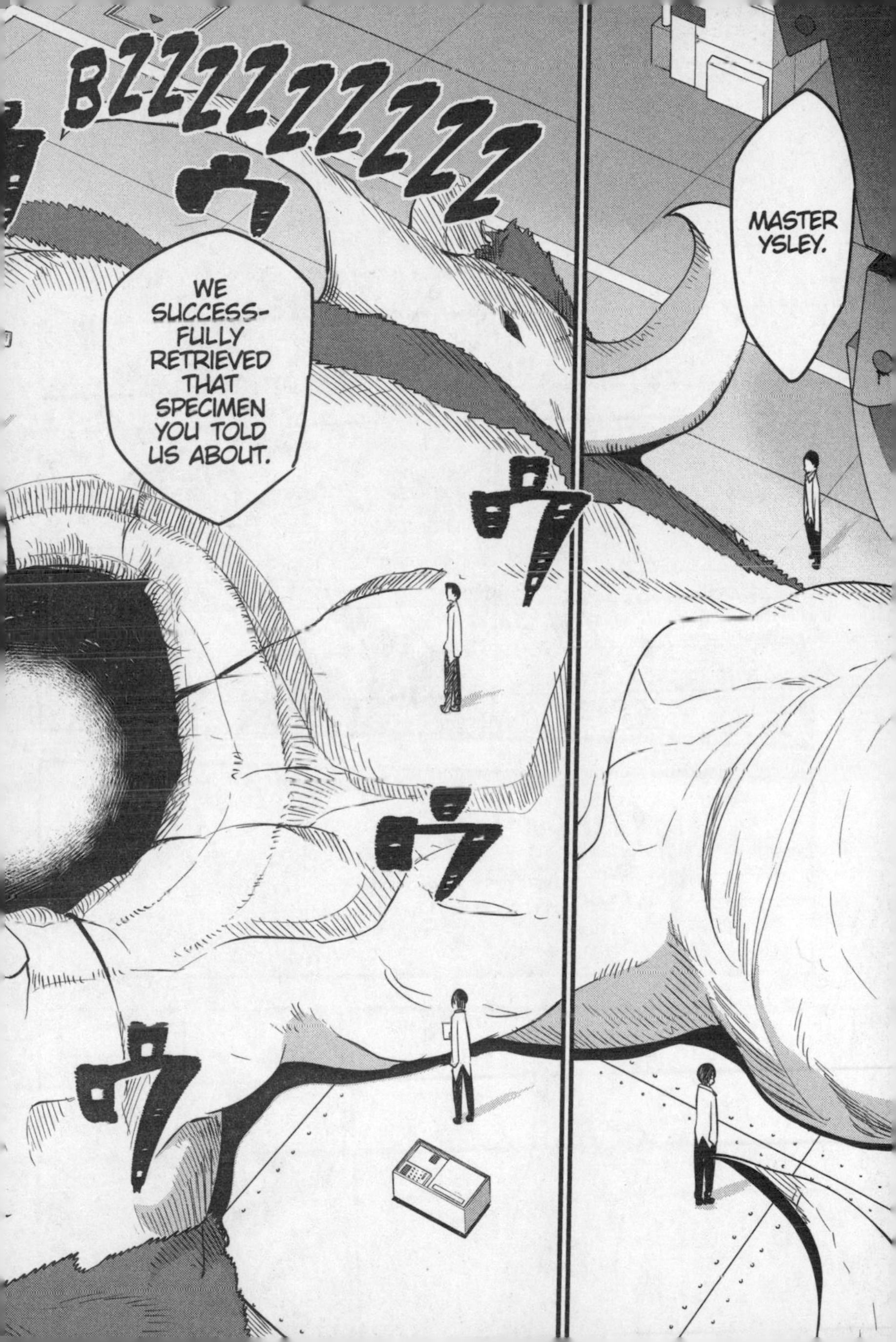
MASTER YSLEY.
BZZZZZZZZZZ
WE SUCCESSFULLY RETRIEVED THAT SPECIMEN YOU TOLD US ABOUT.

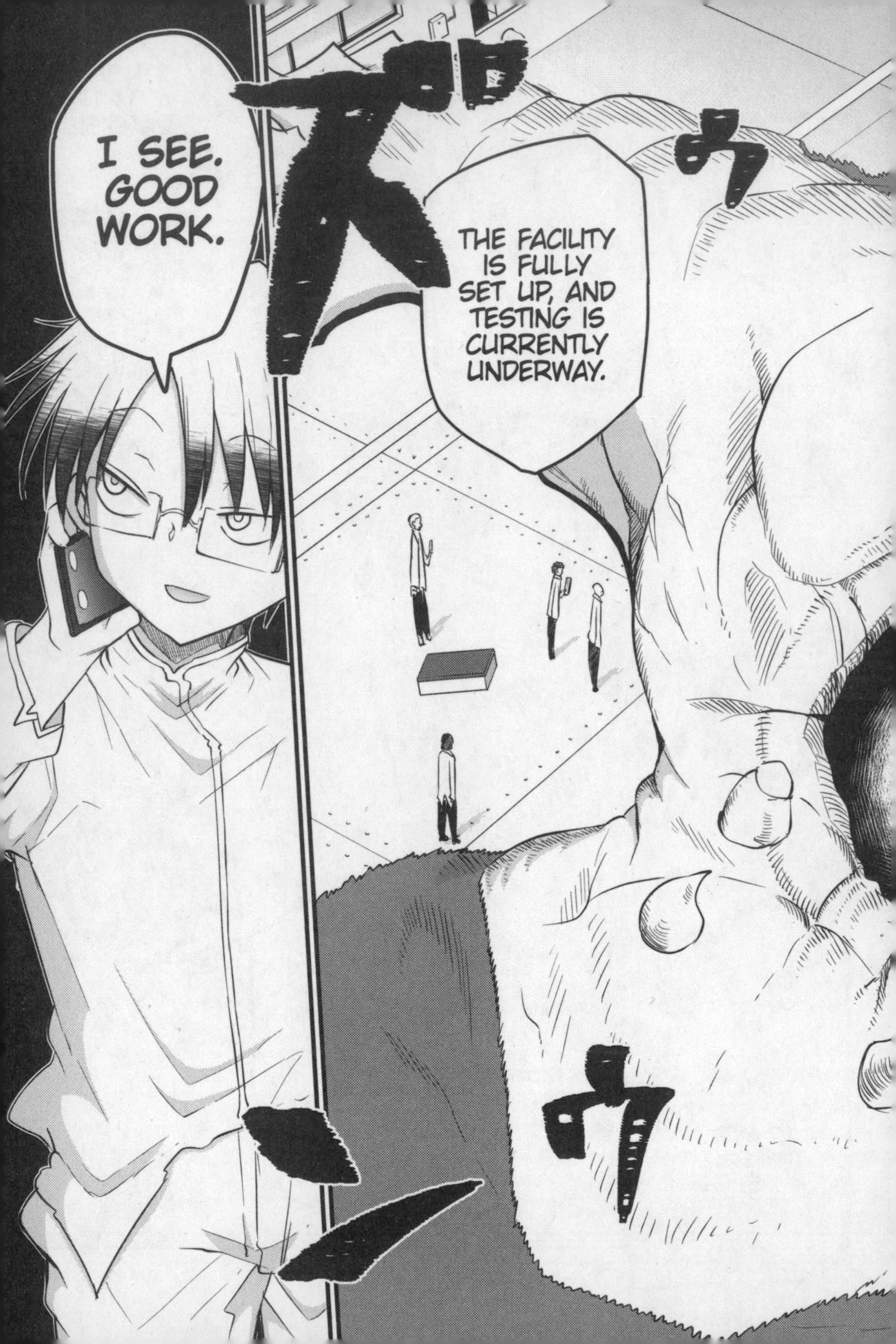
THE FACILITY IS FULLY SET UP, AND TESTING IS CURRENTLY UNDERWAY.
I SEE. GOOD WORK.

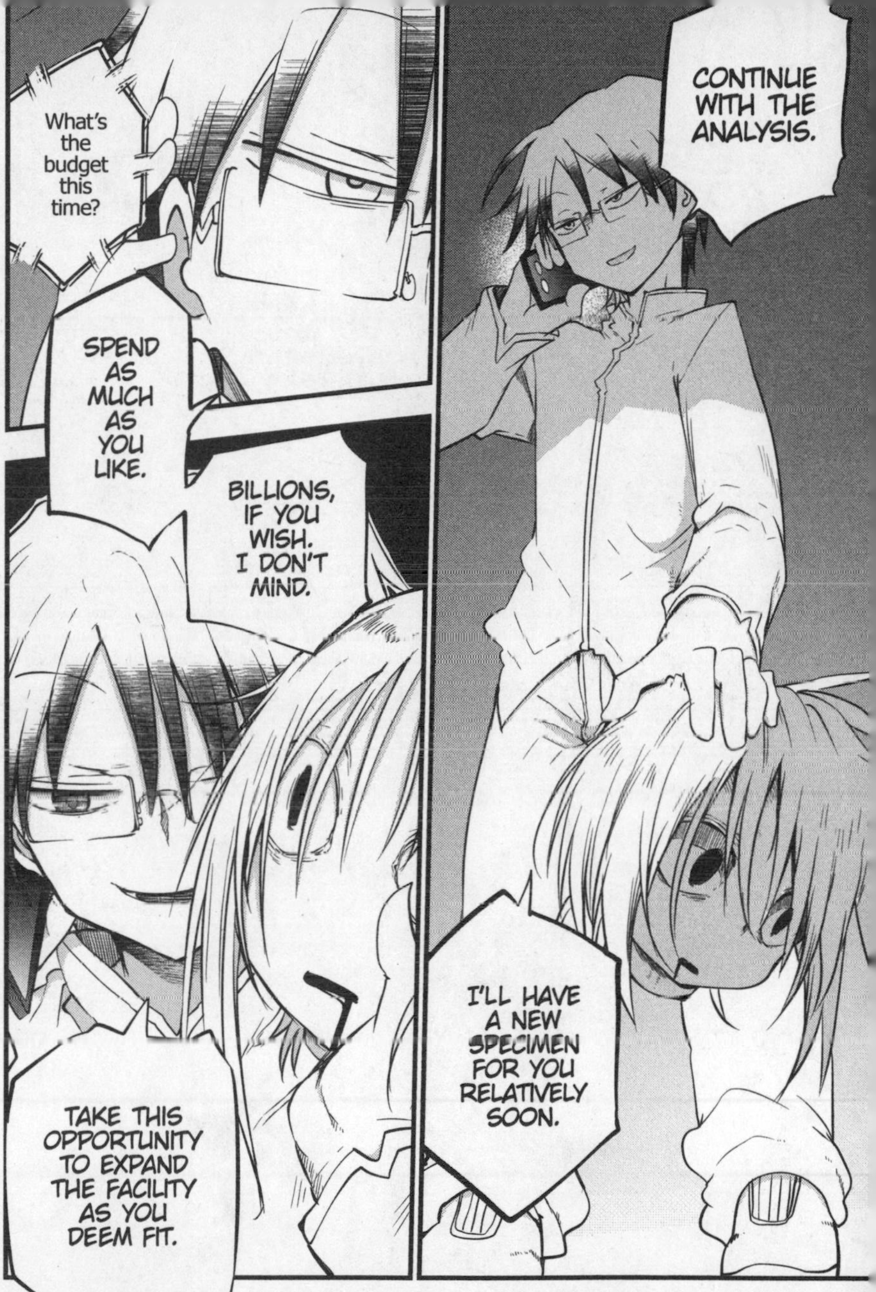
CONTINUE WITH THE ANALYSIS.
I'LL HAVE A NEW SPECIMEN FOR YOU RELATIVELY SOON.
What's the budget this time?
SPEND AS MUCH AS YOU LIKE.
BILLIONS, IF YOU WISH. I DON'T MIND.
TAKE THIS OPPORTUNITY TO EXPAND THE FACILITY AS YOU DEEM FIT.

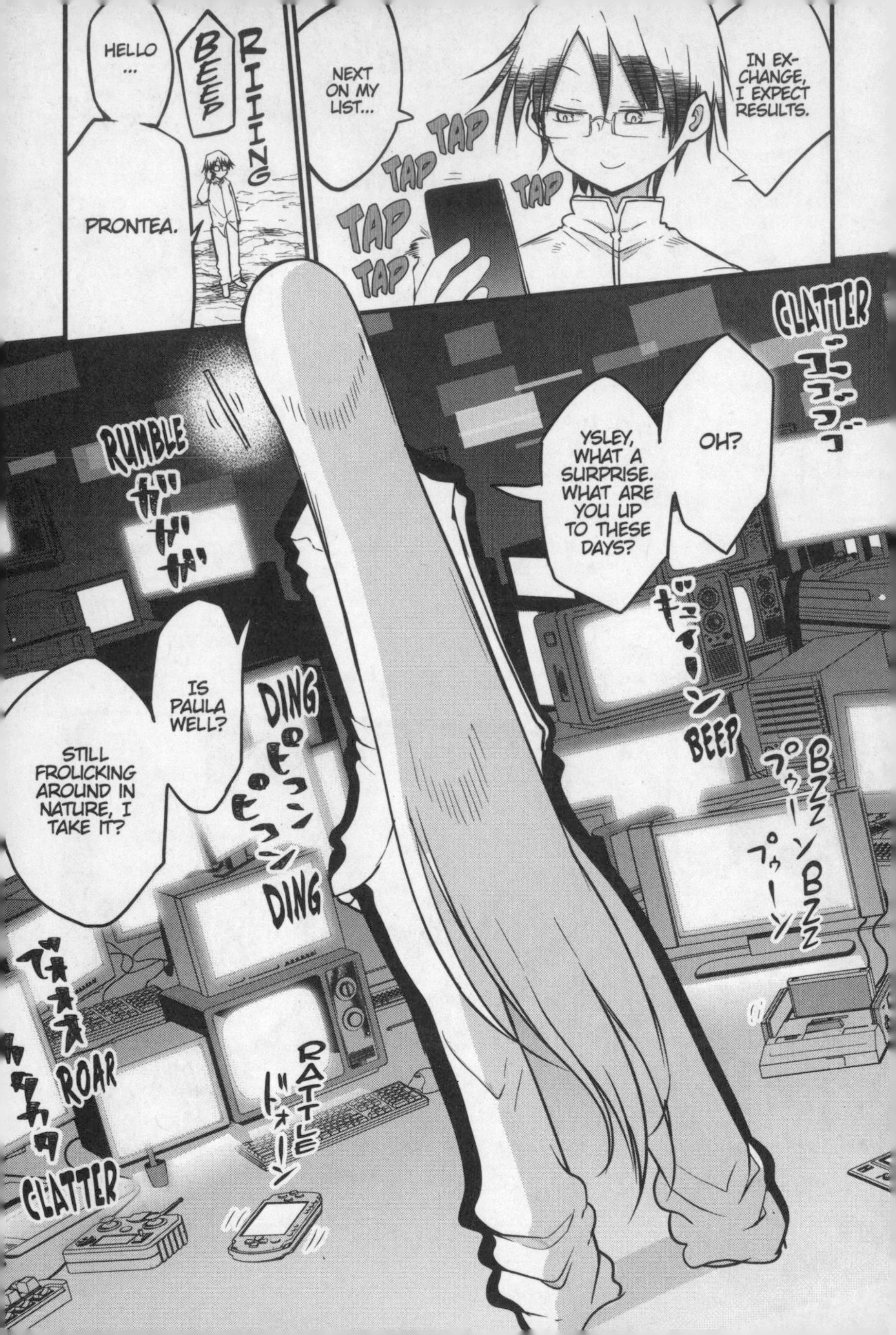
IN EX-CHANGE, I EXPECT RESULTS.
TAP TAP TAP TAP TAP TAP
NEXT ON MY LIST...
RIIIING
BEEP
HELLO ...
PRONTEA.
CLATTER
OH?
YSLEY, WHAT A SURPRISE. WHAT ARE YOU UP TO THESE DAYS?
BEEP
BZZ BZZ
RUMBLE
DING DING
IS PAULA WELL?
STILL FROLICKING AROUND IN NATURE, I TAKE IT?
RATTLE
ROAR
CLATTER

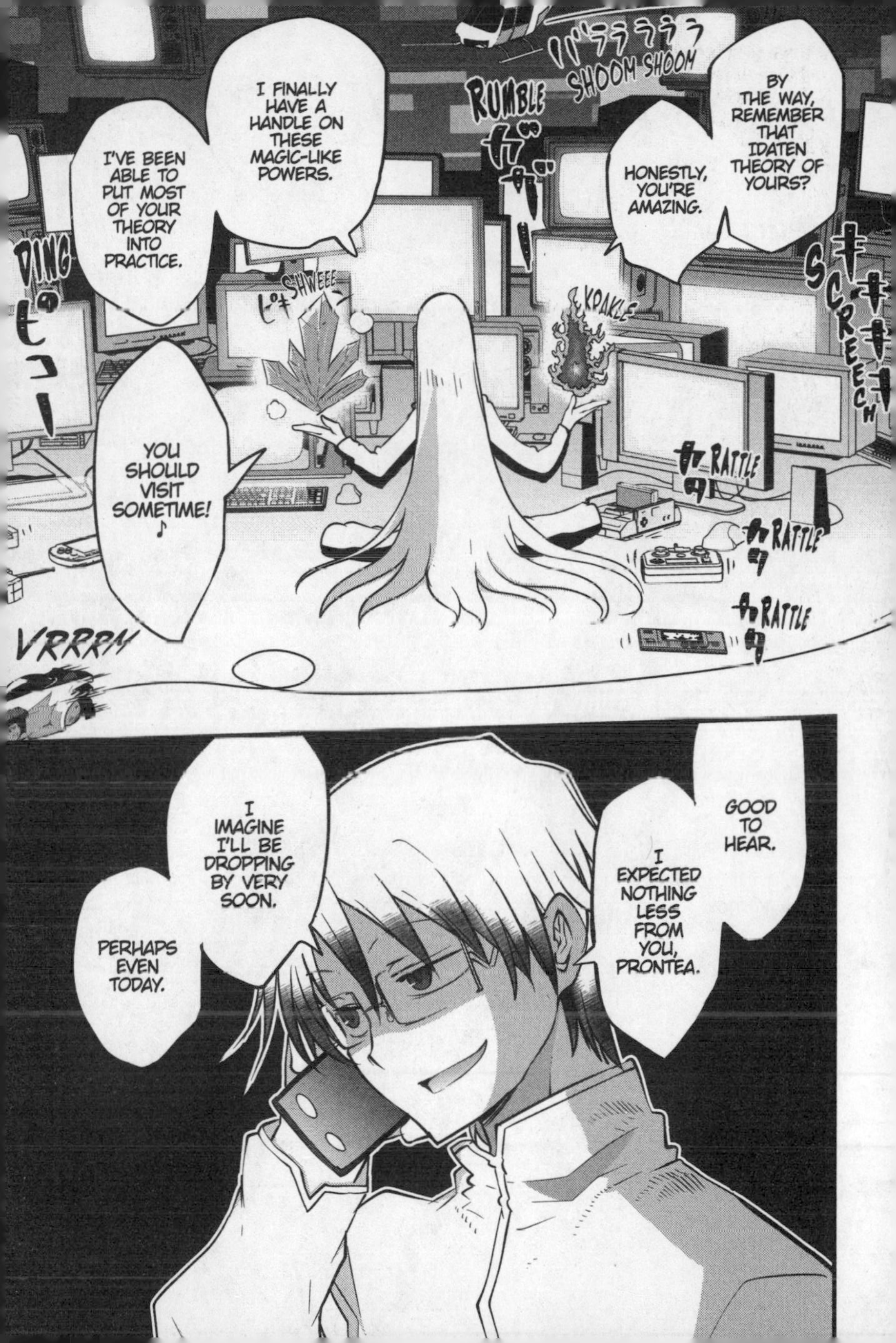
バラララララ
SHOOM SHOOM
BY THE WAY, REMEMBER THAT IDATEN THEORY OF YOURS?
HONESTLY, YOU'RE AMAZING.
RUMBLE
I FINALLY HAVE A HANDLE ON THESE MAGIC-LIKE POWERS.
I'VE BEEN ABLE TO PUT MOST OF YOUR THEORY INTO PRACTICE.
SCREECH
KRAKLE
SHWEEE
DING
YOU SHOULD VISIT SOMETIME! ♪
RATTLE
RATTLE
RATTLE
VRRRM
GOOD TO HEAR.
I EXPECTED NOTHING LESS FROM YOU, PRONTEA.
I IMAGINE I'LL BE DROPPING BY VERY SOON.
PERHAPS EVEN TODAY.

Chapter 15

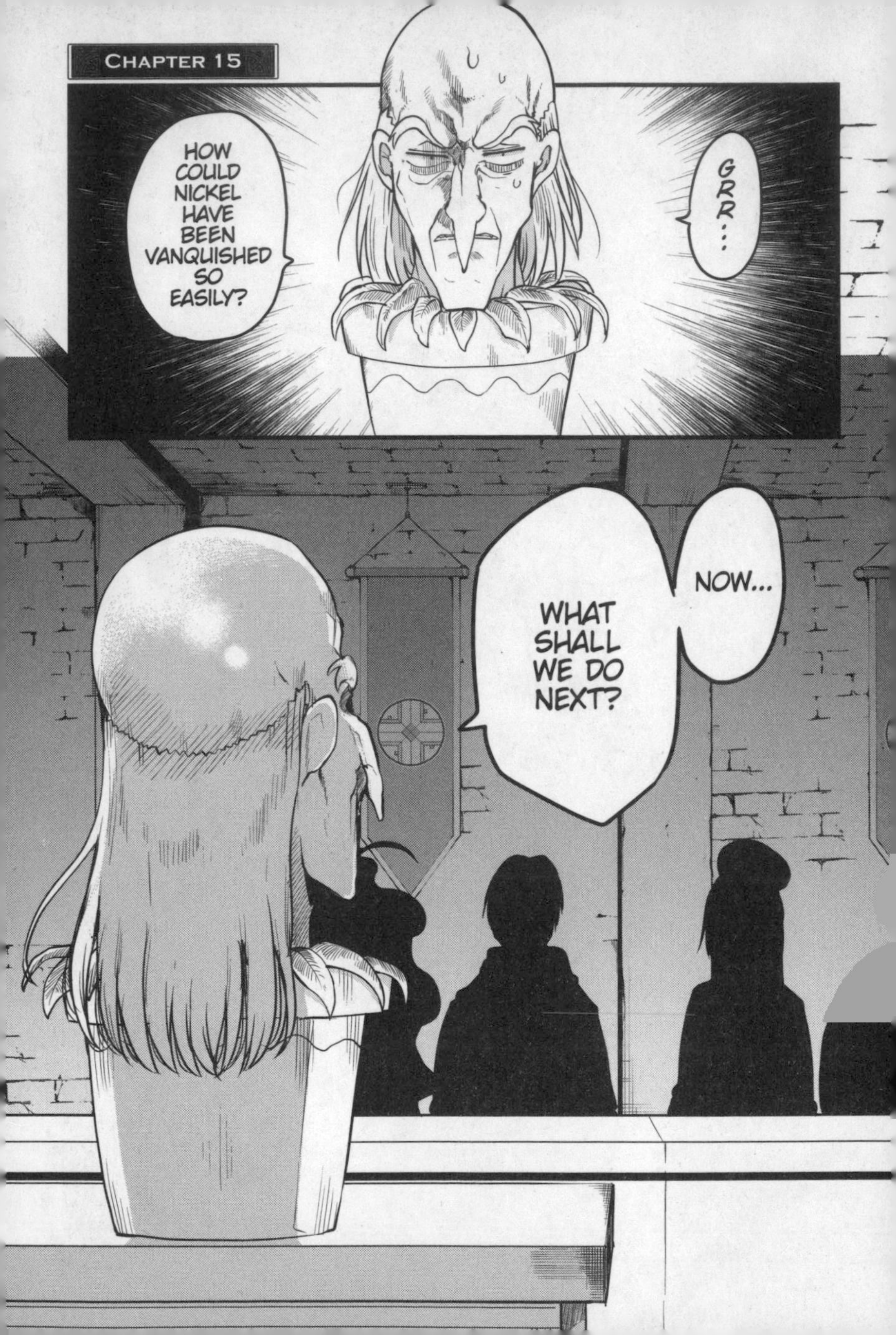
GRR...
HOW COULD NICKEL HAVE BEEN VANQUISHED SO EASILY?
NOW...
WHAT SHALL WE DO NEXT?

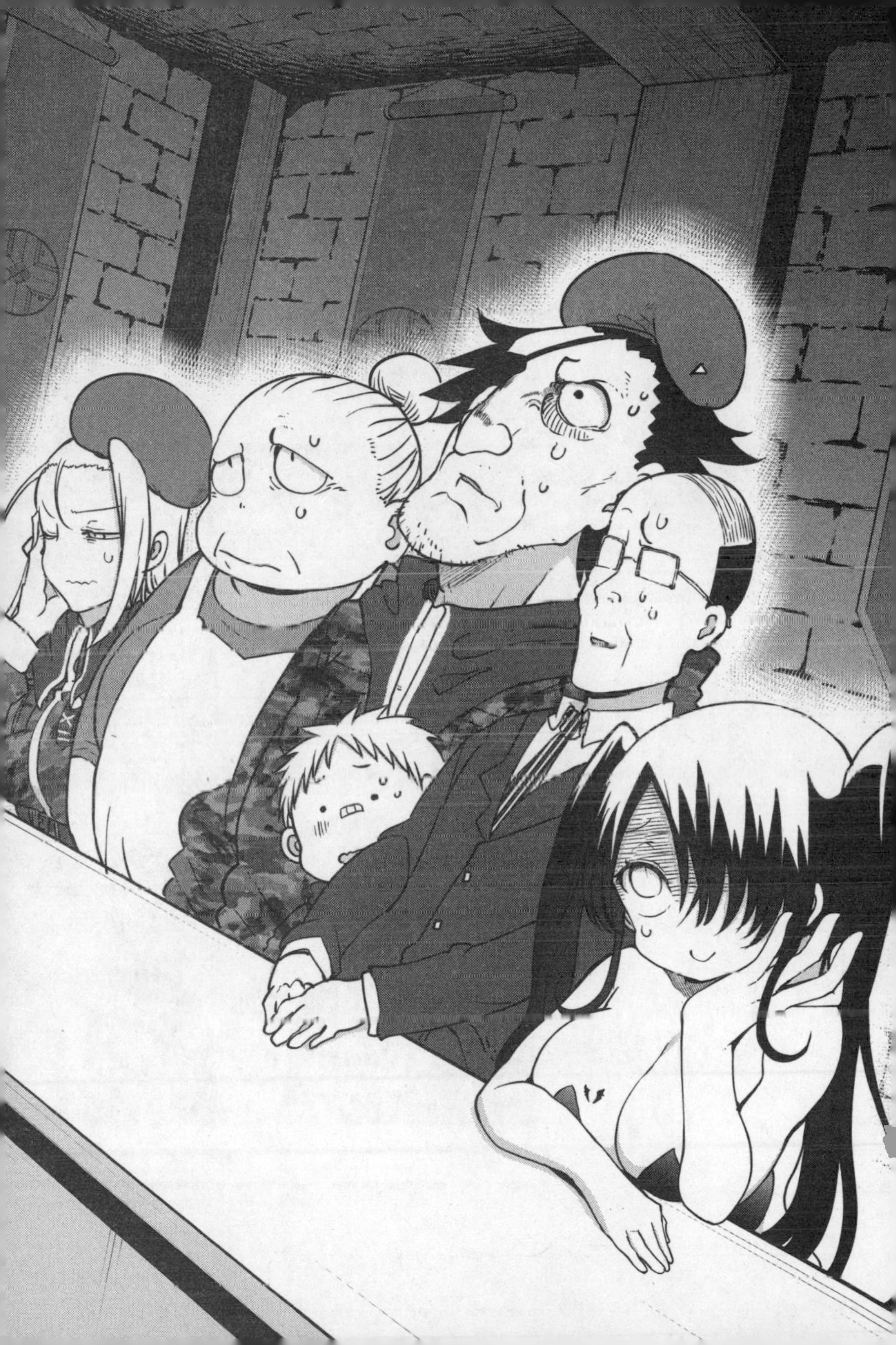

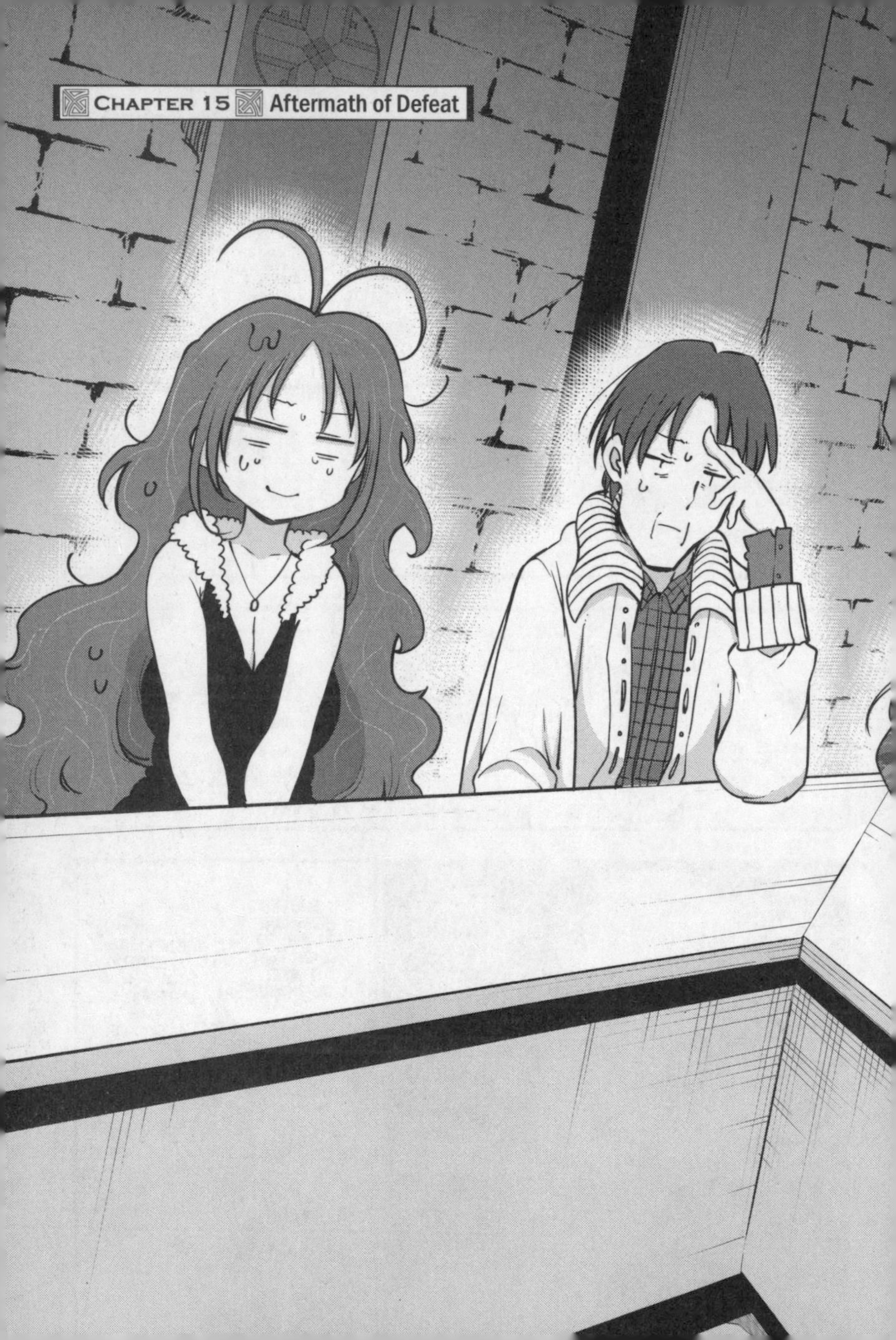
CHAPTER 15 Aftermath of Defeat

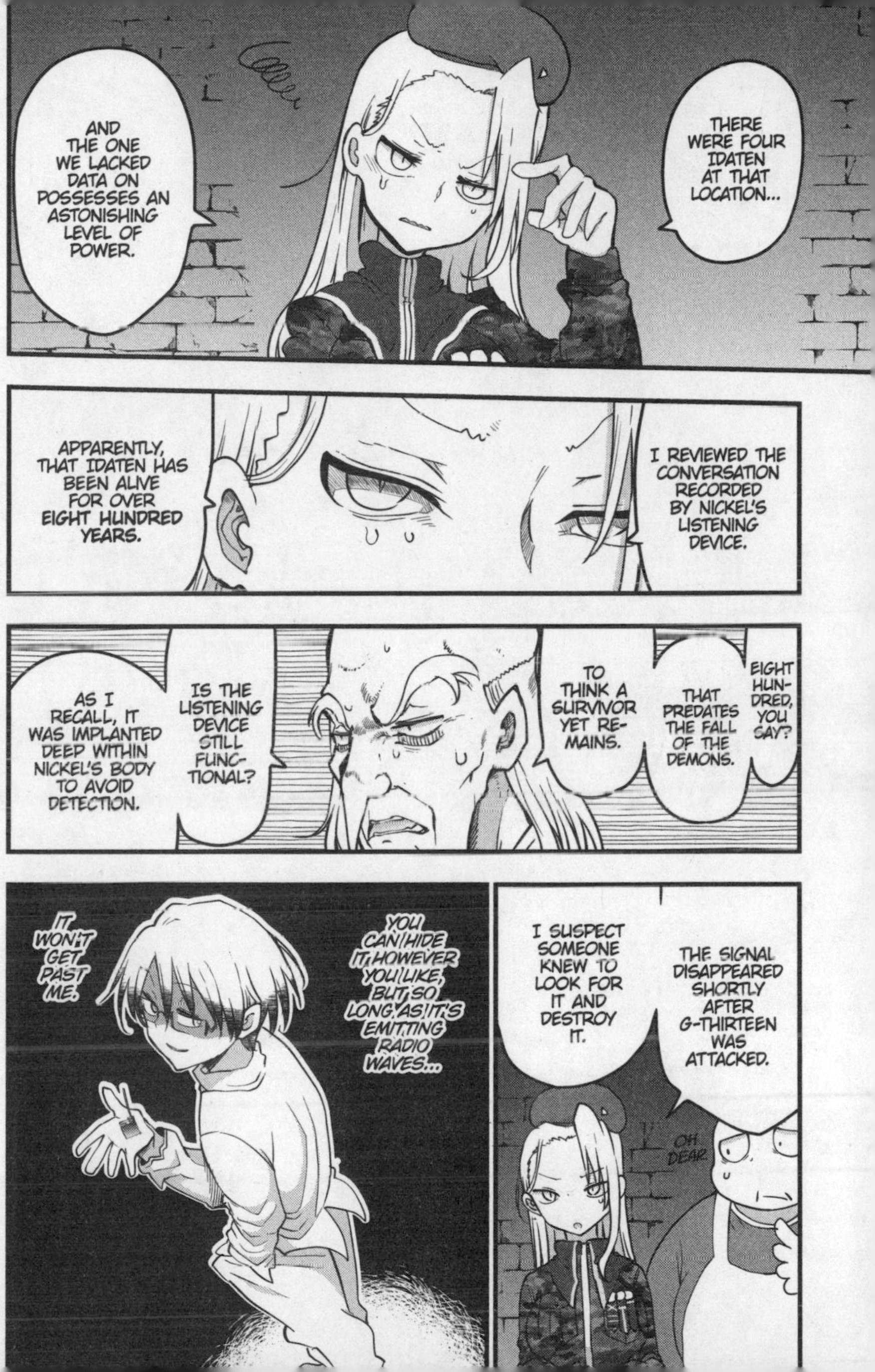

THERE WERE FOUR IDATEN AT THAT LOCATION...
AND THE ONE WE LACKED DATA ON POSSESSES AN ASTONISHING LEVEL OF POWER.
I REVIEWED THE CONVERSATION RECORDED BY NICKEL'S LISTENING DEVICE.
APPARENTLY, THAT IDATEN HAS BEEN ALIVE FOR OVER EIGHT HUNDRED YEARS.
EIGHT HUNDRED, YOU SAY?
THAT PREDATES THE FALL OF THE DEMONS.
TO THINK A SURVIVOR YET REMAINS.
IS THE LISTENING DEVICE STILL FUNCTIONAL?
AS I RECALL, IT WAS IMPLANTED DEEP WITHIN NICKEL'S BODY TO AVOID DETECTION.
THE SIGNAL DISAPPEARED SHORTLY AFTER G-THIRTEEN WAS ATTACKED.
I SUSPECT SOMEONE KNEW TO LOOK FOR IT AND DESTROY IT.
OH DEAR
YOU CAN HIDE IT HOWEVER YOU LIKE, BUT SO LONG AS IT'S EMITTING RADIO WAVES...
IT WON'T GET PAST ME.

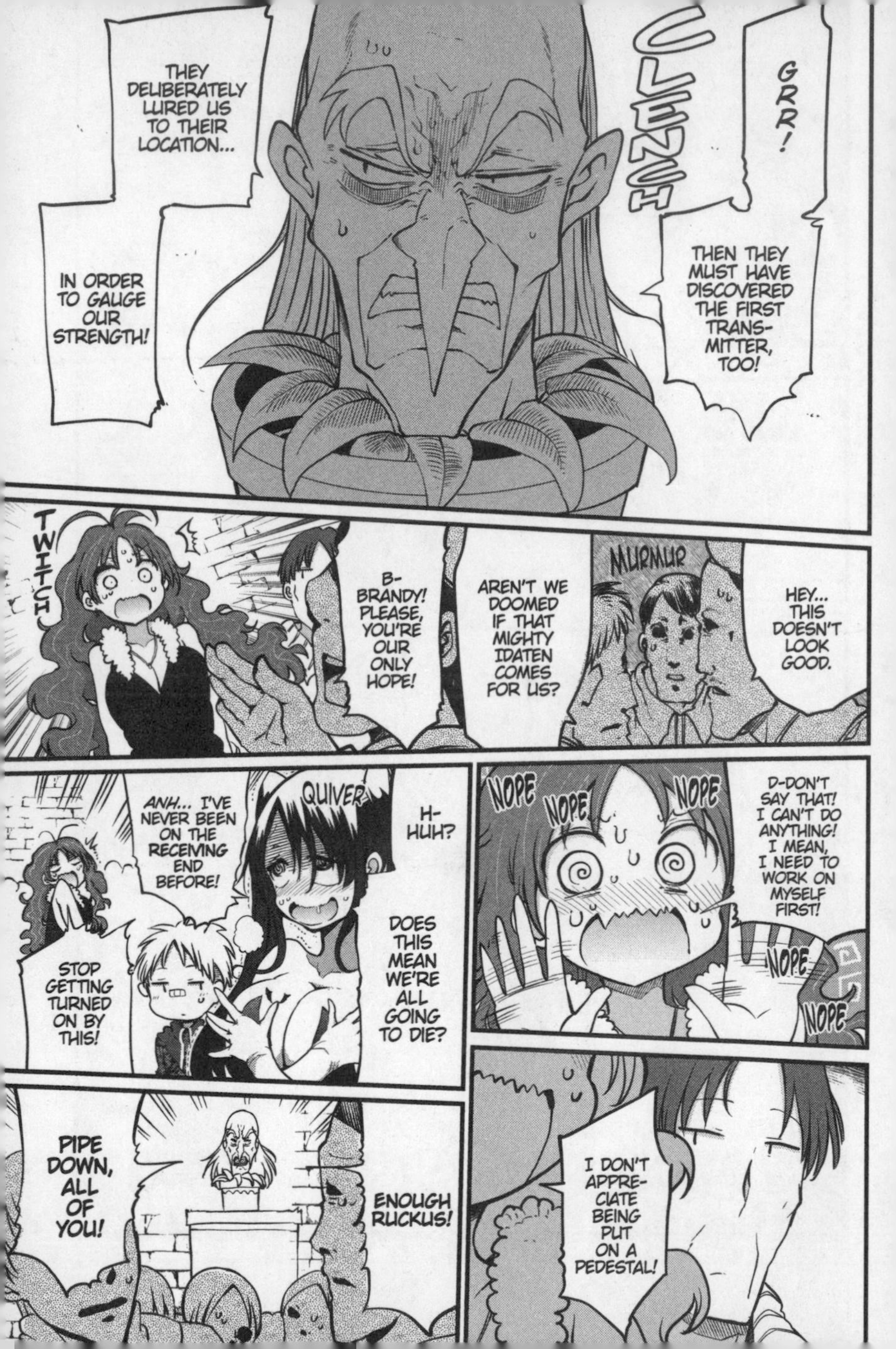
GRR!
CLENCH
THEN THEY MUST HAVE DISCOVERED THE FIRST TRANS-MITTER, TOO!
THEY DELIBERATELY LURED US TO THEIR LOCATION...
IN ORDER TO GAUGE OUR STRENGTH!
HEY... THIS DOESN'T LOOK GOOD.
MURMUR
AREN'T WE DOOMED IF THAT MIGHTY IDATEN COMES FOR US?
B-BRANDY! PLEASE, YOU'RE OUR ONLY HOPE!
TWITCH
D-DON'T SAY THAT! I CAN'T DO ANYTHING! I MEAN, I NEED TO WORK ON MYSELF FIRST!
NOPE
NOPE
NOPE
NOPE
NOPE
H-HUH?
QUIVER
ANH... I'VE NEVER BEEN ON THE RECEIVING END BEFORE!
DOES THIS MEAN WE'RE ALL GOING TO DIE?
STOP GETTING TURNED ON BY THIS!
I DON'T APPRE-CIATE BEING PUT ON A PEDESTAL!
ENOUGH RUCKUS!
PIPE DOWN, ALL OF YOU!

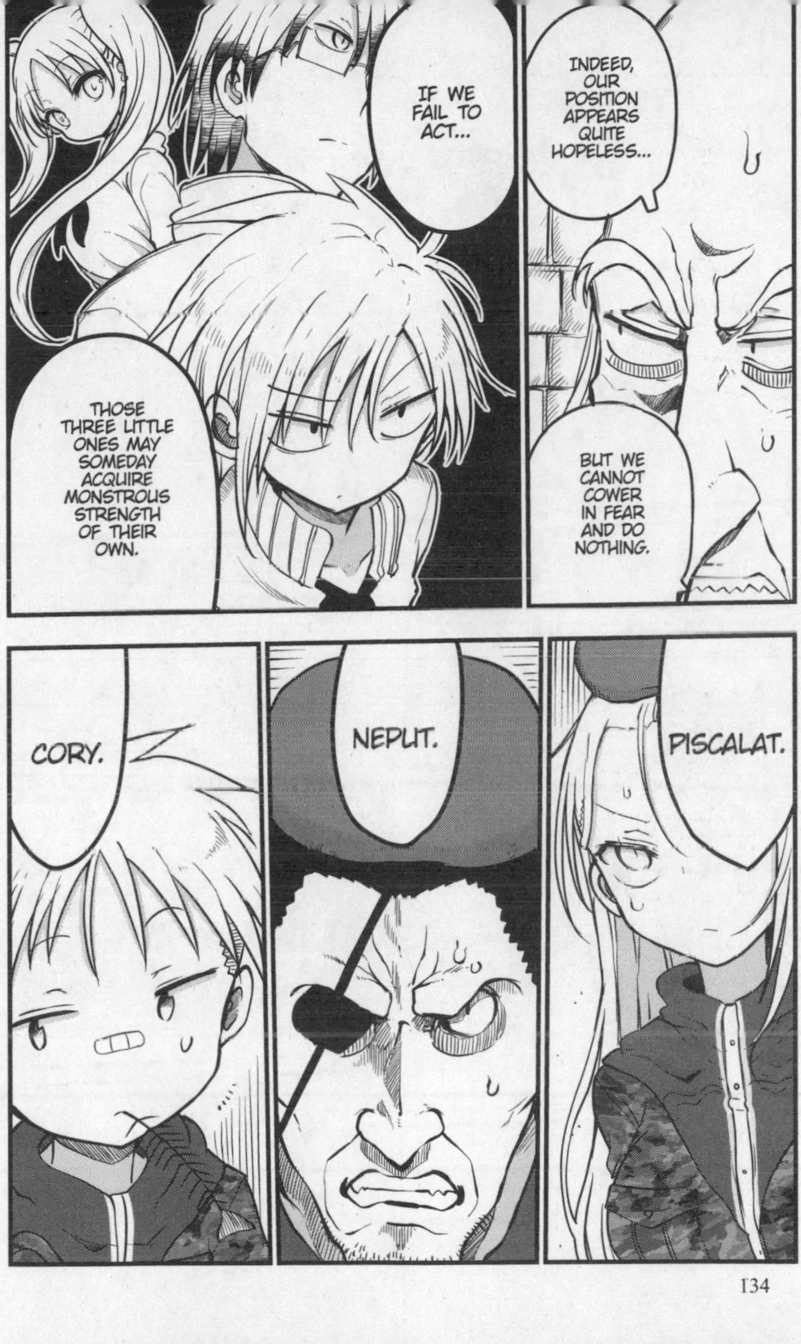
INDEED, OUR POSITION APPEARS QUITE HOPELESS...
BUT WE CANNOT COWER IN FEAR AND DO NOTHING.
IF WE FAIL TO ACT...
THOSE THREE LITTLE ONES MAY SOMEDAY ACQUIRE MONSTROUS STRENGTH OF THEIR OWN.
PISCALAT.
NEPUT.
CORY.

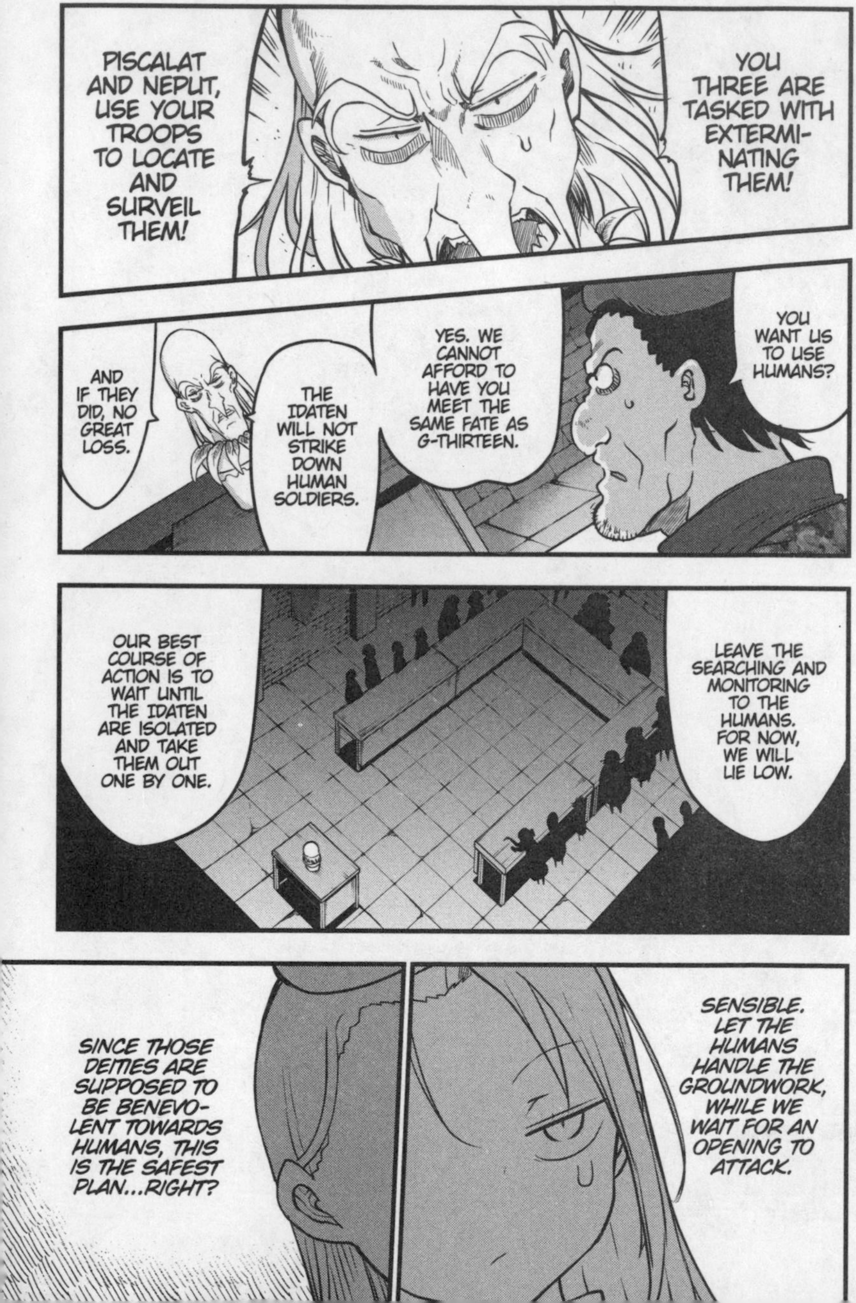
YOU THREE ARE TASKED WITH EXTERMINATING THEM!
PISCALAT AND NEPUT, USE YOUR TROOPS TO LOCATE AND SURVEIL THEM!
YOU WANT US TO USE HUMANS?
YES. WE CANNOT AFFORD TO HAVE YOU MEET THE SAME FATE AS G-THIRTEEN.
THE IDATEN WILL NOT STRIKE DOWN HUMAN SOLDIERS.
AND IF THEY DID, NO GREAT LOSS.
LEAVE THE SEARCHING AND MONITORING TO THE HUMANS. FOR NOW, WE WILL LIE LOW.
OUR BEST COURSE OF ACTION IS TO WAIT UNTIL THE IDATEN ARE ISOLATED AND TAKE THEM OUT ONE BY ONE.
SENSIBLE. LET THE HUMANS HANDLE THE GROUNDWORK, WHILE WE WAIT FOR AN OPENING TO ATTACK.
SINCE THOSE DEITIES ARE SUPPOSED TO BE BENEVOLENT TOWARDS HUMANS, THIS IS THE SAFEST PLAN...RIGHT?

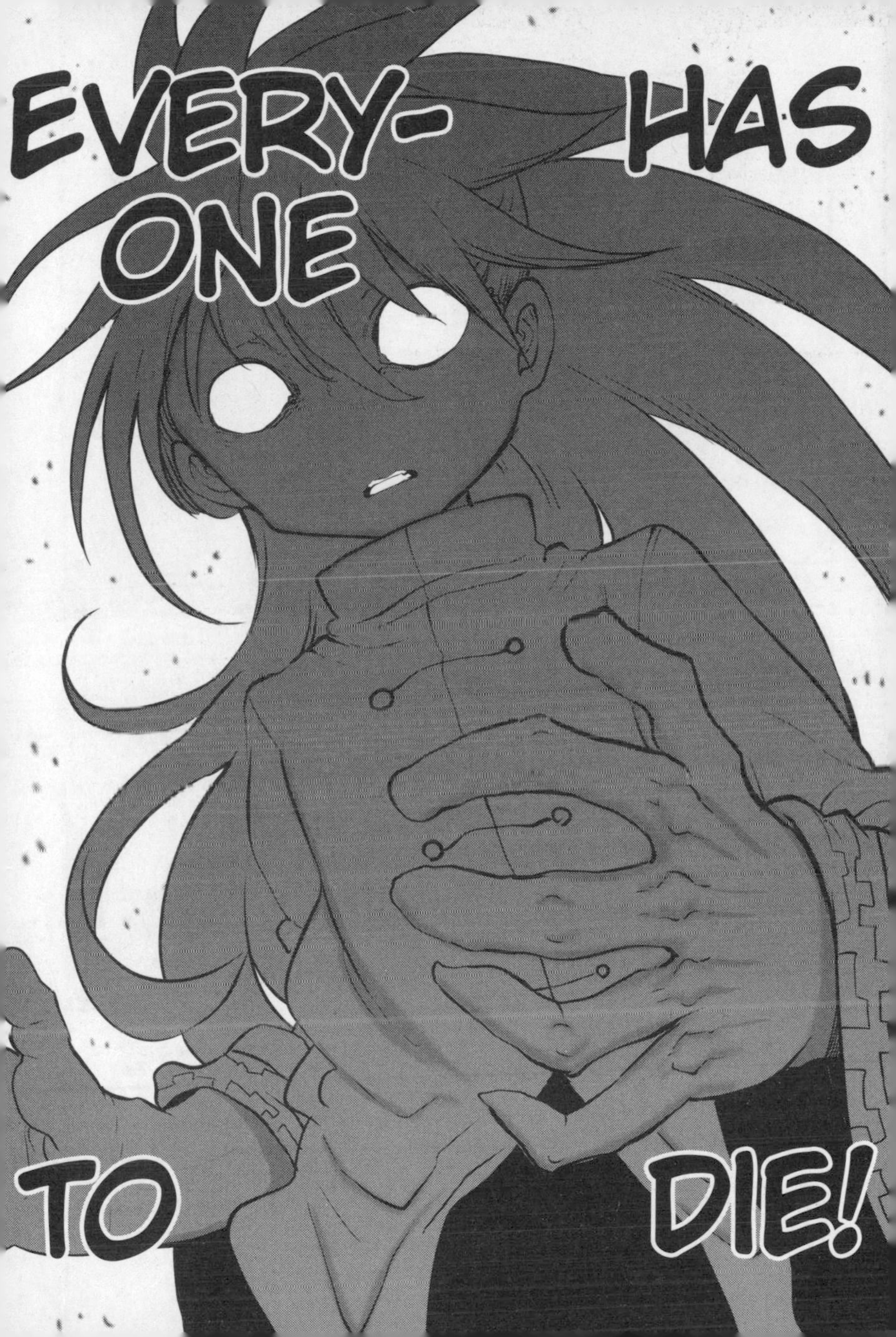

EVERY-ONE HAS TO DIE!

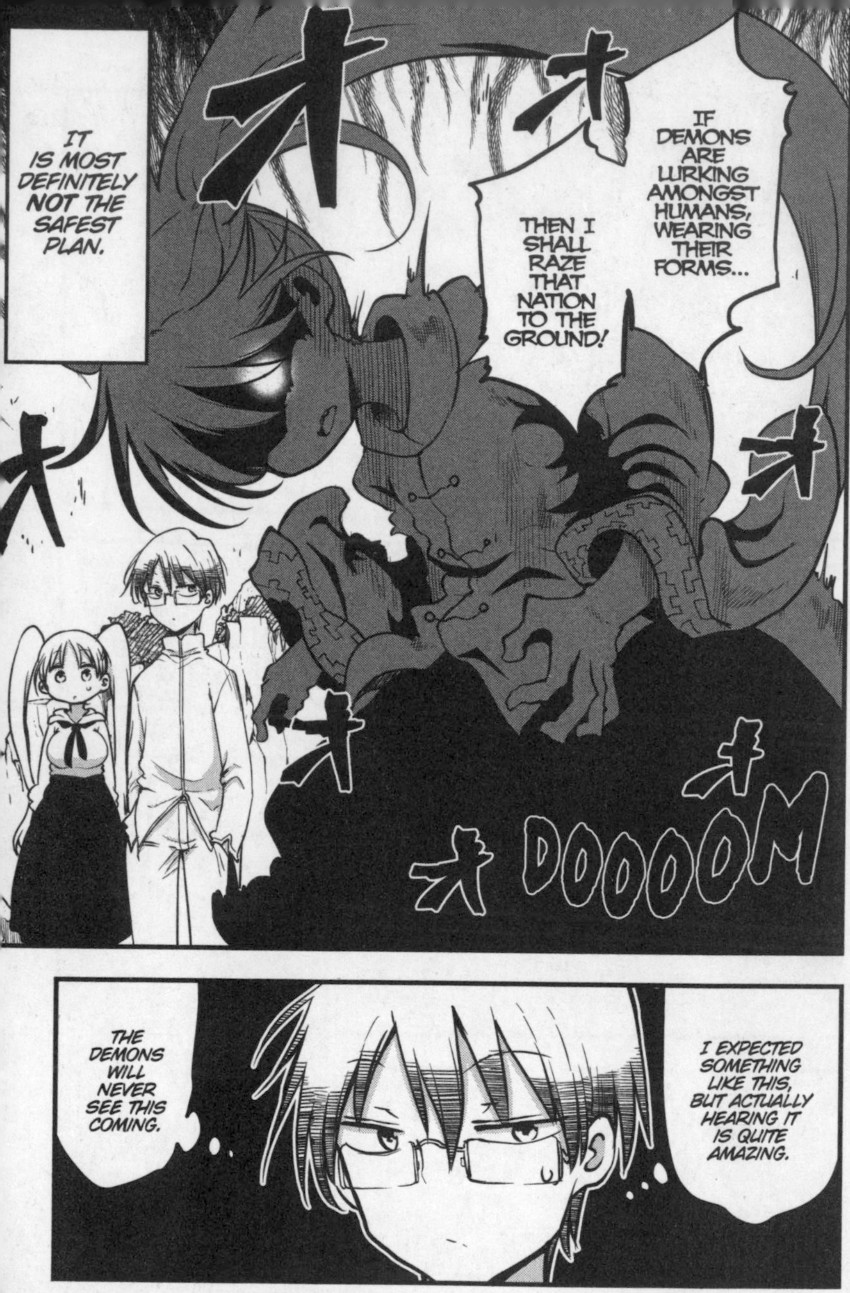
IF DEMONS ARE LURKING AMONGST HUMANS, WEARING THEIR FORMS...
THEN I SHALL RAZE THAT NATION TO THE GROUND!
IT IS MOST DEFINITELY NOT THE SAFEST PLAN.
DOOOOM
I EXPECTED SOMETHING LIKE THIS, BUT ACTUALLY HEARING IT IS QUITE AMAZING.
THE DEMONS WILL NEVER SEE THIS COMING.

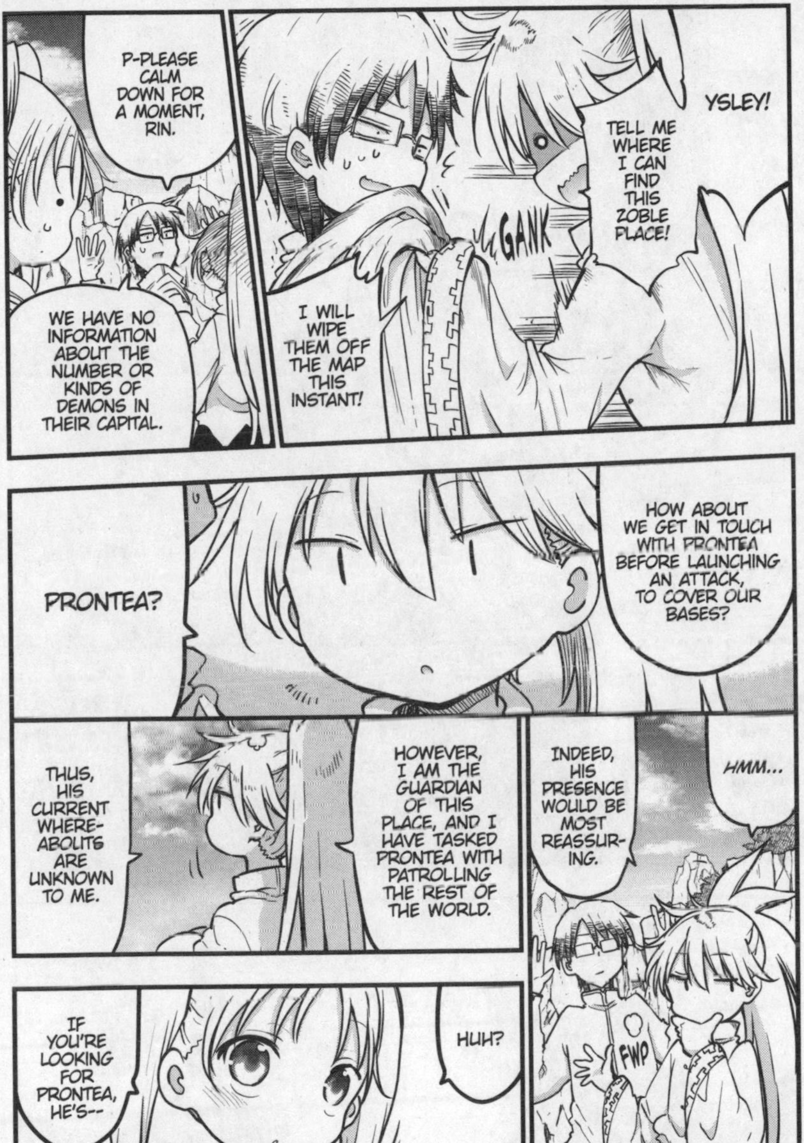
YSLEY!
TELL ME WHERE I CAN FIND THIS ZOBLE PLACE!
GANK
I WILL WIPE THEM OFF THE MAP THIS INSTANT!
P-PLEASE CALM DOWN FOR A MOMENT, RIN.
WE HAVE NO INFORMATION ABOUT THE NUMBER OR KINDS OF DEMONS IN THEIR CAPITAL.
HOW ABOUT WE GET IN TOUCH WITH PRONTEA BEFORE LAUNCHING AN ATTACK, TO COVER OUR BASES?
PRONTEA?
HMM...
INDEED, HIS PRESENCE WOULD BE MOST REASSURING.
FWP
HOWEVER, I AM THE GUARDIAN OF THIS PLACE, AND I HAVE TASKED PRONTEA WITH PATROLLING THE REST OF THE WORLD.
THUS, HIS CURRENT WHERE-ABOUTS ARE UNKNOWN TO ME.
HUH?
IF YOU'RE LOOKING FOR PRONTEA, HE'S--

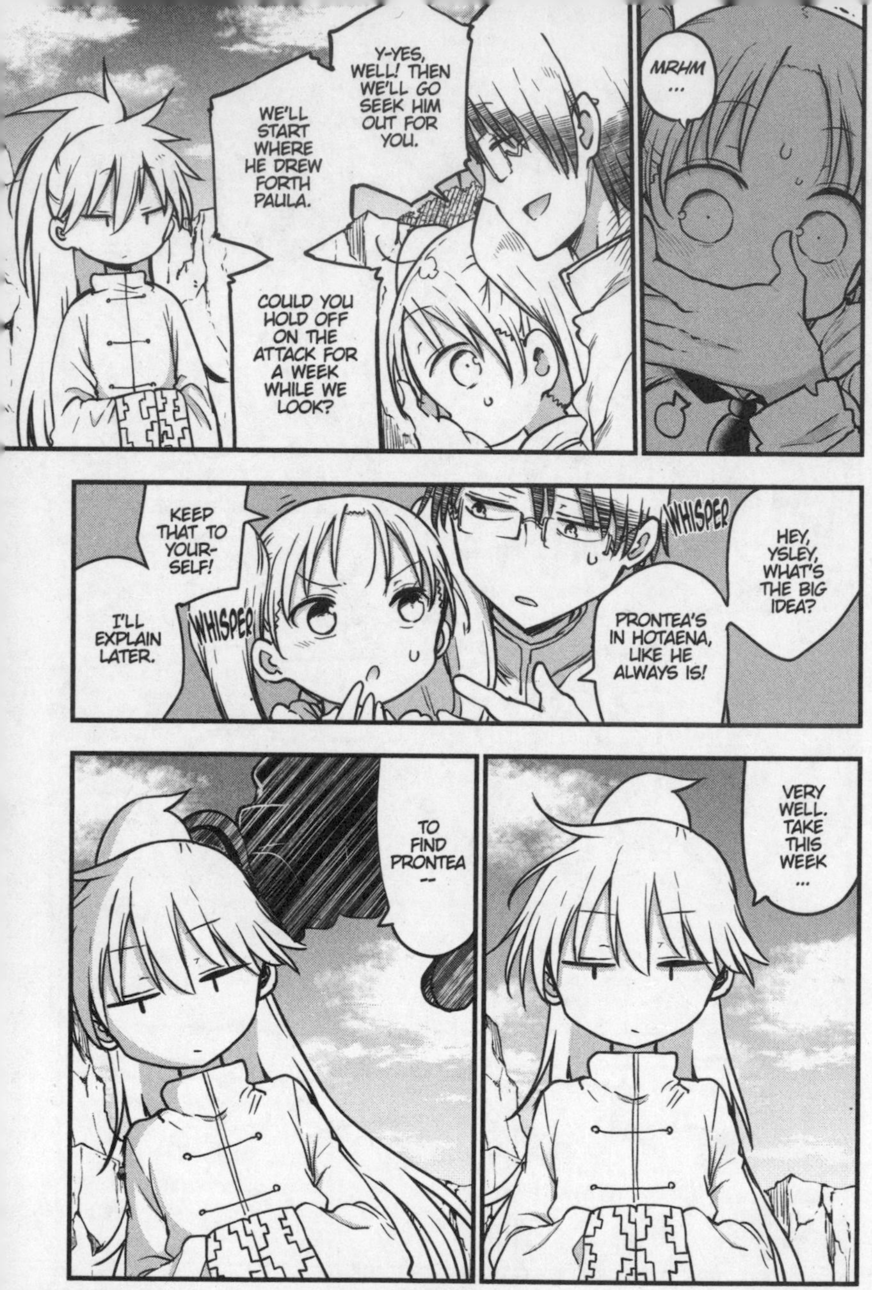
MRHM ...
Y-YES, WELL! THEN WE'LL GO SEEK HIM OUT FOR YOU.
WE'LL START WHERE HE DREW FORTH PAULA.
COULD YOU HOLD OFF ON THE ATTACK FOR A WEEK WHILE WE LOOK?
HEY, YSLEY, WHAT'S THE BIG IDEA?
WHISPER
PRONTEA'S IN HOTAENA, LIKE HE ALWAYS IS!
KEEP THAT TO YOUR-SELF!
WHISPER
I'LL EXPLAIN LATER.
VERY WELL. TAKE THIS WEEK ...
TO FIND PRONTEA --

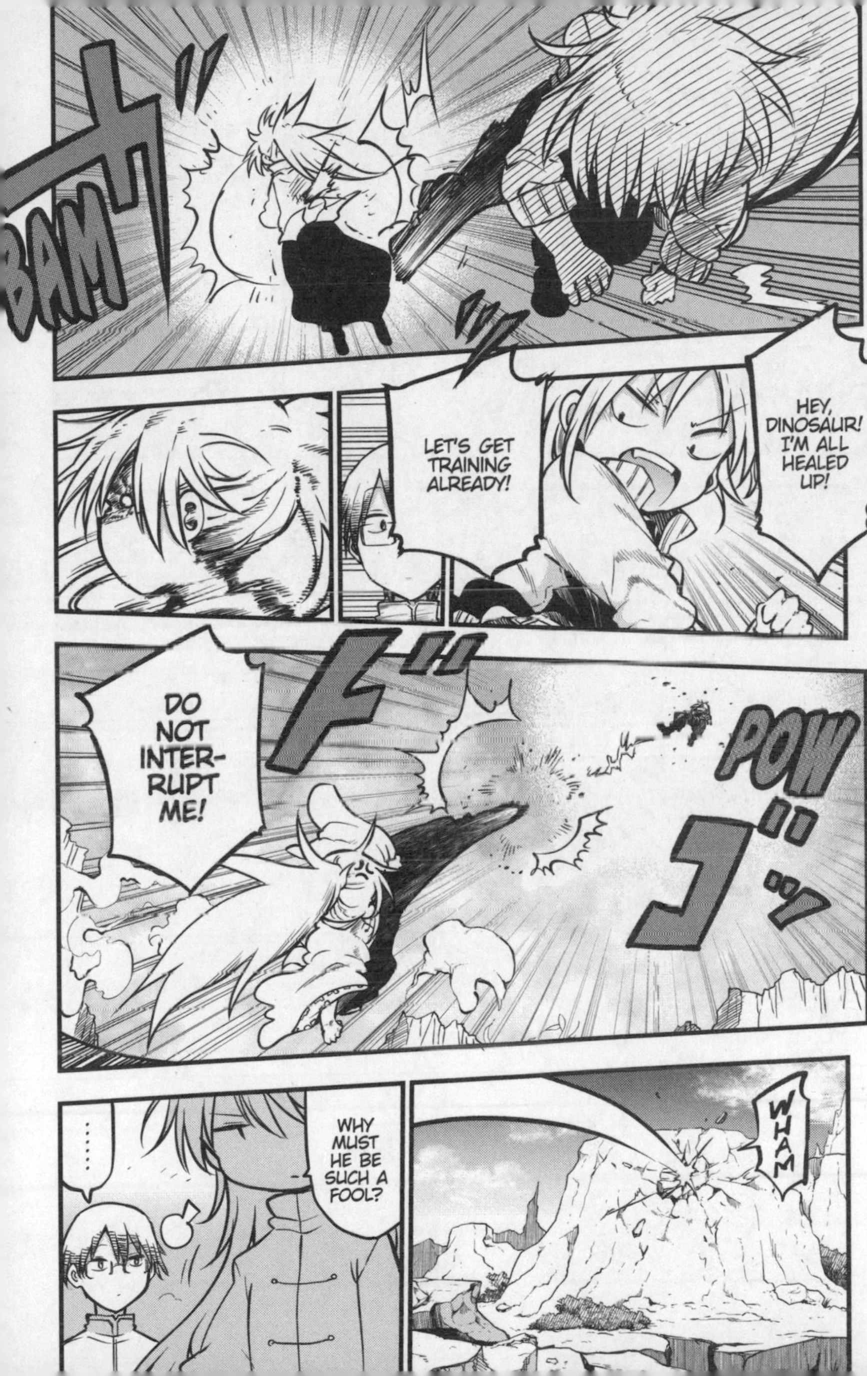
BAM
HEY, DINOSAUR! I'M ALL HEALED UP!
LET'S GET TRAINING ALREADY!
POW
DO NOT INTERRUPT ME!
WHAM
WHY MUST HE BE SUCH A FOOL?
......

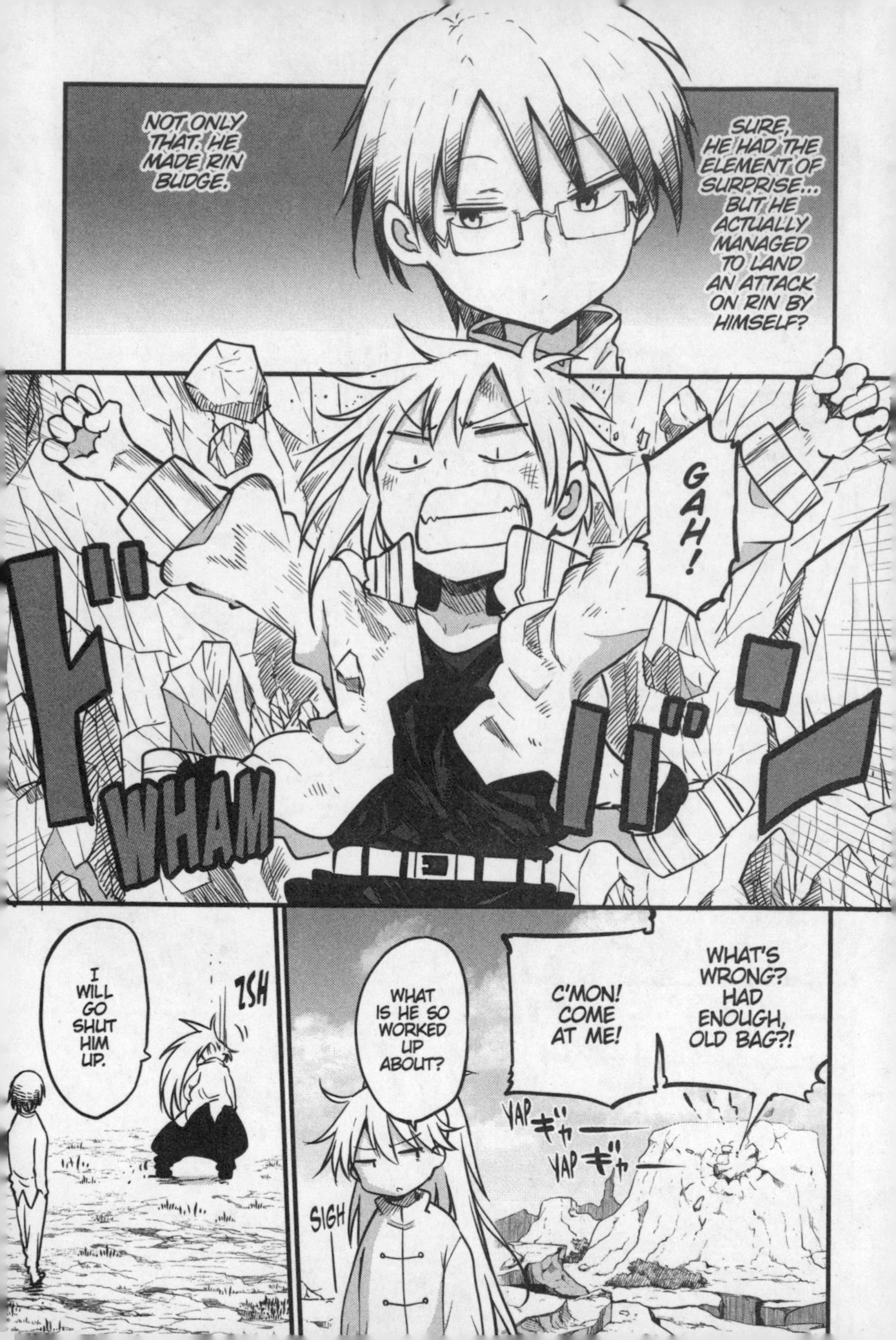
SURE, HE HAD THE ELEMENT OF SURPRISE... BUT HE ACTUALLY MANAGED TO LAND AN ATTACK ON RIN BY HIMSELF?
NOT ONLY THAT. HE MADE RIN BUDGE.
GAH!
WHAM
WHAT'S WRONG? HAD ENOUGH, OLD BAG?!
C'MON! COME AT ME!
YAP ギャー
YAP ギャー
WHAT IS HE SO WORKED UP ABOUT?
SIGH
ZSH
I WILL GO SHUT HIM UP.

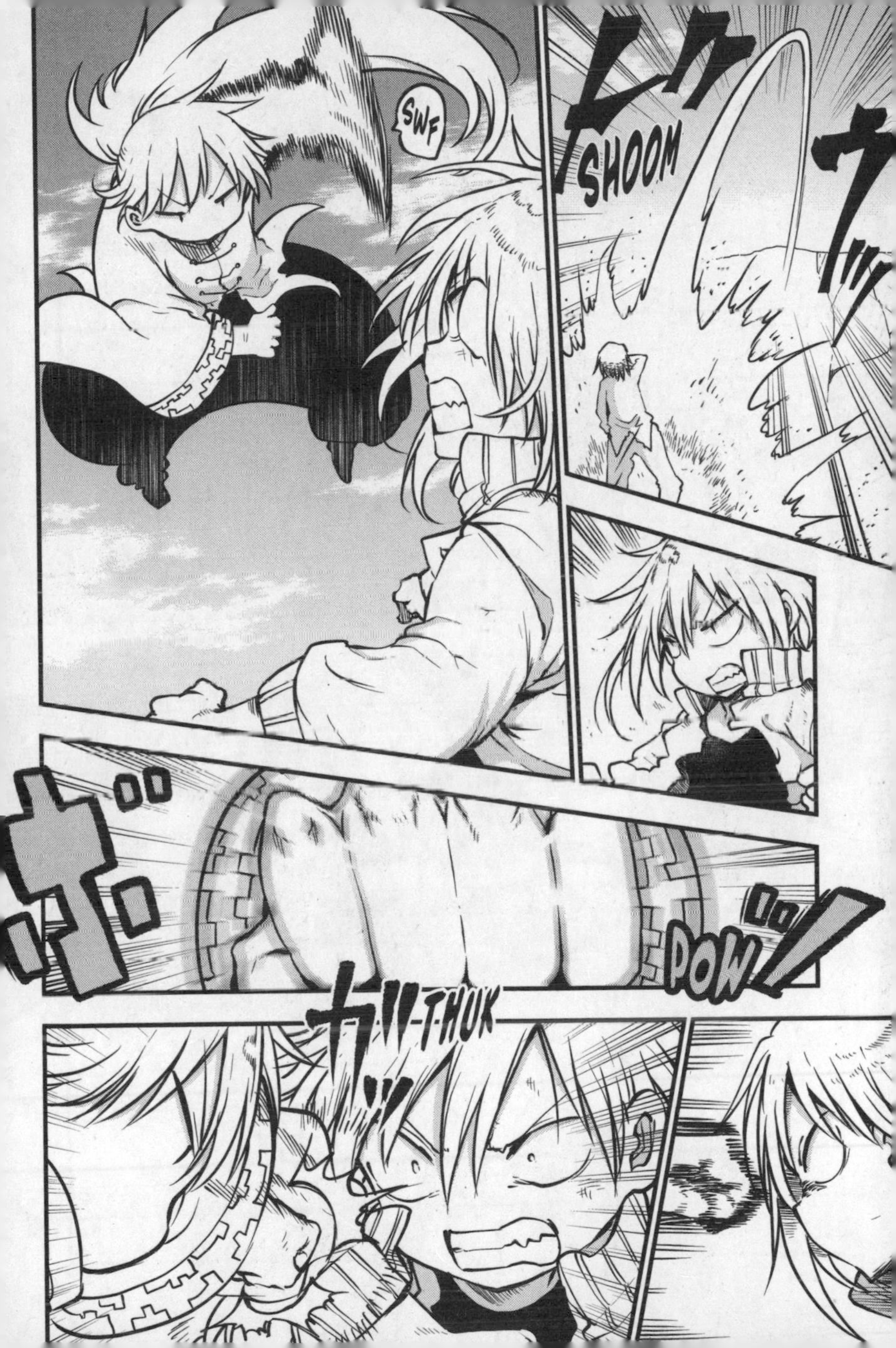
SHOOM
SWF
POW!!
T-THUK

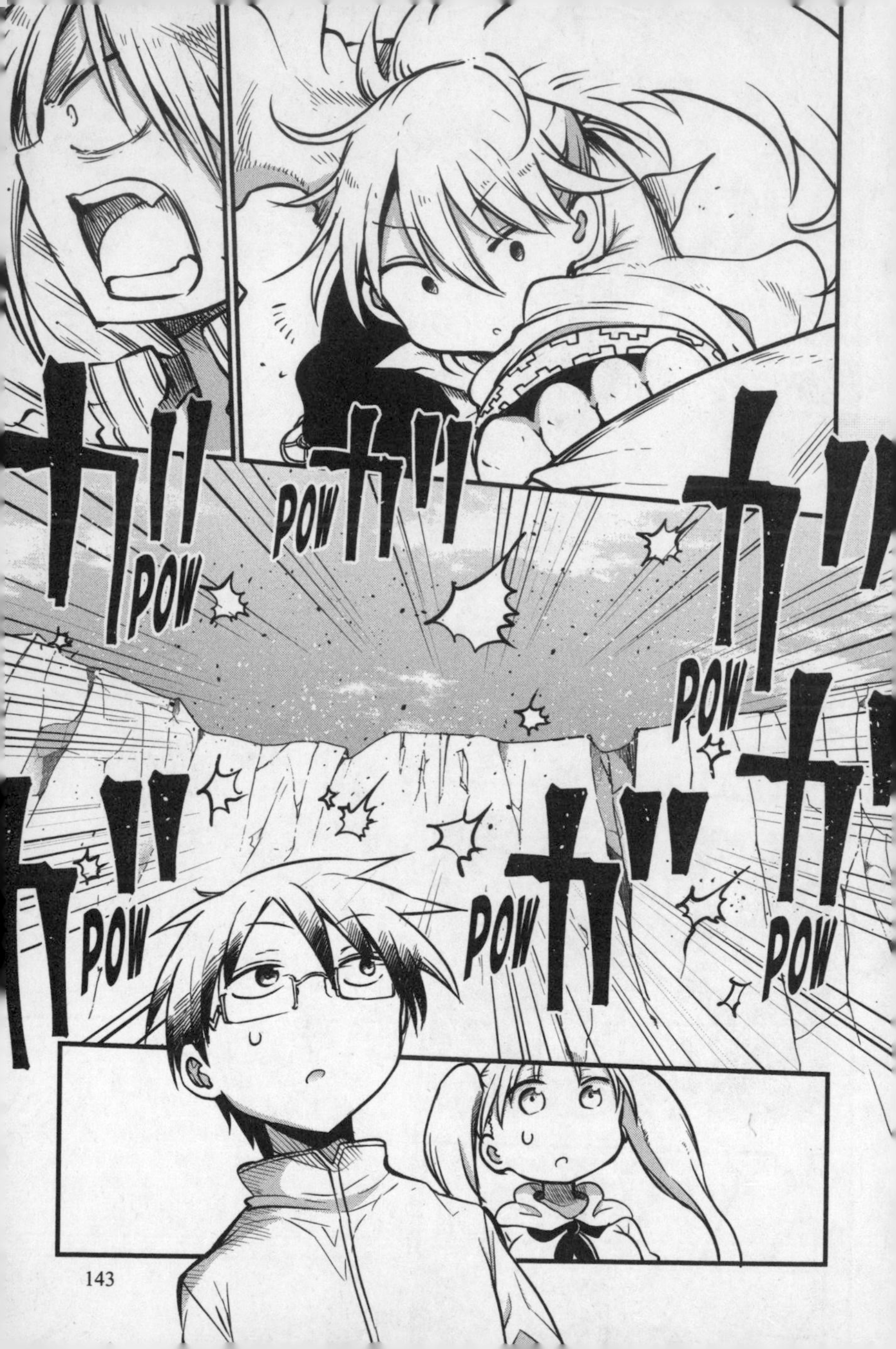

カッ
POW
カッ
POW
カッ
POW
カ
POW
カッ
POW
カッ
POW

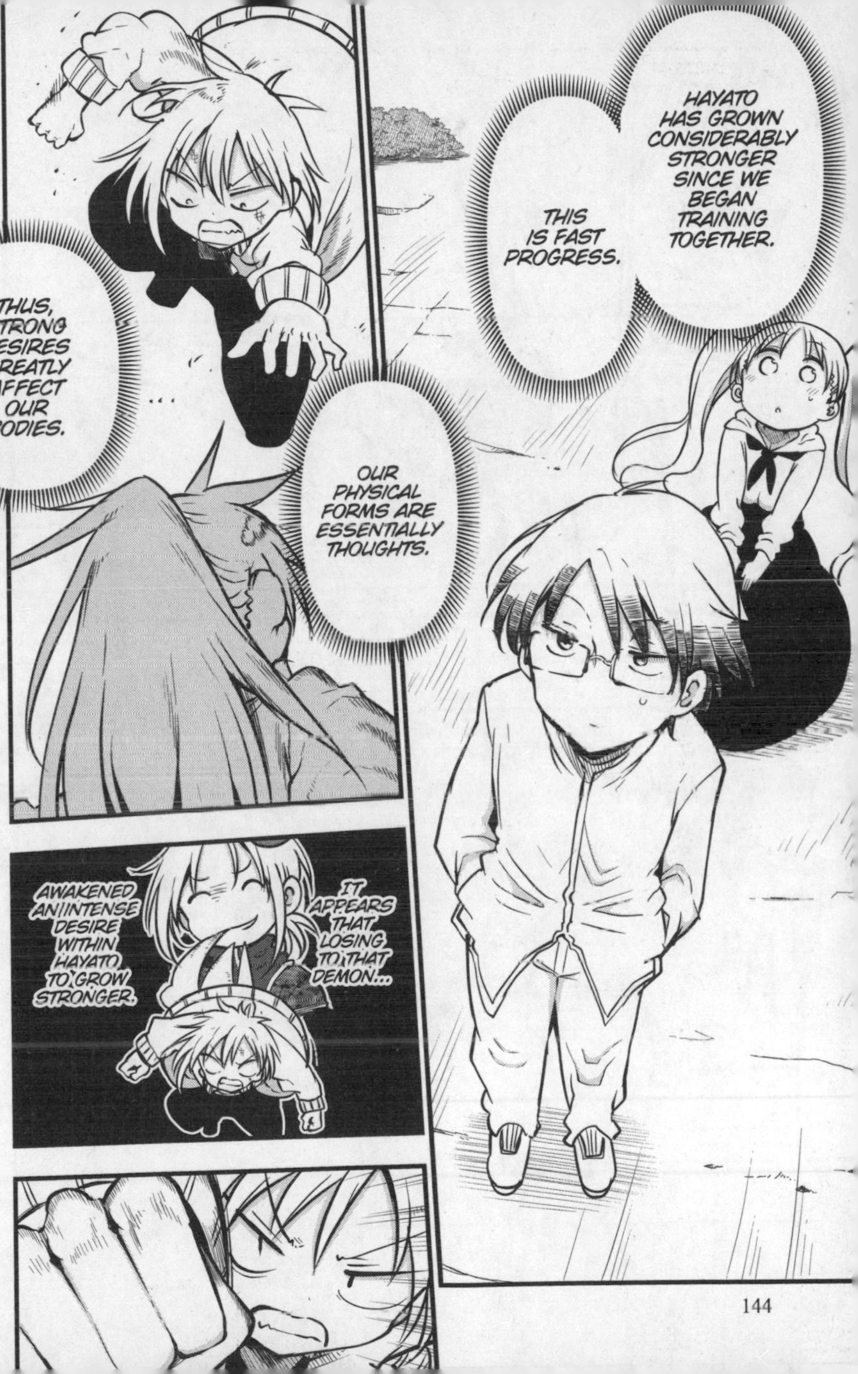
HAYATO HAS GROWN CONSIDERABLY STRONGER SINCE WE BEGAN TRAINING TOGETHER.
THIS IS FAST PROGRESS.
OUR PHYSICAL FORMS ARE ESSENTIALLY THOUGHTS.
THUS, STRONG DESIRES GREATLY AFFECT OUR BODIES.
...
IT APPEARS THAT LOSING TO THAT DEMON...
AWAKENED AN INTENSE DESIRE WITHIN HAYATO TO GROW STRONGER.

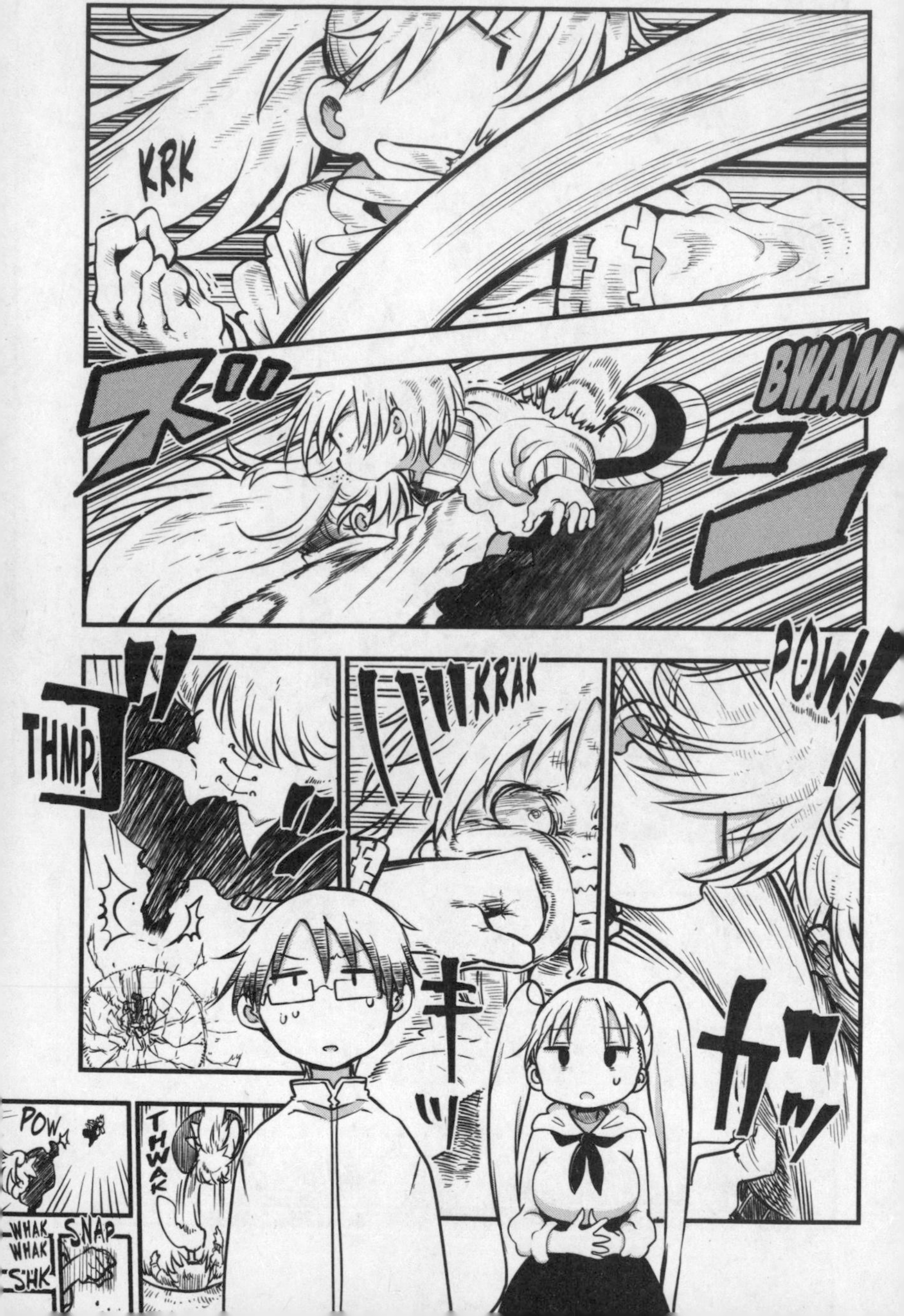
KRK
BWAM
POW
KRAK
THMP
THWAK
SNAP
POW
WHAK
WHAK
SHK

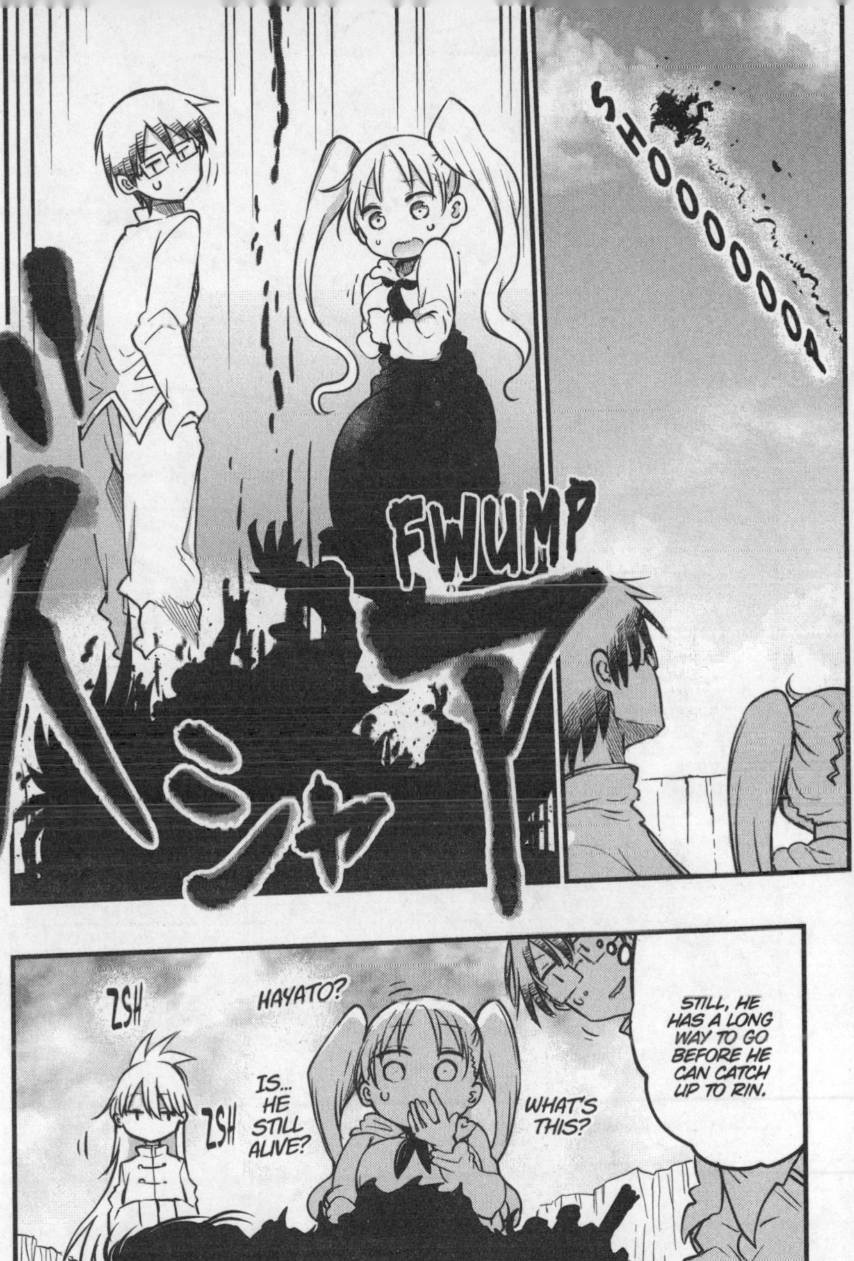
SHOOOOOOA
FWUMP
バシャア
STILL, HE HAS A LONG WAY TO GO BEFORE HE CAN CATCH UP TO RIN.
WHAT'S THIS?
HAYATO?
IS... HE STILL ALIVE?
ZSH
ZSH

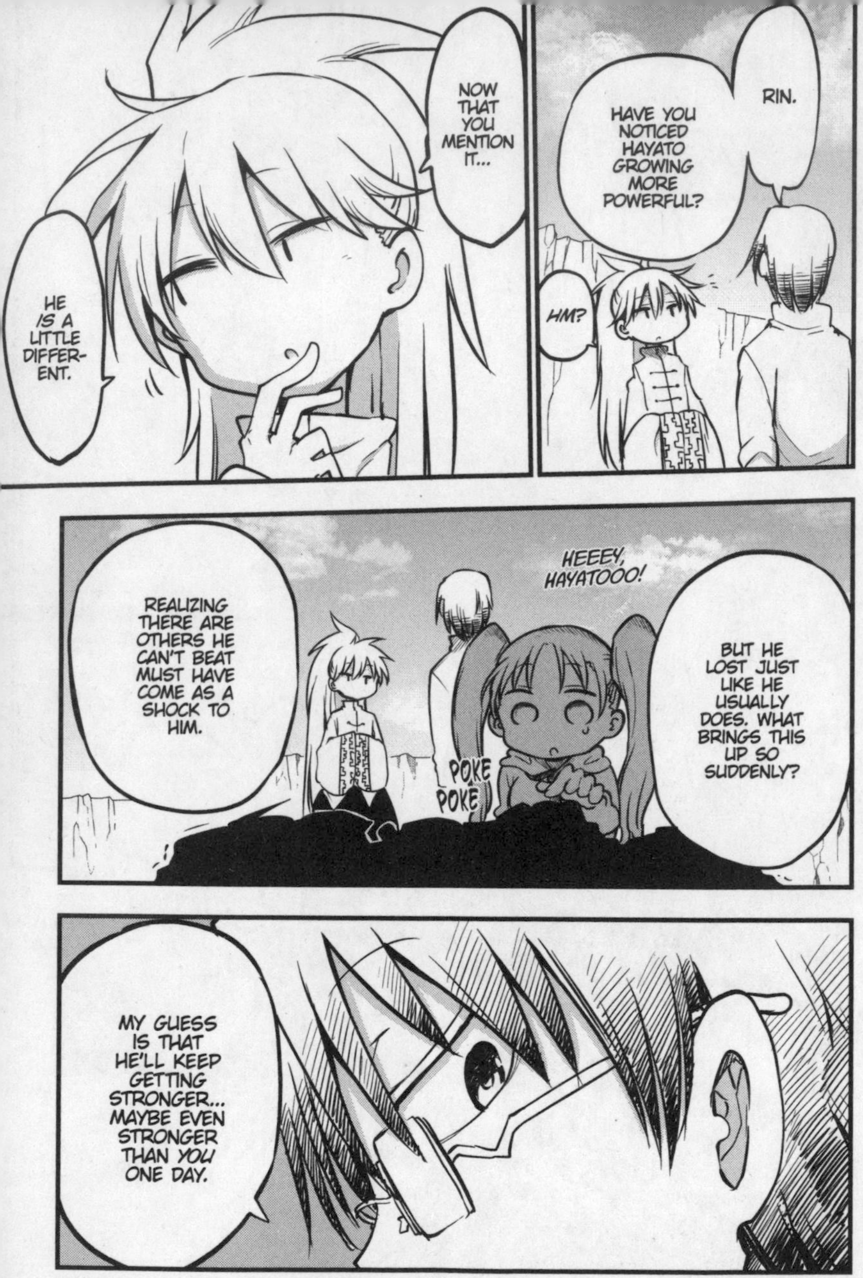
RIN.
HAVE YOU NOTICED HAYATO GROWING MORE POWERFUL?
HM?
NOW THAT YOU MENTION IT...
HE IS A LITTLE DIFFERENT.
HEEEY, HAYATOOO!
BUT HE LOST JUST LIKE HE USUALLY DOES. WHAT BRINGS THIS UP SO SUDDENLY?
POKE POKE
REALIZING THERE ARE OTHERS HE CAN'T BEAT MUST HAVE COME AS A SHOCK TO HIM.
MY GUESS IS THAT HE'LL KEEP GETTING STRONGER... MAYBE EVEN STRONGER THAN *YOU* ONE DAY.

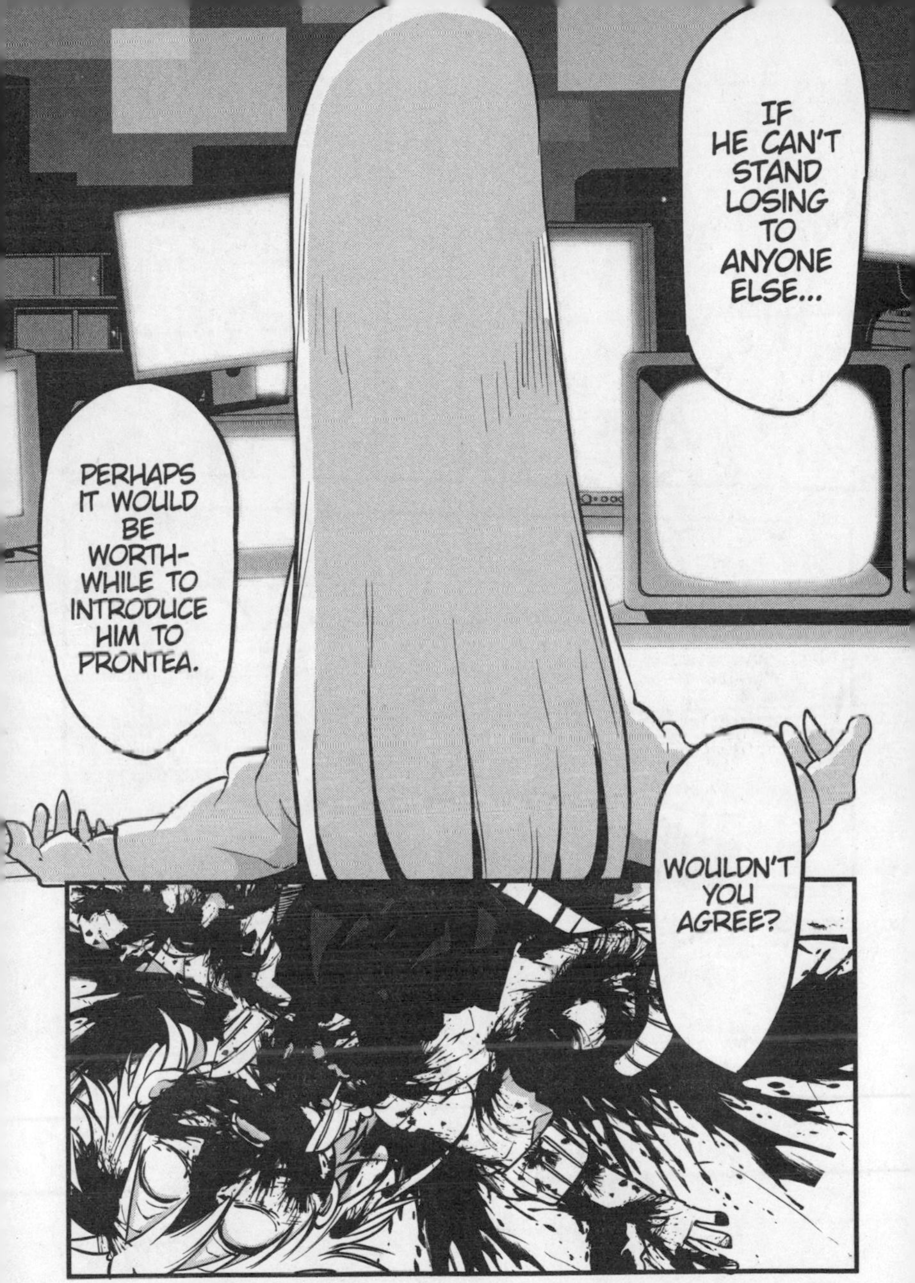
IF HE CAN'T STAND LOSING TO ANYONE ELSE...
PERHAPS IT WOULD BE WORTH-WHILE TO INTRODUCE HIM TO PRONTEA.
WOULDN'T YOU AGREE?

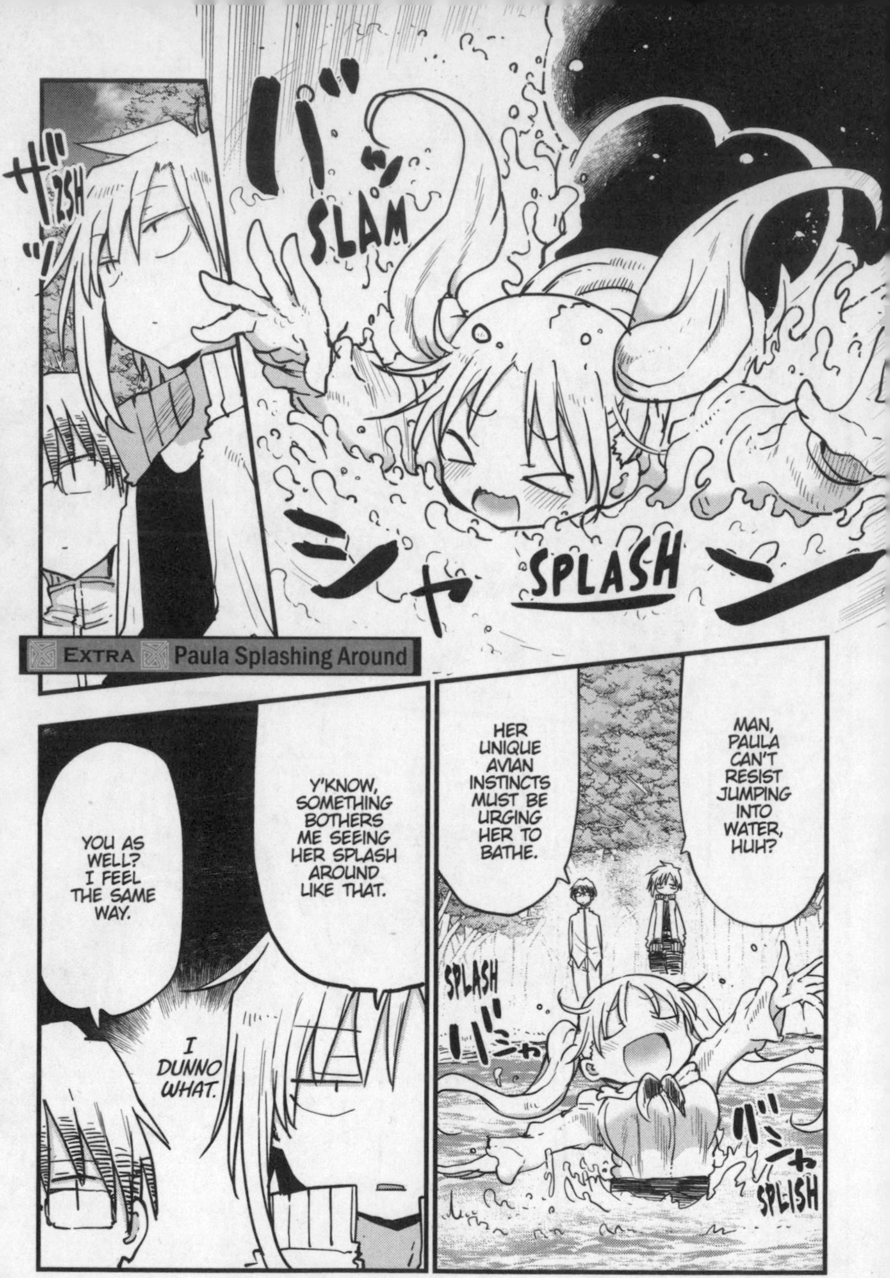
SLAM
ZSH
SPLASH
EXTRA Paula Splashing Around
MAN, PAULA CAN'T RESIST JUMPING INTO WATER, HUH?
HER UNIQUE AVIAN INSTINCTS MUST BE URGING HER TO BATHE.
SPLASH
SPLISH
Y'KNOW, SOMETHING BOTHERS ME SEEING HER SPLASH AROUND LIKE THAT.
YOU AS WELL? I FEEL THE SAME WAY.
I DUNNO WHAT.

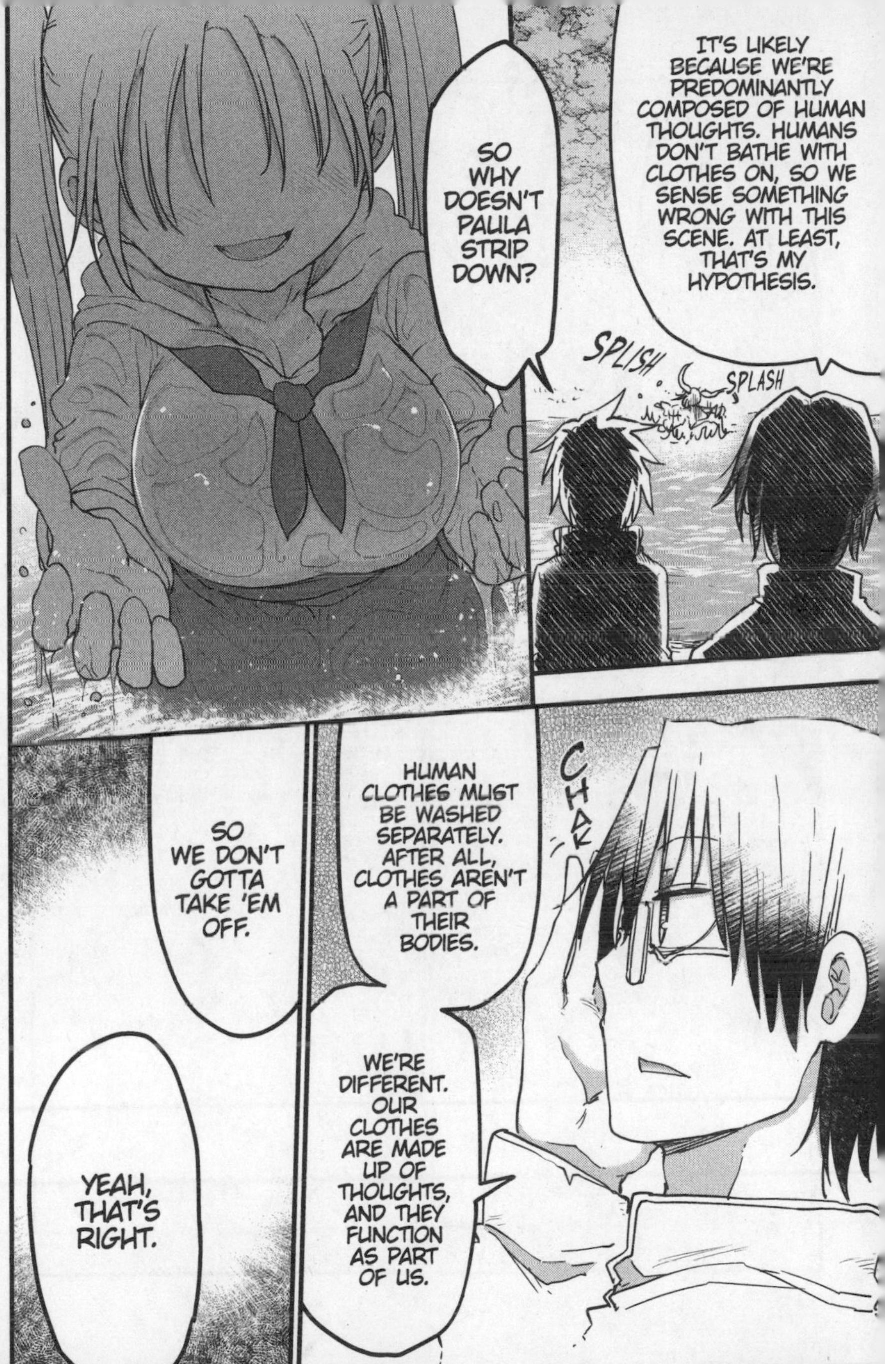
IT'S LIKELY BECAUSE WE'RE PREDOMINANTLY COMPOSED OF HUMAN THOUGHTS. HUMANS DON'T BATHE WITH CLOTHES ON, SO WE SENSE SOMETHING WRONG WITH THIS SCENE. AT LEAST, THAT'S MY HYPOTHESIS.
SPLISH
SPLASH
SO WHY DOESN'T PAULA STRIP DOWN?
CHAK
HUMAN CLOTHES MUST BE WASHED SEPARATELY. AFTER ALL, CLOTHES AREN'T A PART OF THEIR BODIES.
WE'RE DIFFERENT. OUR CLOTHES ARE MADE UP OF THOUGHTS, AND THEY FUNCTION AS PART OF US.
SO WE DON'T GOTTA TAKE 'EM OFF.
YEAH, THAT'S RIGHT.

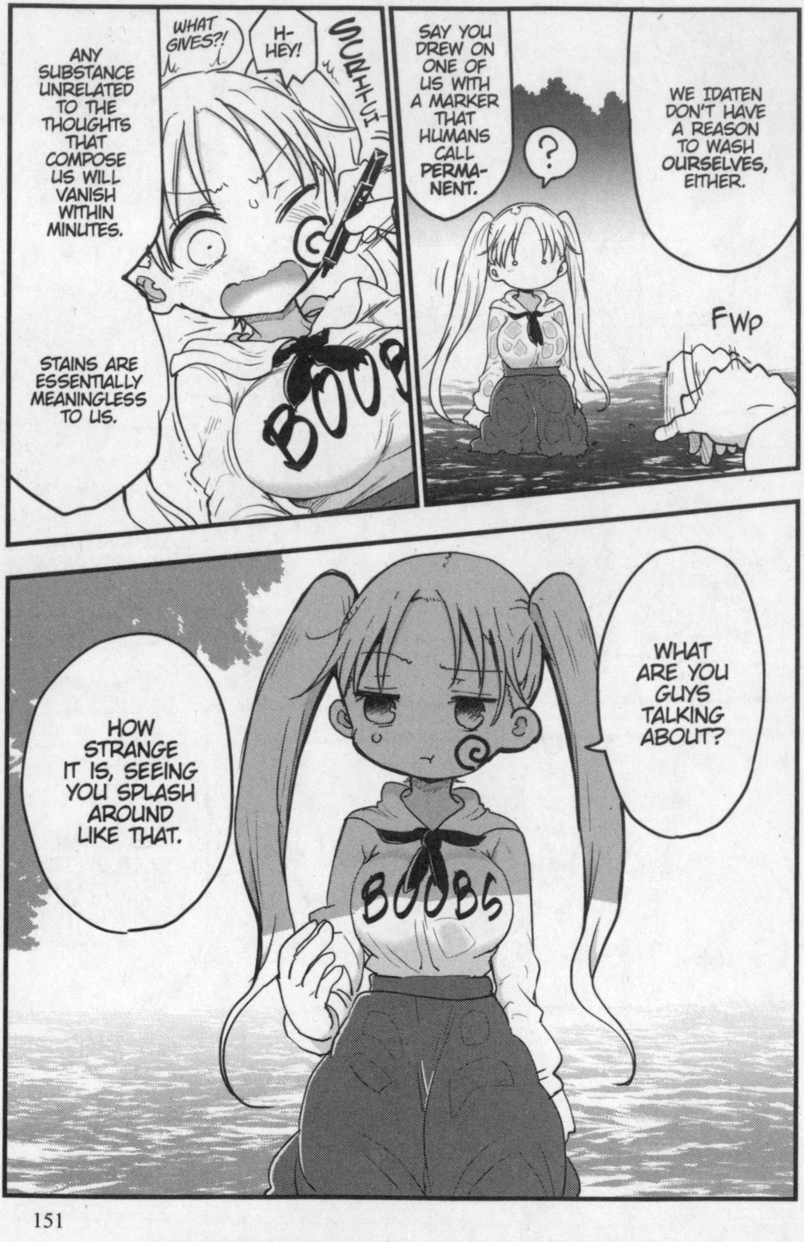
WE IDATEN DON'T HAVE A REASON TO WASH OURSELVES, EITHER.
FWP
SAY YOU DREW ON ONE OF US WITH A MARKER THAT HUMANS CALL PERMANENT.
?
SCRITCH
H-HEY!
WHAT GIVES?!
BOOB
ANY SUBSTANCE UNRELATED TO THE THOUGHTS THAT COMPOSE US WILL VANISH WITHIN MINUTES.
STAINS ARE ESSENTIALLY MEANINGLESS TO US.
WHAT ARE YOU GUYS TALKING ABOUT?
BOOBS
HOW STRANGE IT IS, SEEING YOU SPLASH AROUND LIKE THAT.

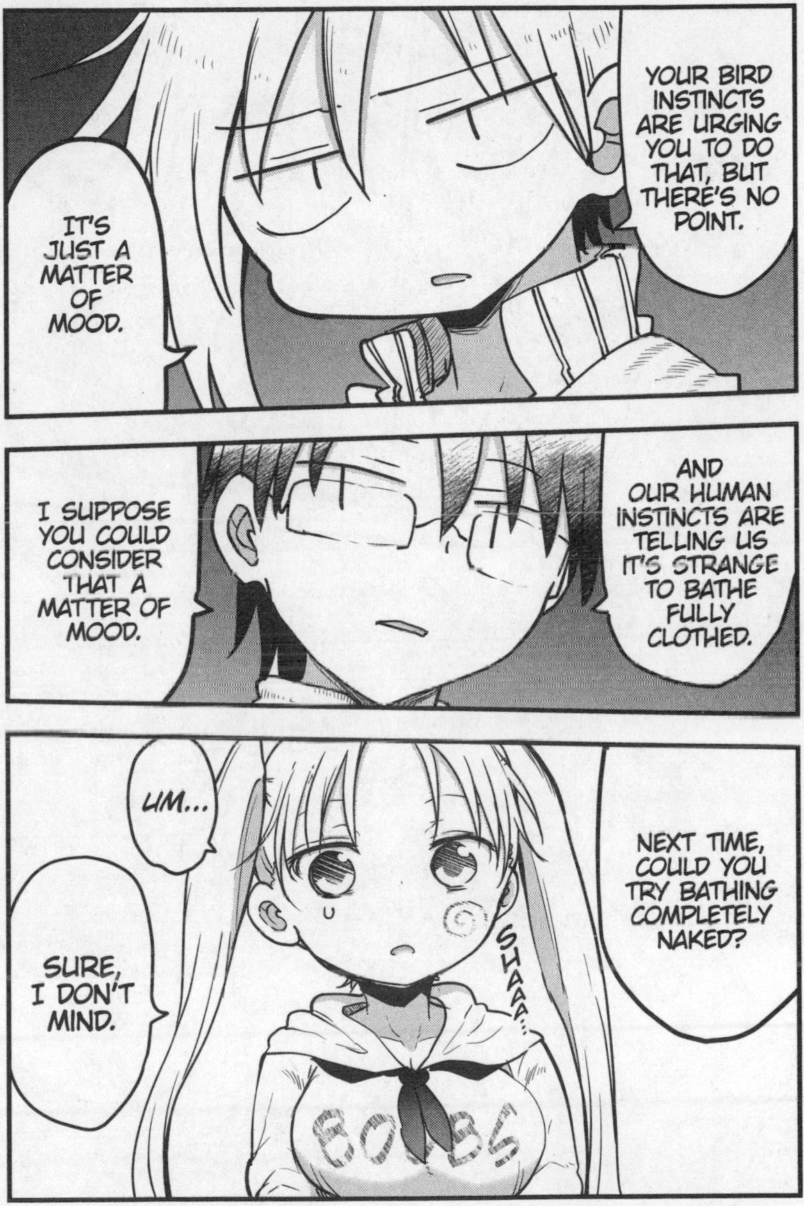
YOUR BIRD INSTINCTS ARE URGING YOU TO DO THAT, BUT THERE'S NO POINT.
IT'S JUST A MATTER OF MOOD.
AND OUR HUMAN INSTINCTS ARE TELLING US IT'S STRANGE TO BATHE FULLY CLOTHED.
I SUPPOSE YOU COULD CONSIDER THAT A MATTER OF MOOD.
NEXT TIME, COULD YOU TRY BATHING COMPLETELY NAKED?
UM...
SHAAA...
SURE, I DON'T MIND.

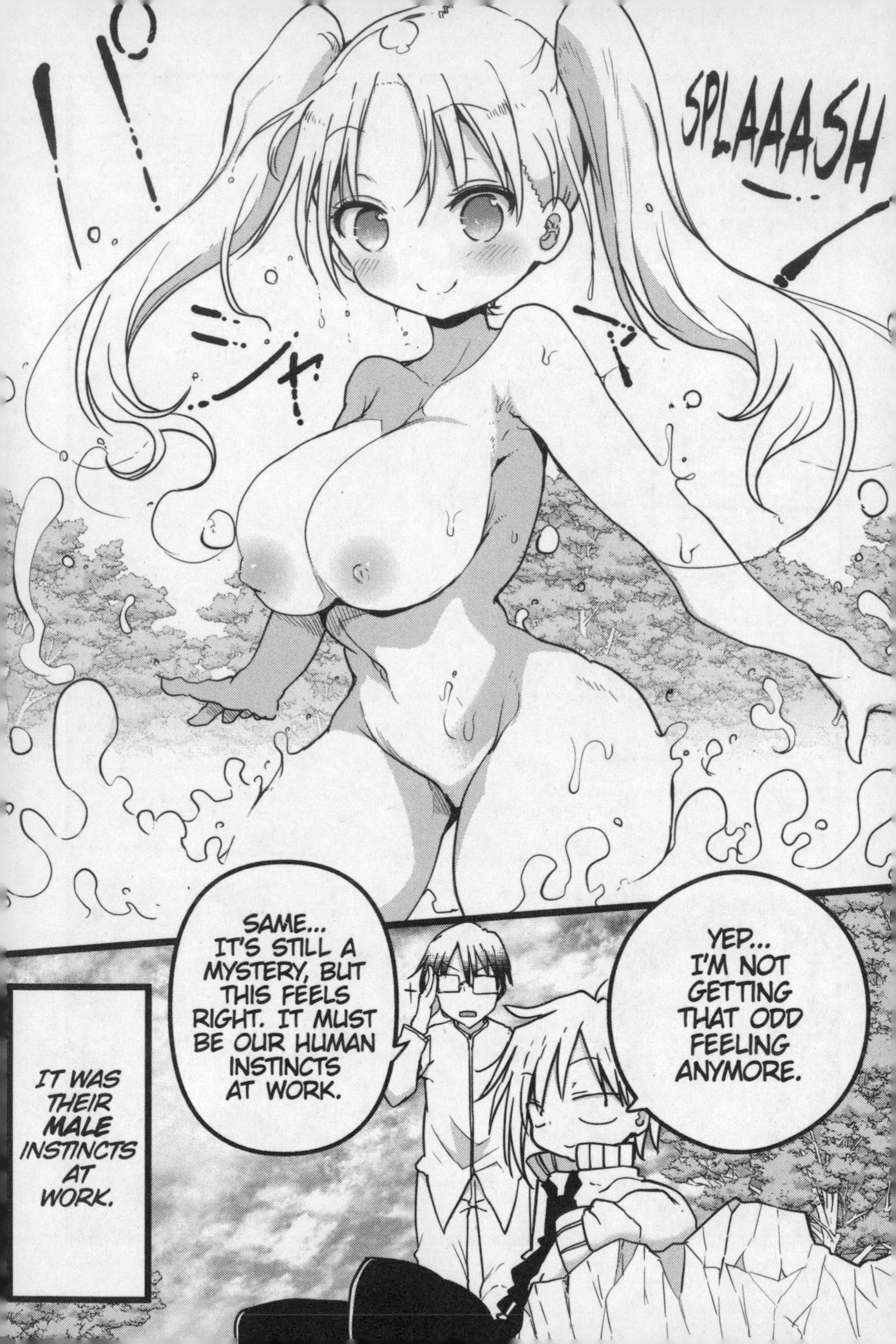
SPLAAASH
YEP... I'M NOT GETTING THAT ODD FEELING ANYMORE.
SAME... IT'S STILL A MYSTERY, BUT THIS FEELS RIGHT. IT MUST BE OUR HUMAN INSTINCTS AT WORK.
IT WAS THEIR MALE INSTINCTS AT WORK.

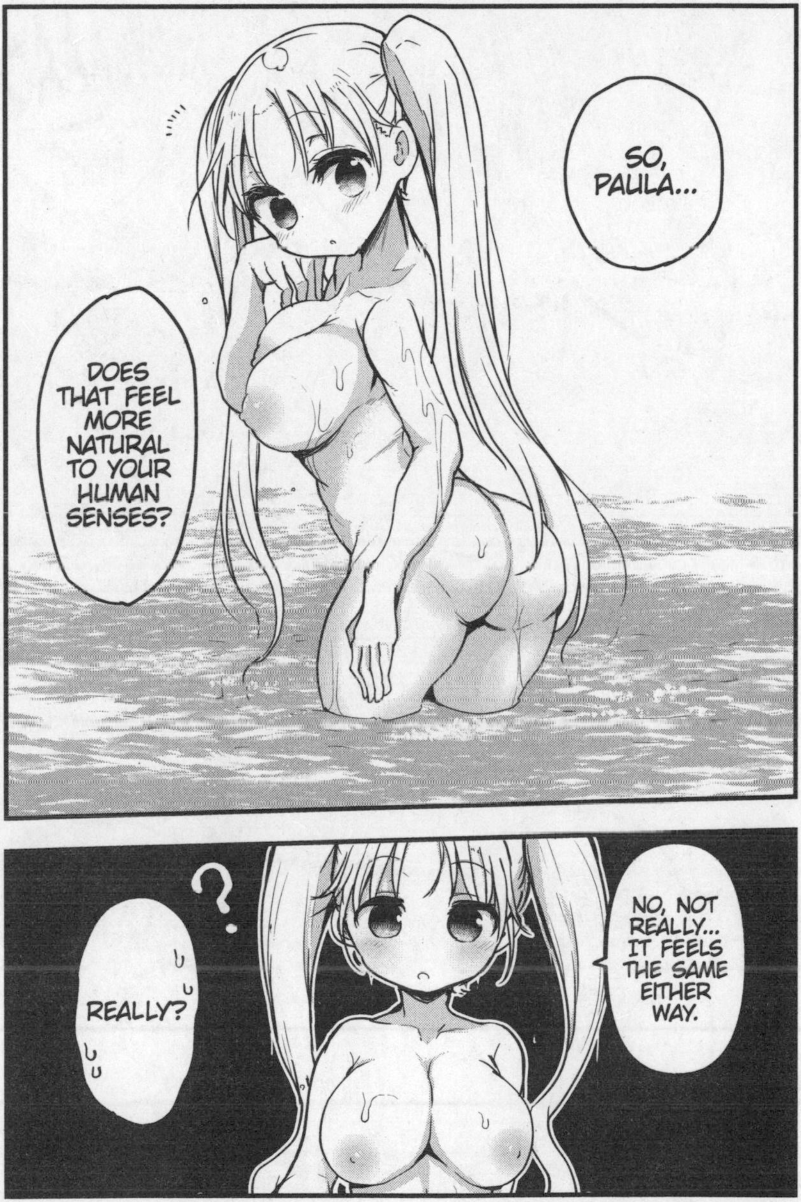
SO, PAULA...
DOES THAT FEEL MORE NATURAL TO YOUR HUMAN SENSES?
NO, NOT REALLY... IT FEELS THE SAME EITHER WAY.
REALLY?

End-of-Volume Bonus

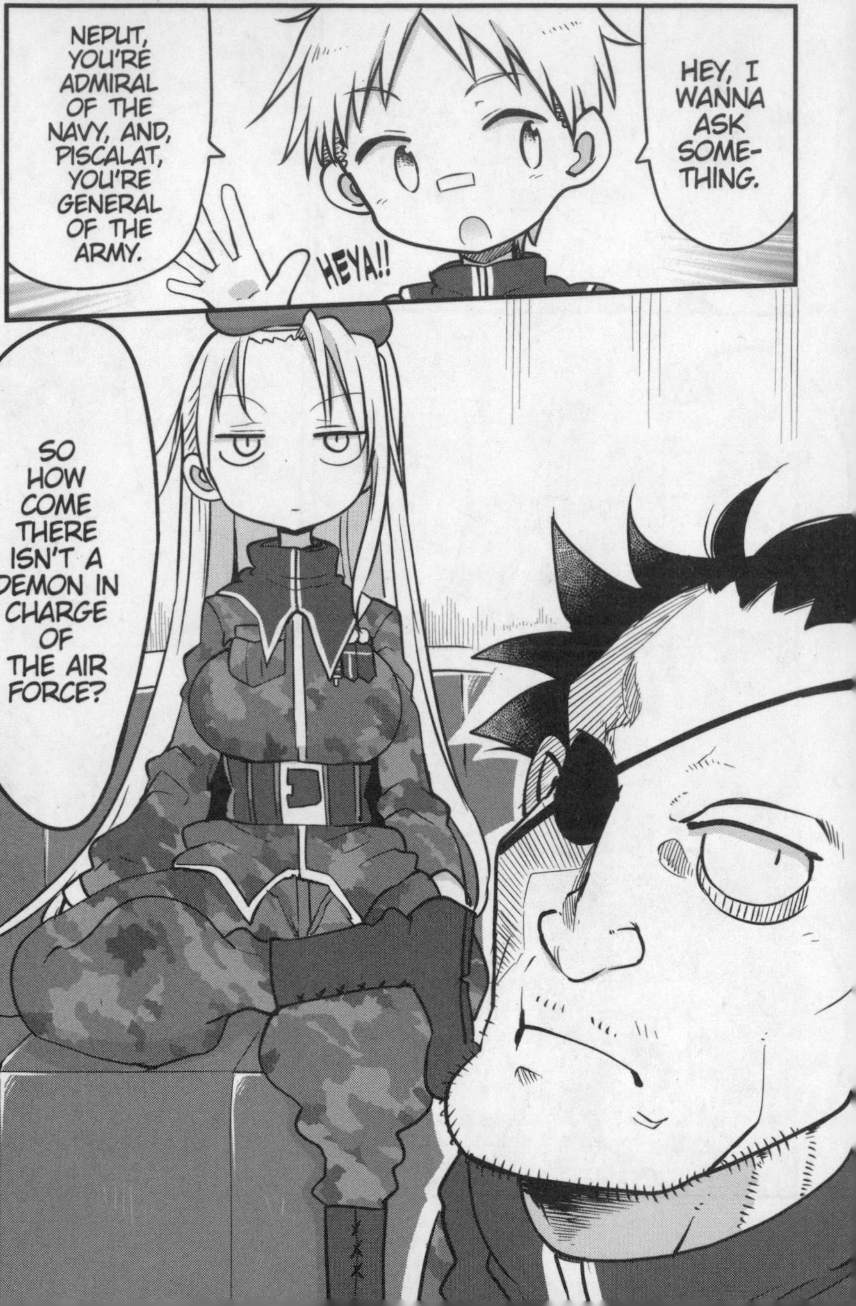
HEY, I WANNA ASK SOME-THING.
NEPUT, YOU'RE ADMIRAL OF THE NAVY, AND, PISCALAT, YOU'RE GENERAL OF THE ARMY.
HEYA!!
SO HOW COME THERE ISN'T A DEMON IN CHARGE OF THE AIR FORCE?

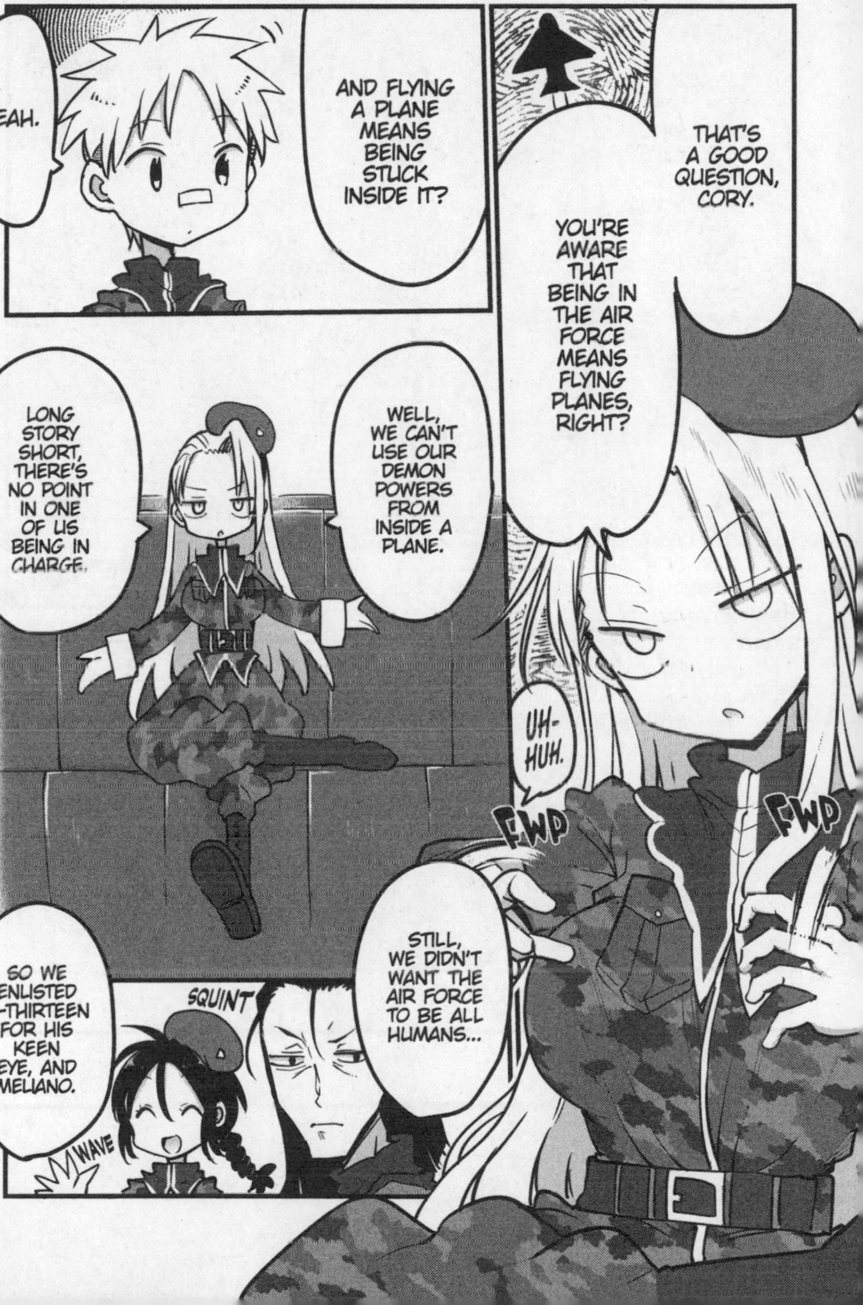
THAT'S A GOOD QUESTION, CORY.
YOU'RE AWARE THAT BEING IN THE AIR FORCE MEANS FLYING PLANES, RIGHT?
UH-HUH.
AND FLYING A PLANE MEANS BEING STUCK INSIDE IT?
YEAH.
WELL, WE CAN'T USE OUR DEMON POWERS FROM INSIDE A PLANE.
LONG STORY SHORT, THERE'S NO POINT IN ONE OF US BEING IN CHARGE.
FWP
FWP
STILL, WE DIDN'T WANT THE AIR FORCE TO BE ALL HUMANS...
SQUINT
SO WE ENLISTED G-THIRTEEN FOR HIS KEEN EYE, AND MELIANO.
WAVE

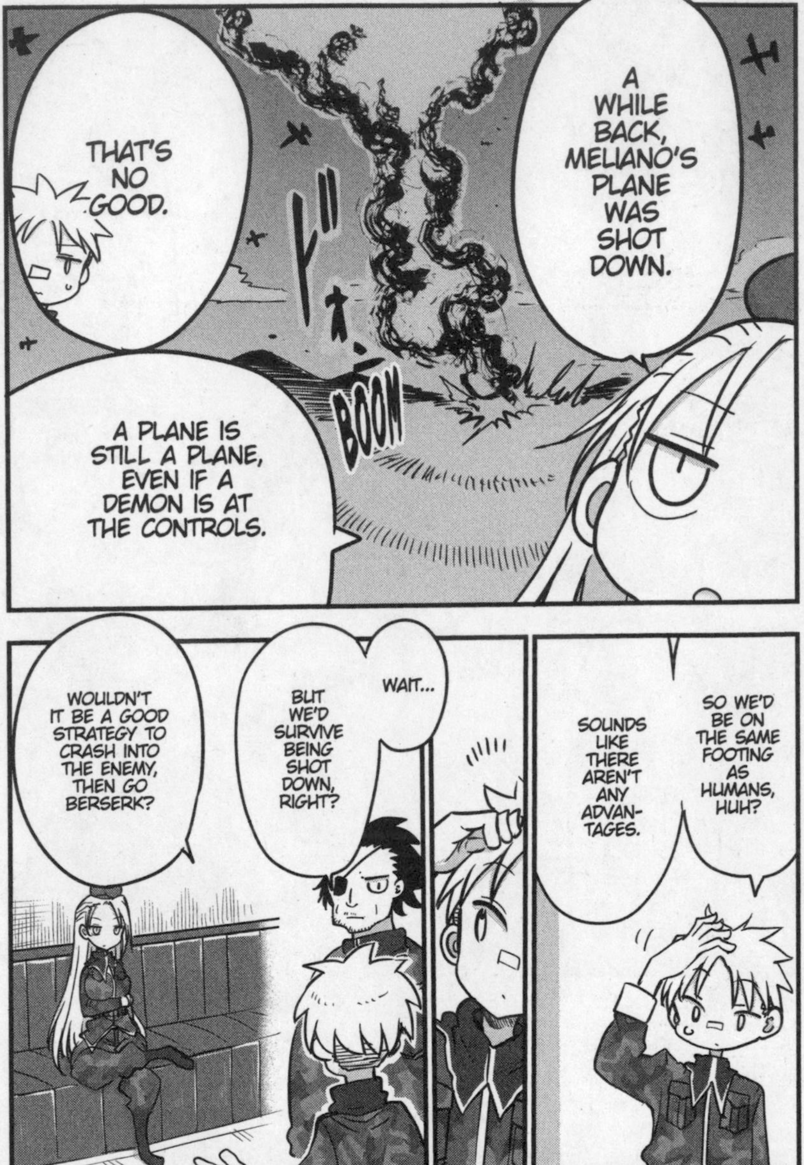
A WHILE BACK, MELIANO'S PLANE WAS SHOT DOWN.
THAT'S NO GOOD.
BOOM
A PLANE IS STILL A PLANE, EVEN IF A DEMON IS AT THE CONTROLS.
SO WE'D BE ON THE SAME FOOTING AS HUMANS, HUH?
SOUNDS LIKE THERE AREN'T ANY ADVANTAGES.
WAIT...
BUT WE'D SURVIVE BEING SHOT DOWN, RIGHT?
WOULDN'T IT BE A GOOD STRATEGY TO CRASH INTO THE ENEMY, THEN GO BERSERK?

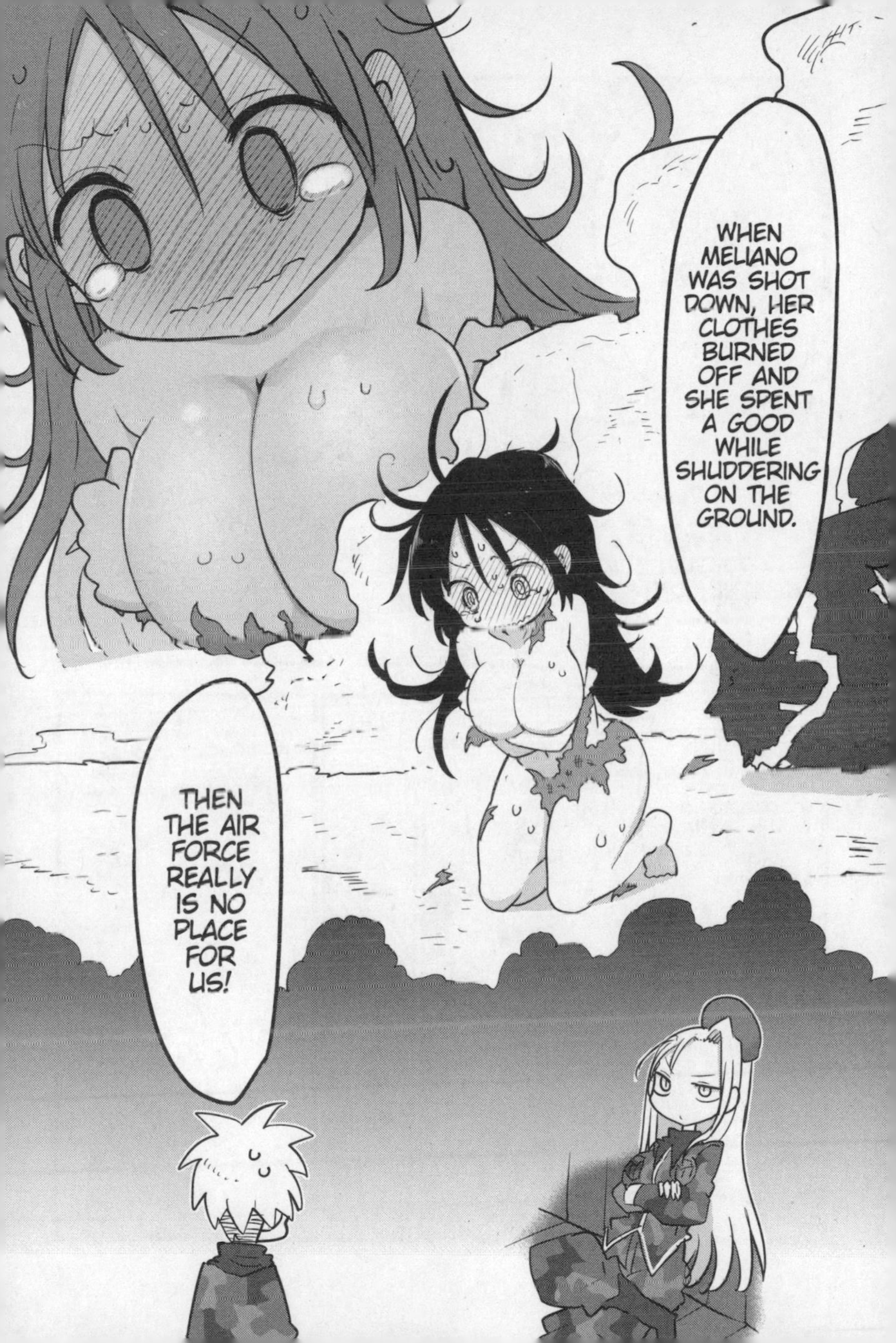
WHEN MELIANO WAS SHOT DOWN, HER CLOTHES BURNED OFF AND SHE SPENT A GOOD WHILE SHUDDERING ON THE GROUND.
THEN THE AIR FORCE REALLY IS NO PLACE FOR US!

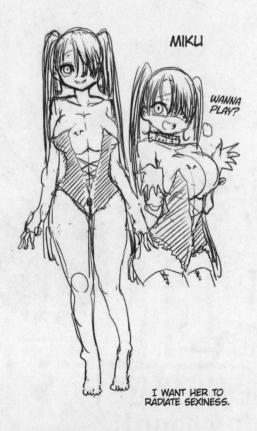

MIKU

WANNA
PLAY?

I WANT HER TO
RADIATE SEXINESS.

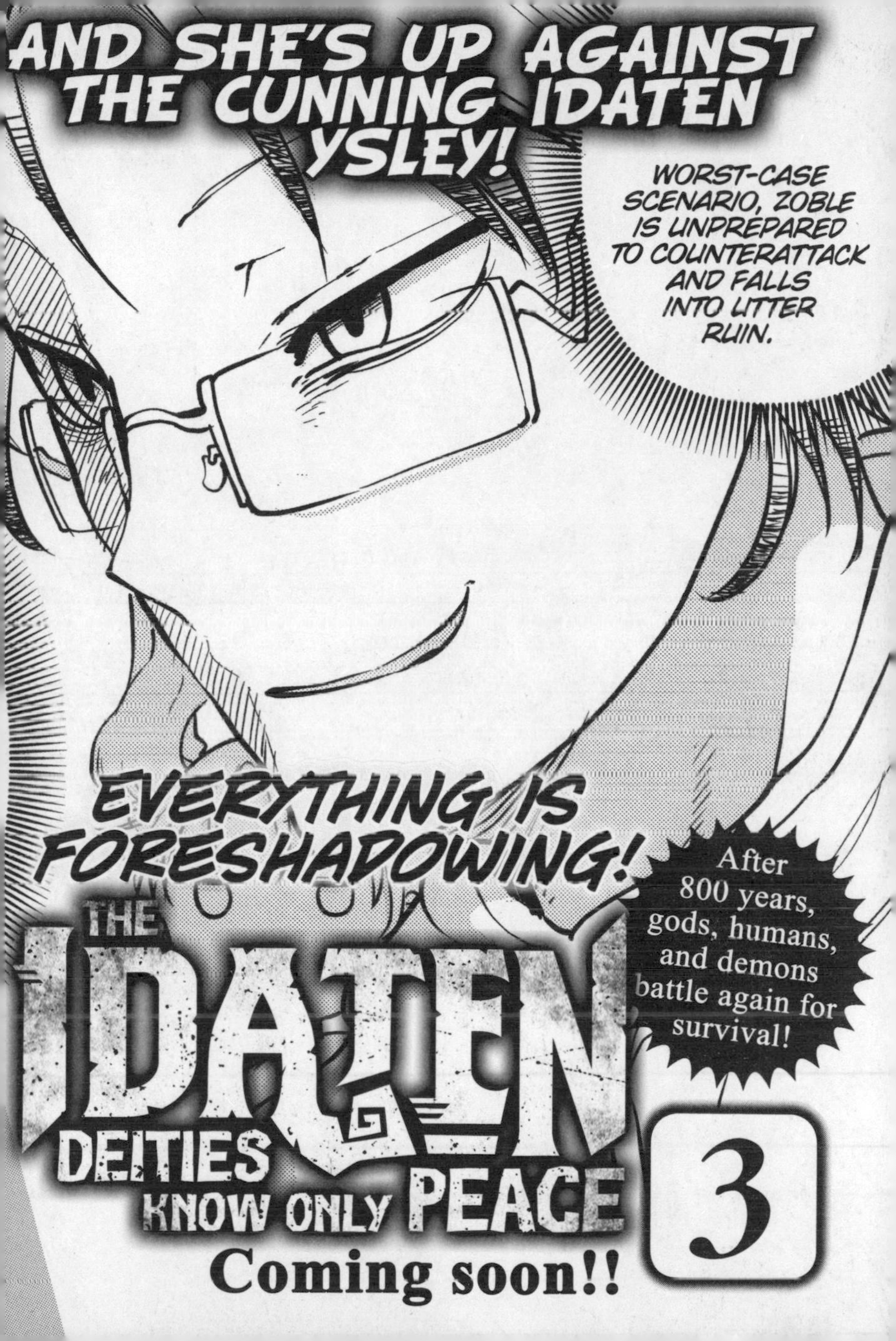
AND SHE'S UP AGAINST THE CUNNING IDATEN YSLEY!
WORST-CASE SCENARIO, ZOBLE IS UNPREPARED TO COUNTERATTACK AND FALLS INTO UTTER RUIN.
EVERYTHING IS FORESHADOWING!
After 800 years, gods, humans, and demons battle again for survival!
THE IDATEN DEITIES KNOW ONLY PEACE
3
Coming soon!!

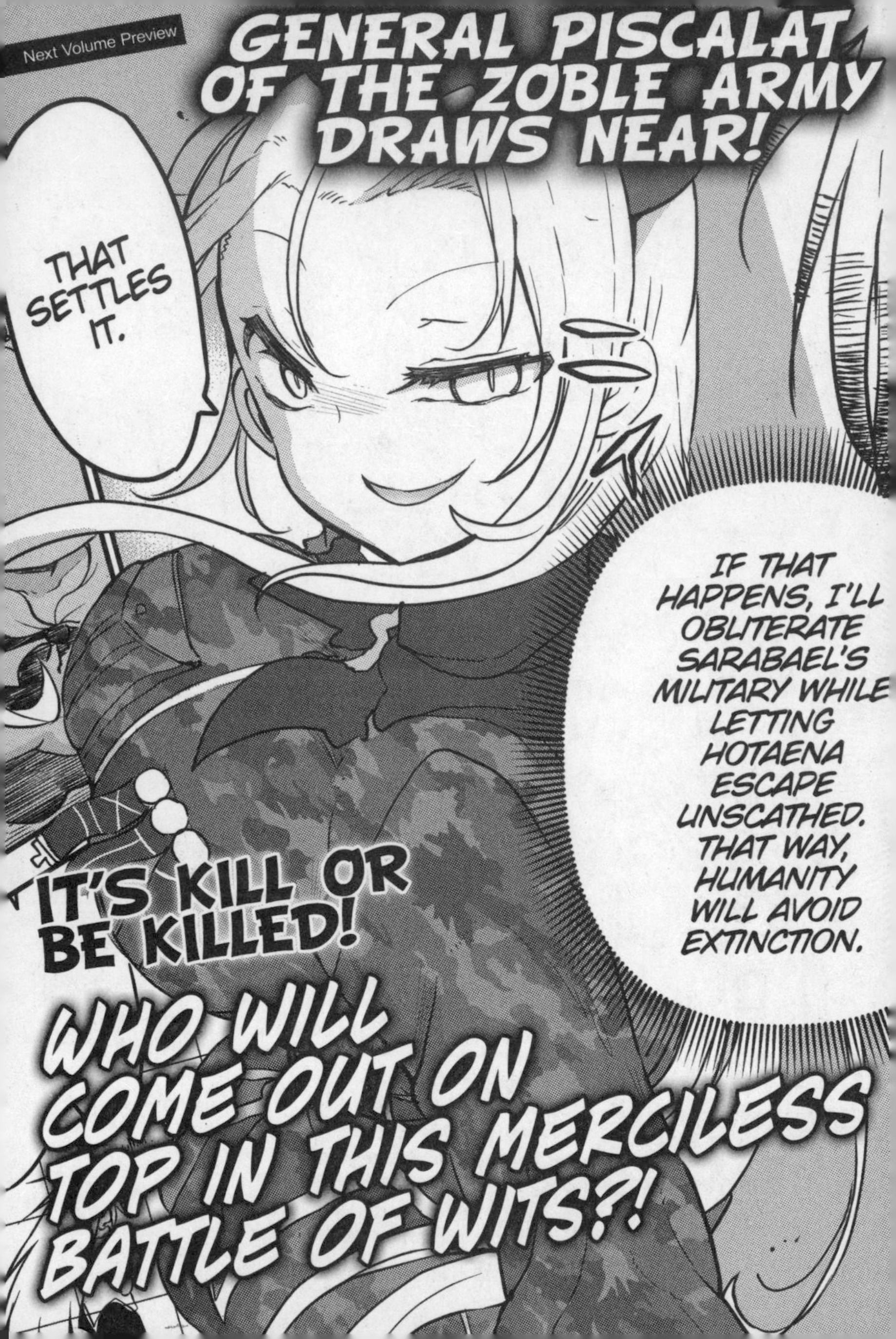
Next Volume Preview
GENERAL PISCALAT OF THE ZOBLE ARMY DRAWS NEAR!
THAT SETTLES IT.
IF THAT HAPPENS, I'LL OBLITERATE SARABAEL'S MILITARY WHILE LETTING HOTAENA ESCAPE UNSCATHED. THAT WAY, HUMANITY WILL AVOID EXTINCTION.
IT'S KILL OR BE KILLED!
WHO WILL COME OUT ON TOP IN THIS MERCILESS BATTLE OF WITS?!

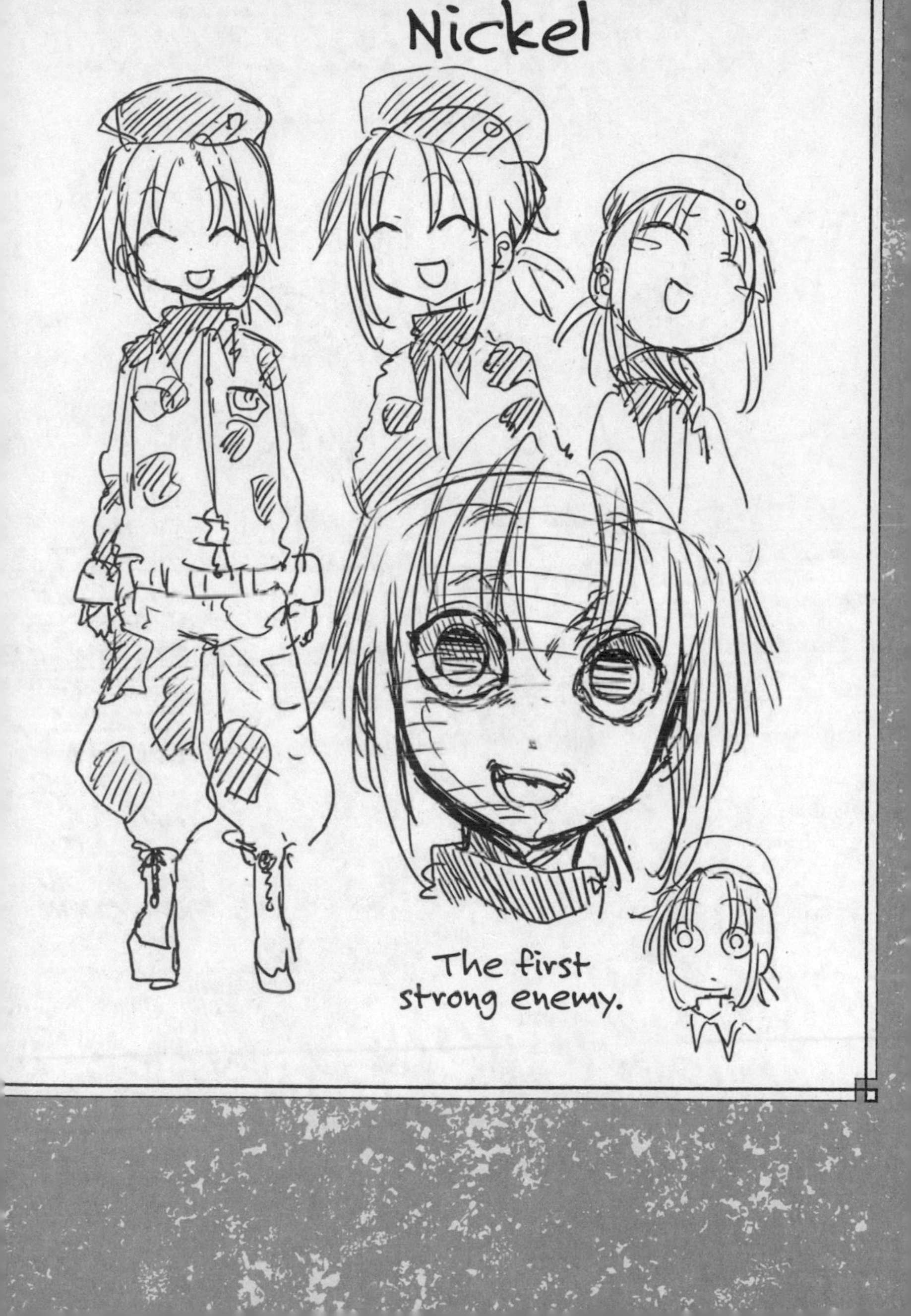
Nickel
The first strong enemy.

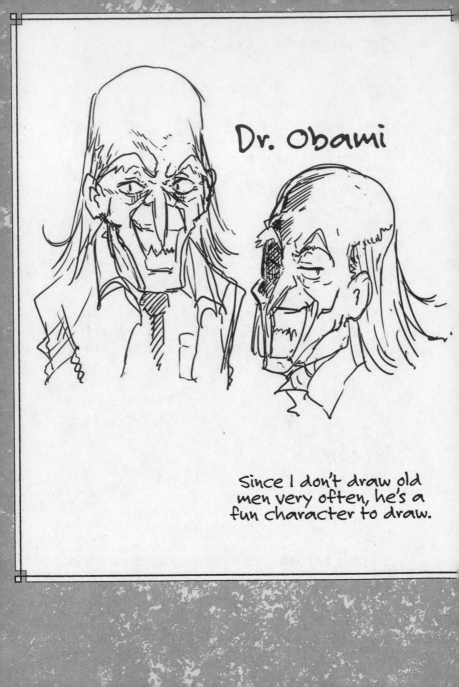

Dr. Obami

Since I don't draw old men very often, he's a fun character to draw.

Piscalat

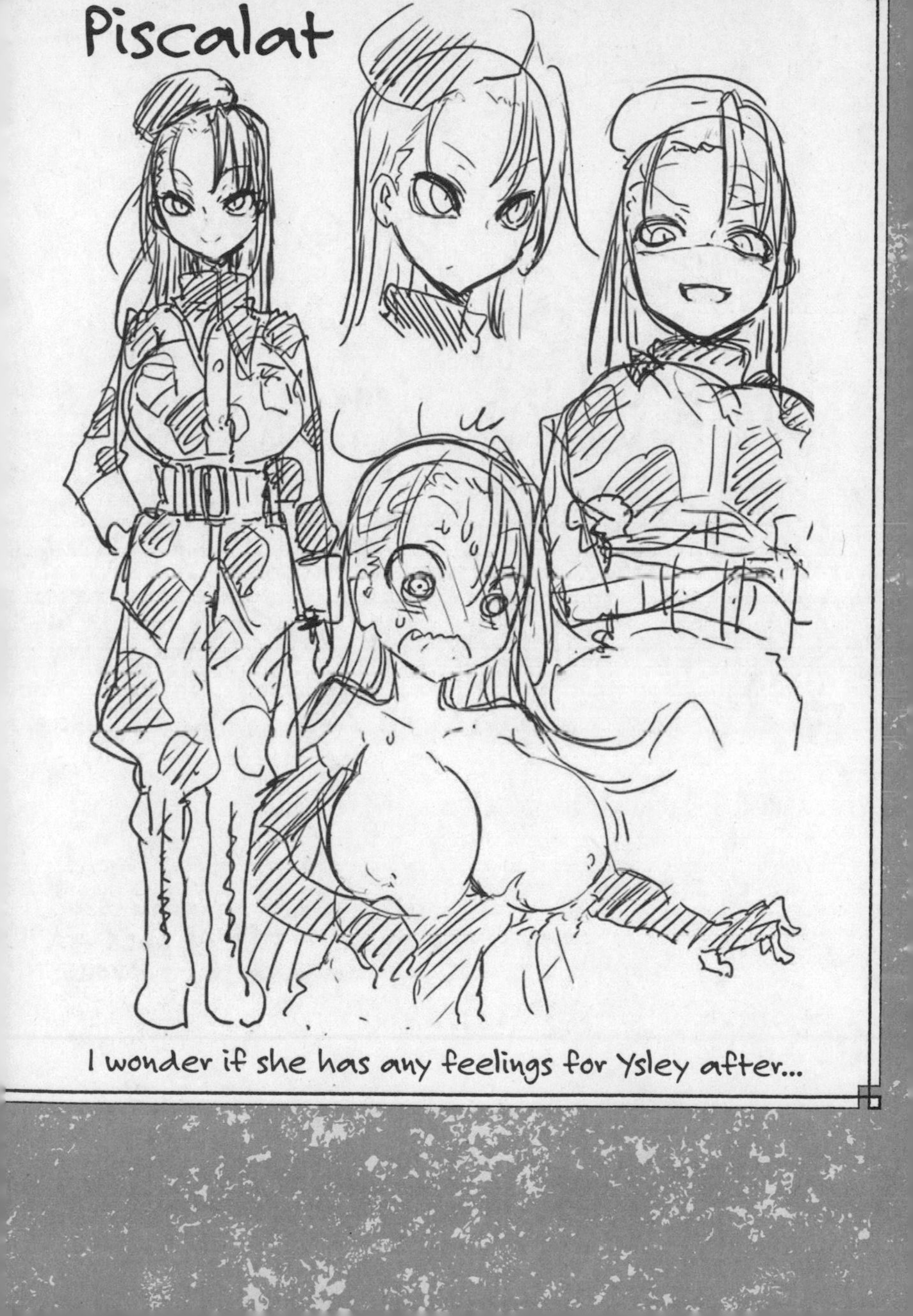

I wonder if she has any feelings for Ysley after...

TALES FROM BEYOND THE GRAVE 2

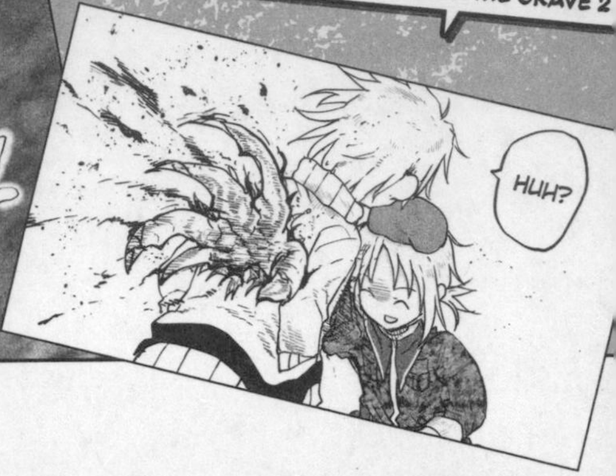
HUH?

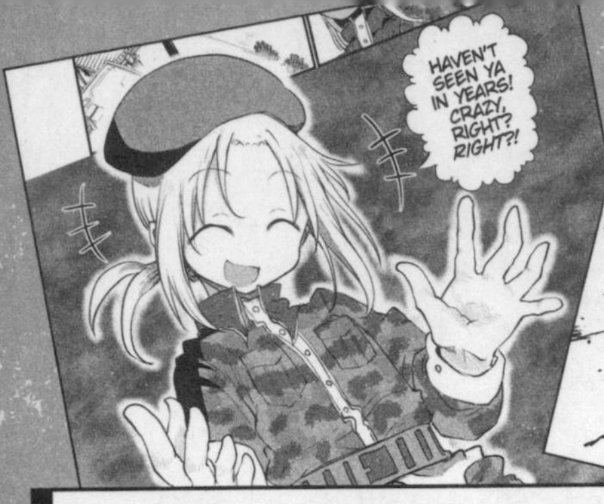
HAVEN'T SEEN YA IN YEARS! CRAZY, RIGHT? RIGHT?!

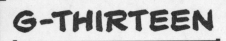

NICKEL

Although Nickel is one of the strongest demons, due to his uncooperativeness—among other traits—he was given zero authority. He spends his days as a soldier in the Zoble Defense Force, napping in the watchtower and anywhere else he can.

His flippant attitude towards his superiors, Takeshita and Neput, along with his annoying speech and behavior towards Piscalat, was meant to set the stage for an ignominious early exit. How very tragic indeed.

G-THIRTEEN

Like Nickel, G-Thirteen is a soldier in the Zoble Defense Force. Since he had the best eyesight out of all the demons and knew his way around a rifle, he was expected to use those skills in the air. Thus, he was made to enlist in the Air Force and learned how to fly a plane. I wasn't sure how I wanted to use this character at first, but I thought he was the best choice to fly Nickel to the battlefield and observe the fight with Rin. With that, his fate was set in stone. If he hadn't been tasked with transporting the doomed Nickel, he might have had a bright future in the Zoble Empire.

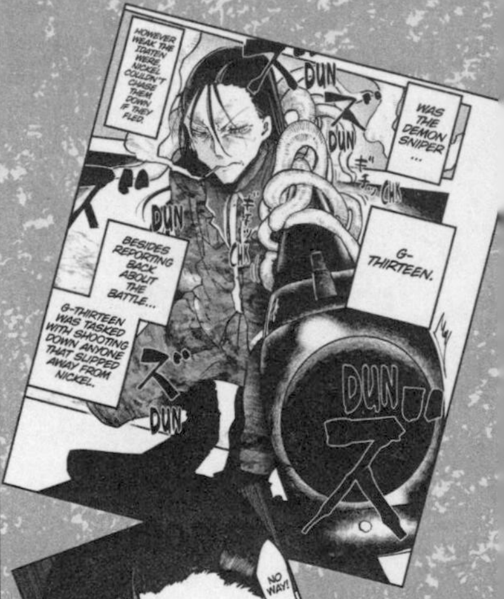
WAS THE DEMON SNIPER...
G-THIRTEEN.
DUN
DUN
CHK
HOWEVER WEAK THE IDATEN WERE, NICKEL COULDN'T CHASE THEM DOWN IF THEY FLED.
DUN
CHK
BESIDES REPORTING BACK ABOUT THE BATTLE...
G-THIRTEEN WAS TASKED WITH SHOOTING DOWN ANYONE THAT SLIPPED AWAY FROM NICKEL.
DUN
DUN

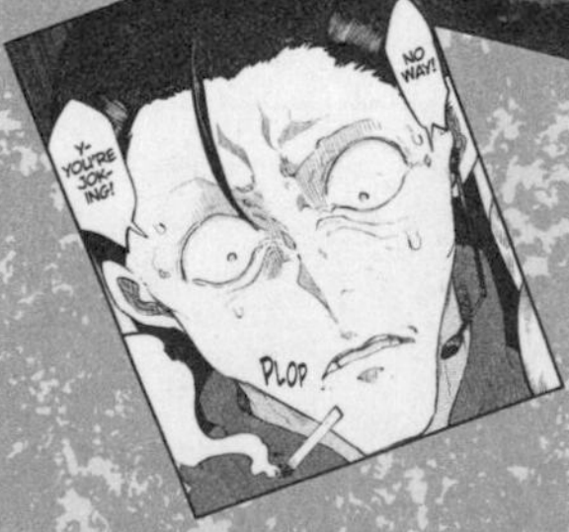
NO WAY!
Y-YOU'RE JOK-ING!
PLOP

THE IDATEN DEITIES KNOW ONLY PEACE

THE IDATEN DEITIES KNOW ONLY PEACE

story by Amahara art by coolkyousinnjya

VOLUME 2

TRANSLATION
Kevin Yuan

ADAPTATION
M. Lyn Hall

LETTERING
Ludwig Sacramento

COVER DESIGN
H. Qi

PROOFREADER
Brett Hallahan

SENIOR EDITOR
Shanti Whitesides

PRODUCTION DESIGNER
Christina McKenzie

PRODUCTION MANAGER
Lissa Pattillo

PREPRESS TECHNICIAN
Melanie Ujimori

PRINT MANAGER
hiannon Rasmussen-Silverstein

EDITOR-IN-CHIEF
Julie Davis

ASSOCIATE PUBLISHER
Adam Arnold

PUBLISHER
Jason DeAngelis

HEIONSEDAI NO IDATENTACHI BY AMAHARA, COOLKYOUSHINJYA

First published in Japan in 2019 by HAKUSENSHA, INC., Tokyo.
English language translation rights in U.S.A. arranged with HAKUSENSHA, INC., Tokyo through TOHAN CORPORATION, Tokyo.

Seven Seas press and purchase enquiries can be sent to Marketing Manager Lianne Sentar at press@gomanga.com. Information regarding the distribution and purchase of digital editions is available from Digital Manager CK Russell at digital@gomanga.com.

ISBN: 978-1-63858-315-8
Printed in Canada
First Printing: June 2022
10 9 8 7 6 5 4 3 2 1

READING DIRECTIONS

This book reads from ***right to left***, Japanese style. If this is your first time reading manga, you start reading from the top right panel on each page and take it from there. If you get lost, just follow the numbered diagram here. It may seem backwards at first, but you'll get the hang of it! Have fun!!

1
2
3
4
5
6
7
8
9

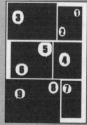

Follow us online: www.SevenSeasEntertainment.com